MATERIAL CULTURE

MATERIAL CULTURE

Henry Glassie

Photographs, Drawings, and Design by the Author

for Erin in Indiana, with affection, Henry

Bloomington and Indianapolis

INDIANA UNIVERSITY PRESS · 1999

Bloomington. March 2000.

The frontispiece shows houses in Bergen, Norway. The plate facing the
table of contents was painted by Nurten Şahin, Kütahya, Turkey, in 1991.
At the end, there is a work of art in wood, a radio with one message,
by Bilal Hossain Bikrampuri of Narayanganj, Bangladesh.

This book is a publication of

Indiana University Press
601 North Morton Street
Bloomington, IN 47404-3797 USA

http://www.indiana.edu/~iupress

Telephone orders	800-842-6796
Fax orders	812-855-7931
Orders by e-mail	iuporder@indiana.edu

Library of Congress Cataloging-in-Publication Data

Glassie, Henry H.
Material culture / Henry Glassie ; photographs,
drawings, and design by the author.
p.   cm.
Includes bibliographical references and index.
ISBN 0-253-33574-4 (cloth : alk. paper)
1. Material culture.   I. Title.
GN406.G53   1999
306—dc21   99-36047

1 2 3 4 5 04 03 02 01 00 99

for
Jim Deetz
and
Warren Roberts

CONTENTS

Rokea Begum displaying a prayer mat she wove for her daughter.
Madhya Lemua, Feni, Bangladesh. 1998

ONWARD

WHEN I PUBLISHED my first book on material culture, exactly thirty years ago, things seemed to be going well. Great anthropologists had led us out of the narcissistic delusions of the old century and taught us relativistic ways to think. Culture was no longer milord's fine taste, but the conceptual orders that all people develop in social association. Modern philosophers had existentialized action. No longer divisible into volitional and instinctual varieties, human beings became actors in their own dramas, freed by will and chained by conditions. Understanding all people to be creators at work in impossibly complicated situations, striving to construct cultures through faulty communication, we were ready to take on the difficult tasks of history and art.

History and art connect in the study of material culture. Material culture records human intrusion in the environment. It is the way we imagine a distinction between nature and culture, and then rebuild nature to our desire, shaping, reshaping, and arranging things during life. We live in material culture, depend upon it, take it for granted, and realize through it our grandest aspirations. Thirty years ago, it seemed that material culture would become the realm within which relativistic and existential thinking would be extended to history and art, the issues of human significance and human excellence.

Then the gears locked, the machine stopped, and began to run in reverse. We slid backward, rediscovering the energies of early modernism and naming our effort—in obeisance to the ideology of progress—postmodern. Humanists busied themselves with the reinvention of ideas they could have learned from

1

the old masters of anthropology. Social scientists struggled to contrive ideas they could have learned by reading the great literature of the past. This retrograde motion was caused by more than adjustment to the conservative mood of the age. Moving ahead on independent disciplinary tracks, we had lost touch with one another.

What has changed can change again; the moment in which I write will pass. Groping over old territory, relocating the critical purpose of scholarly endeavor, rediscovering subjectivity and situation, the diversity of orders and the interconnectedness of things, we will find points of convergence that will become the basis for a new transdisciplinary practice, at once humanistic and scientific. Renewed in oneness, we will be able to get on with our work, fashioning a view of humanity fit to the needs of the world's people.

The concept of culture seems a secure achievement. In the future, history and art, as well as science and philosophy, will be understood to be, like culture, the creations of people who are alike in humanity, but different in tradition and predicament. Problematizing is easy and endless. New ideas are a dime a dozen. What matters is how ideas fare in the world, what they yield in hard application. Our work will recognize the reality of the individual. It will come to judgment contextually, acknowledging the distinctiveness of traditions that unfold only within human control and among uncontrollable circumstances. It will expand through cross-cultural comparisons that bring us understanding at once of the universal and the particular.

Our advancement, unfortunately, will continue to require transitional designations. In the far future, all history will be history, all art will be art. But now we still need words to mark off worthy domains of experience and accomplishment that differ from those celebrated in the academy. Thirty years ago, we called them "folk" or prefixed them with "ethno." We had history plain, the history of the academician, and we had folk history and ethnohistory too. Increasingly annoyed by the burden of old connotations, we naturally press the hunt for better words. Though a folklorist and pleased to be identified with the neglected varieties of excellence that the pompous consider marginal, I find that I rarely call things "folk" anymore. The adjective "traditional" serves me, for both folk art and fine art are traditional. In architecture, "vernacular" has replaced "folk," widening the scope of study, and that term has escaped into new quarters. Certainly, these are only provisional moves, but it is not yet time to abandon qualification.

Without the challenge of folk history or ethnohistory—or black history or women's history or the alternative of memory—history will fail to reach its potential. Without the challenge of folk art, the study of art will collapse again into prejudices of class and gender and race. Neglect persists. Our ignorance abounds. But the goal seems clear. History will be history. Art will be art.

For both reading and writing, I prefer big books, tight in focus, ample in detail, books that submerge theory in rich empirical demonstration and open themselves to dismissal as merely descriptive. This is not such a book. It is composed of essays that roll the theoretical into view. But it is not a random gathering of old papers, nor does it wholly betray my belief that the purpose of theory is to help us approach the real world's vexed splendor, its stretch beyond schemes. A considered assembly, interlaced by theme, this book is designed to illustrate how the study of material culture can bring history and art toward relativistic and existential—genuinely modern—reformulation. I write to get us back on track.

Roman ruins. Yalvaç, Turkey. 1994

·1·

HISTORY

IN TIME, the unified practice of old Herodotus disassembled into disciplinary specializations. Historians became political historians, social historians, economic historians, religious historians, military historians, intellectual historians, art historians, architectural historians, archaeologists, philologists, classicists, orientalists, geographers, sociologists, anthropologists, folklorists. As one discipline closed down, narrowing its scope, another opened up in a compensatory gesture at completeness.

The scholarly discipline teaches discipline. It creates technicians, rigorous in procedure and exposition. Then scholars mature. Finding the world is not divided as the academy is divided, they bumble into territory beyond their expertise and become amateurs committed to a transdisciplinary intellectual practice. So Jean-Paul Sartre taught, and so I believe. To be true to themselves and useful to society, worth their pay, technicians become amateurs. Without betraying discipline itself, the care in their craft, intellectuals break out of disciplinary confinement, abandoning the comforts of youth in order to speak of things that matter. Our work must begin, but it cannot end in our divisive disciplines of nurture.

At work, we shape memory to shape ourselves, to claim a place and gauge our strength. Of history our presence is made. History is a force so potent in our lives that it would be irresponsible to leave it shattered at the convenience of the conservative economy of the academy. It requires transdisciplinary address — seriousness, James Agee would say — and I will launch us on an excursion into history with commonplace observations, beginning simply in the belief that jargon thwarts, but plain talk en-

5

ables labor across the boundaries that hedge the academy to falsify reality.

History is not the past. History is a story about the past, told in the present, and designed to be useful in constructing the future.

The past is vast, and it is gone. Almost all of it is gone utterly, leaving no trace in the mind or archive. We know the past only through things that chance to exist in the present: old books, broken pots, disturbed memories. Yet, even the tattered scraps that remain are too many, overwhelming in their multiplicity, their intransigence, their unfitness to narrative orders.

History begins in the will of the historian, a forked mortal trapped in the unknowable flux. The courageous act of history is the act of the historian who ignores most people and events while selecting a tiny number of facts and arranging them artfully and truthfully in order to speak usefully about the human condition.

That means that writing history is speaking myth. A professional folklorist — that kind of historian in whose province myth lies — I do not use the word sloppily as a synonym for untruth. In line with arguments advanced by Claude Lévi-Strauss, I see the past as a mythic resource for the historian — open to endless transformation during the crafting of engaging narratives, suitable to different philosophical traditions and environmental conditions. In line with arguments about myth advanced by Bronislaw Malinowski, I see the historian as one who composes stories that function as social charters, drawing people together and refining their relations on the basis of a shared cosmology. It is the historian's job to reorder the past while telling useful tales.

Myths are spoken and histories are written to answer needs. People need understanding, help in comprehending their tragedies, and historians earn their keep by telling people about people, by composing resonant stories about other times and places. The goal is — as Robert Penn Warren said, meditating upon America's main event, the Civil War — the goal is to find in historical imagination the options and constraints of human possibility.

Yet, for most people, history breaks apart and fails. Now that Samuel Beckett is dead, our finest stylist of English prose is V. S. Naipaul. In his autobiography, recalling the Hindu community in Trinidad, Naipaul speaks of two histories. One was full of dates, names, and foreign places. It was the history of other people, carefully taught in school. The second was a history of darkness, the unspoken, unknown murk out of which the local people emerged.

To cast light into darkness, we revise the myth. Discovering embarrassing gaps in the universalizing charter we have built out of the past, we choose new facts about new people and attend to new sources, expanding our view beyond the written record to incorporate oral history and material culture. Earnestly, we pluck bits from the world to decorate the old structure, providing a semblance of democracy through the addition of symbolic reminders of history's neglected people, of women and dark people and poor people.

History is picked at, scraped down, patched up, and encrusted with new ornament. In interdisciplinary fervor, we pleasure ourselves in deconstruction, or we scramble through revisions, taking baby steps toward necessary truth. Meanwhile, most people linger in darkness, neglected and vulnerable.

The reason is that, while we seek new people and new sources, we accept them only insofar as they can be accommodated by the rules of narration implicit in the old story we tell. To get the story told, we continue to search for signs of change, for devices we can use to compose our myth, segmenting linear time, then linking the segments along the arc of progress that leads, inevitably, to us.

Nicely confined, art history provides a simple case. Proud of our liberality, we add works by women, by Africans, by Muslims. But if we do not change our definition of art, of what is significant, and if we do not relinquish our commitment to linear, segmented, progressive narration, then the tale might shift and expand slightly, but it still will not include women and men in equal numbers. It still will not include more Asians than Europeans. It will remain false to reality, unable to meet the needs of the world we inhabit.

To say it in the opposite way: if we had an adequate definition of art and adequate expository means, art history would already be filled with works by women, dark people, and poor people. And we would not be flailing about in scholastic affirmative action. Justice would already prevail.

To say it more broadly: if we knew what was important and how to talk about it, history would be useful to everyone. There would be no areas of darkness. It is this matter of what is important and how it is ordered in narration that calls for our transdisciplinary attention.

Central to transdisciplinary hope is the reconciliation of history and anthropology. The contrast between them was purified in a Parisian debate, now past and not yet grasped. Jean-Paul Sartre argued that time is the axis of significance. People participate in the narrative line or they do not matter. They deserve their darkness. Claude Lévi-Strauss countered that time is overvalued by Western thinkers. Nonhistorical action is not only more common among the world's people, it is more moral. Our salvation abides in the darkness.

In following either of these masters, we will find improvement in history. Sartre's progressive-regressive method eliminates the vain hunt for origins, the wild-goose chase of the historian, and it existentializes practice. We meet the subjects of history within their own predicaments. Lévi-Strauss' structuralism doubles history's size, admitting nonhistorical action into scrutiny, and it clarifies the myth-making nature of the historian's errand. In following both of them at once, we find ourselves with two complementary methods and two concurrent histories, one hot, one cool — the hot governed by the secular will to progress, the cool governed by the sacred will to order.

Accepting that history is a simultaneity of the historical and the nonhistorical, the changing and stable, we have begun our quest for better historical constructions. That search should not stop at the edge of the academy where comfortable gentlemen (like Sartre and Lévi-Strauss) confect competing systems that claim the universal and incarnate the provincial.

We should seek disorienting experience in the world, setting our provinciality in relation to the provinciality of others. Wishing truly to understand, we will not merely ask people beyond our walls for facts to assimilate into our schemes. We will learn to engage in collegial exchange with nonacademic intellectuals, discovering in conversation new arts of discourse and new theories of time. I am certain that many of the answers to academic questions — in history and beyond — lie ready in the wisdom of people unconfined by academic convention.

Such a one is Ahmet Balcı. He was born in Ahmetler, a village above the Aegean, tucked in a fold of Kaz Dağı, the Mount Ida of antiquity, where Paris tended his sheep and made the decision that brought Troy to ruin. Ahmet Balcı was also a shepherd in his boyhood. He never went to school, but he taught himself to read and write, and, listening to the old men talk, he became a historian.

Ahmet Balcı tells two histories of Ahmetler. One is a story of change. In Ahmet's account, his ancestors — he calls them the Turks — followed their flocks out of Central Asia in the thirteenth century. Seeking good grazing, they came west along the Taurus range, then up the coast to Kaz Dağı. There they continued their nomadic way, driving the herds to the high pastures in the summer and bringing them down to a glen near the sea in the winter.

Serious in his role, Ahmet Balcı qualifies his story, saying the history is not exactly clear, but counting back through the generations, he reckons his grandfathers' grandfathers settled permanently on the site of their winter encampment about 1760. Early in the twentieth century, having learned the difficult skills of building, they traded their old houses of felt stretched over staked frames for new homes of stone. As the grip of secular reform loosened in the Turkish Republic, and wealth accumulated in the village, the people built their first mosque in 1949.

Ahmet Balcı was born in 1944, and dates become firm when he reports what he has seen. In 1960, a school was added. The people learned to read and write. In 1971, the government built the first road that connected Ahmetler to the world. Before that, all travel was on foot or horseback. Now the wheels rolled. In 1983, electricity followed the road into the village. "Now," he says, "there are televisions, iceboxes, washing machines. In the village, there is everything. After electricity came, the villagers bought everything. There is a television in every house now."

No nostalgia disturbs his evaluation. Ahmet Balcı ends his tale of progress with a smile. *Şimdi, herşey iyi:* Now, everything is good. Thanks to God, thanks to the state, everything is good.

Progress is not the whole story. Change has happened in an unchanging environment. Ahmet Balcı points to the gray mountain ascending above his village and asks how one could farm it. The soil is thin and stony, unfit to the plow. But sheep belonging to the curly race of northwestern Anatolia know how to pick among the rocks for sustenance. Their flesh provides meat, their milk becomes cheese, their wool is sheared, combed, spun, dyed, and woven into carpets to be sold at dawn on Fridays in the agricultural market of Ayvacık. In rational adaptation to the environment, the people of Ahmetler have developed and held to a workable system of exploitation and creation. From the days of our nomadism, Ahmet says, there has been no change in the central tasks of *hayvancılık* and *halıcılık,* of animal husbandry and carpet production, upon which life depends.

The story is double. Life is improved by progress. Life depends on stability. People build mosques and buy televisions, and people cooperate, tending the sheep and weaving the carpets that are the ultimate refinement of the land's constricted potential. "Our women weave carpets, take them to the market and sell them. We buy what we need with this cash. We eat and

Ahmet Balcı

Ahmetler. Çanakkale, Turkey. 1986

drink from the money we earn from the carpet trade." Forward motion, symbolized by the new television, requires adherence to the stable process from which cash is won. Ahmet Balcı believes — and antique examples in museum collections support his contention — that the geometric designs on the rich red carpets of Ahmetler have not changed for centuries.

Ahmet Balcı's two histories cannot be reduced to illustrations of the contrast between Sartre and Lévi-Strauss. They come closer to the ideas of Fernand Braudel. To Braudel, one history is a stream of events, a tale of political succession and economic evolution. In that frame, Ahmet Balcı provides an account of settlement and development in relation to national history. Through this story, his village can be connected to the global structures it is currently fashionable to talk about. To Braudel, another history is that of the long duration, a story of environmental adaptation and deep cultural pattern. In that frame, Ahmet Balcı locates life's center in the stability of stock raising and carpet weaving. His story resists absorption into the new world order of the chic essayist.

Our inquiry will be advanced by Hugh Nolan. Mr. Nolan was a saintly man and the great historian of Ballymenone, a patch of green hills and white houses in the County Fermanagh, just north of the border breaking Ireland. His delight in youth, he said, was listening to the old people talking. From them he assembled the history of his place, and in old age his delight, he said, was speaking the truth.

The truth, he knew, is not the same as the factual. The past is gone, the facts that remain might be wrong, but you learn and ponder, doing the best you can. The truth, he said, is what you are willing to live by, and in speaking only the truth, Hugh Nolan claimed and was granted the name historian. It is the will to truth that makes historians, separating them from other tellers of tale. Mr. Nolan did not falsify by omission. The historian, he said, must tell the whole painful story. Nor did he falsify by generalization. Historians who stretch for grand narratives, reaching from the place they know into places they do not, inevitably, he believed, fall into falsehood. Mr. Nolan stuck to his locality, southwestern Fermanagh, and he spoke its truth. It made him feel good. The lie puts the mind and soul at odds. The tongue stumbles, the brow wrinkles, the body ages. Mr. Nolan kept himself young and content, he preserved the historian's aesthetic and maintained the smooth flow of words, by saying only what he felt to be true.

As it is understood by the farming people of Ballymenone, general history divides. It is a story of change. The greatest change, they say, was brought about by political action, when local folk joined in demands that led to the victory of the Land League. They rallied and marched, Lord Leitrim was slain, and the peasants became the proprietors of the land they worked. Then the land's story rushes forward through technological progress, from mud walls to brick, from thatched roofs to tin, from horses to tractors.

The farmer's tale also tells of stability, of the constancy of the cow. Seeing that grass springs luxuriously from the clay beneath rain-laden skies, farmers know their place was made to be pastoral. It is normally enough for them to repeat what has been done before, doing anew what has been tested redundantly and proved workable. At times they have been forced by the landlord or compelled by the government to cropping, to agriculture, but they have returned again and again, relocating themselves in the land's inbuilt logic of grass and cows. From the ancient epoch of cattle raids to today's toil in the muck, life has depended, as in Ahmetler, on animal husbandry. In Ahmetler, the sheep is the beast, and wool is processed into carpets for sale. In Ballymenone, it is the cow, and milk is processed into butter to bring a little money into the house.

Hugh Nolan complicates Ballymenone's double history. Once when we were sitting in his miserable black house, the turf fire glowing at our feet, I commented that he, a man born in 1896, had seen the arrival of the world we call modern, and I bade him

Hugh Nolan

Ballymenone.
County Fermanagh,
Northern Ireland.
1977

speak of change. He spoke of developments in transportation. He saw the first automobile in County Fermanagh. Before that, he said, people walked or rode horses. "The ass and cart, it was a great improvement in its day. Then came the car, and now there's the helicopter." He paused. The helicopter is a tool of war in Northern Ireland. Mr. Nolan continued, "And there has been a great change in communication." Once news traveled by word of mouth. Then it was riddled out of the rare old newspaper that was passed from hand to hand through the countryside. Now, with the television, people know what is going on in the world instantaneously. "All these changes" — he gestured beyond his home — "have brought a great improvement to the people. All do have the electricity now. And that is a great thing." He paused again. No wires ran to his dark house. Mr. Nolan had repeated the story of progress that we expect, and then he concluded:

"But the greatest change in my lifetime has been that people has lost all respect for authority, civil or divine.

"Today there is neither law nor order.

"And that is the greatest change."

The stream of events entails both progress and regress. Mr. Nolan had little need to illustrate his argument. British soldiers with machine guns stalked the rural lanes. Boys with homemade bombs rode the midnight roads. It was conventional to say, in Ulster in those days, that if you did not adjust to the troubles, you would go crazy, and if you did adjust, you were crazy. Mr. Nolan looked up from the fire and summarized the nature of temporal development:

"Aye, the two things happen at the one time.

"Things get better.

"And they get worse."

The story of change is double, simultaneously a matter of gain and loss. Awash in the fluid, mutable swill, people are charged by intelligence and moral conscience to participate in progressive change and to turn away from regressive change. In turning away from error, people seek stability.

Change, for Hugh Nolan, is double, and so is stability. One aspect of stability is environmental. People, being wise about their work, constantly adjust to the ecological reality. Environmental stability comes from more than conservative acts repeating into continuity. It involves a recursive logic that is necessary to the dynamic of the long duration. Farmers evaluate their situation and return to exploit the potential that God built into their damp, grassy hills at the dawn of time. This is a place for the cow, not the plow.

What seems from afar to be smoothly continuous often appears from within to be a canny series of recursive acts, of little revivals, as people go back to go forward. The narrator repeats the old tale to show children the way into the future. The woman in Ahmetler draws the design for a new carpet from an old one she found on the floor of her village mosque. The ambitious young farmer in Ballymenone, blessed with bright new machinery, finds success by rediscovering his land's old message, following the direction implicit in the sodden slopes rich with grass.

The second aspect of Hugh Nolan's history of stability is moral. It resembles the environmental, for it sets human conduct in relation to an unchanging force, and it counsels adherence to the correct and returns from error. It is similar, too, in that it is emplaced, shaped spatially.

Ballymenone's moral history is built out of events, some of them violent events like those in the conventional history of the academy, but its ordering is radically different. It is local, situated with precision, and its events are not linked by a chronology that distances them from modern people. Events are set on the landscape that people roam across, that they confront regularly and immediately in the course of the workaday round.

Hugh Nolan knew the dates, and he could set events in temporal sequence, but the dates were only facts, and he kept events in order by location. Mr. Nolan's geographical arrangement, enabling him to expand easily from the common experience of place into explanatory narrative, is not unique to him. Native historians in North America and New Guinea, it seems, practice comparably. One of history's greatest texts is the *Seyahatname*, written by Evliya Çelebi, who traveled in the seventeenth century and allowed Ottoman history to accumulate through the stories he told of the places he visited. And any serious history of the world will not be a single tale, but as Fernand Braudel argued, a concatenation of the distinct histories of different civilizations, a product of geographical as well as temporal understanding.

Shelved in the memory by location, not date, the events in Ballymenone's moral history are linked typologically, not chronologically. Mr. Nolan does not invent events. He selects carefully for utility. His goal is to fill out the typology of action, dividing history by human type to illuminate the perplex of existence.

One human type is the saint. Mr. Nolan tells of men and women who embodied God's power, who came to his place in ancient days and marked the land, giving creation its final touches. Causing rivers to writhe and fountains to rise, saints like Febor and Naile left visible signs that witness to the existence of God. The saints were human beings, capable of sin. Columcille was exiled for leading an army into battle. But they sought atonement, they confirmed connections between the Creator and the creature, and they brought the Good News to the people of Ireland, obliging them to moral conduct.

A second kind of historical personage is the warrior. The morality of the warrior's conduct is at question. Warriors are not slaves, the name given in Ballymenone to the passive lackeys of colonialism. As farmers read the environment and come to act correctly, warriors read the political environment and rebel. Through rebellion they become saints, martyrs to old Ireland's cause, welcomed to heavenly glory by the Mother of Christ. Or they become lost. Their actions are retold to classify them, and through classification, history brings understanding of the dilemma in which the people of embattled Ulster construct their wee lives. Achieving no final earthly victory, they will suffer, the saint predicted, until the end of time.

17

Of the many events selected for narration by Hugh Nolan and his colleagues in Ballymenone, two form a pair for consideration: the Mackan Fight of July 13, 1829, and the hosting at the Swad Chapel on August 12, 1868. Were they situated chronologically and absorbed in streams of cause and effect, one would be a minor riot in the train of events that followed Catholic Emancipation, the other would be an instance of civil disobedience in the context of the Fenian Rising. Both would be forgettable details of national history. But set in isolation on the land, one on a slope above the Derrylin Road, the other at the chapel gate in the border town of Swanlinbar, each gains presence in memory, gathers power, and unfolds through story and song to mark the limits of moral action.

The men of Mackan knew no fear: responding to threats to burn their houses, they collected and charged up the hill, killing their neighbors with pitchforks. Their victory brought them death and exile. They were right to stand firm, wrong to commit murder. When the landlord announced he was planning to raze the Catholic chapel at Swanlinbar, thousands assembled. The ballad commemorating their action declares that the Swanlinbar boys will not be forgotten; they were men of honor, guilty of neither crime nor wrong. They stood firm, and God did their work, killing the landlord, turning him black as your boot in his bed.

Circumstances require rebellion, the stories say, but life's eternal commandment is to love your neighbor as yourself. Those who break the commandment with wild words, with threats to burn the home or demolish the house of God, must be resisted, but resistance cannot lead to breaking the commandment yet more violently, lest the immortal soul be gambled and lost. One has no righteous choice but to stand firm. What remains elective is murder, and by his choice the warrior becomes raised to glory or damned to hell.

A third historical class is filled with people like us who exist only in the moral climate created by saints, the heroes of eternal truth, and by warriors, the heroes of contingent action. In

Ballymenone's own history, people like us, men sloughing after the cows, women tasked with the impossible job of keeping the house clean, are exemplified in anecdotes told about the recently deceased. They were, we are, witty. Ballymenone, Hugh Nolan said, was a territory of wits, enlivened by people called stars who sparkled against the darkness, telling comical tales, touched by the absurd, and composing lovely poems about local happenings. In confrontation with figures of authority — the priest, the policeman, the tax collector — the local stars always wittily invert hierarchies of power and gain little victories, proving that their outward poverty tells nothing about their inward genius.

The people who struggle in this place, representing ourselves to ourselves in historical story, are brilliant and artistic, and they are brave. They are people like Mrs. Timoney, a widow who raised her children, kept her house clean, and did the heavy work of a man, wielding the spade in the bog, coping sod on the lea ground. Twice a year, she walked all the way to Ballyconnell to pay the landlord's agent the rent for her insufficient scrap of earth. It makes your blood boil, so it does.

Our poverty is not the result of a lack of intelligence or fortitude. Its cause lies in conditions, environmental conditions (this is no place for agriculture), and political conditions (this is a place of endless rebellion against the invader who took our land and doomed us to penury).

Poor they might be, the people who live in this place, but they are bright and brave, and they are not alone. History's worst moment, the Famine of 1846 that swept a quarter of Ireland's people into death or exile, was no natural disaster. According to the local historians, the cause was English meddling in the ecological balance of Ireland, and Britain was to blame for its severity. At the depth of the Famine, Mr. McBrien, who lived in Ballymenone, turned to the river for food, and God provided him precisely one fish daily for each member of his family. When one child died, the number of fish McBrien caught each day was reduced by one. God provides — the bare minimum. And God takes the lives of innocent children. It is not ours to understand, and the people tell of mystery, describing encounters with the other world, with ghosts, fairies, and tokens of death like the banshee who wailed in despair and clawed the back door at the house of the Widow's Jimmy Owens. Their accounts affirm the unknowable, demonstrating the incompleteness of empirical knowledge and the need for faith. As the saints taught: He is there, surely. We are not alone on our journey.

In Hugh Nolan's telling, the history of change doubles, establishing a context of simultaneous improvement and degeneration within which people must choose, as they say in Ballymenone, a way of going on. His history of stability also doubles to include an environmental realm, requiring intelligent adaptation, and a moral realm that further subdivides into a political sphere, requiring resistance, and a sacred sphere, requiring acquiescence to transcendent law. In the midst of this complexity, one must shape a life. The traits necessary to life are wit (the ability to understand and overturn conditions), courage (the ability to carry on, despite conditions), and faith (a way to endure the unknowable).

Thinking spatially, not temporally, lifting his stories from places on the land, rather than locations in chronology, relating them typologically, rather than setting them into sequences of cause and effect, Hugh Nolan at once tells the history of his small, dark place, and makes history into a description of the human condition.

Hugh Nolan died in 1981. No death hit me harder. We had passed so much time together, he had taught me so generously, that I knew how much the world lost in his dying. He had gathered up his community's history and rehearsed it inwardly to keep it fresh, so that he could tell his neighbors the stories they needed to hear. They came out of the darkness and sat by his hearth. He told tired farmers that their place was rich in history, that people like them had beaten their poverty with humor and art, with hard work and faith. He told the lads who play in the game, who make the bombs that wreck the night in Ulster, that their rebellion was heroic, and that, in rebellion, they were putting their immortal souls at risk. Mr. Nolan's history was designed to make people aware of their conditions and to place upon them the human obligation of choice.

Listening to but two nonacademic historians, we have discovered disruptions in the linear, segmented, progressive order of academic history. If the conspicuous disruption is environmental, the profound rupture in the sequence of change comes with the sacred.

Historians — Marc Bloch for one, Douglas Southall Freeman for another, to cite an odd couple — have recognized the challenge to their craft posed by sincere religiosity. The academic historian seems tempted to dismiss religious people as marginal (which they are to histories painstakingly arranged around secular centers) and to probe beneath religious motives for worldlier goals deemed to be more real. But Hugh Nolan speaks for millions and millions of people who are, like him, religious above all, when he turns history upside down. In history, he teaches, change shapes a domain in which people must endure, seeking adherence to eternal law. Change matters, but less than stability. A narrative built of change must marginalize and misrepresent people whose lives are dedicated to the unchanging.

One among the millions is Haripada Pal. He works in a cramped, damp shop in Shankharibazar, a narrow street, walled by tall buildings, near the waterfront in Dhaka. The capital city of the People's Republic of Bangladesh, Dhaka centers the vast delta that was built by the silt of the Ganges, the Brahmaputra, and the Meghna, as they flowed down from the mountains, met, merged, and ran on to the sea.

Alive in the world, Haripada Pal says he has no choice but to live in time, working to feed the body that contains the soul, as the pen contains the ink, and striving to survive amid confusion and terror. Haripada's time is a massive cycle, revolving through four ages to end in flames and to emerge again from the dampness. Ours is the fourth age, the age of darkness and disorder. There is nothing to be done. We endure the disorder of techno- logical progress that distracts people from God and entices them into the madness of greed. We endure social disorder in which respect for the self and the other dissolves, the center does not hold, and trust becomes untenable. We endure the disorder of political contention, the unending series of invasions, rebellions, and sectarian disturbances that mark time at the far ends of what was once the British Empire — on the Indian subcontinent as it is in Ireland. The political is privileged in academic explanations of life's ordering and history's patterning, but for us, for the people on the ground, political powers gather into a perduring storm of inequity and violence from which we must seek shelter. When the Pakistani army cracked down in 1971, massacring three million Bengalis, Haripada Pal escaped to his village, a mound of jungle above the flood, where he was born in 1946 and learned his trade from his beloved grandfather.

It is, he says, tolerable. He lives in time and finds release in his work. Haripada Pal brings clay from his village to the city, blending and perfecting it to sculpt images of the deities. In con- centration, working the clay, he steps outside of time and unites with God. "Sometimes I become part of God. Sometimes God becomes part of me. I feel God in myself when I concentrate." The God in his soul erupts through his fingertips to fuse with the seed of creation in the clay, investing the image of the god- dess with sacred life. Then the beautiful statue is painted and positioned for worship at the time set in scripture.

In front of the faithful, the goddess descends into the clay. She is welcomed with prayer and garlanded as a revered guest should be. Drums beat, flames dance, smoke flows. The devotee gives flowers, makes the heart's desires known to the goddess, and receives sweets, dining with the deity to seal a con- tract between the worlds, this and the other. Worship ends with dawn, and the statue that took weeks of work is empty, a pretty shell no more valuable than the body after the soul has flown. It

Haripada Pal

Shankharibazar.
Dhaka,
Bangladesh.
1998

is borne to the river and immersed, melted back into the flowing waters so that the cycles of creation and sacrifice can continue.

Haripada Pal works in temporal affirmation of timelessness. His work, he says, is a benefit, a gift to people who need to connect with eternal power in order to receive the blessings of God. His work is a blessing, and it is a prayer, a part of his devotion. His prayer is that he will not be reincarnated into this lower environment where it is hard to concentrate, where the world's derangement makes it difficult to keep the mind fixed on God. In work, Haripada Pal escapes time, and he works to escape time permanently, to please God so that he will be delivered from the cycles of birth and rebirth into a state of timeless bliss.

A Unified History

Now, as is *de rigueur,* I have on stage three French intellectuals — Jean-Paul Sartre, Claude Lévi-Strauss, and Fernand Braudel — and unconventionally I have welcomed into colloquy three impecunious, nonacademic intellectuals, a Muslim, a Catholic, and a Hindu: Ahmet Balcı, Hugh Nolan, and Haripada Pal.

All share the idea of a linear, sequential history, but none is content to stop there. As though recasting and sophisticating the French vision, the nonacademic thinkers have divided time into streams of change and continuity, divided change into progressive and regressive valences, and, limiting time by the timeless, they have revealed continuity to be the consequence of stabilizing actions that exhibit repetitive, recursive, and cyclical patterns.

The shape of time has become complicated enough to allow us to imagine a reintegration of history. The inquiry has barely begun — only six people, none of them women, all from Eurasia — but we have gained some sense of what an improved history might look like, and I will move toward the end by returning to simple talk about big issues.

Since cultures differ, as surely as languages differ, it follows that they will have different histories, different pasts, of course, and different ways of creating understanding of those pasts in line with current needs.

Culture is a mental construct, built by individuals in shifting experience. Moving together in communication, people become alert to problems requiring action. Their thought becomes oriented to key paradoxes around which interpretations coalesce. Agreeing on the importance of certain issues, people come into social association and link their destinies through compatible understandings, at once making a culture among themselves and cutting a collective track through time.

Cultures, like histories, are created by people to serve them during their ordeal. People might be equal in brilliance, but they have not been allotted resources equally. Societies are lucky or not, and their members in interaction build their cultures toward distinct points of value. Cultures accomplish excellence diversely, concentrating energy in different realms of life, this one in technology, that one in philosophy, this one in music, that one in commerce, the other in history.

Difference is interesting, excellence is astonishing, and all cultures are shaped and refined by people who evaluate the familiar in relation to the foreign. Through comparative analysis, cultures seem better in some ways, worse in others. We who have made that common activity into a profession study cultures distanced in time or space not only to record them, celebrating again the variety our species has achieved, but also to learn from them, finding in their excellence hints about how we might face our culture's deficiencies and work toward improvement.

Let me return again, for example again, to art history and the observation that contemporary Western definitions of art retard more than advance cross-cultural study. We might seek answers through review of our philosophical tradition, and Saint Thomas has some of them, but that tradition led us to the dead end we face. It would be easier, and more quickly productive, to seek solutions in other traditions.

During ethnographic inquiry, I found that Turkish artisans held a consistent and excellent definition of art. Western definitions tend to feature media, particular technical disciplines, such as painting and sculpture, that have proved historically more accessible to men than women, making art a male province. Or Western definitions feature functions that separate art from utility and identify it with leisure, making art a province of the rich. Or they feature the response of the connoisseur, replacing creation with consumption, and requiring art to be supported by learned commentary, making it a province of the educated. The Turkish definition, centered existentially in performance, stresses the individual's passionate commitment to creation, despite differences of medium, function, and consumption. It gracefully welcomes women as well as men, the poor as well as the rich, the educated and the uneducated.

One consequence of the tacit democracy of the Turkish definition is that general appreciation gathers at once around calligraphy, created largely by prosperous, educated, urban men, and around carpets, created largely by poor, uneducated, rural women. Another consequence is that, among the world's modern nations, only Japan surpasses Turkey in artistic vitality. Another could be the adoption of definitions in the Turkish style by thinkers in other cultures.

My point is not that the Turkish definition of art is, like the Western academic definition, one among a host of equals in the ethnological spread, different as Turkish culture and history are different. My point is that the Turkish definition is superior, not philosophically perfect for all I know, but pragmatically preferable if the task of the art historian is to engage in cross-cultural analysis during the attempt to create a global understanding of art as part of a unified practice of history.

Turning to history in general, I will grant comparable pride of place to Ballymenone. Hugh Nolan is the best historian it has been my fortune to know. In comparison with academic history,

Ballymenone's is inferior in resources. Dependent on memory, not the written record, it cannot compete with academic history in its stretch or welter of perplexing detail. But built to its place, shaped in oral performance, forever fresh, it is better attuned to the needs of the people. They need understanding. Hugh Nolan's history speaks straight to their dilemma, and incorporating common occurrences that would be ceded to fiction in another tradition, Mr. Nolan's history, like the Turkish definition of art, welcomes people of all kinds and so proves useful to all kinds of people.

With Hugh Nolan in Clio's role, I will venture a sketch of the whole picture. History should be cultural history, geographical at its base so that one culture's history will not expand to become the world's history. The historian becomes a cultural geographer, watching how cultures unfold through time in relation to physical conditions and in exchange with other cultures. As they shift in time and space, cultures seek their own excellence, developing traditions, modes of historical construction.

Traditions collectivize the will, gripping to the significant and reaching for patterns in time. The creators of tradition place the emphasis differently. They might envision time in terms of a tradition of change that begets a trim series of substitutions: the old yields to the new, and one encompassing spirit of the age replaces another, century by century, decade by decade, in the march of progress. Such thinking fits the bellicose, capitalistic West where technology increases the capacity to kill and sequential fashions fuel a hot economy. But the creators of tradition might see time as an expanding accumulation that permits the coexistence of the old and the new in the Japanese manner. Or they might see time as a series of recursions, of returns to propriety through the imitation of refined old models in the manner of Confucian China. Or they might see change as a turbulent frenzy on the face of the timeless depths, as thinkers trying to make sense of India tend to do.

Cultures are built to accord with ideas of time that suit their differing structures of value. The problem is how to compare them in a way that preserves their difference while allowing them to be connected in unified historical understanding. Chronology, the mainstay of Western academic history, cannot be the solution. Cultures do not move to one beat. They do not develop at the same time, or at the same rate, or in line with one temporal pattern. Hugh Nolan's solution, and the solution of the modern ethnologist, is to turn from the chronological to the typological.

Though endlessly variable in detail, cultures are of distinct kinds. Just as their social orders might be patrilineal or matrilineal, hierarchical or egalitarian, just as their economies might be based on barter or cash, their religions on monotheistic or polytheistic precepts, cultures in their histories display different temporal types.

Their traditions stress one temporal way or another, but all cultures rise through time, developing characteristic patterns by combining linear and sequential, fast and slow, repetitive, recursive, and cyclical dynamics. The types are these combinations, distinct fusions of universal urges, and history has become a temporally inflected ethnology.

An ethnological history would have as its task the assembly of a systematic array of temporal types. The array would collect real cultures, each with its own clock, each on its own course, but related, one to the other, by temporal pattern. Cultures dedicated to continuity would cluster in one group, cultures dominated by rapid change in another. We would probably find highland pastoral societies in one cluster, industrial societies with far-flung colonies in another. But by the complexity and impurity of their mixtures of developmental dynamics, all would connect, and each could be set into a coherent display of historical possibility — a story of stories.

The big picture — this systematic array — could be detailed endlessly. Any act in time, and they all happen in time, could be added, and as they accumulated, the system of connection would expand, complicate, and grow in its power to embrace and unify. But the ultimate goal would not be the refinement of a science of time that would reveal real cultures to be transformations of a limited set of abstract types, each the yield of a dialectic of tradition and conditions. That would happen, and with no great difficulty. But the ultimate goal would be a unified history that grants to each of the world's cultures its own place in time.

To compare cultures historically, to array them typologically (reconciling history and anthropology into the bargain), we need comparable data. It would be most polite to encounter each culture through its peculiar excellence, let us say its art, defining art for the historian as a culture's most radiant and integrated expressions of its values. Art would offer the proper entry to culture, and history would become art history. But some arts are evanescent, leaving no phenomenal residue to use in understanding how cultures shape through time. Memories run out of detail as time deepens, and the analyst in the present is reduced to material culture, to artifacts that, surviving from different eras, remain to be arranged in temporal series as illustrations of progress or regress, of repetition or recursion.

Surviving artifacts might bear inscriptions. They might be books, say, that are novels or diaries or government reports. In comparative study, the obvious limitation of inscribed artifacts is that some cultures have them and most do not. The focus on writing, while natural to the writer, violently distorts history, marginalizing cultures without writing, leaving most of the past's people out of account, lost in darkness. We are back where we started, composing histories of no use to most people. The subtler limitation of the written record is that writers are odd ducks who choose to pass their time in isolation instead of decently among their fellows. How far does their knowing go? At question is whether writers speak only for themselves or whether, as John Milton said of himself, they articulate the common murmur. Stuck in the flux, writers seem always to speak of their times as times of change, which they are, of course.

It is true, but hardly news, that all is changing in human affairs, that everything is fluid, negotiable, emergent. But in reconstituting intentions and tracing consequences, we learn to get beyond the complexity of incidents. Through compassionate analysis, we come to understand whether the actors in the mutable moment were working toward minor adjustments, major alterations, or stability. The product of performance, the story told, the book written, the pot thrown, is the stuff of history, and following the consequences of the act, tracking its success, we will find out whether this event, flowing in the stream of events, leads to profound change or loses itself in the flutter of incident through which stability is maintained.

Vexed or excited by change, writers call their moments transitional. Their texts prove handy to historians who, being writers themselves, need change in order to make narrative, and who need period voices to support their own cases. But even in the hot history of the West, revolutionary moments are separated by long stretches of stabilizing adjustment. And even if history were reduced, as it often is, to the literary history of the West, these questions would remain: For whom does the writer speak? Is the writer's change mere change — part of the important and engrossing normal state of affairs — or profound change? Is the writer's moment of transition enmeshed in a revolutionary or stabilizing trend? Literary creations require context to become sources in cultural history.

In her deft handling of Martha Ballard's diaries, Laurel Thatcher Ulrich provides one splendid instance of how historians use close contextual reading to convert written texts into cultural documents. But at the edge of the record stand shadowy images of those who did not write, the majority even in literate societies, and beyond them spreads an immensity of darkness. Only a human being's own creations can be interpreted into a fair representation, and we are driven by care for our craft and respect for humanity past the limits of the literate.

The sources we need for a new history will carry us, at once, far back into time and out across space into every place. Seeking understanding from those who did not write, as well as from those who did, we are faced with uninscribed artifacts, with landscapes, settlements, and buildings, with knapped flint, engraved bone, carved wood, beaten steel, woven wool, molded plastic, and clay shaped into pots and gods. History becomes a kind of archaeology. Artifacts assemble into general patterns, providing context for writing and oral testimony, and cultures become temporal types, displays of different ways through time, as they collide, converge, and diverge.

Instead of collapsing along one narrative line to accommodate some cultures and not others, to serve some powers and not others, history expands into an array of real cultures, each understood in terms of its own development toward value and located in a geographical frame genuinely global in scope. Neoevolutionary possibilities open for the scholar. Freed from the confines of a universal chronology, able to compare cultures in virtue and circumstance, scholars could contrive surprising theories of causation. At the same time, by enfolding all cultures, by including all kinds of actors and acts, this new history could help people gain some sense of their place in time.

There is not a chance in the world that history will reunify, becoming a cultural history that uses artifacts to lay a geographical foundation and build upon it a system of temporal complexity in order to meet a diverse humanity's need to comprehend the predicament of existence. Disciplines have ground into comfortable grooves. Running in separation, disciplines are convenient to bureaucratic efforts to propagate a culture of management in service, at last, to economic power. But in resistance, or in oblivious devotion to the delights of their work, intellectuals remain free to entertain improvement in their fine, private endeavors. To them, I offer this piece of concluding rhetoric for consideration while they get on with the important task at hand.

A More Complicated History

If some historians, call them academic, see history as a succession of changes and view the changes to be the creations of actors with whom they identify, then other historians, call them nonacademic, living hard up against reality, see change less as a creation of action than as a context within which creative action is framed. Change is, for them, like the weather. It is ferocious or benign in the instant, repetitious over the long haul, a force to which one adjusts, living day by day.

When history is equated with changes that fit into narrative orders, when the myth is progressive, then most people are left out. History describes, not them, but their conditions, the climate in which they endure. They remain in darkness.

History's purpose cannot be to sort people into classes: on the one hand, a few, bright angelic beings whose lives are built by volition, and on the other, a vast, undifferentiated herd of beasts whose lives are governed by conditions. In granting humanity to all of its subjects, history will begin inside, at the point where all people have the power to shape their lives against circumstances. Then it will reach toward unifying patterns. Unity may lie beyond realization, but greater complexity does not; history can stretch beyond the chronicle into a patterned account of creative responses to change.

One pattern is accommodation. Playing the role of the masses, of the oppressed, people align with progress to gather the crumbs under the tables of privilege.

A second pattern is opposition. A clear, exemplary type of opposition is revitalization. In revitalization, people react to the new by returning to the old, scanning the past to imagine the future. The historian who profits from progress misreads revitalization as insignificant or decorative or regressive. Yet, in our world, the process of modernization — the progressive urge to the individualistic, the materialistic, and the international — is countered repetitively by revitalization, by work toward the communal, the sacred, and the local.

We have collected the disparate signs of modernization into a single force because they fit the logic of progress in our historical narrative. We have not done the same for revitalization, for the logic of recursion, because its abundant signs do not fit the story. Happy to generalize to the world from the narrow situation of the self, we miss the absurdity in confident sentences that begin, "Now that everyone has a computer..." Meanwhile, outside on the ground, the observer is witness to a global revival, mounted upon the sacred and shaped by local politics in opposition to progress, even deploying modern machinery to negate modernization. In the linear, segmented, progressive tale, revitalization is anachronistic, out of time, unreal. In the world that historians must describe, revitalization is a massive modern reality.

Patterns of response include accommodation, opposition — and continuity. Despite change, people keep to the right path through life. Their myth is the *Bhagavad Gita*.

Continuity has an environmental dimension. The one who occupies a clean space, heated against the cold, cooled against the heat, feels comfortable in neglecting the environment as a historical force. But most men and women remain at work in the world; there are, remember, more peasants in the Indian subcontinent than there are people of all classes in the United States and Europe combined. Their myths pit culture against nature, their history is a terrain of conflict between local knowledge and technological progress, and they find balance in difficult, willed acts of continuity. The farmer might be described as rooted in timeless process, but he maintains his tenuous hold on the land by intense exertion, repeating today what worked well enough yesterday.

33

Continuity has a social dimension. Despite the revolutions, there is the humble, fulfilling continuity of daily life among family and friends. The great historian E. P. Thompson told me that here lay folklore's challenge to history, the basis of a powerful critique. History in its commitment to dramatic change, he said, had no graceful way to deal with the continuity that characterizes normal existence as people pass the time, working and eating, loving and fighting, and fading away. A history incapable of describing most of life is no history at all. One thing that makes me a folklorist, one kind of historian and not another, is exactly that. I do not find it difficult to understand how small and common things matter, nor difficult to see how history should be a story of continuity as well as change. Another thing is that my discipline encouraged me to take nonacademic creators seriously. Though I have gone off in directions my teachers did not suggest (history being one of them), I have remained alert to continuity, and I have sought guidance from uncredentialed intellectuals like Hugh Nolan, who was not my equal, but my superior, my master.

Most profound, and most disturbing to the chronicle of change, is continuity's sacred dimension, exhibited in repeated prayers, cyclical rituals, and recursive works of art. Historians must learn a way to speak of this truth. For many men and women the goal in life is not compliance with time, a loss of the self into the fluid give and take, but a firmness in relation to the eternal, a commitment to timelessness.

Timelessness: continuity is not a strong enough word. There is continuity from sacred act to sacred act in the cycle of life and around the calendar, but in the sacred moment, connecting to the eternal, the prayer is to be without time, balanced, perhaps, at the midmost point of cosmic space, or translated from this vale of tears to the land of unclouded skies. The old-time Christian sings, "This world is not my home, I'm just a-traveling through. . . . Traveling, I'm traveling, trying to make Heaven my home." In that bright land to which we go, there will be no setting sun, no sorrow or death, no time.

Hearing the hope for a home without time, the historian, time's keeper, returns to the quotidian, remembering that time is but one axis in existence, and the other — space — might be its equal in experience and the construction of culture. Living at once in time and space, people use history to locate themselves in time, seeking their fortune in the temporal, and they use history to situate themselves in the wideness of space, seeking a home, a place of belonging.

Siraj Ahmad told me the history of his place. His place is the Swat Valley, rising and narrowing toward the mountains at the middle of Asia, where Afghanistan stretches to touch China, separating Pakistan and India from Uzbekistan and Tajikistan. He did not link his stories by time, nor lift them out of chronology. Like Hugh Nolan, Siraj picked them off the landscape.

Villages of rock and wood cling to the slopes. The land below is split into fields of green and gold. Mighty rivers roll down the valleys. Here, Siraj says, every man is a *khan*. If the sky could be divided as the land is divided, it, too, would be equitably apportioned among the people. Siraj Ahmad is the man of power in the town of Khwazakhela, and his stories, while celebrating the local and the virtuous, are meditations upon power:

A wicked king taxed the people without mercy. He warned them that he controlled the waters and he would send a river to crush them if they did not meet his demands for wealth. They took their complaint to the Buddha. The footprints of the Buddha remain on the rock where he stood and, with a sweep of his hand, sent the river to destroy the king and free the people of Swat.

Traveling here, a Persian king became lost in the forest. He knew a great thirst, and a woodcutter gave him a drink of clear, cool water. Journeying on, the king found a palace in ruins, heaped with treasure. Thirsty again, he returned to the woodcutter, received another refreshing drink, and to repay his generosity, the king told him about the treasure. The woodcutter said he knew the place. His father knew of it, and his grandfather before him. But wealth always leads to killing, he said, and he was content with the good life of a cutter of wood.

The British asked the king of Swat if they could build a road through his domain, saying that the road would bring improvements — schools and hospitals — and the people would become rich. The king took the English general on a walk, and told him to pick stones from the ground. Every stone he lifted was pure gold. You see, we are already rich, the king told the general, and we have no need for the improvements you promise.

Warriors for the faith laid siege to a Hindu fortress. There was no break in the deadlock until the leader of the army dreamed that he should surrender his power to the first man he found reading the Holy Koran. The next morning, he passed the turban of command to a pious, handsome youth. While the young man, a general now, was riding beneath the castle walls, a princess was smitten, and she sent him a message, saying that if he would promise to marry her, she would betray the secret of the citadel's water supply. He agreed, found the underground pipes, and broke them. A great thirst settled upon the people of the castle. The king realized the siege would succeed, and he sent his troops beyond the gates and into battle. In the furious clash of arms, the young general's head was cut from his body. When he lifted his head and continued to fight, the Hindus surrendered and embraced the true faith. At the tomb of this hero, who secured the land for Islam, Siraj in his youth sacrificed a sheep every Thursday evening.

A Muslim cleric once became jealous of a Sufi saint who attracted throngs of disciples. The cleric went to the king of India and asked him to make the saint come and submit to authority. The saint refused, saying his business was no business of the king. Enraged, the king commanded the saint to come, or his head would be parted from his body. The saint replied that kings do not have the power to know who will have a head tomorrow, and that night the king found himself unable to piss. His mother, knowing the saint to be the cause, went to him, beseeching him

Siraj Ahmad

Swat.
Pakistan.
1997

to stop her son's terrible pain. The saint said he would come only if the king granted him his kingdom. In misery and desperation, the king agreed, found copious relief, and took up his cloak to walk. The saint stopped him, saying he had no interest in the nasty job of king. The king could retain his position, but he must remember the rules of kingship: to remain humble and available to the people.

When they were building the great mosque at Kalam, the carpenters fashioned a beam too big to raise. The people went to a saint, asking how it could be set into place. He replied that, if it was God's will, the beam would be in place at dawn. It was, and it remains, and I have seen it, an architectural miracle.

Power, Siraj says, is God's. It is manifest among people in the acts of the saints. Siraj says that the saints, having purified themselves of desire, partake of the sacred and mediate between God and the common people. Saints are powerful. Kings, by contrast, think they are powerful. Kings, Siraj says, are always stupid.

Swat is a long way from Ballymenone. Their pasts are dissimilar, but their histories are like enough to suggest how history can welcome difference while seeking unity. Swat has kings, Ballymenone has landlords, but both histories fill with saints, warriors, and workers. Both are arranged by location. It matters less when something happened than where it happened, and it happened here, within our circle of experience. Both histories lace into unity not by time, but by theme, typologically. Hugh Nolan would understand Siraj Ahmad's tales. In them, worldly powers take wealth and offer wealth. They threaten destruction. People endure in the context of the rage and vanity of the king. Their need is for cool water and healthy bodies, for honest work, humility, and the faith that puts them in touch with true power.

The days passed, the stories piled up. His retainers came and went, pausing to smoke and listen. His youngest daughter brought our meals from the kitchen. In the shade of the veranda, Siraj relaxed on the roped bed where I slept at night, and he spoke of power. Like the great seventeenth-century historian Geoffrey

Keating — and like Herodotus two thousand years before him — Siraj Ahmad did not edit his heritage, omitting stories because they seem untrue to the scientific mind. All the stories reiterated the deep truth that the final power is not human and people should conduct themselves correctly.

The stories came off the land. They fit into our long conversation, rising to distinctiveness in narrative line and clarity of implication, and then they returned, sinking back into the land. As space absorbed time, it became particular, rich and holy — a place worthy of habitation and defense. This is where Alexander faltered, this is where the British were stopped. Siraj Ahmad has seen Paris, but this is where he knows the history, this is where he belongs.

If history reduces to a linear, segmented tale of change, it falls into alliance with the forces of oppression. If history can be a myth that entails progress and opposition and continuity, a story that is spatial as well as temporal, moral as well as factual, gentle to diversity, then it can serve its people.

The myth we need will leave no areas of darkness. It will teach us to understand change and lead us to the mature view that the two things happen at the one time, that things get better, and they get worse. The myth we need will help us know that we should adjust when it is to our advantage, and that we should not adjust if it means surrendering our rights to work worth doing and lives worth living.

Subel Koşar and Nezihe Avcı weaving together.
Karagömlek, Çanakkale, Turkey. 1986

· 2 ·

MATERIAL CULTURE

MATERIAL CULTURE is the conventional name for the tangible yield of human conduct. It is an odd term, material culture, for culture is immaterial. Culture is pattern in mind, inward, invisible, and shifting. Material things — red wheelbarrows, for instance — stand solidly out there in the world. But I have become accustomed to the term over time, and I even find virtue in its ungainly conjunction of the abstract and the concrete, for it cautions us to recall that we can know about culture only as it cycles in flashes and scraps through the sensate. We have things to study, and we must record them dutifully and examine them lovingly if the abstraction called culture is to be compassed, if the striving of the human actor is to be met with fellow feeling.

Material culture is culture made material; it is the inner wit at work in the world. Beginning necessarily with things, but not ending with them, the study of material culture uses objects to approach human thought and action.

Art is a better word. In his early essay *Nature*, Ralph Waldo Emerson defined art as a blending of nature and will. Emerson's art is material culture exactly: the unity in things of mind and matter. But in oneness with those who create, learning about *sanat* in Turkey and *shilpa* in Bengal, I have come to think of art as a special realm within material culture, its center and peak.

In exchange with nature, men and women make things, tracks in the mud, scud missiles. Those are the things of material culture. Things are works of art when the act is committed, devoted, when people transfer themselves so completely into their works that they stand as accomplishments of human possibility. They are, those works, so filled with the human that, as Robert Plant

41

Armstrong argues, we encounter them as affecting presences —
as subjects, not objects — wondering, as Michael Baxandall argues, how they came to be. Art embodies, and insistently exhibits,
personal and collective identities, aesthetic and instrumental purposes, mundane and spiritual aspirations. Around art — the most
human of things — material culture gathers, blending nature and
will, and beyond material culture spreads the merely material,
the unhuman.

Seeking the human, the artful in the cultural, the cultural in
the material, we go into the world and find things. They will not
let us mistake people for vapors of consciousness. Artifacts set
the mind in the body, the body in the world.

The world enters the artifact in materials, abiding in stone,
mellow and gray, in swirls of woodgrain and the luster of silk.
Materials carry the scars left by the body in motion: the rhyth-
mic chips of the chisel and scoops of the adze, the twists of spun
fiber, the dainty pricks of the needle. Artifacts recall the technology by which nature was made cultural, and they incarnate the
creator's mind, holding in form and ornament the plans that
preceded them and the decisions committed in their making.

Consider the wonder of the Japanese teabowl. It is a thing of
clay, dug from the earth and still gritty. The sweeps of its maker's
fingers run in the slow spiral of its raising. Its moment of dampness, when it stood in pliable uncertainty, lingers in the wobble
of the rim. Scorches remember its time in the fire when it grew
firm. The glaze that melted in the flame seems molten still, blis-
tered and flowing. The footring, fine walls, and upright form
speak of the scheme in the master's mind. The cracks fastidiously filled with gold lacquer hint of subsequent travail and car-
ing. The bowl was filled with hot liquid and passed from hand
to hand, filling the cup of the palm, warming the palps, joining
people in ceremonial conviviality.

The teabowl embodies a relation to nature. It plucks an instant out of transitory experience. It materializes its maker's desire for beauty, and it awaits use as a tool to forge social affinity.

Teabowl named the Thunderbolt.
By Gonbei. Izumo, Japan. c. 1677

Teabowl. By Norio Agawa.
Hagi, Japan. 1998

Material, a part of the world, the record of bodily action in nature, the artifact perpetually displays the process of its design, the pattern in the mind of its creator. It incorporates intention. Intentions need not so register in consciousness that they can be brought forth in orderly commentary. Their reality does not depend on words.

There are people who say that people think in words. A friend of mine, a linguist, says that the idea of a tree forms first in his mind as a word, "tree," beyond which he must stretch to bring real trees into thought. For me it is the opposite. Visions come first, of cypress and pine and oak, of the roughness of bark and the blackness of limbs in winter, then I must work to recover the idea that gathers all of that and confines it in a word. I cannot be alone when I think in images, quicker and larger than words, and then must exert to transform them into the conventions of language. Only some of the thinking of some people gains presence in the record when linguists reduce social interactions to speech or historians find evidence only in stripes of inscription.

The clearest case for material culture is historical. The literal mind can know only the history of a prosperous, literate minority. The history of most people, preserved in unwritten artifacts, escapes into oblivion. I have argued that point for more than thirty years, and it remains a tenable position, but now, reflecting more, I worry that studies focused on words, whether written or spoken, omit whole spheres of experience that are cumbersomely framed in language but gracefully shaped into artifacts. We miss more than most people in recent times, and everyone in the most ancient days, when we restrict historical research to verbal documents. We miss the wordless experience of all people, rich or poor, near or far.

I need to be more specific. Suppose life's sociable center is full of talk, ranging from formulaic greetings to twisted philosophical discourse. Converting spoken moments into verbal documents presents no great difficulty. But at one end of the spectrum of experience there are the small, silent tasks without which life would be unendurable. The little pleasure of the little job well done appears clearly in the artifact — the trimly weeded garden, the table set for dinner, the clean manuscript, the smooth plank — though it baffles all but the greatest masters of language. It takes a James Joyce to make doing one's daily work a fit topic for verbal elaboration. At the other end of experience, silent again, alone again, people bend before eternal power. Rote prayers fail their emotions. Thousands of fervent couplets composed in mystical ecstacy can only point at the deep mood of the soul that the artist captures suavely in the placid face of the Buddha or in the whirl of stars on the dome above.

Things composed of words and things crafted out of scraps of the world differ in the experiences to which they bear clear witness. But in the ambit of the excellence of theoretical linguistics — which we owe to thinkers of the magnitude of Noam Chomsky and Dell Hymes — and as befits my job of writing words and yours of reading them, it is useful to entertain the similarities in language and material culture.

Were we to call things made of words and things made of earthy bits both texts, we would be reclaiming for material culture a term like many others — line, verse, and stanza, for examples — that was borrowed from the realm of handwork to clarify verbal actions. The text is an entity woven together out of other entities, a textile, and the process by which texts are created, through mental and physical effort in social life, brings material culture and language into connection.

Visited by a feeling that deserves communication, the mind directs the body to move, and it does, using the environment to send a signal, comprehensible (it is to be hoped) to another. Using light, the shoulders shrug. Using air, the tongue bobs to make meaningful sounds. Using stone, the hand moves to shape the body of a god. From that simple observation, flows one special quality of material culture. Since the artifact blends the mind with permanent materials, with stone rather than light or air, only artifacts last beyond the event, and only artifacts — books, crockery, projectile points — provide the basic resource for the historian.

My advocacy of the artifact should not be taken to mean that I am opposed to the use of documents in history. That would be silly. After all, documents are artifacts, and any serious historian will use sources of all kinds to get the story told. What I do oppose is the idea that there can be no history when there are no documents, which leads drearily to the idea that the only real history is that of the literate. If it were, most people would have no place in time, history would serve the power of a privileged few, and it would be better to have no history at all, no guidance from the past about conduct and order. Maybe chaos would bring justice.

When documents accompany artifacts, it would be foolish to ignore them, but it would be no less a mistake to assume that they say the same thing and that the document is the more reliable source. Documents and uninscribed artifacts want separate analysis, followed by comparison to locate their points of complement and conflict. There are times when it is clear that the artifact should lead the investigation. A building is a far grander thing than a building contract. An artist's paintings are richer than his titillating letters. More often we find both documents and artifacts to be insufficient and difficult to understand. Then, growing weary, losing heart, we are tempted to follow the document because it seems easier to read and to reduce the artifact to an illustration of an argument compounded of words. It would be more fruitful to reverse the procedure, turning first to the abundant and democratic resource of material culture, assembling artifacts into independent systems, letting them have their own muffled say, and then returning to the documentary record, the work of the wordy observer, to develop explanations.

Material culture is as true to the mind, as dear to the heart, as language, and what is more, it reports thoughts and actions that resist verbal formulation. Like a story, an artifact is a text, a display of form and a vehicle for meaning. Both stories and artifacts arise out of concentration, both are created in time and shaped to cultural pattern, but they differ in apprehension. The story belongs to temporal experience. It moves in one direction, accumulating associations sequentially. The artifact belongs to spatial experience. It unfolds in all directions at once, embracing contradictions in simultaneity, and opening multiple routes to significance.

Artifacts rarely mean in the manner of lucid prose. Poetry, explosive with ambiguity and uneasy in the confines of time, comes closer to the artifact's mode of significance. Music, moving more than allusive, repetitious in transformation, comes closer still. At last, the artifact has its own way to meaning, and in learning it we begin to hear the voices in things, the screams of the stone gods prisoned behind glass in the museum. Then we accept the strange responsibility of putting into words that which is not verbal.

Method

There is nothing easy in our work, but its basic strategy is not hard to state. We seek pattern. Patterns imply intentions and carry toward meaning. The skeptic will ask for the meaning of a single thing. What, say, does a lone motif on an oriental carpet mean? The rigorous answer is: nothing. In this, too, material culture resembles language. A lone word means nothing. It is an assembly of sounds as the motif on the rug is an assembly of shapes. The word comes to meaning within the structures of contrast and association in a particular language. Things and words are empty in isolation, arbitrary. Arbitrariness leaves them as they gain places in systems of interrelation.

Our work requires quantity, complexity, and a way to proceed. The old pair of text and context can serve to order the endeavor. All objects are simultaneously sets of parts and parts of sets. They are texts, sets of parts, to which meaning is brought by locating them in contexts, by analyzing them as parts of sets.

As a text, every object can be broken down into its parts and read as a composition. The greater the object's complexity, the more decisions its composition required, the more it fights us, rising before us into a thing created by another, a presence in its own right. We may not know what the object means, but it can be described. The description — the product of the Cartesian operation of dismembering and reassembling — becomes an account of intention as patterned relationships consolidate into a whole.

What makes a text, where it begins and ends, how it is to be represented — these are not simple questions, and for two centuries the progress of my discipline, folklore, has been marked by steady improvement in the recording and depiction of the integral unit of the text. Context, though, is harder. It is the ethnographer's temptation to reduce context to the observable, watching bodily motions while subtle meanings escape. It is the archaeologist's frustration to be denied direct access to most contexts, for they are inward and transitory more than palpable and lasting; they are cultural more than material. Texts have limits, meanings do not, and the analyst on the hunt for meaning will gather as much information as possible to construct as many contexts as possible. Then as the text is located in context after context, associations will assemble and multiply. The reading becomes rich. The artifact swells with meaning and accomplishes its mission.

One way to schematize the contextual variety, to arrange the categories of information within which artifacts absorb significance, is to envision contexts as a series of occasions belonging to three master classes — creation, communication, and consumption — that cumulatively recapitulate the life history of the artifact. The object is a carpet. The creator is Aysel Öztürk, weaver in the village of Karagömlek in northwestern Turkey.

First is creation. Aysel leans forward in concentration. Before her rise the dense white lines of the warp. She lifts yarn with one hand and ties a knot with the other, placing on the warp one

Aysel Öztürk and her daughter, Yasemin.
Karagömlek, Çanakkale, Turkey. 1990

Aysel and Hanife Öztürk, with Şükran Öztürk between them,
weaving a carpet at home in Karagömlek. 1987

Çınar yaprağı carpet. By Aysel and Hanife Öztürk. 1985

fuzzy, colored dot that will join thousands of others to make the design she holds only in her mind. The carpet comes, she says, *kafadan*, from her head. That instant in which she translates herself into wool, when thought becomes material, is central, fundamental, and it gathers a host of associations that fuse in the act of creation.

The associations are social. Aysel's social associations have a vertical dimension. She learned in girlhood from her mother, Hörüye, and she honors her teacher in creation. Her mother is absent physically, preparing dinner in another room, but she is present conceptually, continuing to guide Aysel's hands. Social associations have a horizontal dimension. Aysel works as one in the sisterhood of weavers in Karagömlek, young women who move from house to house and sit to chat at the loom.

To be human is to be alone and not alone, at once an individual and a member of society. During creation, Aysel is alone in concentration and part of a team at work. Her younger sister, Hanife, sits beside her, learning the art and giving her help. Others will credit the carpet to Aysel, for she is the master, but she will use the first person plural in describing the carpet as a collaborative effort. In social exchange, learning, teaching, and cooperating with her friends, Aysel has mastered a technical discipline, piled weaving, and she commands a range of forms, holding them at the ready for improvisatory action in the creative instant.

Form divides into basic and ornamental varieties. Ornament further divides into color, the inevitable consequence of materiality, and decorative detail, which is dependent, ancillary in application, but, like basic form, derived from a set of conceptual possibilities. A building displays its basic form in a composition of volumes. Realized in materials, it is always ornamented by color, by the natural hues of stone or wood, say, or by coats of brilliant whitewash. Colored form might, then, be decorated and consolidated by moldings that run around the openings and along the eaves. Comparably, a story has a basic architecture, a plot that must be realized in some vocal tone, taking on color, and that might be molded and ornamented by poetic conceits.

In Aysel Öztürk's carpet, the basic form is the pattern of the field, an assembly of shapes that embodies one of the abstract types by which the weavers name and classify their carpets with a rigor that would satisfy any scientific purpose. It might be the *çınar yaprağı* or the *altın tabak*, the *kızıllı*, the *çarklı*, or the *turnalı*. The figure of the type is achieved by alternating colors in the knots Aysel ties, filling the ground in red, the signal color of the Turkish carpet, or in white to display the gleaming sheen of the hand-spun wool that makes her carpet superior to those woven of dead, dull machine-spun wool. As the building is ornamented by repetitive, continuous forms that encircle openings and embrace the whole, Aysel's carpet is edged by borders, by runs of motifs that she calls streams.

Aysel holds separately in her memory, then brings together in creation, ideas of technology, basic form, color, and formal ornament. Each is ordered by a dominant desire — technology by smooth execution, basic form by a symmetry of drawing in both part and whole, color by harmony, borders by regularity of repetition. An aesthetic of smoothness, symmetry, and balance unifies the carpet. At the same time, each aspect of her compositional act consists of a discrete set of relations, offering internally a range of transformational options, and unfolding through performance into new combinations. Every carpet, Aysel says, is different.

Centered in the present, in the instant of concentration when Aysel, managing multitudinous possibilities, chooses to tie exactly that black knot, the act of creation, occupying time, reaches at once backward and forward, becoming historical.

Reaching backward, Aysel's act collects the whole of her biography. Her carpet's harmonious coloring remembers an early moment when she crawled around the loom, across the carpeted floor, and played with the scraps of wool from which she extracted a palette of hues: three reds, two blues, green, gold, black, and white. The carpet's technique, two smooth shoots of weft between trim rows of knots, remembers her learning, her mother. That motif, not quite right, remembers her teaching, her sister, and this one, intentionally reversed, recalls the day when Sevgi came and helped, knotting a memento into their fabric while talk flowed between them. In its wool, the carpet remembers the sheep that Aysel, with a staff in her hand, a black dog at her side, drove to the high pastures. Her father brought the sheep down and sheared them. Her mother spun the yarn that Aysel lifts now to make the pattern. The pattern is one of the types that are emblems of her village and region. In its size, her carpet is a *seccade*; it is a prayer rug, a tool for sacred ritual, and its lovely field bordered by streams evokes the garden with streams flowing by that is promised in the Holy Koran.

Through the particulars of her biography, the life of a young woman in an agricultural village, a Muslim in modern Turkey, Aysel's carpet assembles cultural history, and then history swings forward as she imagines the future. The carpet will be sold. Someone else will own it, use it, and she will have gold, securing her economic position in her new home when, years later, she marries the son of the owner of the sawmill and moves to the village of Bozeli.

Aysel's carpet means time at the loom, work and home, fire in the hearth, sheep on the mountain, the soft floor of the mosque, a mother's touch, a sister's love, a baby girl yet unborn.

The act of creation bundles up distinct sets of relations within each of which the object gathers significance:

There is the context of concentration, when Aysel sat quietly through a short winter's day, between hewn beams, and made thousands of decisions that abide in the finished carpet. The yield of concentration, of her devotion to her *meslek*, her profession, the carpet is, to Aysel, *sanat*, a work of art.

There is the context of learning, when she watched, wanting to work, and then sat at her mother's side, receiving the instruction that she had, in turn, received from her mother. There is a context of teaching, when Aysel transferred her mother's instructions to her sister, preserving the high technical standards for which her home and village are locally famed. And there is a context of cooperation, when she worked with Hanife, with her cousin Nejla, with her friends Sevgi and Şükran, weaving their separation into oneness, materializing their affection in beautiful carpets.

There is a context of technology, in which natural materials were transfigured into a cultural product, and Aysel's carpet can be evaluated by the precision of its weave. And a formal context, in which she chose replication or innovation, arranging dots of color to shape the busy borders that play against the repose of the center, symmetry upon symmetry.

There is a context of memory, where biographical fragments remain sharp and particular, yet drift toward the general, opening toward the whole of life in a family, the family of Mehmet Öztürk, who came as a shepherd, rebuilt a mud-walled house, and ascended to the status of a farmer; of life in a sociable village, where nomads from the east settled in the nineteenth century and all young women weave, forming among themselves a sisterhood of professional practice; of life in an agricultural place, where teams of workers at harvest bend and go, cutting with reaping hooks in the golden grain; of life as a Muslim, for whom the universe is ordered by the will of the one God.

And there is the context of hope, in which the future is imaginable, the carpet will be sold, and a better life seems possible.

All of that comes to focus and fusion in the instant when Aysel chooses to tie this knot. Here, in the multiplex context of creation, meaning begins, but it does not end.

The second master context is communication. In some kinds of performance, creation and communication coincide. The storyteller composes and presents the tale while communicating, transferring the story directly to another whose presence conditions creation. Certainly when Aysel weaves she displays her skills before the immediate audience of her collaborators, but her main communicative act resembles that of the writer who tells the story in isolation, committing it to sheets of paper that are later, perhaps much later, taken up and read. Like the writer, Aysel works to an imagined response and receives reaction slowly and indirectly through multiple channels.

Aysel Öztürk might weave a donation to a mosque in commemoration of a deceased loved one. On the floor of the mosque, her carpet represents her, her skill and taste and grief, her family and its bonds of love unbroken by death. Then, in time's passing, she will be forgotten, though her carpet will endure to help symbolize her village, the corporate entity from which she drew her art and to which it returns, her carpet becoming, perhaps, a model for a weaver in the future. The art of the village cycles in the mosque from the collective, through the individual, and back into the collective. The mosque is a place of prayer and remembrance, and it is the village's art gallery, its collection and exhibition, its resource for new creation.

More often Aysel's carpet escapes the circle of the village through economic exchange, leaving her, never to be seen again. For Aysel, as for the writer, the main context for communication is framed by commerce. Sold and bought, the artifact is transferred to another who will never understand all of its associations, and who, therefore, must be struck by its inherent properties. The writer's work, designed to approach and impress unknown others, must be clearer, more coherent and self-contained, than the storyteller's. In Aysel's thinking, the qualities in her carpet that will seize the attention of the buyer are its neat weave, its lively color, and the symmetry of its drawing. These are legible signs of intentionality. They signal excellence and bespeak the human: a body in control, a soul at play, a mind at work.

The contexts of communication make a series, in each of which the consumer is less knowledgeable, harder to reach. There is a context of collaborative performance, in which the creator reveals her art before colleagues who understand her effort. A context of donation, in which the carpet is given as a gift to family, friends, or the people of her community who know her personally or at least know much about her tradition and conditions. A context of commercial exchange, through which, in setting after setting, she is gradually erased and replaced by the buyer.

Beneath its busy surface the marketplace is structured by economic realities, limited by the knowledge of the participants, and shaped by the social conventions of bargaining. Differing in dynamic by gender and class, bargaining — in Turkish, *pazarlık etmek*: to do marketness — entails trades of numbers and facts while a price emerges that reflects the distance between seller and buyer. A relative pays less than an acquaintance, an old customer less than a new one, a native less than a foreigner.

Women with carpets in their arms meet the buyers at dawn in the weekly agricultural market in town. Aysel has agreed with the other weavers on a price to ask and a price to get. They hold firmly at a certain point, set in relation to the international price of gold that is published in the newspaper. It is not frivolous cash they want, but gold. The man who buys from her, in a quick procedure governed by the etiquette of gendered interaction, knows the selling price in the city. A local man, he knows, too, about village life, and, though a man, he understands something of the weaver's aesthetic. Not enough, says Aysel. The buyer stresses the fineness of the weave and neglects other qualities in the carpet that she deems more important: the play in the color, the sobriety in the drawing.

Her carpet lies on the dusty street between them. A tractor rattles past, hawkers call out the prices of vegetables, a crowd has gathered. He kicks over a corner of her carpet to see its weave, asks her price, and counters with a lower number. Her hope is for a price higher than the one she will take. The price she will take repays her time at the loom. It allows her to go slowly, maintaining her high standards and preserving the pleasure she finds in her work. To dip below the minimum, to break the price, they say, would disturb her art and disrupt the sisterhood that agreed on the prices for today's business. She lives with them and depends on them for help. She wants their affection, not their enmity, and they stand around her now, watching. In solidarity, they resist the buyer's pressure and slowly push the prices upward. They move together, listening. Prices carry information that might influence future production. The weavers learn quickly about shifts of fashion in faraway places from the arguments that accompany the numbers they hear in the weekly market of a small Anatolian town. Local commerce connects them to the world.

A local man takes Aysel's carpet in a bundle on the bus and sells it, at a small profit, to a wholesaler in the big city, Istanbul or Izmir. That buyer, a city man who knows little about the lives of the weavers, will sell it at a higher profit to a retailer with a classy store in a prosperous urban neighborhood in Turkey, or perhaps to a foreign buyer through whom it might come to rest any place on earth.

Through the channel of trade, Aysel's carpet leaves her and money comes to her. With the money comes information, anecdotes and generalizations that have passed through a long series of buyers and sellers. From the information, she develops an idea of the consumer that will help her in crafting commodities to venture in future markets.

In communication, the object goes from its creator to its consumer. Consumption, like creation, collects contexts in which the meanings of the artifact consolidate and expand. Communication and consumption always mesh, and in consumption the sequence of contexts continue within which the meanings of the creator are eclipsed by the meanings of the consumer.

Within consumption, in the context of use, the consumer's reaction overlaps with the creator's intentions. A wealthy man in the city, appreciating the qualities in Aysel's carpet, purchases it. Understanding the function implied by its size, he chooses to use it in his home as a prayer mat for his private devotions. Aysel and this man do not know each other, but they share enough in culture, in aesthetic and religious orientation, for his act to be seen as the completion of her plan.

Use is the first, but not the only, context in consumption. In the context of preservation, the consumer, while missing the particulars of association, recognizes the object's deepest meaning. This is the outcome of effort, a human thing, worthy of care and conservation. Aysel's rug is kept clean, protected from decay and destruction.

Finally, in the context of assimilation, the carpet is important for its connections to its owner. A German couple buys a carpet in the Covered Bazaar in Istanbul. It becomes a souvenir of their trip to Turkey, a reminder of sun on the beach, and then it becomes one element in the decor of their home, a part of the assembly that signals their taste. Their son saves it as a family heirloom. To him it means childhood. Germany replaces Turkey. The weaver's memories of village life give way to the memories of an aging psychiatrist in Munich for whom the carpet recalls a quiet moment when he lay upon it and marshaled his bright tin troops on a rainy afternoon. Then his son, finding the carpet worn, wads it into a bed for the dog, and his son, finding it tattered in his father's estate, throws it out. It becomes a rag in a landfill, awaiting its archaeologist.

In the context of use, I place a carpet by Aysel Öztürk on the floor to beautify my home. In the context of preservation, I bought a carpet by Aysel for the permanent collection of the Museum of International Folk Art in Santa Fe, New Mexico. In the context of assimilation, I use her carpet to compose an argument on the complexities of context that is interesting to me and maybe to others.

Contexts of creation teach about creators. Contexts of consumption teach about consumers. Contexts of communication connect the two, balancing creation against consumption, enfolding their similarities and differences. Meaning has its center in communication, at the point where intention and response link, where the consumer receives the creator's gift and continues creation in use. Where it is centered, meaning might logically stop, but lacking a common vocabulary for orders of meaning, we follow meanings in both directions, moving away from the center into the associations developed independently in the silent minds of the creator and the consumer.

Meaning is the sum of relations between objects and people. Accounts of meaning can begin anywhere in the object's history, though I think they are best begun in creation. From its place of beginning, the quest for completeness will assemble associations around the acts of creation, communication, and consumption, and then slide past every limit as the imagination plays tricks in the memory and the object becomes all it can be.

All objects exist in context. There is no such thing as an object out of context. But contexts differ greatly in their ability to help us understand the artifact at question. In some contexts, objects beam us deep meanings from other human beings. In other contexts, we find the reflections of our own tired faces. Seeing a composition of steel and wood, we pull it into our idea of the axe. We make it imaginatively into a thing for the chopping of timber and cease pondering it. A tool, we say. But for the man who forged and helved it, the axe was more — the realization of his tradition and skill, a device to honor his master and serve his neighbor. And for the man who used it, the axe might have been a token of status, not to be lowered into wood and mere utility.

I feel that I have already schematized context in the best way, but now I will summarize by cutting through the issue at a different angle. The text does not have one context; it has many.

One kind of context is the last stage of consumption: assimilation. It is the context we shape for things out of our own worries and concerns. As we shift a statue from its setting in a temple, where its associations were sacred, and place it in a museum, where its associations become aesthetic, and then imaginatively pluck the statue out of the museum and relocate it in the progressive sequence of art history, so we lift the axe out of a village ceremony, where it served as a mace of honor, and situate it in the category we have built in our minds for axes and dismiss it as a tool. Old meanings are replaced by new ones that seem convincing because they are derived from the culture we share with our readers. We think our work is done. It has not begun.

A second kind of context is conceptual. In it, the object exists within the sets of association that constitute the minds of its creators and users. This context could be called cultural, for it holds the meanings shared, if incompletely, by the people who made the thing and those who put it to use. It has also been called abstract, since it is invisible, an arrangement of forms and principles, not of tangible objects. The conceptual context does not exist out there in the world, posed for a photograph. It abides in the mind that creators shape as they struggle through the whole of life. Having watched his elders at work, having seen axes lying about and used in sundry projects, the creator abstracts from experience an idea of the axe — a basic form attended by a range of variations and enlivened by associations — that is enacted in the creative moments when the axe is made and used.

A third kind of context is physical. It has been called behavioral, for its contains bodies in motion, and it has been called particularistic because each one is unique, a specific assembly, while the conceptual context is principled and redundantly applicable. The physical context accumulates the pertinent pieces available to the senses. The axe rests on a bench amid oily rags and wood chips. It is lifted by a hand with knuckles and veins and allowed to fall into a short section of tree. All this is external; we watch, take notes and photos, and learn about axes.

As a thing of parts, the object perpetually represents its composer, the man who pounded steel and shaved wood. As a part of things, an element in a larger composition, the axe might or might not provide us further information about its maker. Found at a flea market, an old axe continues to babble about the creator it contains, but from its setting in the market, we are not drawn closer to him, but farther away, distracted into intriguing thoughts about the merchants and collectors of antique tools.

Out of conceptual context, the object remains in some physical context, visible among other things. These things, the other objects in the sensate ambit — the chips in the workshop, the labels in the museum — may aid in interpretation when the object, having been seen, is taken into the mind and given significance through association. The act of association is the key to our work. The associations might rise from our culture, assimilating the object to our needs, confirming our right of ownership. Or they might be gathered out of diverse categories of evidence in order to reconstruct the conceptual context, making the object into a creation by another person to whom we decently grant the right to be like us in humanity and unlike us in culture.

The second is the nobler task. We record texts, making precise records of real things, and we assemble contexts around them that lead us toward the intentions of the creator. The problem that remains is the relation of text to context. For the creator they form an experiential unit. The analyst approaches unity through two distinct moves, one compositional, the other associational.

In the compositional move, the text is located in a set with other texts that belong to the same time and place, that can be understood as products of one process of composition, manifestations of the same culture. The construction of the set is a crucial step. Noam Chomsky began the work that would lead to the splendid theory of transformational grammar with thousands of English sentences. Vladimir Propp discovered the formal principles of the folktale in a collection of Russian stories. Robert Plant Armstrong came to his new view of aesthetics through contemplation of a collection of Yoruba sculpture he had assembled in his beautiful home. I have built sets for analysis out of fieldwork by gathering data on all the barns in one county in New York state and all the houses in one area of Virginia, by recording all the stories told in the Irish community of Ballymenone, by seeing all the rugs on the floors of the mosques and on the looms of the weavers in a few of the villages in Çanakkale, Aysel Öztürk's region of Turkey.

The text is broken down, all the texts in the set are broken down into their parts, and what varies among them is separated from what does not vary. Then, the variable and the invariant are structured together into a single principled statement that defines the set as a system enclosed by rules of transformation. The system, a kind of grammar, becomes a theory of composition, an account of the process employed in designing the integrated range of forms that stand before us. Each form — story, house, or carpet — realizes the mind that was capable of creating all the forms in the set. The text is a revelation of consciousness, and it embodies a cultural style in its particular ratio of the variable to the invariant.

During the creative act, something will change to meet the needs of the creator who is always changing, always operating in new moments, and something will remain the same to meet the needs of communication: the wholly new thing would be incomprehensible. Intellectual proclivities bring different attitudes to the unity of the text. The geographer might be attracted to the invariant, to the typological in form and the continuous in historical action, while the historian is drawn to the variable in form and the changing in time. But the object, as part of a compositional set, will always display both stability and variability — matching the folklorist's old definition of folklore as that which, in seeming paradox, holds steady while varying fluidly with personalities and occasions. So it is for everything. Creation always blends the repetitive and the inventive. The text, the yield of creation, is no longer alone. It belongs to a compositional set within which it is comprehensible as a form.

Meaning remains. The text, now a historical entity — an assembly embodying a relation between stability and change — is located among mutable associations. Associations coalesce into contexts, sets of data within which the particular formal properties of the text, its uniqueness and its redundancy, can be explained as part of cultural history. Contextual limitations, options, and desires register in the text. The text invades its scenes of being, gathering contexts.

In the associational move, analysts logically employ the procedures that worked in the compositional move. The sociolinguist orders social exchanges systematically, the structuralist does the same for cognitive transformations. The results are clear. They become exquisitely, excruciatingly complex. They remain incomplete. I am reminded of a joke told by a rodeo clown at a county fair in Indiana, which I also heard in the cycle of witty tales about Nasrettin Hoca in Turkey. Coming home late at night and having lost the key to his door, a man is down on his hands and knees, hunting in the light under a street lamp. Asked if he lost his key there, he replies that, no, he lost it in the darkness farther down the street, but the light beneath the lamp is better for his search.

With Noam Chomsky, I believe that some of meaning can be revealed through the tidy, bright techniques that work in compositional analysis, but the reach for all of meaning demands courage as much as rigor, a willingness to grope in the dark, using the expansive, intuitive tactics of the novelist as well as the reductive, systematizing procedures of the scientist.

We have come to one of the many places where the labors of the ethnographer and the historian that seem so different — the subjects of one being alive, of the other dead — are at last alike. Ethnographers can elicit reactions to their theories, historians cannot, but both can test explanations in new settings. Both can record texts, both can collect texts in sets and analyze them formally. Both can search widely for unpredictable and astonishing associations — historians by reading diverse texts from the period, ethnographers by accumulating random experiences in the field. The goal of both is to learn enough to imagine the text's wild life of meaning.

A fragment of the spatial and temporal whole, the text gestures toward infinity, and playing on a field so vast that it can never be mapped, the analyst will, at some point, surrender to serendipity and consider any wacky fact, daring to speak of things that cannot be proved, since so much of meaning lodges in the deep fissures of memory, even using memory's tricky tropes while braving the dark places in order to explain the peculiar act of an individual who forced upon the world an object to trouble the mind. To meet meaning's expansive, subtle reach, the method trades rigor for seriousness.

Twice saved from the absurdity of isolation, now a part of a compositional set and a set of associations, the artifact stands ready for understanding. The first challenge is to describe things so well that their complexity will prevent us from associating them with things they do not belong among, as, say, folk art ineptly described becomes associated with the makings of children, madmen, and Sunday painters. The second challenge is to join texts correctly with their contexts.

I hope it is out of affection for the world, and not merely because they seem easier to describe, that analysts are drawn to physical contexts more than conceptual contexts and even use the word context synonymously with setting or scene. Only some of the setting is context (the part that goes with the text) and most of the context (the assembly of associations that lend the text meaning) is not visible in the scene. Ethnographers are naturally thrilled by settings of creation and scenes of use, and they are obliged to describe them — one might say completely, though complete description is impossible; the task is to select swiftly and intuitively the salient facts that will prove useful during writing to provide a semblance of reality while accounting for creative action. What excites the ethnographer befuddles the historian whose struggles to restore physical contexts drift into fiction, draining time away from work on the conceptual contexts in which, for ethnographers and historians alike, the explanations lie.

If we are lucky enough to encounter things bound as their creators intended them to be bound with other phenomena, we will learn much by puzzling the physical context together. But even when artifacts have sprung free from their scenes of creation and use (which, being material, lasting, and often transportable, it is in their nature to do), they can still be located in conceptual contexts, where, as incarnations of intention, they carry us toward the other people we need to meet if our notion of humanity is to be sufficiently rich.

When we want to learn about other people through their creations, the work, as I said, is not easy, and I have allowed the argument to grow complicated in harmony with reality. Early on, I arranged contexts to tell the artifact's story, setting before you this sequence: creation (concentration, learning, teaching, cooperation, technology, form, memory, hope), communication (collaboration, donation, commerce), and consumption (use, preservation, assimilation). Since I do ethnographic study in material culture, I know that such a list can guide a productive program for fieldwork. I also do historical study in material culture, and, while I feel it is good to understand such complexity, for it brings our limits into awareness, I know, too, it is frustrating to realize how little we can know when we face the artifact in isolation. But the work must go on.

So, with the historian in mind, I recast the contextual variety to argue that, though the ethnographer can watch creation and use, and the historian cannot, both of them, when developing explanations, will focus on the unseen, reconstituting conceptual contexts in two analytic moves. These moves enable us to imagine two of the contexts of creation. The first is the formal context, in which the particular object is seen to be one option in the transformational set of possibilities in the creator's mind. The second is the context of memory, which the analyst will subdivide and organize into categories of data — biographical, social, economic, political, religious, geographical — that bear upon creation. The job is, in essence, to connect formal properties in the object with cultural data from beyond, allowing each to explain the other, in order to understand the act that left us an artifact.

The artifact is described, analyzed in a compositional move, made meaningful in an associational move, and the final step is to comprehend the unity of creation by looping composition and association — text and context, form and meaning, structure and function — together. Their connection is often pictured sequentially. The object is made and placed into the world to accrue associations. That happens, but the central act of creation is portrayed better through the theory of performance formulated by Dell Hymes. In performance, an idea of context, of a thing's fit in the world, its uses and meanings and functions, precedes and sparks the enactment of compositional competence. The historian Antoine Roquentin in Sartre's *Nausea* discovers in amazement a seat beneath him. It is a wonder to ponder. People gathered materials and went to work with the idea of making a seat. When they were done, that is what they had made. And there it is, a thing to sit on, the marvel of the seat.

A new acquaintance in a bar does not tell a joke that just happens to be funny. He wants to amuse you, to connect with you, and he recalls a joke to that end. A builder does not employ the grammar-like rules for architectural design to erect a building that chances to shelter its occupants. Instead, a wish for shelter, among other desires, prompts the architectural capacity. The architect belongs to the world. His ability to compose merges with his knowledge of conditions — with his responsibilities as a moral being who must build to bring improvement, environmentally and aesthetically, socially and politically. He performs knowingly in a field of consequence; he builds to build culture. His house is designed to fit the world, and as it is built, the process of construction is adjusted delicately to make it fit better, and once it is finished, it is modified continually to keep the fit right.

Functions precede, guide, and follow structures. The object, a structuring of the variable and the invariant, might be followed by the unforeseen consequences that Robert K. Merton called latent functions. The axe is used to fell a tree to make a basket; the toppled tree contributes to the denuding of a hillside that leads to a mudslide that destroys the cornfield, eliminating the need for baskets at harvest time. The object will probably have latent functions, and surely it will collect associations unimaginable to its creator as it is situated in scene after scene, life after life. But other functions and meanings are planned, then built into the object during creation. Creation entails use: Aysel Öztürk weaves a beautiful rug to be used in prayer. Ideas of composition and association, of form and function, interpenetrate and unify in the performative act, so the object is not only in context, context is in the object. Art is not a pure projection of the mind. It records the mind busy in the world.

Once we have seen things for themselves, then seen them in connection, and then looped their aloneness with their connectivity, we have come to artifactual systems. Comparing systems spatially, we have ethnology. Comparing them temporally, we have history. Put ethnology and history together and you defeat the fractious academy, returning the study of humankind to the level of its beginnings in old Herodotus.

A Text in Time

Like the maker of a carpet or axe, the writer of a book works amid colleagues at the end of a tradition, historically, while looking ahead with hope. This chapter had its origin in a talk that closed a conference on material culture, organized by Gerald Pocius and held in St. John's, Newfoundland, in 1986. Written twice —in 1990 and again in 1998 — to fit the times, this paper belongs to the history of material culture study in North America.

The study of material culture is, in academic terms, a transdisciplinary movement designed to expand and integrate the study of art. It uses historical and ethnographic techniques to understand art as a part of common human experience. It adds the anthropological idea of culture to art history in order to make art a part of history in general. It adds the art of the people to general history to make it more democratic. It gathers archaeological and geographical, historical and ethnographic evidence to locate art in the world.

In practice, the study of material culture is the study of creativity in context. Through consideration of things as grand as whole landscapes, as modest as teapots, it opens to analysis the dialectic of will and conditions, discovering the reciprocal connections among individual desires, social orders, and environmental possibilities.

Philosophically, material culture study is founded upon the genetic right of human beings to create and the manifest reality of delimiting conditions. It upholds a meaningful relation between the conceptual and the physical, the personal and the social, the cultural and the historical. Framing human conduct culturally and materially, it conjoins aesthetic and moral evaluation.

Politically, the study of material culture confronts prejudice and seeks justice, resisting forces that deny art or history — excellence or significance — to human beings on the basis of gender, say, or race or class or culture. It demands the construction of an idea of art and an idea of history that can meet the needs of all people during their struggle to shape for themselves fulfilling and decent lives.

Looking backward, the historian of material culture finds the view dominated by the monumental figure of William Morris. Others are there in the distance, beyond him in time — medieval aestheticians in Europe and Asia; those great Greeks with whom intellectual histories are supposed to begin — but closest stands John Ruskin. He wrote, Morris said, "one of the very few necessary and inevitable utterances of the century." In it, explaining the nature of the Gothic style, Ruskin brought art into life, unifying aesthetics and ethics, pointing, Morris said, the road to the future. William Morris had been on that road since childhood, thrilled by Sir Walter Scott's novels and by his first glimpse of Canterbury Cathedral, and he would follow it for the whole of his intense, impatient life.

Morris read Ruskin, he scanned the Middle Ages for inspiration, and he created new works in an astounding range of genres and media, from ballads and visionary novels to stained glass and textiles. Morris read Marx, took heart from a trip to Iceland,

William Morris

and he used his experience of art and his great historical imagination to wage holy war on the age of ugliness and greed in which he was trapped.

William Morris marched and spoke, rallying his fellow socialists, and he was an astute businessman, purveying handsome commodities to prosperous customers. An environmentalist, he strove to protect ancient buildings, engendering the modern movement for historic preservation. A collector of art, he brought magnificent objects from Asia into the new museum in South Kensington to inspire English artists, and he wrote that the carpets woven in Aysel Öztürk's very region of Turkey "are designed on scientific principles which any good designer can apply to works of our own day." He sat at the loom himself, and working from close analysis through direct practice toward pattern and principle, he created the crisp, rich objects that form the foundation for modern design. Last came his typographical adventure; at Hammersmith in London, he printed the most beautiful books of the age.

Amid all that, especially in the decade of the eighties, Morris wrote with passionate clarity a series of essays on material culture. William Morris died in 1896. Those essays are over a century old, but they remain the best writings on the topic we call material culture and he called popular art. Filled with wisdom and hope, his essays glow with a love for art, for the delight we find in our work, and they smolder with hatred for a system — not for innocent machinery, but for the "profit-mongering" system that used machines to enslave workers and steal the pleasure from their work and the satisfaction from their lives.

William Morris told us to cease thinking of art as the rarefied expression of a mystically talented few, or as the peculiar possession of rich men. He argued that work is the mother of art, directing our study to carpets as well as paintings, axes as well as statues, and he bade us consider our own work as a source of insight into the work of others. With him, we come to wish that the painter in the loft, the scholar at the desk, and the industrial laborer on the shop floor might know the joy of the peasant girl at the loom.

After Morris, material culture gathered great students: Ananda Coomaraswamy and Soetsu Yanagi, Sigurd Erixon and Richard Weiss, Ruth Bunzel and Gladys Reichard, Estyn Evans and Fred Kniffen. They prepared our study to enter an expansive new phase in the 1960s.

I was there. My spare time in those days was divided between measuring weathered old barns in the hills of Pennsylvania and marching through clouds of tear gas in my nation's capital to advance civil rights and stop a horrid war. Those activities, the one antiquarian, the other youthful and optimistic, fit together in my mind.

The mood was angry and alive with hope. Freedom seemed possible. Black and white would march together and overcome some day. It seemed possible to stop the war, chanting in our thousands, "Hey, hey, LBJ, how many kids did you kill today?" Within the general mood, we shaped an intellectual climate by bringing the recreational reading of our undergraduate years into our scholarship. We had read Sartre and Camus, or poets and novelists who had read them, and existentialism reshaped our thinking. Sartre described existentialism as imagining a world without gods. Adjusted for scholarly consumption, that means seeing a world in which the active agents are not superorganic forces, but folks like us. People were cast back upon themselves, denied excuses, and charged with responsibility.

Once, scholars played minor roles in processes scaled beyond their ken. They could contribute to knowledge, but power lay in a tradition called the discipline to which one submitted. Now, scholars became heroes, responsible for the construction of their own styles of study. Issues of ethics arose, and transdisciplinary work became obligatory. The study of material culture gathered historians, art historians, architectural historians, geographers, folklorists, archaeologists, anthropologists, sociologists, artists, curators, dealers, and collectors in a common cause.

The cause was understanding human beings through their creations. Once, they were slaves of the subconscious, creatures of culture, bearers of tradition, beings blown about by historical forces. Now, they were responsible. Our goal was to know them as creators amid conditions, as historical actors.

We were aided by writers on the left, like James Agee, Oscar Lewis, and E. P. Thompson, who brought us close to people, to individual men and women with their own problems and understandings, and who — both the writers and their subjects — reminded us of our own creative potentials and political responsibilities. Novelists, ethnographers, and historians pushed us into the real world, where we learned the falsity of neat scholastic schemes. Structuralism drew us into the mind. No longer to be described in psychological terms as snaky, sick, and beyond control, the mind was celebrated by Claude Lévi-Strauss as gloriously logical in its complexity. Historical hierarchies toppled and colonialism lost its rationale as structuralism revealed the human mind to be one.

People are stuck in one impossibly complicated world, just as the Buddha taught. They belong to one species. Battered old barns bore evidence of the creative humanity of the dead. As for the living: we marched to liberate ourselves from the system that denied our rights and sent us to death in war. We called it the military-industrial complex, we called it capitalism, and most often we called it the system or the establishment. It was, in our minds, maintained by the government to benefit the rich.

Secular power had crushed community, undermining local support and leaving individuals vulnerable to manipulation by the propaganda of the mass media. Industrial capitalism had cramped creativity, convincing workers to trade happiness for cash and banishing artists into social irrelevance, making them exotic oddities — like the beasts caged in the zoo, said Lévi-Strauss. Without communities to nurture and receive their art, without serious outlets for their urges to creation, people are reduced to mere consumers of goods that bring wealth to a privileged minority. The issues of community (the immediate context for creative action) and creativity (the exploration of human and cultural potential) oriented our work.

Political purpose and empirical study unified in the material culture movement. We sought artifacts to build a better history, one that would reveal general creativity and explain the changes that made the system that ruled our world. In critique of that system, the system that brought us prosperity and gave us the time to pursue our studies, we went to people from whom we could learn about alternatives, gaining appreciation for the anachronistic virtues of community and creativity — fellowship and good work, William Morris would say. Ralph Rinzler went to visit Cheever Meaders, a potter in Georgia. Michael Owen Jones visited Chester Cornett, a chairmaker in Kentucky. I visited William Houck, a basketmaker in upstate New York.

They taught us ideas of art that reminded us of our radical and romantic heritage. We reread William Morris and he made great sense, for he had worked hard at art and thought about it seriously. His writings fit with what we were learning in the field. They nerved us to continue, moving deeper into the lives of the people who made the things, learning from them better ideas to guide our study.

That was thirty years ago. Since then, the whole show has gone to the right. The signs in the United States seem numberless: the return of capital punishment, the widening gap between rich and poor, the destruction of necessary social programs, the resistance to raising taxes, the failure to develop a reasonable national medical program, the blockade of Cuba, the bombing of Muslims. Those are mostly government actions, and there is nothing strange in governments moving to the right. What is strange is that the intellectuals have followed. The journalists whom we allow to tell us about ourselves say we have become more conservative. It does seem that people have retreated from responsibility, seeking causes in biology or political power to excuse their failings, but whether or not it is true of the population in general, it is true of scholars. We have become more conservative.

The material culture of a past age.
Kansas City, Philadelphia, and
Washington, D.C. 1968–1971

In saying conservative, I mean something quite specific. It is the willingness to accept arguments spun out of the self. Satisfactory political policies, moral codes, and views of the world are derived from limited personal experience. My life is like this, so everyone's life is like this, or should be. Thought collapses into the context of assimilation. It is enough to know ourselves. Such self-centered thinking spawned oppression at home and colonialism abroad; it created the need for anthropology, sociology, folklore, and a multitude of compensatory histories: black history, women's history, subaltern history, artifactual history. When the life of the English gentleman was life itself, when his society was society, his taste was culture, then the history that had made him was history. But when his society became only one of thousands, we had to learn about new people, people with little political power perhaps, with little wealth perhaps, who left scant trace in the documentary record. So we went to work and built a treasury of empathic new methods. Now, if we let ourselves define life by our lives, we tumble into the old trap, losing all we have gained.

The new conservatism shows up diversely in our scholarly actions. Some return to the safe confines of the old conventions, abandoning transdisciplinary exchange. Others choose to write in a thick dialect known only to scholars, qualifying little arguments into defensive briefs abristle with citations of higher authority. Some adopt a democratic rhetoric of diversity and inclusion, and then continue to tender serious study only to things that resemble the canonical creations of the same old dead white males. Others turn their analytic energies away from the world and its big questions to focus on the petty sins and successes of the academy, composing tiny histories of disciplinary trends in order to chastize the ancestors and confirm their own superiority. Some refine theory past any empirical need, displaying academic virtuosity, while the world fades from attention and their careers advance. Many assert the priority of their own interests, making reality submit to the glamorous obsession of the moment. This week it is nationalism, next week globalization. Something called power and something called the economy gather superorganic strength and drive facile arguments, while the workaday realities of the millions cease to concern us.

Things are, of course, not so bleak. Some among us have held to the old faith. Furthering the radical and romantic, existential and empirical traditions, we have moved from theorizing to intimate study designed to reveal the genius and pain of other people. Dell Hymes formulated performance, bringing emphasis to social action in linguistic theory; he pointed the way to the future in *Reinventing Anthropology*, and then he got down to his greatest work, building a monument to Native American artists through his close, poetic analysis of their myths. In his shadow, I have come into increasingly intense collegial relations with the people whose works I study, listening to their explanations, following their directions, finally letting their interpretations dominate my own.

Narrowing now to material culture study, I find one symptom of change in the word chosen to name things. The old word was "artifact," the word I use. It evokes the artisan's act, the conversion of the natural into the artificial, and it associates all things with art, gesturing toward creation. The new word is "goods"; things are commodities and possessions. Trading the old word for the new, we participate in the general drift, shifting emphasis within the domain of material culture from creation to consumption. Once, in a spirit of opposition, we sought to temper the power of capitalism through affirmation of creation. Now, we accede to its dominion, and display our conservative self-interest, in studies of consumption. The justification for conservatism is realism, the egocentric tradition of depicting the world from the prospect of the observer.

Nobody, we say, makes things by hand anymore. Now it is all industrial production and consumption. It can feel like that because we are consumers more than creators. We buy houses, clothes, and electronic devices, not knowing who made them or how. And we forget, it seems, what a small portion of the world we represent. At work in the United States, I met old people plying their trades and young people excited by revival, but still I tended to think of material culture in the past tense. Then I went to Turkey, where handmade excellence is neither a memory nor a peripheral pleasure but a vibrant part of modern life. I went on to Bangladesh, where eighty percent of the people live in villages, in handmade houses, where urban as well as rural people depend on objects beautifully made by hand in small workshops. Before you dismiss such places as minor, or employ the haughty style of the realist to center the world in the self and declare them marginal, consider that the population of Turkey is twice that of Canada, and the population of Bangladesh is twice that of Turkey, and to the people in those places, we are marginal. And before you say that places with vital artistic traditions must be economically backward, note that — by the most telling measure of advancement (the number of people in poverty) — Japan is ahead of the United States and yet wonderfully rich in traditional art.

No, the world we inhabit abounds in handskills. The reason to come to grips with industrial production and consumption is not because they define the modern world (even if they characterize our corner of it), but because a complete idea of material culture must encompass industrial production as well as handcraft, consumption as well as creation.

Our conservative drift, then, has revealed a fine new focus for material culture. And, upon reflection, I find the change in my own work, from my book on Virginia houses, written in 1972, to my book on Ballymenone, published in 1982, where I announced a turn in vernacular architecture study from male house builders to female homemakers.

In the days when this paper was composed, the particular topic that vexed us was the consumption of industrial commodities. Industrial production was not the concern, for we do not think we are industrial workers. When I visit factories, I find more handwork of a more challenging sort — more continuity with elder practice — than Chaplin's *Modern Times* would imply. Industrial production should claim our attention, but consumption was the concern, for we are consumers. I will open the issue by expanding upon the idea of use that lies at the intersection of creation and consumption.

All artifacts are multifunctional. Among their functions, some are instrumental. Things are made to use. The painting is made to pass the time; it works to save the painter from madness and boredom. It is sold to bring cash to the painter and prestige to the painter and patron. It is used to decorate the home, to display taste, to represent its creator and consumer, helping to configure their fields of social relation.

Some of use belongs to creation. It is predicted and framed into the object, coercing response. If the object is used as the creator intended, it unifies the maker and user in a communicative bond. Through the useful object, the creator and the consumer, who normally do not meet, form a relation of mutual trust. Things that work poorly or break easily, things with value in commerce but not in use, symbolize societies in disarray. The well-made tool is an emblem of social order. But it depends on the honor of its creator.

In making a tool, the creator builds into it an idea of the consumer. That idea might be vague, it might be exact, but even when a patron provides detailed instructions, it is the creator who realizes the work. The patron is, during the creative process, only a phantom in the mind, a part of the conceptual context of creation, and the object speaks for its maker. Use is submerged in the artifactual process, much as the reaction of the audience is incorporated into the telling of a story that exists, at last, with only the teller to blame.

Try as we might to credit works of art to their patrons, to find consumers in commodities, or audiences in stories, things tell us of their creators. A new Ford automobile expresses its designer and manufacturer, just as an antique chair does. The makers might have anticipated use, imagined users, but the car and chair will be bought and used for thousands of reasons that were no part of creative intention and left no evidence in the world. We may make the Ford into a symbol of American culture, but it comes from a few creators who built their vision of the consumer into their process of design and manufacture.

Now put the thing into use. The car is purchased. It is polished, dented, wrecked. From rubbing or rust or patterns of wear, we might recover hints about use and users, but not much, and not much of importance. Most of the car remains the possession of the Ford Motor Company. The consumer exists as stains and scratches.

When we begin to learn about users is when they abandon the role of consumer and become creators. Then we watch people drive, and from their conduct gain notions about their personalities, and if we spend enough time with them, we will note stable and variable patterns that allow us to speak of cultures of automotive operation. The English ride cars like horses; Americans steer them like ships.

During ethnographic study, the car becomes an instrument in a creative act. It is to driving as a fiddle is to playing. From the fiddle alone, from scars on the neck, we might learn something about the habits of the fiddler, but the yield is slight. The fiddle tells us mostly about fiddle makers, their ideas of technology and form. Fiddling tells us about fiddlers, their ways of attacking a tune in performance. Driving tells us about drivers who are not consumers of cars, but creators of automotive behaviors.

When we watch consumers in action, we are observing the use of industrial commodities, but use is a creative act that employs the product of the creative act of another: the driver uses the car, the basketmaker uses the axe, the shopper uses money. Little about shopping behavior, or the culture of shoppers, can be learned from the shapes of bills, their colors, or the pictures they carry of dead presidents. Money expresses the designers, engravers, and printers at the mint.

It turns out that our old focus upon creativity, learned by observing and interviewing men who made baskets and chairs out of wood, remains apt. Here is the argument. The old man uses an axe to split wood for a basket that he hangs outside his shop as a sign of his trade and ability. The young woman uses a car to drive to market and park at the curb as a symbol of her success as a worker. To see the archaeologist's problem, take the person out of the picture, leaving only the basket, only the car. The only people we can learn much about are the ones who made the things. The consumer is reduced to an idea in the creator's mind and a few smudgy fingerprints.

But suppose that the consumer, in using the object in a creative act, remakes it. In my day, no self-respecting teenage boy would drive his parents' car. The kid who bought a Ford used the profit from his paper route to buy an old one. Then with help from Manny, Moe, and Jack, he reinvented it, removing the opulent chrome ornaments of the adult, filling holes with lead, painting the body with splotches of barn-red primer, and almost never giving it the lacquered finish of his dreams. Thus recreated, the Ford became an expression of a second culture. The culture of the Ford Motor Company and the culture of the teenager came to coexist fitfully in automotive fabric.

The customized car (that is what we called them), like the old house modified over the centuries, like the whole vast landscape, embodies creative layering. It expresses simultaneously the wills of many makers. One way to approach the material culture of the industrial age is through attention to rebuilding. Fresh work in the study of vernacular architecture brings urban row houses and suburban ranchers into consideration, then concentrates on the way the row house has been remodeled and redecorated to signal ethnic identity, or the way tract houses are made livable by their inhabitants. Walls are moved, windows enlarged, garages added. The user's will endures in the creative act of alteration.

The purchase of a house is conditioned by too many variables. Statistical correlations between the forms of houses and the demographic profiles of their owners are suggestive, though only patient interviewing can lead us into an understanding of the motives for consumption. But a house, somewhat changed, somewhat not, filled and decorated with objects, becomes a repository of information about its user, who is not its consumer, but one of its creators.

Use becomes creation as objects are altered. And use becomes creation when objects become parts of objects, when the physical context becomes a creative composition. You buy a Ford. In the Ford abides information, not about you (you would be properly represented by a Jaguar), but about the Ford Motor Company. But if you buy a Ford, and then make it an element in a set, gathering commodities into a household unit, you have shaped a new entity, which is — as a whole — your creation. Such units are what archaeologists hope to recover in laying bare one stratum of a dig to expose diverse fragments — a rusted buckle, some coins and pipestems, a few shards of earthenware and china — that belonged once to a single household.

The old man went into the woods. He selected a tree he did not make, felled it, split it, and wove its bits into a basket. The consumer goes to market, selects a car she did not make, drives it home skillfully, and there incorporates it into a unit that is her creation. Structurally, the process seems similar, but it differs emotionally. Rich in instants of manipulation, the basketmaker's act included both selection and composition. The consumer's act included selection, but the work is not done until the collection has been assembled into a composition, a display of the self. The car posed in front of the house becomes a display; commodities arrayed into a unified domestic environment become a display. Even if we do not make cars or customize them, we can locate cars in sets of possessions, and while the particular elements tell little about us, the set is, as a unit, ours, and it becomes an expression when it is built into a display, a new composition.

William Houck.
Vernon Center,
New York.
1965

Stanley Lamprey. Braunton, Devonshire, England. 1978

It is not the food bought, but the food processed and made into a meal — it is not the shirt bought off the rack that is you, but the shirt as a component in a composition of attire that informs on you. Whole meals, sets of clothing in action (the soft architecture of the environments that go near us), and collections of commodities assembled into domestic settings — these are the key creations in the material culture of industrial civilization. They are our mirrors; we see ourselves in them. They are our lenses; others read us through them.

Marcel Duchamp moved a snow shovel from one physical context to another to make a tool into art, to challenge art, to show that new meanings rise when objects become part of new assemblies. Joseph Cornell built miniature stages, boxed ensembles of found fragments and memorabilia. Framing and reframing, Flann O'Brien recycled characters out of old books to compose new novels. Recently in America, hip disc jockeys in the cities have melded commercial recordings into sizzling electronic performances, and women have joined in a massive revival of quilting, piecing purchased scraps of industrially manufactured fabrics into orderly new beauties.

In montage, collage, pastiche, and assembly, twentieth-century artists have shown that the collection, the new unit composed of gathered bits, is a major expressive mode of industrial civilization. The painting expresses the painter. The collection of paintings expresses the collector. The television expresses its Japanese manufacturer. Purchased, the television becomes part of a collection that is arranged into a home to express its creator, the homemaker.

Collecting is easy to mock as a luxurious hobby, but in the United States, it is an intense interest for people of all classes — from the homeless woman with her shopping cart of fastidiously folded paper bags, to the trucker with his documented arsenal of Civil War weaponry, to the wealthy lawyer with her shelves and closets crowded with old folk pottery. Collecting can be seen as a neurotic disorder or as a heroic attempt to create some order, some place of personal control and satisfaction, in a world gone haywire.

By consistently using the word "artifact" during material culture analysis, we implicitly stress one dimension of all things. They are made. By using the word "goods," we stress another. They are traded and possessed. All things are artifacts, all are goods, and material culture study needs both orientations. The student of artifacts engages them as creations, blendings of nature and will, and slights use and commerce, avoiding the moral issues raised during contemplation of economic systems. The student of goods encounters things as commercial cyphers, slighting creators and avoiding the moral issues raised through consideration of systems of production. The new conservatism provides a valuable corrective to material culture study. We become interested in the men who repair and sell carpets as well as the women who made them. We become interested in the women who ornament the interior of the house as well as the men who built the walls. The artifact's story fills out, but an exclusive concentration on goods would betray our humanity and subvert our intellectual tradition.

Studying creation with the old basketmaker as our guide, we need to add to the basketmaker's performance other varieties of creativity. His is the creation out of nature, the prime artifactual act, but it is paralleled in two other acts that should draw our attention now: rebuilding, when the car is customized and the house is remodeled, and collecting, when new things are made — not out of bits of nature, but out of sundry commodities.

It is wrong, I believe, to call one of these acts creativity and the others use. Each is a creative act that brings forth a new composition — a basket, a customized car, the decor of an office in a university building — that exhibits a mind at playful work.

The times change, but the study of material culture continues to develop along traditional lines, its goal being to keep the idea of art broad, open, democratic, and historically useful. In adjusting to its moment, study has come to focus on our own lives as well as those of other people, featuring industrial commodities and consumerism as well as handmade objects and creativity. The expansion is beneficial, but it should not mislead us into rejecting our intellectual heritage, for it prepared us adequately to deal with new phenomena.

Among the new things, the most important, I believe, is the collection: the assembly of gifts, souvenirs, and commodities into a home — the domestic environment in contradistinction to the house. The collection represents a victory over disorder in industrial times, when the flood of goods threatens to sweep us to madness in a rising tide of irrelevant trash, just as the house of stone represented a victory over disorder in the days when people lived close to nature, when the lean wolves came down from the heath and the night winds wailed. But we should not be confused. Today, while we create things out of things made by other people, all across the globe, people in no way less real or alive are going up into the woods and down to the riverside. They are chopping out chunks of nature and fashioning artifacts that display their spirit and serve the serious needs of their neighbors.

Our responsibility is to keep the idea of art wide and useful, so that the old man's basket, the kid's chopped coupe, the old lady's beautiful kitchen composed of cheap goods, and our own earnest writings will be taken seriously. The job is to get up, go out, and find the things that will help us learn how others manage in the world we share. We need to learn about their work and values so we can improve our own. We need to meet them, joining in appreciation of their creations, in hatred of the forces that thwart them, overcoming our separation in a oneness of humanity.

3

One Life

IN THE LIVES of working men and women, the history of the world is written. This is the story of one man, his growth from an apprentice tailor into a master of carpet repair. It is also the story of contemporary Turkey, of country people moving to the city, and of the United States, of immigrants adapting, and of the Armenian people rising bravely to success in a hundred foreign lands.

This is Hagop Barın's story. We met in 1983, soon after his arrival in the United States. He had found a good job, repairing oriental carpets for a retail dealer in Philadelphia, but he did not know English. I had been to Turkey and wished to return for serious fieldwork, but I did not know Turkish. On Sunday evenings, we ate together at my home, and beginning with a simple sentence — "This is a glass": "*Bu bir bardak*" — we traded languages.

During the years of our friendship, Hagop told me the tale of his life in bits and pieces. I came early to believe that his biography should be written. He is a master of his trade, and his story would tell of one man's life in material culture. We had talked on occasion about that project, and in the winter of 1987, we set aside the time. After dinner, we went upstairs to a quiet room, followed by my daughter Ellen Adair. I set up the tape recorder and we began.

Hagop knew that I knew about his life already, and since I had been to Turkey many times, once living for eight months in the very neighborhood of Istanbul where he settled as a boy, he could count on me to catch quick references. So I interrupt the run of his narrative, digressing to expand his story with my understanding. Our friendship is enmeshed in Turkish, so we spoke in his native tongue.

As a folklorist, I am professionally committed to accuracy. I believe in the particular, relish the verbal detail, and I offer you our conversation, transcribed exactly in Turkish, and then translated into English. While I worked, listening to the tapes over and over, I took care not to erase the qualities of spontaneous speech, nor to eliminate the peculiar feel of Turkish in the ear.

With a small shy laugh, for he is not a man of words (his art lies in his hands), Hagop begins the story of his life at the beginning:

"In the year one thousand, nine hundred and forty-nine, I was born in a small town near Kayseri. There were six brothers. It was a small town with the name of Sarıoğlan. Our work there was farming. Then I began primary school.

"After primary school, we moved to Istanbul. After that — "

Hagop interrupts himself and asks me to ask him a question. At that time, my richest field experience had been in rural Ireland. Among the Irish country people I knew, questions were shunned. Conversations advanced by indirection through comments that could be handled like questions or left to stand as simple statements. In Ireland, I had learned to begin interviews with a wordy request for information, an invitation to verbal creation. Then I held back, and, abiding by the local courtesies, I allowed long silences to thrust upon my teachers the obligation to instruct me. In Turkey, conversations proceed directly. Straight — *doğru* — speech is a virtue. The frank exchange of straight questions and straight answers is normal, and I have had to learn a new style of interviewing.

So I ask Hagop questions, and when I do not, Hagop asks himself questions. Typically, his response commences in a flurry of short, unconnected assertions within which he discovers the path to his answer. Then speed increases and his statement gains coherence — and sometimes passion — while he crescendos to a conclusion.

Hagop Barın at work.
Philadelphia, Pennsylvania. 1984

Hagop is fourth from the right, next to his grandmother.
Sarıoğlan, Kayseri, Turkey. c. 1953

Now, I ask him to tell of village life. Hagop's birthplace, Sarıoğlan, is a town, a *kasaba*, not a village, a *köy*, but Turks generally call rural life "village life," and they speak of country people as "villagers," because the Turkish landscape remains, like the old landscape of lowland Europe, a place of villages, of houses densely clustered around a religious building, beyond which the fields spread wide. As his silence continues, I suggest he begin by describing his home, and he does:

"We lived in a house made of earth. It is in that picture."

He alludes to a snapshot he showed me once in which his family is gathered in front of the earthen walls of a house.

"So, it was a six-room house. Earlier all my uncles and so on lived in the same house. Later they moved to Istanbul. It was my grandfather's house, and my grandmother's. We lived together with them. Later, after their deaths, we moved to Istanbul.

"Life in the village: generally people farmed. And they wove carpets. There was a loom in every house. But, for example, they wove these Kayseri carpets — Bünyan, floral — those carpets."

Hagop is speaking of piled carpets — *halı* in Turkish — and he names their types after places. Kayseri is a *vilayet*, a state in central Anatolia. It contains the city of Kayseri, the ancient Caesarea, as well as the towns of Sarıoğlan and Bünyan. The carpets woven in Sarıoğlan are named in the trade after the state, Kayseri, or after another town, Bünyan, forty kilometers to the south that is famed for weaving. "Kayeri" or "Bünyan" carpets are not necessarily made in the city of Kayseri or the town of Bünyan. Like the carpets called Kars or Konya or Bergama, they exemplify a type, named for a place but distinguished by certain features of design, palette, and weave, and they are made in many locations. In this case, the carpet is one with a fine weave and a Persian floral medallion. Hagop continues:

"In our house, I saw them, I mean my mama's. I saw her making root dyes; I saw her making kilims."

Kilim contrasts with *halı*. The pattern of the *halı* is made by tying knots in different colors on the warp, between the shoots of weft that bind the web. The *kilim* is created by varying the color of the weft, as in a tapestry, or by inserting extra wefts or warps to make the pattern. The Turkish word *kilim* has been adopted in the West, but Westerners generally restrict its reference to tapestry-woven rugs, while Turks call all flatweaves kilims. The *kilim* is one class of rug, the *halı* is the other.

For her kilims and carpets, Hagop's mother dyed her yarn with root dyes. Root — *kök* — means specifically madder root, the main source of the red that dominates Turkish weavings, but by extension, root dye — *kök boya* — names the class of all natural dyes. It contrasts with synthetic dyes, usually called *paket boya* or *toz boya* — packaged or powdered dyes.

Dyes are often used by scholars to date rugs. Naturally dyed carpets are shoved back into the nineteenth century, raising their value, and the recent return to natural dyes is overpraised as the revival of a practice long dead. But I have found in Turkey, in places as separated as the Aegean coast on the west and the mountains of the Iranian border on the east, that natural dyes were still in use after the Second World War, less than a generation before their current revival, and Hagop attests to their use in central Anatolia in the early 1950s. Synthetic dyes came into use late in the nineteenth century, but people adopted them slowly and sporadically. For nearly a century, natural and synthetic dyes were used simultaneously and mixed in particular rugs, so they fail as reliable guides to dating. About all that can be said for certain is that a carpet with exclusively natural dyes was probably not woven between 1960 and 1980.

After a pause for a thought, Hagop starts anew. He generalizes from natural dyes to a whole natural way of life, and he intensifies our relationship in the conversation by addressing me appropriately (for I am his elder) as *ağabey* — abi — big brother:

"I swear to God, how can I explain village life, Henry Abi?

"We lived without machines. In my childhood, for example, I remember that there was no electricity in the village. And life was completely sociable and natural. Natural. Everything was fit. For example, there was every kind of animal for a person's use: sheep, goats, horses, cows; you know, everything, dogs.

"Then, as I said, when I was a child of seven years, I began primary school. I finished primary school there. After finishing primary school, we moved to Istanbul. Generally, my brothers grew along the same path, but there was always something: the schooling there was not good. There was this Armenian issue.

"In that town earlier, it seems, there were many Armenians, but my family, our family, were the last Armenians. Other than us, there were no Armenians.

"There were about five hundred households: two thousand, seven hundred people were living there at that time, in my childhood. The last Armenian family was our family.

"But much earlier there were many Armenians. I remember a few, but much earlier, it seems, there were very many."

I ask how he learned his religion in a Muslim town. He replies:

"There was probably a church before, in the past, but I saw none. There was none. There was no church, but from the adults — for example, you learned religion in your family; that fashion, I mean."

With soft sadness, Hagop repeats that his was the last Armenian family:

"There was not another family. There was only us."

I return him to his home.

"My grandad and grandmother lived in another house nearby. The fields were ours, and their house was called a *konak*. When speaking of their house, it was always *konak*. It had two stories. Only theirs was called a *konak*; it was made of stone, and generally I stayed with them because they wanted a child constantly by their side. I stayed with them.

"The other houses were made of earth. They had one story and flat roofs."

Hagop has classified the houses of Sarıoğlan. The usual house was the *ev* of one story, with earthen walls and a flat roof. The fine house, the *konak*, was imposing with its upper story and its walls solidly, permanently built of stone. Buildings teach history. The lofty *konak*, where Hagop lived to serve his grandparents, was owned by the town's last Armenian family; the Armenian past was not one of deprivation. Differences of wealth register in architectural fabric, but — as is usual in the countryside — differences were more of degree than kind, for when I ask Hagop to describe the interior, he leads us into a typical central Anatolian house:

"There was a hall, a hall. It was that wide in the center."

He gestures to a breadth of about eight feet and says that rooms opened off each side of the hall:

"At that time, one room, the *tandırevi*, you know, for making meals, baking bread — the *tandırevi*. For example, one room was for storing wheat, for storing dried beans, lentils, yogurt. The other room was for guests — like that, I mean.

"Generally there was a *sedir* made of earth, made of earth, and on top of it there were pillows and there were cushions. Men come. Everything is good."

The house collected agricultural and domestic functions under one roof. Running from front to back, through the middle of the house, the hallway was a place for work and informal socializing, and it provided for circulation among the rooms. Some rooms were given to the storage of farm tools and sacks of grain. One was a *tandırevi* — literally an oven house — where food was cooked. Another was for guests, the *misafir odası*, the finest room in the house. Its decoration, its color and pattern, lay in its textiles. There were kilims on the floor. There were stuffed pillows and cushions on the *sedir*, a stepped ledge, built into the house to provide seating around the outer walls. In Turkey, those pillows and cushions — *yastıklar* and *minderler* — were made in every technique used to weave rugs, and cut free of their backs, they become the miniature rugs that are prized by collectors and placed in odd spots in American homes. I ask Hagop to describe them in more detail.

"The *yastıklar* were piled, but the *minderler* were made of cloth, with wool inside, genuine wool, but they were made from normal cloth, from shirt cloth.

"On the floor there are reed mats, there are kilims. The kilims were made around there, and they were plain, plain."

The plain kilims, like the flat roofs of the houses, spark a warm, reminiscent little chuckle for Hagop. Both are signs of poverty, both are reminders of a sweet and vanished childhood.

While the word *kilim* calls boldly patterned tapestries into the mind of the rug collector, in Turkey, gathering all flatweaves, it includes the ubiquitous, simple striped rugs that are analogous to the rag rugs of rural America or Scandinavia. A layer of reed matting between the earthen floor and the kilims softened the step and made the floor comfortable for sitting at meal times, when people gathered around a tinned copper tray. I ask Hagop to speak about his life as a child.

"I swear to God, Henry Abi, what did I do when I was a child? Generally in Anatolia the boys worked at farming in the summer — only not me. Among the people who lived there, generally there was a family, all right."

Hagop points to my daughter playing quietly at the other end of the room.

"For example, Ellen is a child of four; it is possible to find work for Ellen. In that family, in the life of that village, there is work for everyone because there are no machines.

"How can I explain it? I remember herding the sheep, feeding the sheep. After that there is much work on the farm — tending the garden, herding the sheep — there is always that kind of work — at that time there was, I mean.

"This farming is not easy work. A family, a crowded family, is necessary. Our family slowly dispersed. The family dispersed in this fashion. After finishing primary school, it was not easy to find another school *for us*. Because of that: Istanbul. All of our relatives moved to Istanbul, those who finished primary school moved to Istanbul; for example, my big brother came to Istanbul, then another came, and so on. Our family grew small.

"Then there was another thing: we sold our farming equipment to them. Then I began to try other work — work other than farming. After that, there was a friend for me: a tailor. Then, in the winter I would go to school. In the summer, there was nothing to do. It was very important for us to learn an art."

There is one word — *sanat* — for art, craft, and trade. In Turkish (as was once the case in English), no crude distinctions, based apparently on medium but actually on social class, separate art from craft and confuse those who would understand the nature of creative action. Hagop's family had grown small, there were not enough hands to do the farm work, the tools were sold "to them," to their Muslim neighbors, and Hagop had to learn a nonagricultural art. Fortunately, Hagop's father knew a man who was a tailor:

"My father talked with that man. At his side I began to learn tailoring. At that man's side. Tailoring to order, village tailoring, that is. He was a good tailor, though. He had a shop in the town. I did the work of an apprentice."

The style of training is of great importance in the understanding of art. During education, culture is transferred, and artists learn to find a way for themselves that fits their personal needs and meets the expectations of others. By simply dichotomizing education as formal and informal, much as we separate art from craft, or fine art from folk art, we misapprehend the complexities of learning. I need to know more, so I ask Hagop to expand on the progress of his apprenticeship. He responds with excitement:

"He was a man of terrific discipline. For example, that man's teaching was not easy for every man because there was great discipline. That man frightened us. In apprenticeship, what did we do? For example, clean the shop, then tea — you know, I brought tea for the guests all the time from the coffeehouse. Then, the *needle*, how to hold — I learned how to hold the needle for perhaps one month. I got used to that. Then, little by little, I began sewing work and so on. But for *one month*: a threadless needle and empty cloth."

With a blank expression on his face, Hagop imitates himself as a lad, passing again and again a needle attached to no thread through a piece of cloth. He laughs, and goes on:

"Then, after one month, Henry Abi, there was thread in the needle."

The memory tickles him once more to laughter.

"Then I began to work together with thread," he says, laughing still.

"After that: sewing. I would pointlessly sew a piece of cloth, a useless piece of cloth. Empty sewing, do you understand?"

Hagop assumes the harsh tone of his master: "'Sew like this,' he said. 'Do like this.'" He reenacts his master demonstrating the making of a hem:

"Then, there was a very important job: basting hems. At that time there was no machine. Everything was done by hand, everything. Then I began to baste hems."

I ask him to tell more about his master.

"That man did every kind of tailoring for males, not for women. Pants, coats, shirts, everything, I mean — hats, everything for males.

"At that time, that man was probably thirty-five years old; thirty or thirty-five, I don't remember. He seemed very big to me at that time."

"But he was not an Armenian," I comment.

"No, he was not an Armenian. Generally the people of the town were Muslims. There were a couple of Kurds and Alevis. We were the lone Christians in the village."

When Hagop had finished primary school and learned the tailor's trade, when he was twelve years old, his family, his father, mother, and two younger brothers, followed his older brothers. They left the old home, and moved to Istanbul:

"We took the train. It had a coal-fired engine. They had them at that time. The trip continued for three days and three nights. It was a very very strange trip. Then, we came to Istanbul. The beginning was very very hard for us at that time. The family was crowded.

"We took a room in Istanbul, in Kocamustafapaşa. We stayed a while in a very small house. Then we found a bit larger house in Kum Kapı. Then we went there, we lived there, and I began carpet work."

Kocamustafapaşa is a neighborhood near the walls in the southwest of the old city. It surrounds a Byzantine church that was converted into the Mosque of Koca Mustafa Paşa, where people come to pray at the tomb of the saint Sümbül Efendi. You find their requests for help in family matters and school examinations penciled on the window frame of his *türbe*. The area is called, too, Paşalar, for it contains as well the mosques of Davut Paşa, Hekimoğlu Ali Paşa, and Cerrah Paşa. It is a lively neighborhood with an excellent hospital and a large weekly market, and it remains a place where country people come and begin the process of adjustment to urban life that is the big story of modern Turkey.

Farther east along the slopes descending into the Sea of Marmara, downhill from the Covered Bazaar, lies Kum Kapı. The district gave its name to fine, courtly carpets woven while the Ottoman Empire crumbled, and it is famed now for seafood restaurants. There is music in the streets at night, and few things are finer than a fish stew in Kum Kapı. Among the reinforced concrete apartment buildings, a few old wooden houses remain. In one such, Hagop's family found rooms to rent, which Hagop remembers as drafty, as noisy and cold:

"Istanbul was a wholly empty world, a beautiful world, suitable, wonderful, but it was not free. For example, in the village it was different: there was openness on every side: mountains, rocks; I would roll downhill and run and race. For example, in Istanbul there were narrow streets. Then, there were more houses, many people; that kind of people: without awareness, without importance. Then: foreignness — we talked much about that in Istanbul."

Hagop recalls a long conversation we had once, walking through Istanbul, when he described his feelings of "foreignness," of alienation. In Sarıoğlan, he did not feel that he belonged, for he was an Armenian and "they" were Muslims. When he came to Istanbul, "they" were *şehirli*, city people, but he was *köylü*, a villager. Again he did not fit. He describes the Istanbul of the early 1960s:

"Istanbul was not today's Istanbul. Generally city people lived there. For example, people in Turkey are classed into two kinds: they are called villagers and city people. Perhaps you would ask, what are the villagers like, what are the city people like? Do you understand? For example, clothing. City people always, every day, shaved and wore suits and ties. They spoke a different Turkish. I don't know. Anatolian people were looser; for example, in their way of sitting, in their way of eating, in other things. City people were different. They were closer to Europe. They copied Europe; they tried to do things like Europeans. For example, three million people were living in Istanbul at that time, and few people were coming from the villages. For example, when a villager would come to Istanbul, he was immediately understood: this one came from the village. His clothes were different, his walking was different. Do you understand? His shoes were loose, I mean. Disorderly.

"This was very hard for me. Do you understand?"

I do. He did not fit. Hagop told me once that when he came to Istanbul, it was dominated by city people who laughed at the villagers, but now it is exactly the reverse. The city is dominated by country people. When they meet in the streets, they ask one another where they come from, and, though they might have lived in the city for years, they answer with an Anatolian locale. Young men in the city choose brides, or have brides chosen for them, from the village. Married couples return for annual visits to the home they maintain in the village. Stones above the graves in the city's cemeteries name the dead by country places. Now Istanbul is dominated by villagers, says Hagop, and they laugh at the city people with their silly, polished style.

"But," he continues, "besides this there were beautiful things.

"So, Istanbul was like that. So then, we tried to be like them. We tried to live like city people, because it was very hard in our places of work when, for example, we spoke Turkish with them. They laughed at the Turkish we spoke. They looked down on us, belittled us. Then, we began to do things like them, and we learned. We began to speak cleaner Turkish. We changed our shoes. Slowly, we began to change."

It was not easy to change, and the effort seemed ludicrous at times. With a distanced laugh of remembrance, like that which accompanied his account of village life, the flat roofs, the plain kilims, Hagop pauses. In time, they learned, he said, and when people in America ask Hagop where he is from, he answers Istanbul. In Istanbul he would say Kayseri, in Kayseri he would say Sarıoğlan. I ask him to tell the story of his beginning in the carpet business.

"The story of my beginning in the carpet business, Henry Abi: for example — tailoring was my trade. Then they said — there was a very big worry upon my father: 'I have so many children. What will I do? Life in Istanbul is very very hard.' I knew tailoring. They said, 'This is all right. No problem. It can go.' And I began to work at tailoring, because my sister's husband was a tailor. Then I went there and did everything very easily, because that master was a very good master — one month with an empty needle."

He laughs again at the severe training he received, but his village master was a good one who gave him the skill that would enable him to succeed in the city.

The pattern is a general one. Boys who come from the Black Sea region with a knowledge of woodworking can attach themselves to masters in the Tahtakale district of Istanbul who came earlier from the same provinces and established a trade in wooden household goods. Boys from places with a copper-working tradition similarly find work in the ringing ateliers of the coppersmiths. The traditional craft, learned in the country-side, can smooth adaptation to urban life. At his master's side, Hagop learned good habits: his hands came to know how to move smoothly, automatically without constant conscious direction. He learned, too, the discipline that would serve him as a worker and then enable him to teach when he became a master respon-sible for the education of wild young boys. His training with the tailor of Sarioğlan laid the foundation for his successful adjust-ment to the big city. Hagop remembers:

"But being a real lad, I did not like that work at all, Henry Abi.

"In that period, my big brother was living in Istanbul. He came from Anatolia earlier than us; he was going to school. And by chance he was working beside a carpet dealer. (He worked in the summer; in the winter he went to school.) He was a very big carpet dealer. And my big brother knew something: that I did not like that work: tailoring. Then, for example, when school opened in the winter, and it was necessary for him to go, he knew that a man was needed for working at the carpet dealer's. And he said to me — because he knew well that I did not like that work — then, he said, 'This is very hard. Don't you want to work at the carpet dealer's?' I said, 'Sure.' I was very pleased.

"After that, I went there. It was very beautiful, everything was beautiful. The carpets were beautiful, the people were more beautiful; it was more comfortable, so clean. The money and so on was good. Everything was very very beautiful. I began.

"But on the first day I loved the men greatly.

"Then the matter of my beginning in the repair business was very funny. For example, the sales area was down below in Zincirlihan."

Built near the ancient Forum of Constantine, between the great mosques of Beyazit and Nuruosmaniye, the Covered Bazaar cen-

Kapalı Çarşı: The Covered Bazaar.
Istanbul, Turkey. 1994

Zincirlihan. 1983

ters the old city of Istanbul. At its center, the Old Bedesten, a hall for trade, was built in the days of Mehmet the Conqueror, who took the city in 1453. In time, the streets around the Bedesten were vaulted, and today more than three thousand shops are roofed together within the Covered Bazaar. Commercial buildings, called hans, stand around the market's edges, supplying spaces for storage and work. One of them is Zincirlihan, the Han of the Chain, that opens off the side of the Bazaar at the end of one of the streets given today to the carpet trade. Like other old hans, Zincirlihan piles balconied floors around an open courtyard. On one side of its gateway, tea is brewed for boys to carry through the Bazaar, warming friendly chat and oiling the machinery of commerce. On the other side, stairs ascend to the lofty floor above. The courtyard, focused by a pretty Ottoman fountain, offers a calm, sunny counterpoint to the thrilling, shadowy tangle of the Covered Bazaar. Here Hagop fell in love with carpets. Here he began:

"The shop for sales was below, right beside the fountain, across from it. The han had two stories; there were three storerooms. There in the storerooms the women and so on worked, doing carpet repair. Elderly women, Armenian women."

"Women?" I ask in surprise, knowing that today in Istanbul most rug repair is done by boys and young men. "At that time was it generally women who did the repair?"

"No," Hagop answers, "there were also males."

We pause to change the tape. I open Hagop another beer, and ask him to describe the work of carpet repair when he first came to Zincirlihan.

"So, my work there — he was an Armenian carpet dealer. He was a very very good man. Bogos Varjebetyan was the man's name.

"Then — but it was very very funny — they gave me an end to sew, my first job. All right, but, Henry Abi, they did not know that before that I had wielded an empty needle; they did not know that I had wielded an empty needle for a month. They thought I would be dong that job until evening. Do you understand? Then, for example, ten minutes later, I said, 'Finished.' They looked."

He laughs.

"But there was also another thing: for example, when you begin work in a new place, you always work fast to show yourself positively. Isn't that so? They, they looked."

He imitates their surprise, their approving nods and clicks of the tongue, their appreciative tone:

"'Ah, very beautiful.' 'It is not wrong.' 'The sewing is all right, and everything is all right.' 'How did he finish it?'

"I swear to God, then I finished one or two more jobs early — terrifically quick. Then I was very free there. Very free. After a few jobs, they said, 'Go below.'

"I said: 'Sure,' I said."

He chuckles with satisfaction. Being sent down to the sales area was a victory. His skills were quickly recognized and rewarded.

Today in Istanbul, big dealers generally maintain rooms in inexpensive hans, set away from the shop for sales in the Covered Bazaar. In the rooms, rugs are piled and a repair atelier is arranged. There a master repairman manages the operation, assigning the tasks, keeping watch over speed and quality, doing particularly difficult or interesting jobs himself, and training the boys who sit around the room, bent over the rugs on their laps. The master is valuable, his time cannot be wasted, so a gifted, industrious boy is chosen from among the repairmen to sit in the shop, to run for tea, to open rugs for display when the customers come. When they leave, he rebuilds the piles of rugs, straightens the shop, and then continues to work on a repair project of his own; his work does not require supervision. To be called out of the repair atelier and into the shop is to be invited to take an important step in the ideal career that leads from apprentice repairman to rug merchant. While the dealer and his customer sit on a *sedir*, draped with a kilim, drinking tea in the hospitable, mock-domestic style of the Bazaar, and the boy silently opens rug after rug for them, he is observing, learning the rug merchent's trade.

So, Hagop chuckles with satisfaction and describes his new job:

"When customers came, I would open rugs, go here, go there, and there was much work. Do you understand? For example, going to the tax office — 'Go. Take this. Take that. Take this.' *But,* Henry Abi, in this period I came to love *carpets* and *carpet repair* so much that I cannot explain it. I did not stand idle for a minute, and the men loved me terrifically. I mean, everyone was surprised. The neighbors they saw, I mean, would ask, 'Where did that man come from?'

"Then — perhaps this is also interesting: when time would remain for me — for example, men did not always come, or when there was no 'Go there, Go here,' when there was nothing for me to do, when there would be a little time for me, I would go above and do a little repair. Then, together with my other work, I began to do repair below. Alone, in the room below. For example, a customer comes. For two hours I open rugs. One hour I am idle, so for one hour I do repair. And so on, like that.

"So I learned. I forgot nothing. I was unable to find nothing to do. I opened a hole in a carpet or *yastık*. I cut it, made a hole, then I threw in the thread, worked at the loom, I began to repair it."

Hagop is amused by the memory of making work for himself, and he laughed as he described working at the loom to repair a hole he had made. The word he used, *tezgah*, means loom. It is the word used for the looms on which carpets and kilims are woven, but the repairman's *tezgah* is a small frame, made of four pieces of wood nailed into an open square. The piece to be repaired is tacked taut to the frame. New warp, when it is necessary, is also tacked in tension to the frame. As evidence of the central significance of the women's art of weaving in Turkey, male craftsmen may call any immediate working space their loom. The potter's wheel is his *çark*, but it is also affectionately called his *tezgah*, his loom, as is the businessman's desk. The Turkish man is smitten by loom envy. As a young boy in the village, before he left the warm house to work with the men, he watched his mother and sisters work miracles on the loom. Come to the city, bearing memories of weaving, knowing how to weave, though he has not done it, he becomes a repairman, working at the periphery of Turkey's great traditional art.

It is essential to know how arts are learned. We casually say that the continuity of the traditional arts is maintained as skills are passed from father to son, mother to daughter. The implicit contrast is with the formal education of the schools. But the traditional arts are learned in diverse ways. Some artists say they learned from a particular master, as Hagop learned from the tailor of Sarıoğlan, or as a girl might learn weaving from her mother. Such an education can be as strict, as staged and disciplined as it is in the academy. Other artists teach themselves, imitating the models to which they are exposed, copying, botching, improving, until they have shaped through practice a personal style that is embraced by their native tradition. Traditional artists — fiddlers in Ireland and metalworkers in Bengal, as well as rug repairmen in Istanbul — have described their education to me in both of these ways. I ask Hagop if he learned repair in Zincirlihan from a special person.

"Earlier there was a special person. For example, there was another thing of great importance: the affection of the people. This is also very important. Perhaps I was a bit childish. In those times — it is possible to see that today in Istanbul every boy works — but at that time it was not so. Do you understand? For example, I worked much, helping everyone, bringing tea, this and that and so on. I don't know. For example, above there was a Jew. His name was Jaques. That man has appeared on television and in the newspapers in Turkey. He is a very very famous carpet repairman. Impossible: that man would not show to anyone. He was the most famous, but hiding his work, he made it impossible to see. He sat so."

Hagop turns away from me so that his shoulder blocks my vision, making it impossible to see his hands at imaginary work. The word he chose — *göstermek* — is precise. Teaching was not a matter of abstract precept and verbal instruction. As it was for the Navajo weavers who taught Gladys Reichard, teaching was a matter of "showing," of demonstration by concrete, visible example. The most important of Istanbul's repairmen worked in Zincirlihan, but he would not show his techniques to the boy who thirsted to learn:

"He would show to no one. He was not a good man. Do you understand? He would teach no one. No one. I know well.

"So, during a break, I would go there to see. He had a more honest workman."

The word I translate as workman is *kalfa*. The apprentice is *çırak*, the master *usta*. The *kalfa*, a journeyman, is fully competent. He has learned the art, but he is not a master. The master knows the art, and in addition he manages the shop and teaches his apprentices, teaching being a natural part of responsible management, as well as a moral duty of the accomplished artist. The famous repairman's *kalfa* did help:

"He was an elderly man. Sometimes — he was a little bit friendly — sometimes he would come down and show me a little. Then there were other women beside that man; they were better than the men who worked with us. I learned a little from them. That is, at last, I prepared myself, Henry Abi. You have a little taste, then you have a little talent, you know, then bit by bit, you are all right.

"Then, it went like that. I worked almost six years until I went into the military service."

The life of a Turkish man is patterned into stages. In childhood, he plays around the house that is run by the women. Then school begins, and with school, work begins. The gentle company of women and a carefree boyhood blend into a sweet memory. He leaves the warm, soft confines of home, and joins the big, tough men. After school and in the summers, he learns to work. When his schooling is over, the full responsibility of a man is delayed, boyishness is indulged, until military service. Conscription is universal, and after his military service, it is time for marriage, for a serious career, for dedicated and ungrumbling industriousness. Working hard, he hopes to ascend from labor to management. Then after the pilgrimage to Mecca, or an early retirement, a new maturity comes upon him. His commitment to work loosens, religiosity deepens, and he assumes the clean and placid, powerful role of a moral leader in the family and community. His work is less economic than social, and then life ends, again at home in the care of women.

While he moves from manly duty to manly duty, a memory lingers of a boyhood home. That memory suffuses carpets with feeling, making the soft, colorful creations of women into evocative signs of a time of warmth and affection.

Hagop served in Thrace because boys are sent to a part of the nation far from home, and his home for official purposes was Kayseri, not Istanbul. His learning lay in the years before his military service. He had six years to learn; I ask him how long it took.

"I learned everything, every job. Years are not important. I mean, it is hard to say. You will learn in six months, six months. Years are not necessary. You can learn everything in six months, but in six months — how can I say it? For example, I will show you, and if you learn in six months, still your work will not be beautiful, will not be good. You will have only learned the techniques.

"I swear to God, in essence, you learn out of yourself, Henry Abi. I brought it up out of myself. For example, generally, I learned from how I did it.

"Let us say that, all being spoken — it is very long and wide. Today, for example, I see something; I see something I have not seen. I have not made such a thing, because such a thing as this carpet — how can I explain it to you? Generally, in the things people make are their feelings, their tastes, their thoughts — all of that which is in their heads. The thing is made by one person."

Hagop is consistent, his understanding is sophisticated. He was trained in the beginning, he was shown things as he learned, but, at last, he taught himself. He learned his art out of a personal accumulation of experience, and when he faces a carpet he recognizes it to be the creation of a person who is, like him, unique, and whose work projects a singular synthesis. The job of the repairman, like that of any serious student of material culture, begins in acknowledging the distinctness of the creator of the object lying before him. Then it proceeds to success through engaged empathy, as he maneuvers into relation his personal style and the style of the creator.

Carefully, warily intervening in a thing made by another, the repairman is poised to discover that other person — the subject in the object — and to learn from a thing as one would from a teacher. In the American Southwest, many of the artists who have recently revived the tradition of carving images of the saints began by repairing old works. There were, for them, no living teachers, but the works of the dead taught them, enabling them to carve and paint in the style of the pieces they repaired. The historian of art works comparably, reconstituting from objects the procedures and values of their creators. Looking is not enough. I follow John Ruskin by making careful drawings of the things I study, and while I draw, I imaginatively recreate the object, learning as Hagop does when he probes into a rug, picking it apart mentally in order to know it completely, so he can create as its creator did.

Hagop's characteristic feelings of alienation serve him well in his trade. He begins by generously granting the right of otherness to the weaver whose work he reworks. Students of art should follow his example, resisting the notion that they can grip the essence of an artwork immediately. In doing so, they absorb others into themselves in a sort of intimate colonialism, when they should work as Hagop does, discovering the creator's style through patient analysis, and then using their own skills to bring the skills of the creator into new wholeness.

Consider, for comparison, architectural restoration. In the United States, restorationists are beginning to learn what Europeans have long known: the restoration of old buildings to some fancied early state is an act of violent appropriation. The building rebuilt becomes a monument to the restorationist's taste; the building's builders are obliterated. The opposite goal is to intervene minimally in old fabric, preserving the building with all its cranky mixtures of style, all its patchings and modifications, for all are historic evidence, signals sent from the dead. Courteously removing themselves from the building, restorationists stabilize it as an historical document. But restrained preservation can yield fragile objects that must be protected, removed from the touch and bump of daily life, and it can lead to a decadent affection for ruins, to a fascination with useless fragments. The middle course is to preserve all that can be preserved, rebuilding what is missing in a way that is consistent with remaining fabric, so the building can both honor its creators and serve its modern users. And that requires recognizing the gulf that lies between the artist and the analyst, but knowing that the gulf can be bridged by compassion.

In Turkey, continuities in the trades permit artisans at work on great monuments to ply their talents freely. When repair is necessary, masons are called from the Black Sea to Istanbul to work on the Süleymaniye, the sixteenth-century mosque of Süleyman the Magnificent, designed by the great Sinan and one of the world's architectural treasures. The old building belongs to history, and it serves the devotional needs of modern people. The masons come. They carve new pieces and lay new stone, they say, just as their ancestors did when they built the mosque. Turkish restoration crews leave Ottoman monuments looking fresh, scraped, and new, and carpet repairmen, who have known rugs throughout their lives, happily turn tattered old carpets into sturdy, usable new things. Belonging to the society that created the carpet in the first place, sharing in its tradition, they claim the right to rebuild it in accord with their intuitions, patching it soundly, improving it perhaps.

But Hagop considers such efforts to be butchery. Fitting his personality to his experience, he understands that he is not the carpet's creator. His mastery is rooted in the assumption that he and the weaver are different people. He must use clues in the carpet to guide his gingerly reconstruction of its particular weave. While working to preserve the rug's character, which is the materialization of its weaver's personality, Hagop finds a connection between the carpet and his experiences, so blending them that his work becomes invisible. He is proudest when even he cannot locate his contributions within the restored rug. His art is to know the art of others.

All rugs, being the expressions of individuals, are different, so every one must be approached cautiously. It must be queried for hints that will enable a tempered modern restoration, one that is respectful of its original character, while recovering its wholeness, and so bringing it back into usefulness.

Hagop illustrates his ideas with the rugs at our feet. He points to the tight, demure selvage of a Kurdish *yatak*, then across the room at the flamboyant selvage of a shaggy prayer rug from Keles near Bursa, so extravagant that it looks like a piled rug has been placed upon a kilim. Then he points to another:

"For example, such a selvage. Look at that carpet's selvage. Then look at that one's selvage. Then look at that one's. There are differences among them all. Do you understand?

"But, for example, if I found only a tiny part of that selvage, I would know a little. There is a little bit there, a fragment. Looking at it, I would say, 'All right.' But if there is not much there, then more must come from within yourself. You bring it up from within yourself. Do you understand?"

I do. The more you have experienced, the more different rugs of different kinds you have handled and repaired, the more you will be able to fill in the missing pieces correctly. It would take a lifetime to be able to do this well.

"It is hard to say it to you, though I am saying it to you. But, Henry Abi, I could teach you in three months."

"So," I say, "you were not a student with a master. You watched, asked, and taught yourself." I am thinking of a general pattern in the education of traditional artists. While they are described simply as learning from their parents, they will often describe themselves as having taught themselves, as having developed a personal style out of practice. And I am thinking of repairmen I know in Istanbul like Ahmet Opçin, who had a job as a boy in the Covered Bazaar, where he saw repairmen at work. He was intrigued by what he saw, so he tried to weave a little kilim of his own. It was a failure, but he learned from the effort, and, teaching himself by watching others, and more by examining old rugs, and still more by trying his hand at the job, he became a master of kilim repair. "So, you were not a student with a master," I say. Hagop answers:

"No. It was not like learning from a master. Your own taste — how can I say it?"

He points again to the rug on the floor. "Look, for example. You learn to sew whatever is in that carpet. There is a technique: you throw the weft, you seat the weft, you take it from the loom. The carpet, at last, comes into being from three things: warp, weft, and knots. I mean, I could show you that in a week, and you would be all right. Then you could do everything on your own."

Now that is funny, and he laughs while continuing:

"How can I explain it? There is only so much that can be shown, then the rest is up to you."

There is more to repair than getting the weave right, but that is the first thing. The repairman must do with the needle what the weaver does with her fingers, learning, as Hagop said, "to *sew* whatever is in that carpet." When the weaver ties the knots along a row, nothing lies above them on the warp. She has room for her hands to move. But the repairman inserts warp, weft, and knots with a needle, often working in cramped spaces. Making the knots with a needle, he loops the thread after each warp pair in a continuous sewing motion, so the effect of the pile is not accomplished until the loops are snipped.

The last step in repair involves delicate work with the scissors, cutting, smoothing, prying and poking with the needle to disguise the patch and blend it into the whole. It is called *tesviye*. Some repairmen, like Hagop, also call it *rötüş* — retouching — though others reserve *rötüş* for the dealer's shortcut of painting worn spots. On the dark back streets of the Covered Bazaar, you will see boys touching up the worn spots, the white dots of exposed warp on rugs, with indelible pens that come in sets. But painting is anathema to the master repairman. The Holy Koran teaches that the potter who patches a cracked vessel and represents it as sound does evil. Painting is deception, desecration; it is not repair. To repair — *tamir etmek* — is to reweave.

Reweaving is the beginning, it is technically honest, but it can be done poorly. It takes sensitivity and practice to reweave in a way that melds new work into a carpet's texture. Incompetent reweaving is often tight and lumpy. A master of *tesviye*, like Hagop or Nuri Ayhan, can improve things with the scissors and a needle and a gentle touch of flame, but proper reweaving is the foundation. Even accurate reweaving can yield a bad result. By using the wrong wool, especially wool taken from the hides of dead sheep and spun in a factory, repairmen leave dull, rough patches in shiny, smooth surfaces. That is the most common defect of contemporary Turkish repair. It is a common error because proper wool is hard to find in the city and because, though the rug does not look good, nothing has been done wrong — in the moral sense. The rug is strong, usable, and it contains no deception: the technique used to create the rug has been used to repair it. Reweaving is basic, wool selection is important, and obviously, the dyeing of the wool is critical. Poorly dyed wool — bad dyes or good dyes badly prepared — fade more quickly than the old dyes, leaving the surface dappled and splotched. And the colors must be matched exactly. Conscientious repairmen in Istanbul will dye their own wool, especially to get rare colors, like the gold and purple of the old rugs from Konya.

When I lived in Istanbul, I would walk downhill on Sundays to Yedikule and visit Mehmet Ali Akın. Our daughters would play together while I learned about his work. After the death of his father in a farming accident, Mehmet Ali left Sultanhanı in the central Anatolian region between Konya and Niğde that is famous for rugs. He came to Istanbul and learned repair from a relative. A man of tremendous energy, Mehmet Ali established an atelier where he received boys from his home region, feeding them, providing them with a place to sleep, and training them in the repairman's trade. As his nephew Osman became capable of running things in their atelier in a han near the Covered Bazaar, Mehmet Ali spent more and more time ranging through the Bazaar, dealing in rugs.

While I was visiting him, Mehmet Ali built an atelier in the building where he lived in the shadow of the towers of the old city walls. There the boys continued to work on the seventh day. He had built a *boyahane*, a room for dyeing, in the basement, and he would place the carpets he was repairing in the sun near his dye vat, so that he could try and try again to mix colors that matched so closely that when he placed a piece of dyed yarn on the carpet it would become lost to the eye. He dyed yarn in great quantity, and the boys carried the hanks steaming to cool and dry on the stone wall that ran beside the railroad tracks skirting the Marmara. He dyed far more than enough for his own needs, and he supplied many of the repairmen in the hans around the Covered Bazaar. His success was their failure. He matched the colors for his own work exactly, but the men who used his yarn, since they did not dye themselves, had to be content with the

The Opçin brothers: Hasan, Ahmet, Zeki, and Halil.
Çorlulu Ali Paşa Medresesi, Istanbul. 1989

Osman Yiğen and Mehmet Ali Akın. Yedikule, Istanbul. 1984

colors they bought from him. If they were lucky, the match would be perfect. If not, close would have to do, and slight differences of shade prevented the repair from melting into the unity of the rug. So, I ask Hagop if he dyed his own wool.

"Sure, sure," he answers in English, and then returns to Turkish: "At that time, I did dyeing, Henry Abi, all the time.

"At that time there was no prepared wool for sale. Let's say first, perhaps second: mine was among the very best dyed wool in Turkey. My dyed wool was superb. It came from Europe, though — the dye. It was not root dye, but it was very beautiful. It was packaged dye, but it was good dye. I made that. For example" — he points again to the rug on the floor — "this apricot color that appears to you, I would pull it out, and I could make it the same. This blue — I would make whatever you wish."

I think of Mehmet Ali's operation, the stinging steam from the great copper vats, the hundreds of hanks of dyed yarn draped over the wall by the tracks. "Where did you do the dyeing?" I ask.

"I dyed in the shop. There was a small balcony at Zincirlihan, but at that time I did not dye so much. After military service — I came out of the military in one thousand, nine hundred and seventy — then I worked for three months or so beside a man. Then I opened a shop in Çarşıkapı."

Outside of the Covered Bazaar, on the Street of the Janissary Corps, stands the early eighteenth-century *medrese* of Çorlulu Ali Paşa. The rooms of the theological students have been taken over by sellers and repairers of rugs, including my friend Ahmet Opçin, who has one room for sales and another for repair. Across the busy street, another leads down to Kum Kapı and the Marmara shore. On that street in Bizim Han — Our Han — Hagop opened his own shop:

"After military service, I worked for a short while with a man. He was a carpet dealer, and I did the repair. Then I opened my own shop. It was a small shop. There was much work. But at that time, I began to make a very beautiful name. At that time, I began to make my name.

115

"I worked with my brother and another partner, a boy who was a painter. Today he is in Canada.

"Then my younger brothers learned in that shop. At that time, my oldest brother was in Germany. The others were in Istanbul. My next oldest brother, as I said to you, went to school, then to the university. Only I worked. Then we opened the shop. At that time my brother was going to the university, but we also worked together and so on. After that, my younger brother began.

"Before that, for example, I would work for a carpet dealer. Then before school and after school and during the summer, my brothers would come, and we would work together. Every summer. They began like that. They learned the work like that from me."

The process of education, begun in the shops of others, continued when Hagop opened his own shop. He secured the jobs, and his brothers would help him, and in return he taught them. He had become a master. It is like that in the villages. Two women work at the loom. The older one directs the work and owns the result. The younger one contributes her work in return for her education. Later she will own the carpet, and she will be obliged to train the younger woman at her side.

Hagop was his shop's master, its artist, its manager, its teacher. It is the master's obligation to transfer his hard-won skill, easing the way for younger people. Hagop trained his brothers. As they learned, Hagop was freed to spend more time in the rug trade, becoming a merchant. Having taught himself, Ahmet Opçin then taught his younger brother, Hasan, who became a wonder of speedy repair. Hasan Opçin now manages a large repair atelier in Izmir. In the past, once he had learned, Hasan could train the boys in the workshop, leaving Ahmet with more time to scout for rugs and chat with customers. As his nephew became capable of managing the boys in his atelier, Mehmet Ali Akın could be absent longer on the hunt in the Bazaar. The ideal course of the repairman's career leads toward profit and independence — from learning to mastery, from teaching to dealing, from work for another to work for oneself.

You learn, and as your mastery increases, you teach. As your students grow in competence, you work less and less at repair. You become a social force, a station on the route to urban adjustment, receiving immigrants from the countryside, guiding their lives and training them to do the work, so you can wander through the Bazaar, drinking tea, buying the pieces that your men can repair to sell at a profit. As capital increases, you become a merchant. Hagop continues:

"After that, for example, after opening the shop, they began to know me very quickly. Everyone looks at the work. 'Oof, oof.'"

Hagop repeats their sounds of approval and their excited words:

"'I have work, I have work, I have work.

"'Come, Hagop. Hagop. Look, look. Look.' But it was very quick. Suddenly, 'Look, look, look.' Very quick."

Hagop became a master of carpet repair at a time of great expansion in the rug business. I know that there are hundreds of repairmen today in Istanbul — Hagop estimates there are at least two thousand — and I know that there were few at the time he began. I ask him how many.

"When I began, there were few repairmen. There were ten, say twenty, twenty or so people — summer workers, young, old, all kinds taken together, twenty or so. After my military service, there were perhaps fifty, and I was almost the most famous."

He does not exaggerate. The young repairmen in Istanbul today generally do not know him, but they all say they have heard his name. They are always surprised to learn that he is so young, since he is, for them, a legendary master from the dim beginnings of their art.

"I am telling no lie, but I do want to explain one thing. There was that Jaques. He is old now, retired. To say it straight, he was the most famous. Straight speech is necessary. But later they came to know me, and they said that I was better.

"At that time, I began to earn much money. All right, Henry Abi."

He interrupts himself with a brief meditative chuckle.

"I began a night life. Night life. Women. I don't know: this and that: whiskey.

"Since straight speech is necessary, I will tell you that before that I had not seen much money. Then money and so on came, and there was another thing, concerning psychology. After military service, you are from then on a male. Before military service, let's say for example that I would make fifty *lira* a week. I would give forty *lira* to the household. Ten lira would remain for me to spend the whole week. That was the rule. After military service, I still gave, but only a little. For example, I earned a thousand *lira* a week. I gave one hundred *lira*. All right: nine hundred *lira* was mine. Beautiful clothes, then, as I said: beautiful restaurants, beautiful women, bars. I swear to God."

He laughs and goes on:

"Despite the night life, there was much work."

He assumes the whining, pleading tones of his customers:

"'Hagop, Hagop.' It was strange. Everyone talked about Hagop. In the Bazaar. In the street. I mean, that is how it passed.

"In that period, the repair work continually improved. I knew. Others didn't. But I understand. I could see that I improved. There is another thing, as I said, Henry Abi: I loved carpet repair and carpets very much. It was that way in the beginning, and it was always so: I tried to do well.

"I warned myself constantly from the inside: Do better, do better, do better. I mean, artistically. I thought about the artistic. I tried to do well. Always. From the inside, I mean.

"And I saw that it was so. For example, I would see a Kurdish carpet that I had repaired a year ago, and now my work was more beautiful, I mean. The others failed. I improved. I saw that myself."

The flood of people from the country carries rugs with it. Couples come through the back doors of the Covered Bazaar, bringing rugs from home, treasures from the dowry that they must sell now to get through another week. As village populations dissolve, heirlooms once passed on to the next generation are sold to roaming pickers, and as people leave for the city bringing their rugs to sell, rugs from different places come to dominate the Covered Bazaar for a while, providing the market with a pattern.

But in general, the dealers complain, quality has declined, the supply has nearly ended. *"Bitti,"* finished, they say, for the rugs that are brought now, though praised by their sellers for their sturdiness and the quality of their wool, the rugs that come now contain wild synthetic colors, making them of little commercial value. The dealers send the rugs back to the country to kill them — that is the word — by spreading them on fields in the sun. Clever repairmen will pluck out bad colors — pink and orange — and reweave using yarn raveled from old kilims, making the rugs seem older than they are, rendering them valuable, saleable. Dealers know chemical tricks to change hues, and there are wash houses in the suburbs where baths leave rugs with faded colors and whites the shade of weak tea. A short bath "washes" rugs, a long one "kills" them. Their corpses bear the faded elderly look favored by many tourists. There are tricks aplenty, but the older dealers remember better times when deception was unnecessary. They have turned increasingly to the revival of natural dyes, less because of the excellence of the new rugs than because of the dwindling supply of handsome antiques. I ask Hagop if there were beautiful rugs in the market at that time.

"I swear to God, Henry Abi, it was astonishing. I saw very very beautiful carpets. Many, I mean. I always repaired very beautiful carpets. Always. Very old, the most beautiful carpets. Not every kind; they were generally Caucasian and Turkish carpets. (You know the Turkish market.) Sometimes there were Iranian, sometimes other carpets, but generally Turkish or Caucasian."

I ask, "Which did you like best at that time?" He answers:

"Among the Turkish carpets — let me speak straight with you — I most loved Sivas carpets. To me they were the most beautiful. But, when speaking of Sivas carpets, there is another thing.

For example, if you look at a Konya carpet, generally it has the Konya air. The carpet says, 'I am from Konya.' Konya carpets are similar to each other, but great differences were made among Sivas carpets. For example, there were city carpets, there were very strange carpets. Konya-like carpets were made. There are superb carpets with mihrabs. How can I explain it to you? I also loved those of Konya. I loved all carpets. I loved Bergama carpets, for example, very much. Beautiful. But it is hard for me to say. Sometime I loved Kazak carpets very much. But I loved Sivas carpets the most.

"I learned about carpets. In every carpet there is a different hand. Every hand is different. For example, for an idea, when you look at the back of a Konya carpet, you understand it quickly. How can I explain it to you?

"If I would give you the same wool and the same things, and if the two of us wove two carpets, there would be a difference between our works. They would resemble each other, but if I looked closely into them, I would see differences. In the carpet, in the wool, the weft, the warps, the knots, the pile — in everything that I would see, *you* would remain."

Viewed from afar, works of art fit general types. They belong to schools, movements, periods, regions, traditions. When understanding is slight, as it often is with folk arts, they can seem to be anonymous expressions of general concepts. Up close, however, seen from within the tradition, all works of art contain signature, the unique impress of their individual creators. The natural ratio between type and example, between the general and the specific, the conventional and the individual, produces much of the power of art. That is clear in the oriental carpet when the connoisseur appreciates a work at once for its stability, its adherence to recognizable form, and for its variation, its incorporation of its particular weaver.

Richly entailing the qualities found in all art, the carpet has come to global appreciation. Only Chinese porcelain rivals the oriental carpet in universality of acceptance. The carpet's order extracts the orders discovered in nature, the implicit symmetries of the blossoms and beautiful beasts of the earth, of the wheel of the stars in the sky, and these are matched to the ordering principles of human consciousness, the inherent will to sequential and parallel arrangements within balanced schemes. The patterns hidden externally in nature and internally in the mind merge and consolidate in traditional forms, forms that are lifted to view by individuals who use the world's substances while working within the particular limits of time and space and talent. So natural, so human a thing, the oriental carpet exhibits a person: her environment in its materials, her mind in its design, her hand in its execution. In its materiality, in its ratio of pattern to execution, every carpet, like every human face, is symmetrical to the mind, lively to the eye — one of a kind. The weavers say that every carpet is different, and Hagop agrees.

Every carpet, Hagop says, is different, and once he told me that in every carpet there is something to love. With that assertion he placed himself in opposition to rug dealers who, during arguments over prices in the midst of a purchase, focus upon a rug's failings, its weak design or bad colors — the imperfections that keep prices down. Hagop's eye is always drawn to the detail, perhaps minor, that makes the rug singular, lovable, worth repairing. I remind him of his saying that there is something to love in every rug. His response veers off into a valuable commentary on the meaning of rugs — especially valuable, for it issues from within the carpet tradition:

"I swear to God, Henry Abi, how will I explain it to you? If you love something, it is very hard to explain it openly.

"There is this kind of thing, Henry Abi. In my childhood, there was a life. The life I passed in the village, in my childhood, I see that when I look at a carpet.

"Now, I am a cooked apple, or a cooked quince. I am able to see everything better. Those times were different. It is not possible to understand. At that time, in the period of my village life, it was different: those people, their feelings, their thoughts, their plainness, their cleanliness. All right? Now, when I look at a carpet, it is as though I see Fatma, our neighbor Fatma, a woman I loved, our other neighbors, the people, their clean feelings, their thoughts, their humanity, the differences among them."

Swept up in the emotion of his answer, Hagop stops. His answer embraces the idealization of a lost rural life. It conveys an attitude that the cynical often attribute to the comfortable outsider and dismiss as nostalgic or romantic. But I have found in decades of study among country people that they hold such sentiments more passionately than any outsider. They know, after all, what has been lost. They know, too, what has been gained. Now that he is experienced — "cooked," not raw — Hagop knows more, understands better, but among the things he understands is the virtue of the rural life abandoned in the quest for the good life — for him, an exciting, luxurious "night life" in the city.

Artifacts, being human creations, bear meaning, but how artifacts mean is a difficult, delicate question. The bookish turn things like oriental carpets into texts that can be read, making motifs into words, carpets into narratives. But the meanings in carpets elude the literal mind. They are associative, indirect. For Hagop, the rug is an emblem of village experience, the epitome of a way of life. He pulls out of it what the women wove into it: their thoughts, he repeats, their feelings.

Once in a shop where he worked, an old prayer rug from Bergama hung on the wall across from his table. He told me that he saw in it a village among the hills. There was no village, and there were no hills, but he gathered out of the carpet a feeling about a mountain village.

When I asked him how he separated good carpets from bad, he made no reference to design or weave, color or age. He said that looking at a carpet was like experiencing a landscape, like taking a trip. The bad carpet was like being lost in a forest. Too many details, an unclear overall design prevented you from moving through it comfortably. It was crowded, dense, your feelings were confused. Other carpets offered no surprises. They were too clear, mechanical, uneventful; your feelings were dulled. The best carpet, he said, was like standing on a low hill, surrounded by an inviting countryside. As your eye moved, you did not become lost. The general pattern remained clear, but on your journey through it, you encountered pleasant incidents, little details that enlivened your senses while you were in their company.

His answer was based on a Turkish notion of pleasure. The best things are not too exciting, nor are they dull. They do not create thrills, but feelings of contentment, of relaxed interest, a sense of being at rest and satisfied and alive. His answer was also as good a comment as I have ever heard on the aesthetics of the oriental carpet. Its art lies in a proper ratio of pattern to detail, which is analogous, not to the complex, busy, multivocal life of the city, nor to the monotonous drone of the factory, but to the confident, unexciting life of the village, where basic patterns are solid and clear, but where room remains for diverting incidents, pleasurable occasions, and small personal joys. In the rug you see the symmetry of enduring tradition, and you see the little variable motifs of a happy, personal existence.

No, the carpet is not like a book written with a direct communicative purpose, yet its appreciation is analogous to reading a good book in which momentary surprise is contained by a unity of plot. It is more like a poem than a novel, though, for its meanings are associative and incomplete, more affecting than intellectual, and it is still more like music than any thing of words. Music gathers you in and takes you on a trip that enlivens the senses and creates a mood without necessary reference to worldly detail. Letting your eye travel across the carpet is like letting your ear follow the course of a symphony.

You might tell yourself a story out of the moods created on your trip. Of all rugs, Hagop most favors prayer rugs. Their religiosity moves him. He sees in them, in the best of them, an aspiration upward. As the eye rises to the peak of the mihrab, so the person grows upward toward a more perfect life. Hagop has two prayer rugs that he will not sell. Both came to him in terrible condition. They have demanded so much work that no sale could repay him for his contribution. They contain, like children, the complete release of affection, a giving without restraint or need for repayment. One is from Konya, the other is a Kazak, a little Caucasian rug out which he tells himself the story of a long life's struggle for maturity, through a passage of labor toward a state of spiritual calm.

Most good rugs, though, tell him no story. They create a mood in him, a mood like that he knew in the village before he was cooked, when it was as though he stood looking across a lovely landscape, clear in its wholeness, delightful in its detail. Moving down from the hill, across open meadows, into copses aflutter with light, feeling the sun on his neck, the good earth beneath his feet, meeting clean, calm, smiling people, people like those he loved in childhood, Hagop takes a trip.

Any particular trip might be likened to flowing along with a symphony. But rugs are not music, for music moves in one direction, and though it might battle temporal limitations through thematic inversions, counterpoint, and harmony, still music goes on from the beginning to the end, like a work of literature. But the rug can be traveled in any direction. It is not like music, it is like the land, open to trips of all kinds — quick or slow, left to right, bottom to top, center to periphery, now melodic as you follow its pattern, now harmonic as you attend to color. You are free to move or linger as chance or whim or taste suggest.

The rug is a little landscape, inviting exploration, and the best rug, in Hagop's mind, is one like a village landscape, orderly, cultivated, and alive with incident — not wild, thick like a forest, nor confused like a city, nor monotonous like a factory, but open and interesting, like the landscape of his childhood.

At last, carpets symbolize to Hagop the clean and pleasant life of the village, removed from the sophistication and corruption of Istanbul.

To get himself back on track, he returns to his statement that I recalled for him: all rugs contain something to love:

"Here are three carpets. In this one's color there is a beauty. In that one's mihrab there is another beauty. In that one's center there is a beauty."

The word I translate as center is *göbek*, literally navel, but figuratively "center" as in the Turkish proverb, "The woman is the *göbek* of the family." *Göbek* is one of the words used in Turkey for what the rug books call a medallion. *Medalyon* is another, often used in the trade in Istanbul, and *gul* is, like *göbek*, a common country term. People with a weak grip on Turkish try to rationalize *gul* into *gül*, rose, or *göl*, lake, both of which make metaphoric sense, but a *gul* is not a rose or a lake. It is the Turkish word for a rug's main motif, synonymous with *medalyon* or *göbek* when the rug bears but one. Hagop continues:

"Really, beauty lies in their art. It is hard to explain. In every carpet there is a person's heart — not the person's dirtiness, but their thoughts and feelings, their extreme cleanliness. Because of that, I see them, I love them.

"Not the people who bought and sold and used carpets, but the people who made carpets; they were extremely clean people. I mean, so plain, so light, so free of the smallest badness. I mean, Henry Abi, when you make this carpet you are far from every thought, from badness, from everything. You carry only sweet, pleasant things in your mind. For example, when you weave a flower into a rug, there is not another thing in your head. I mean, you think this, you carry this in your head, you make this. A bad meaning is impossible. It is impossible to think something bad, I mean. Their hearts, their thoughts are in their rugs; I love their hearts, their thoughts, I mean."

The weavers, Hagop believes, put the best of themselves into their work — their plainness, he says, their cleanliness. And when Hagop looks at a rug, that is what he chooses to see. His brave, generous act harmonizes with the Sufi spirit. At a time when the television's news overflooded with terrorism, my friend Abdülkadir Uçaroğlu, a potter in Kütahya, painted a plate with a monster below and a canopy of beautiful flowers above. He told me that the choice is ours. We can stare at the monster, at terrorism, losing ourselves into the ugliness of the world, or we can look up and find the world's beauty. Seeking beauty, we follow the Sufi way and find God. Hagop imagines the weavers creating out of pure spirit and investing their works with beauty. When he looks at a carpet, he is drawn by its beauty into oneness with the weaver. His positive evaluation meets her positive effort. He does not fixate on the rug's defects. He searches for the beauty, no matter how slight, that every rug contains, and there he concentrates the emotion of love.

Hagop gestures again to the rugs at our feet, repeating that there is a different hand in every one. It was hard to say, but he said it well, providing us with a native interpretation superior to the efforts trapped in rug books. In the rug, in its weave, there is a particular hand, trained by experience to certain habits. Into the rug, that hand brought the weaver's spirit, her feelings, her pure thoughts, her ideas of the good and the beautiful, making her rug a particular instance of the plain and engaging life of the village. That is what Hagop sees in the rug — a hand, a heart, a clean country place — and that is what he loves. The rug is a woman named Fatma. It contrasts, for him, with the sullied sophistication of urban life. As though he could look through the rug, like a magic lens, and see once more the lovely, free life of his childhood, Hagop repeats:

"It is possible for me to see. That thought, those feelings."

In silence, he looks through the rug into his childhood, through his childhood into himself. We are quiet together. I change the tape and ask him to continue the history of his career.

"After opening the shop, Henry Abi, I worked with my brother. I was working well, and I would continually go to the Bazaar. It was nearby, you know. There I came to know a German man. He loved my work. All right. He was a collector.

"Then I went to Germany. I worked there four and a half years. Then I returned to Turkey."

"But," I say, "you told that too quickly." With a laugh he agrees. He has no wish to speak of the unpleasant. In his life, as in rugs, he concentrates on the positive. I ask him to tell how he got to know foreign rug collectors.

"I got to know them from the Bazaar. For example, they would buy a carpet from a carpet dealer in the Bazaar and so on. Then I met this German. He bought carpets continually from a carpet dealer. Then he had a carpet he wanted to be repaired. Then I did the work. He loved it. Then he wanted to know me better. He came to the shop. He drank tea, he drank coffee, we talked. Then other work and so on — he always brought a carpet in need of repair. I would do it, and we became very close friends.

"He was my big brother — from the angle of age, I mean.

"Then, he asked me, 'Will you come to Germany?' And, I answered, 'I will come.'"

I ask what he was thinking when he decided to go to Germany.

"Germany was a Christian nation. Then also, I was interested to see another country, another world. Generally, there are not many blonde girls in Turkey. Yellow-haired, blue-eyed, tall, long-legged women would come from Germany as tourists."

He laughs, saying it is improper to speak of such things, then turns abruptly serious:

"This is the real reason, Henry Abi. I have not told it to many people. All right. For example, being a Christian, life was not comfortable for me. You understand, but perhaps you do not understand. In Turkey, there was, from childhood, a discomfort inside of me. It came from Christianity. Then I thought, Germany is a Christian country. I will go to Germany, and everything will be all right. But I went to Germany, and I saw something: it was very different. It was not like I thought.

"The Germans were against foreigners. There was no sympathy. They were against the Turks, and nobody would call me Armenian; it was always, 'Turk, Turk, Turk.' Then I thought to myself: in Turkey I was an Armenian. I came to Germany, and I am not an Armenian. Everyone living here calls me Turk, Turk, Turk.

"Then I returned. I returned again to Turkey."

Hagop's family came to Istanbul early in the tide of immigration that would make the old city into a home for Anatolians, but he went to Germany at the peak of the immigration of "guest workers," when Germany's unemployment rate was down to one percent and the government signed agreements with foreign nations to bring in workers to do the bad jobs. Of all European nations, Germany has the most foreigners, and the foreigners are from Turkey more than from any other nation. One and a half million Turks lived in Germany in Hagop's time. Polls showed that the Germans did not project great criminality or laziness upon the Turks. Their objections were largely aesthetic. Turks were seen as loud, dirty, clannish. Nearly half of the German people did not approve of the foreigners among them, and prejudice against Turks took many forms, some subtle, some so shocking as to remind the Germans of their treatment of the Jewish people. I ask Hagop to describe life in Germany.

"Life in Germany. From the standpoint of art, I lived a very closed life in Germany. When I say closed, I mean this man was not a carpet dealer. He was a collector. For example, how can I say it to you? I worked for a private man for a year. He was not a collector; he was the collector's brother, a very very rich man with a terrific house. For one year I repaired that man's carpets. Do you understand? He had *so* many carpets. For one year I worked for that man. Then one year I worked for the collector.

"In Germany, I had a beautiful house, but not much social life, and my artistic life was not much. I mean, it was not important. How can I say it to you? I worked. It was normal.

"I swear to God, let's say that it was strange. For example, when I came to America, I wanted nothing from America. Because of that, I am content in America. But when I went to Germany, I wanted much from Germany. I imagined a fantasy. I created a fantasy but found nothing. Do you understand? Because of that, I was not content. Perhaps if, when going to Germany, I came like I did when I came to America, it would have been much better for me.

"Then with such feelings of discontentment, I returned to Turkey. But how can I explain life in Germany to you, Henry Abi? It was a very plain, simple life.

"The people were good. The men were lovers of art. I would do repair, and they would be pleased. But how can I say it to you? I had nothing to show for myself. I had no position for myself."

Hagop went to Germany with his hopes too high. He hoped for acceptance in a Christian nation, but he found rejection. He was hoping to move along the conventional course of success, from repairman to independent merchant, but he saw a future full of nothing but endless labor for others. He clarifies that second goal when I ask him if he thought he would stay for his whole life when he, like his brother before him, left Turkey for Germany.

"No. When I went I didn't think so. I went to work, but I went without deciding for how long or what I would do. I went without thinking. But then, there was another thing in Germany, Henry Abi: I understood that I would do something. (Do you understand? I am discontent with this thing against foreigners. All right.) If work over there prolonged for me, I would stay, then later when I returned to Turkey, it would be a very good thing that I went. I would earn more money, and slowly I would make a beginning in buying and selling and so on. But how can I say it to you? It was like falling from high to low. Do you understand? Because of that, I was not content. After that, I returned.

"There is one thing I understand: I lost much in Germany. I understood this when I returned. Because — I don't know exactly, but I stayed there four or four and half years. That was a very good time for me. For work. For earning money. My strongest times, my best times passed over there. Then, whiskey and women — I don't know, this and that, you know, night life in Germany and so on. I understand the things I lost.

"Then, Turkey had changed a little. Do you understand? What was this change? The carpet business grew. New people and so on."

I understand. While he was wasting his best years in Germany, the Turkish rug trade surged forward without him. I tell him that.

"Of course," he replies. "I saw that it was so when I returned. But then again, slowly I began to work, but it had become different. There was more buying and selling. I had several men working for me. The others from my family had gone abroad.

"At that time, one brother was in Turkey, in Istanbul. He had finished the university, but it was hard for him to find work, so he did carpet repair. One was in the military service. Then, the others were in Europe. One was in Germany, one was in France, one was in England."

I ask where they are now.

"Now — we are six brothers — one is in Germany. He works in a factory. Then, the one younger than him is a carpet dealer in Italy. Then, the one younger than him works in France, repairing, buying and selling automobiles; that kind of thing. The one younger than him is me. The one younger than me is a carpet dealer in New York. The one younger than him is a carpet dealer in London. Like that."

That is the end of the tale of the migration of an Armenian family from Kayseri. The mother is dead. The old father remains in Istanbul. The boys have scattered to Germany, Italy, France, England, and the United States. Hagop continues:

"After Germany, I slowly began again to adjust to Turkey. Again, I had my name, again I had my work, again jobs came easily because there were always men who knew me. It was no problem to find work. It was no problem to earn money. Everything was easy.

"I began to work anew. All right? Everything was beautiful. I worked in the same shop as before. When I was in Germany, my brothers stayed in the same shop.

"Then, later it became a little different. For example, a little less work, more buying and selling, I mean, like that: cleaner people, more beautiful money, an easier life.

"So, to speak the essence — in that period, the other brother went abroad and no one other than myself remained there. And then, this thing began. There was more terrorism, you know, Henry Abi. A diplomat was killed. My family, my mother, began to worry. Something dreadful might happen. The middle of life was ruined. There were terrorists."

Hagop pauses. Armenian resistance had escalated from words to bombs. A fearful unspoken history and memories of violence fill the silence. Slowly, he says quietly:

"Then it was clear, Henry Abi.

"Then America."

I ask him how he decided on America.

"My decision about America — I had heard a few things about America, but it was like nothing. My coming to America was by chance, Henry Abi. All right. When I took the road out of Turkey, I thought only one thing: I was leaving Turkey. But, for example, I thought every country other than Germany was possible. Luckily for me, I was taken to America. By chance you could say.

"Then, I really did not know much about America. I am speaking straight. I came to America by chance. What kind of chance? My brother and one or two friends were in America, and they told me about America and so on. I imagined a different world. You know.

"I came to New York. I stayed there a while. Then, I looked for work. There was nothing.

"Then, my friend and I were in my brother's house. I remember that day as though it were today. A carpet dealer came and he gave my friend a kilim for repair, and my friend said I had just come from Turkey and so on. Then that carpet dealer called a friend of his, and he called my friend — my friend's name is Zeron; you know him — and that's the story.

"Then we came to Philadelphia, my brother, Zeron, and I. Then we talked, I saw the shop and so on. Then I said, 'All right,' and began."

I ask him to tell how America seemed to him when he arrived.

"All right. I will tell about it. One thing was very very strange, Henry Abi. Let's say, I know very little about European countries, but getting to know them is very easy. The reason is that the people are all of the same stuff. It is as though they were cut from the same pattern, as though they came from the same factory.

"Turkey or America — it is one thing for me. Before I was in Istanbul, I was in Anatolia, then I adjusted, and I got used to Istanbul. So I could adjust to America because America is not like Europe.

"In Turkey, there are places that resemble America. How can I say it to you? There are dirty streets here, all right: unclean, sorry, wrecked houses, bearded, unshaven people, all right. It is the same. But beside them are clean, cultured ladies and gentlemen. It is the same: beautiful women, ugly women. It is a very mixed up place, a little like Turkey.

"Then when I came, believe me Henry Abi: when I came I loved America very much. It was like this. On the first day I was here, it was as though I had been living here for ten years. It was as though I had lived here before. Everything went so easily. Everything.

"And then, I thought, Ah" — he breaks into English, "America is the right country for me." Then he returns to Turkish, "This is the place for me. All right. I can live here.

"But I had no idea about America. I had no idea at all. I knew nothing at all.

"So then, as I began to learn a little English and so on, slowly I began to know America. After a year.

"And there was a difference.

"Do you understand, Henry Abi? There was a difference. I came to know about the lives of the people, about unshaven people, dirty streets, sorry wrecked houses. What was the difference? My mood was very different. Do you understand, Henry Abi?

"The summer is too hot, the winter is too cold, and I don't know. It is a very different country, very hard to describe.

"The second year was very hard because slowly I began to get used to America. For example, the first year everything was new, everything was new. For example, there is always something to see. Your time fills. You look at this street for one month, at that street for one month. You have no time to think of other things. Do you understand, Henry Abi? For example, you look two times, three times, five times, then you know. Then you know you did not look well into yourself. Food and the like, family life. In Turkey there is extremely clean food, beautiful food. Then here, for example, the same food and so on is hard to find. It is not normal.

"I am not a child. My confidence faded, my bones weakened. Do you understand? I became depressed, rebellious.

"Everything grew worse. Generally I love America very much, Henry Abi, but I am saying it straight to you.

"I cannot speak about this business to everyone, Henry Abi. I do not like saying this to a person's face. In the past, I kept my unhappiness to myself. I hid it. I did not behave well and I did not like it.

"You are a good man, my Henry Abi, so I did not like to say it to you. Do you understand? I am saying it straight. But you are very close to me, closer than anyone, so it was a thing you could see. You knew how I was then, and you know how I am now. Then I was depressed, but slowly I have gotten used to America. My mood and attitude are better. I am stronger and able to do things."

Hagop describes himself as a man of low energy. He means he is not bouncy, optimistic. His laugh is bemused, thoughtful, undercut by knowledge of life's tiring imperfections. His most common comment, his summary during gaps in small talk is, "So, it is like this. We work." Hagop is tenacious, dogged, and he is contemplative. He broods. During his second year in America, he missed his mother. He missed the fresh, delicious food of Turkey. He missed the easy camaraderie, the talk and tea and constant socializing that kept his mind off himself. Through his brooding, angers swirl that he usually contains bravely, but

133

he can erupt and harm himself. His words call sad events into our minds separately, and I remind him of an Armenian woman who befriended him in Philadelphia and gave an old immigrant's warning to a new immigrant:

"She said it very straight. That woman said to me — she was an Armenian woman from Russia — I was working in the shop, and she came and she said to me, 'Are you an Armenian?' 'Yes,' I said, 'I am an Armenian'. Then she said, 'How long have you been here?' I said, 'Three years.' 'Ah,' she said, 'a little more time is necessary for you.'"

Hagop laughs. "'How is America?' she said.

"'Beautiful,' I said.

"Then she said, 'America,' she said, 'after five years is beautiful. The first year,' she said, 'is very very beautiful. The second year,' she said, 'is a little hard. The third year is harder,' she said. 'The fourth year, if someone asks how America is — you have gotten a little used to it, of course — and "How is America?" they ask. You say, "Ah, it's all right," and you go on.'"

When Hagop reported what she told him, he imitated her bland, unenthusiastic tone, and he added a shrug of dismissal. Then he repeats her concluding words: "'After that, America is very beautiful.'

"And very straight that woman said it. Straight and true."

Hagop stops, smiles, and provides his own conclusion:

"So. Now I have decided.

"When I left Turkey, I thought nothing. I did not think whether I would stay all my life or only a short while. But now I think," Hagop shifts into English, "America is my country."

I was there when he decided. Walking together through Kum Kapı, his old neighborhood in Istanbul, we came upon a teahouse owned by a man irreverently nicknamed for the call to prayer. They had played on the same soccer team years ago, and the teahouse being crowded, he brought a couple of crates from inside and upended them on the sidewalk. There we sat, drinking tea and enjoying the sun, while Hagop told me of his life's search.

His search began in his feelings of estrangement. As a boy, a member of the only Armenian family in an Anatolian town, he did not feel that he fit. It was not that he was held back. His grandparents lived in an exceptionally fine house — a *konak* of stone. A Muslim master trained him. It was not that he was caught in a web of hostility. The rugs he loves are emblems for him of people he loved, like his neighbor Fatma (her name is emphatically Muslim). Village life, as he describes it, was free and clean, sociable and natural. His problem was not oppression or prejudice — forces from without — but feelings that rose from within, feelings he calls "foreignness." As we sat there that day, sipping tea together in the sun on a bright and busy street in Kum Kapı, this is the story he told to explain his feelings to me:

Once he was taking a trip by bus through Anatolia. He stopped in a small town and entered the hotel. When he signed the register, the young man behind the desk commented on his unusual name. The family name is not unusual. Barın is a Turkish name. But Hagop — Armenian for Jacob — struck the man as strange. Hagop explained that it was Armenian, and the young man became excited, saying his father had told him about Armenians, how intelligent and talented they were, but they had all gone, and the young man, having never seen an Armenian, made Hagop join him for tea and a long conversation. That is what Hagop did not like. It was not mistreatment, but treatment as though he were not part of the community. He was made to feel as though he were strange.

Coming to Istanbul, knowing that many Armenians lived there, Hagop hoped at last to become a part of a community — a community like the one that Muslim Turks enjoyed. But he found the Armenian community fragmented, nothing but a collection of selfish individuals, and he found his friends, as he had in Sarıoğlan, among Muslims like the man who cheerily kept us in tea while our conversation continued.

Christian among Muslims, villager among city people, he did not belong in Istanbul, and he hoped the Christian nation of

Hagop's Istanbul. 1983

Germany would provide what he was looking for, but there, as a Turk, he became the embodiment of a negative stereotype. The Germans did not like him, and Germany did not suit him. At night, he said, the windows were shuttered, the streets were silent. Living in Kum Kapı, he came to love the sound of the streets. The word *ses* means both sound and voice, so I let it mean voice and listened as Hagop told of his love for the voice of the streets. I heard the laughter of children at play, the calls of the vendors, the rattle of wagons, the moan of the ships on the Marmara. We stopped and listened to the voice of the streets, the vital pulse of Istanbul. He missed that dreadfully in Germany.

The Germans did not like Turks. They seemed all alike, as though cut from the same pattern. Again he was made to feel different.

When he came to America, he bore no inflated hopes. As he came to know America and weathered a bout of depression, he found that he had a home. In Philadelphia there was noise in the streets, the kind of confusion he had learned to enjoy in Istanbul. Here he found a home, not because he feels that he belongs, not because America has provided him a warm community within which he can be at last integrated, but because America lacks community. It is not homogeneous like Germany. It is a place for people who have no place. America, says Hagop, is filled with people like himself, people who do not fit.

The conclusion is not a happy one, but it is balanced, realistic. America, he says, is my country because it is no one's country. It is a place to succeed or fail.

In America, Hagop can live with his feelings of alienation, and in America he has been able to follow the career of the repairman to its logical end. He was stifled in Germany. There he would repair carpets for all time. But in America he has opened his own store.

In Philadelphia, he worked as a repairman for a retail dealer, learning English, coming to know America and the American rug market, meeting people, building a reputation as an artist.

In the self-sacrificing, austere style of the immigrant that has subtly supported the American economy for centuries, Hagop lived modestly in a spartan room and saved his money. As it had in Istanbul, the skill and discipline he learned in the Turkish countryside enabled him to adjust to a new environment and to accumulate cash enough for advancement. At last he announced that he was going to quit his job and go into the carpet business.

We all warned him that he might fail, that he would make better money as a repairman, but he was adamant. He would go into business for himself. It did not matter if he made less money. He wanted to be his own boss. Repair would provide a foundation, but he would have his own shop, and he would buy and sell.

He opened his store, he says, with no money. But he ordered a sign with his own name on it: Barın Oriental Rugs. His stock was slight, but he piled it in neat heaps along the walls. I cut an Ottoman arch out of plywood to decorate the doorway that divided the space (it had been a dry cleaning shop). Hagop hung his best pieces on the wall, and placed copper vessels from Turkey on a kilim beneath the sign in the window. He created an American shop with the Istanbul feel.

To keep the cash flowing during the store's first year, he did much carpet restoration, but sometimes, he says, when someone would bring him a repair job, he could taste his liver in his mouth. Repair is his art, but he hates to be obligated, hates to do work that is not interesting. He should be teaching younger men. They should do the dull jobs, leaving him with a few interesting tasks and with time to spend as the manager of a business, a trader in carpets.

In his shop's second year, Hagop did less repair, and he devoted more time to buying and selling. As time passed, he took on an apprentice, a young American woman, and he taught her well. More than a decade has gone since we sat in my house with the tape recorder between us. We stay in touch, chat in Turkish. His stock of antique carpets has grown. Hagop's is the only shop in America where I can still find old Turkish rugs to suit

Hagop Barın at Barın Oriental Rugs. Philadelphia. 1998

my taste at prices I can afford. Hagop is a merchant, a success, an American.

When customers come, he buys drinks for them, Istanbul-style, and lets them sit and talk without worrying whether they will buy. He wants people to come, to feel relaxed. Perhaps they will buy. If not, he likes the company. He has his own mode of business. He will pay too much to a picker, sell too cheaply to a customer. He wants them to return. He pays full prices for beautiful old Turkish carpets, which he finds somehow, and he does not worry about the money he has given for them. If they never sell, he enjoys having them around him. He loves them, he is doing well enough, and he always has his work.

A few days after our interview, I passed Barın Oriental Rugs on Pine Street, in Philadelphia. The street was dark, the other shops were closed, but light flowed out of the big window where Hagop sits to watch life pass by while he is working over a carpet. I stopped in and told him it was past six, time to go home. "I know," he said smiling, "but I love my work." As I left, he bent again over the rug, and continued to nudge it slowly back toward beautiful wholeness.

Now that he has a home where he fits because no one does, now that he has become a successful rug dealer, he knows two distinct rug markets well, that of Istanbul and that of Philadelphia. I ask him to compare them, and he answers:

"For example, the carpet business in Turkey. The Turkish people use carpets and love carpets. The American people are different.

"In Turkey, the carpet dealers who sell carpets to the outside generally sell to tourists. There is this kind of thing, for example. In America — and I would say it is the same in the countries of Europe — when they think of Turkey or Iran, they think of carpets. But, for example, most tourists have no idea about carpets. Then they come to Turkey and they buy a carpet. All right. They can give a thousand dollars easily for a carpet. There is a beautiful story in it, and a picture, an old picture in it. The wool is soft.

"They come to buy a carpet and they buy atmosphere. They buy a story.

"In Istanbul there is something. It is possible to sell everything over there. Because people come from all over the world. They have diverse tastes.

"So Istanbul is like that, I mean. Generally carpet dealers working in Istanbul sell to foreigners — to America, to Europe — to foreigners. But generally in America carpets are sold to Americans, and Americans have one taste. Generally Americans look for decorative carpets. Color, they look for color. And, like a fashion, the color always changes. For example, pastel colors, then dark colors. Everything goes like that."

Hagop has a home and a store. It seems that his quests are complete. I ask him to think of the future.

"Now my life is becoming very beautiful. And it will become, I believe, more beautiful.

"The future is a strange place, a strange country. Everything takes time. You know that well. It is not so easy.

"But everyone has a fantasy in their thoughts — half thought, half fantasy. Since I am normal, what there is in a normal person there is in me. I swear to God, I will buy the most beautiful carpets. I will repair the most beautiful carpets. I love carpets very much. Carpets are a big part of my life.

"What do I think of my coming life? I swear to God, I will do everything. Together with carpets, Henry Abi, I will do everything.

"God alone knows."

Norio Agawa. Hagi, Japan. 1998

4

THE POTTER'S ART

VIOLATING NATURE in the hunt for resources, working and reworking materials to rebuild the world, people intend to make things better. The wish to improve, to advance the human cause, invests all artifacts with value.

Coming into being, the artifact inevitably creates relations — relations between nature and culture, between the individual and society, between utility and beauty – and governed by desire, the artifact's construction answers questions of value. Is nature favored or culture? Are individual needs or social needs more important? Do instrumental or aesthetic goals dominate in the transformation of nature?

Artifacts rearrange nature to embody values. The more values that the artifact contains, the richer its display of purpose, the more it is to be addressed as a work of art. Attitudes in the ambit of art imply value. Art is gauged in economic terms: the object's worth as art is established in the gap between its price and the cost of its materials. It is judged philosophically, the object's worth lying in its ability to provoke and sustain argument. Veneration divides things: this one is used and discarded, that one is dressed with the blood of sacrifice or elevated on a pedestal in an atmosphere controlled for heat and humidity. Works of art bring cash, inspire discussion, and request respect, but their inherent worth does not depend on response. It abides in the gift made to them by their creators. Artists bear down in devotion, and their works fill with the human and swell with value.

One way to describe the study of art is to say that it is the process of discovering through objects the values of their makers and users. In the ethnographic study of art, I have found, it is best to attend to the full range of media, noting how values obey and ignore the limitations of particular craft disciplines while people express themselves and shape their culture. But in cross-cultural study, the conventional art-historical concentration on media bears merit. We can hold the medium steady, learning how people who are biologically alike use the same materials and similar techniques to realize cultural difference and human unity.

The chief problem in the study of art is learning to value the unfamiliar. Born into an environment filled with pictures, trained to understand how paintings contain value, it is natural for us to travel the world with the easel painting in mind. Then, encountering other people and assuming their traditions to be like ours, we tend to miss their best effort altogether and select their minor works because of a fancied resemblance to our own. We welcome other people into study only to dismiss them as inept makers of pictures and affirm our superiority. No matter how important the painting is in the late West, it is uncommon in world history. It would be more just, truer to reality, to begin cross-cultural study with textiles and ceramics, neolithic victories that are genuinely global in distribution. The result would be chastening. The industrial West would not fare so well — we have no textiles to match Iran's, no pots to match Japan's — but we would be closer to comprehending the human urge to excellence. In this essay, I will tell a few stories about the potter's art to illustrate how common clay is made to carry value.

Bangladesh

I will begin on the other side of the world, in Bangladesh. The land is lush and flat. Through it rivers run from the mountains to the sea. Their silt has built the world's widest delta. Having much money, we grade the world's nations by wealth, and Bangladesh lies near the bottom, but if clay were the basis for ranking, Bangladesh would stand at the top. It is a beautiful green place, rich in clay.

The very earth is the common resource upon which life is built. Farmers plow the fertile soil and plant it to rice so that people might eat. The clay beneath the surface is dug out, borne in headloads, and heaped into the foundations that lift the villages above the flood. And clay is mined and mixed, shaped and baked into the tools that people use to get through another hard day.

In Bangladesh, there are six hundred and eighty villages of potters, nearly half a million people who use clay to make art because clay is what there is. The nation is predominantly Muslim, but the potters are predominantly Hindu, members of the craft-caste of the Pals. Potters — Pals — divide themselves into two kinds. One kind, they say, makes *kalshis*, the other *murtis*.

The *kalshi* is a globular water jar, but makers of *kalshis* make utilitarian pots of all kinds — vessels for cooking food as well as carrying water. Symbolized by the elephant, water is a terrible force in the delta of Bengal, bringing life in rain, death in flood, and the potter's prime creation is the one capable of containing water, the *kalshi*.

They begin by blending two kinds of clay — one black and sticky, one white and sandy — into a smooth new substance. Then, women and men use different techniques to accomplish identical forms. Women raise the *kalshi* in a sequence of three dishes, turning them by hand, while adding coils to fashion the shoulders, neck, and lip. Men use the big *chak*, the hand-powered wheel that requires postures unbecoming to women. They throw the *kalshi* in two sections, then paddle the parts into unity. The goal is to achieve the maximum of internal volume, and the minimum of weight, while crafting a thin-walled jar for the transport of water. The need is real, and it has long endured. Terra cotta tiles nearly two thousand years old show *kalshis* in the modern form being carried by women in the way they are carried today, with an elbow crooked around the neck and the body of the pot pressed into the hollow of the waist.

Fired on an open, wood-burning kiln, the *kalshi* becomes a commodity. It is made to sell. It is bought to use. In commercial

Malati Rani Pal.
Kagajipara, Dhamrai, Bangladesh.
1989

Gauranga Chandra Pal.
Rayer Bazar, Dhaka.
1995

Kiln and *kalshis*.
Norpara, Shimulia, Bangladesh.
1996

exchange, potters get cash, customers get tools, and they join in a bond of interdependence and trust, founded upon the honorable ethic of utility.

Among the Pals, most men and women make *kalshis*. In the villages I know, one household out of ten contains men who make *murtis*, images of the deities for worship. They begin with a prayer, repeating a mantra of praise to the deity that calls a vision into the mind. As the artist of realism works to render an image that appears on the retina, the sculptor of *murtis* strives to realize a direct revelation of the divine that appears to the mind's eye. He splits sticks to build a frame, wraps it with rice straw, bound into form, and then covers the straw with a thick coat of the clay blend used to make *kalshis*. Next comes the time of concentration, when the *murti* is detailed to completeness through sprigging and modeling by hand.

In the moment of concentration, as the sculptor Haripada Pal describes it, the artist withdraws from the quotidian and unites with God. Called Bhagaban, called Allah, God is omnipresent and formless. God follows prayer into the mind in the form of a particular deity.

The deities each have their powers, their missions. First is Devi, the Great Goddess, manifest as Durga in triumph and Kali in rage. She is the Great Mother, attended in worship by her children: Saraswati, the goddess of wisdom; Lakshmi, the goddess of wealth; Kartik, the beautiful god of war; and Ganesh, the Lord of Beginnings, with his opulent paunch and white elephant's head. Next is Shiva, called Mahadev, the Great God. He rises in pure energy as the phallic, black Linga. He dances alone, his dreadlocks flying; in one hand, he holds the drum that sets the tempo of existence, in another burns the flame that will extinguish the world at the end of its current phase of misery. Shiva embraces Devi in her wifely embodiment as Parvati. He lies, a dozing dandy, beneath the feet of Kali. Third of the great deities is Vishnu, the Lord of Life. In devotion, Vishnu is eclipsed by Krishna, his eighth avatar, the third incarnation of time, who sways with his lover, Radha, and lifts his flute to call humanity to love. And there are others: Bishwakarma, the god of the artisans; Sitala, the goddess of smallpox; Manasa, the goddess of snakes. Out of the infinite, the deities coalesce to give form and special purpose to the single power of God.

God fills the mind with living form, and in working to recreate his vision in clay, the artist becomes a conduit for universal power. The clay in his hands contains the seed of all creation, the presence of God that springs to life with prayer. The clay of his body contains the immortal soul, the drop of God that enables all action. During creation, at one with God, working to pull God's image out of God's substance, Haripada Pal caresses and massages the clay, pressing into its softness, while the power in his body surges through his fingers to fuse with the seed of creation, effecting a reunion of the divine and impregnating the image with sacred force. Haripada says that his work in the clay is part of his devotion to God. It is a prayer.

As I watched Sumanta Pal, sculptor in the village of Kagajipara, create a *murti* of Saraswati, the goddess of wisdom, I saw how his every motion was pitched toward perfection. His steady hands, trained to repetition in common work, figured pieces into neat patterns. His mind, capable of seeing the form beyond the form, brought shapes into singing symmetry. Sumanta's Saraswati swells with fecund youth like the wooden gods of Africa. There is no sign of age or strain, no tug of gravity. She is weightless, inflated with power and radiant with beauty. The abstract and idealized qualities in Sumanta's statue — qualities found generally in what is called folk art — do not eventuate from a failed effort to depict a woman out of the world. This is a goddess. Sumanta's work is a prayer, its result is a splendid materialization of eternal power.

The aesthetic of the *murti* is built upon the sacred and oriented to the transcendent. Nature's implicit patterns and geometry are extracted and brought to perfection in manifest symmetries. Nature's roughness is erased in smooth, dampened

148

Basanta Kumar Pal,
shaping the straw form
for an image of Saraswati.
Kagajipara, Dhamrai, Bangladesh.
1998

Sumanta Pal,
sculpting a *murti* of Saraswati.
Kagajipara. 1995

Saraswati.
Puja at Dhakeswari Mandir.
Dhaka, Bangladesh. 1987

and sanded layers of fine clay. Nature's dullness, the dark tone of the earth, is hidden by a coat of white paint, thickened with boiled tamarind seeds, that serves, like the gesso of the carved Latin American saint, to seal the surface and provide a bright base for the application of luminous color.

The *murti* is not burned. Fire would kill the power of the clay that abides in its dampness. The damp interior is for power. The surface — symmetrical, smooth, and bright — is for beauty.

Powerful and beautiful, the *murti* makes sacred wisdom visible. Haripada Pal was trained in his art by his grandfather Niroda Prasad Pal, and he was instructed in esoteric interpretation by a saintly ascetic, Surendra Chandra Sarkar. He knows one hundred and eight distinct images of Kali, the goddess in wrath. They are brought to order in myth.

In the story Haripada tells, beautiful Kali — black in color to her enemies, the blue of the deep sky to her devotees — set out to destroy the evil in the world. But with her success, in the midst of her rage, she lost the difference between good and evil. Wielding the sword in her left hand, she began to destroy everything. In terror, the people went to Lord Shiva, beseeching him to do something. Shiva positioned himself in her path and fell asleep. Continuing on her wild course, Kali stepped on him. Her foot knew Shiva's flesh. Her tongue lolled in shocked embarrassment and sudden understanding. Recognizing the wrong she had done by putting her foot on her husband's body, she remembered her duty to him. Particular understanding became general: the sword switched from her left hand to her right as a sign of her recognition of the wrong she had done to the world, and of her duty to humankind. It is Kali in this instant, her foot on Shiva, her tongue hanging, that Haripada shapes of clay. His statue embodies a narrative. It carries myth and wisdom, and it is poised for ritual.

Kali is caught in the flash of awareness. With the sword in her left hand, she is Shamakali, strong and enraged. Her devotee asks for protection, praying for the annihilation of the devils in the world, the criminals and terrorists who make life miser-

Rakshakali.
By Haripada Pal.
Shankharibazar, Dhaka.
In process, 1998

Rakshakali. By Haripada Pal.
Shankharibazar Kali Mandir. Dhaka, Bangladesh. 1995

Shamakali.
By Haripada Pal.
Shama Puja.
Shankharibazar,
Dhaka. 1998

Kali is fed before her sacrifice.
Shama Puja. Tanti Bazar, Dhaka. 1998

able. With the sword in her right hand, a split instant later in mythic time, she is Rakshakali, strong and benign. Her devotee asks for personal blessings. This is the Kali, Haripada says, that people can approach with prayer, offering gifts and requesting worldly favors.

Haripada Pal calls the *murti* a mediator. It is made to bring people toward God so their lives will improve. The beauty of the *murti* works like a litany of praise to attract the deity into the clay, as the artist's mantra called the deity into his mind. The beauty of the *murti* draws people toward the deity so that they can communicate with God.

On the day set in scripture, the *murti* is installed in a tented pavilion. Invited by prayer, pleased with the beautiful image prepared to receive her, the goddess descends into the clay. The *murti* is made to signal from afar, obliterating the distance that divides people from God. The large eyes in the large head pull the people, and they crowd forward, straining to take *darshan*, connecting eye to eye with the goddess. Their eyes meet: the water in the clay of the body of the devotee connects with the water in the clay of the body of the *murti*; the soul in the devotee connects with the goddess in the statue. Contact is made, communication becomes possible. While the deity is delighted with throbbing drums and dancing flames and the sweet smell of incense, people make their wishes known to the goddess. In sacred exchange, they give flowers and receive sweet cakes and fruit, palpable, consumable signs of wishes to be granted.

With the cool light of dawn, worship ends. The goddess is gone, the beautiful statue is empty. Practice differs for each deity. Worship lasts seven days for Durga, one day for Saraswati, then after a week in the case of Durga, a year in the case of Saraswati, the painted *murti* is fed, garlanded, and borne to the river in a jubilant, carnivalesque procession. Incense fills the air, the drums pound, and at last, to the ululation of the women, the image is drowned, melted back into the running water from which it came. The clay of the *murti* decays into the silt out of which the *kalshis* and *murtis* of the future will be shaped. The rivers go on flowing, the cycles of birth and rebirth, of creation and sacrifice, continue.

In the contemporary United States, ceramic artists divide. Some make utilitarian vessels, others make sculpture, and the difference between them can stiffen into contention. But the potter in Bangladesh creates both useful ware and lovely statues. They say that some make *kalshis* and others make *murtis*, but in practice most of the Pals who work in season to sculpt icons of the deities fill slack time with the manufacture of utensils of clay.

The separation of *kalshis* from *murtis* seems to align with the Western division of craft from art. Western critics sunder the utilitarian from the aesthetic and pose them in opposition, demeaning work and lifting some artifacts with some people into an idle elite. But most people work; it is their lot, their burden, their delight, and they appreciate help during the labor of their days. For the world's working majority, utility is a high value, the merely decorative seems trivial, and their greatest creations blend the aesthetic with the useful, just as the good meal blends flavor and nutrition. The potters of Bangladesh make useful pots and beautiful statues, and they call them both *shilpa*: art.

Murtis lift the sacred to view in beauty. The *kalshi* is for use. And yet the *murti* and *kalshi* share in affect. Both are symmetrical, smooth, and bright. Like the *murti*, the *kalshi* is pulled away from nature during creation. It is raised to geometric form, its surface is fastidiously smoothed, and it is slipped. The slip, a solution of special clay, serves no utilitarian purpose. It sheathes the pot with color and sheen.

If holes are poked through the coating of straw and mud that covers the pots on the kiln, the *kalshi* comes buff from the fire, and its surface glows with the rich red of the slip. If the fire is smothered, an atmosphere of reduction is established, and the *kalshi* emerges blackened from the kiln. Slipped passages shine, the surface plays from silver to sooty black. And the *kalshis* were stacked on the kiln so that the proximity of other pots would produce pale clouds on their sides that are desirable marks of beauty to their makers and their buyers.

Utility dominates, but much time is given to making the *kalshi* handsome as well. Trim rows of dents are hammered around the shoulder to ornament the pot, to clarify the impurity of its commitment to utility, and in color, smoothness, and symmetrical form, the *kalshi* embodies the aesthetic that crosses the boundaries between media to bring the material culture of Bengal into unity and to bless the world of work with beauty.

The decorative impulse that is subdued in the working pot becomes conspicuous and dominant when the *kalshi* is painted. Hindus paint *kalshis* with scrolling forms borrowed from *alpanas*, designs women draw on the floor for auspicious occasions, and painted *kalshis* are arranged beneath the *murti* to hold holy water during worship. Muslims paint *kalshis* with abstract floral patterns that evoke the promised garden of the Holy Koran, and painted *kalshis* are sold as souvenirs of sacred occasions at the shrines of the Muslim saints. Painted, the *kalshi* declines in utility while increasing in ornament. Then ornament gathers meaning, replacing service to the body with service to the soul in its gesture toward the sacred.

The *murti* completes the reach for the sacred in beauty. It is shaped by the aesthetic. But the purpose of the *murti*, according to Haripada Pal, is instrumental. Haripada has worked hard and traveled widely to make himself the best sculptor in Bangladesh. He makes *murtis* to please God, to achieve release from the cycles of reincarnation, and he makes *murtis* to make money. The executive committee of a temple raises funds from the community to commission a *murti*. Haripada is paid to sculpt images that serve his community, making it possible for others to receive the blessings of God, as he has received the blessing of talent, the source of his art, his livelihood, and his hope. The *murti* works to bring people into connection with power, so their lives on the earth will be better. A bridge between the worlds, the *murti* is, like the *kalshi*, a tool.

Kalshis. Khamarpara, Shimulia, Bangladesh. 1995

Murti of Radha and Krishna. By Babu Lal Pal.
Khamarpara, Shimulia, Bangladesh. 1996

The *murti* binds beauty to utility through the sacred. Makers of *murtis* also bring the decorative qualities of the *murti* into dominance when they employ their modeling skills to craft things called toys, small clay statues of birds and animals that are slipped and fired or fired and painted. Utility seems to have disappeared. Yet, the toy sold at the market is useful to the potter — as the painting is useful to the painter — in providing cash. The toy is used by the child in play or by the adult to decorate the home, and playful and decorative things retain a potential for significance. The most common toy is a pottery horse on wheels. Pulled along until it breaks, the horse brings a message, for it is a symbol of the noble, perishable body that carries the soul through life as the horse bears the rider over the land. And toy horses are made as votive offerings at the rural shrine of Ghora Pir, one of the saintly horsemen who brought Islam to the delta of Bengal in the thirteenth century.

Bright clay toys are things for pleasure, but, like painted *kalshis*, they can serve as reminders, helping by religious suggestion to keep people on the right path through life. This little bird might be no more than an ornament, but it might be the symbol of the immortal soul that is conventional in Sufi verse. That gaudy lion might be a simple plaything, or it might be the *vahana*, the vehicle and symbol of Durga, the goddess in the fullness of power, the prime deity of Bengal. Patently decorative, toys and painted *kalshis* are subtly oriented toward the center of the potter's system of creation, where magnificent *murtis* and working *kalshis* differently apportion the mix of beauty and use.

The *kalshi* and the *murti* are both vessels. One holds water. The other holds sacred power, symbolized by water. Both are used, then discarded. Their difference lies in their spheres of operation. The *kalshi* is fired to be useful in daily life. The *murti* is left unfired to be useful in the sacred moment when people approach God and ask for worldly blessings. Useful pottery is central to life in Bangladesh, helping to shape two great relations. It connects the creator and the consumer into a society. It connects people with the deities into the cosmos. Its values are ethical and religious.

Useful pottery is also art. Among the potters of Bangladesh, and generally among the world's workers, art is founded upon skill. Developed through training and practice, dedicated in the creative instant, skill eventuates in forms that vary by tradition and need. Difficult accomplishments, *kalshis* and *murtis* differently incarnate the skills of their creators. Testing themselves constantly, potters strive for excellence, shaping natural materials toward beauty. The works of their hands — water jars and statues — witness to their devotion and bear aesthetic value.

Where use meets beauty, where nature transforms into culture and individual and social goals are accomplished, where the human and numinous come into fusion, where objects are richest in value — there is the center of art. That center is touched daily by the hard-working potters of Bangladesh, but it seems to have disintegrated into the haze of the past in the West.

Sweden

For a more familiar story, come west into territory where pottery is decentered, where it no longer meets practical or sacred needs. The pottery at Raus in Skåne was founded in 1911 by Ludwig Johnsson. With the death of the founder, Hugo Anderberg became master of the works in 1947. As the need for salt-glazed stoneware declined among the farming people of southern Sweden, Hugo decided to let the pottery die, rather than pass it into incompetent hands.

Then he met Lars Andersson, a city boy who had taken classes in pottery and worked as a teacher of ceramics. Hugo became to Lars as a grandfather, teaching him all the tricks of the big kiln before he was killed in a motorcycle accident. Lars has installed a museum in the pottery where old objects validate his practice for the visitor. Surrounded by models from the past, Lars has

Lars Andersson. Raus, Skåne, Sweden. 1993

Crock. By Lars Andersson. 1993

narrowed his action to the replication of traditional forms. His handsome brown jugs and crocks are sturdily utilitarian in appearance, but no one puts them to work. They are amazingly exact sculptural representations of useful pottery.

At Raus, in a big brick building, using Hugo's old wheel and Hugo's huge kiln, Lars Andersson finds satisfaction in his work. Then cleaving to old techniques and forms, he answers the responsibility of tradition, connecting himself through new works to his revered teacher, Hugo Anderberg, and to the wider history of his place. His customers do not need crocks to store milk. They need to avoid anomie and gain connection, reaching through the things of their region to their history, joining Lars in the spatial — Scanian and Swedish — identity that his pots embody.

As for value: the salt-glazed crocks of Raus fulfill Lars Andersson's artistic desires, and his customers find them to be, like other works of art in the late West, objects that are decorative and historically evocative.

America

A similar story, set nearer home, can be told about Mossy Creek in Georgia. The pottery founded there by John Milton Meaders in 1892 was revitalized in the 1930s, when, at a low point of local need, outsiders discovered John Milton's youngest son, Cheever Meaders, still at work in the old way, digging the clay, throwing it on a treadle wheel, firing it in a wood-burning tunnel kiln, making ash-glazed utilitarian ware. In 1967, the year of his death, Cheever burned his last kiln for the Smithsonian Institution, and his son Lanier, recognizing the new market provided by collectors of folk art, left his bad job in a mobile home factory and took to pottery full time.

In the early 1970s, it seemed that Lanier would be the last in the line, but when he fired his final kiln in 1991, others were at work. Lanier's younger brothers, Reggie and Edwin, had re-

Lanier Meaders. Mossy Creek, Georgia. 1991

Pitcher.
By Lanier Meaders.
1967

David and Anita Meaders. Mossy Creek, Georgia. 1991

Face jug.
By Anita Meaders.
1991

turned to the trade. His cousin C.J. retired, came home to north Georgia, and refined the ash glaze that ornaments the family's ware. With his wife, Billie, C.J. made a hundred commemorative pots to celebrate a century of continuity for the Meaders family's trade in 1992. His son, Clete, followed his father into the clay, and when the Olympic games were held in Atlanta, Clete amusingly joined in the commercial frenzy by declaring his to be the official folk pottery of the Olympics. Meanwhile, Lanier's nephew David, a truck driver, built an old-time kiln in his yard to fire the pots thrown by his wife, Anita, and then they moved their operation to the old family site, using Lanier's shop and kiln, and asserting a claim to a central role in the family's tradition.

C. J. Meaders is not bothered that his customers do not buy his pots to use, but because, in his words, they want to own "a piece of history." Like Lars Andersson, C.J. holds firmly to old forms and technology, and he works to make each pot better than the last. His churns stand tall beneath their skins of streaky green glaze. They could be used.

Needing money, just as you do, potters work to the market. In the past, their customers wanted many churns and crocks and jugs, and the potters for sport made a few comical pots, at once jugs and grotesque human heads. Collectors might term them face vessels, but the potters call them ugly jugs, and "face jug" is the usual compromise. From their customers, the potters have learned a history of the form, and they repeat it during commercial exchange. The story is that the face jug was developed by slaves who worked as potters in South Carolina. Then the idea was carried up to the highlands — maybe by an ancestor of Chester Hewell, a potter in Gillsville, Georgia — and assimilated into the Appalachian cultural mix. It used to be acceptable to maintain fantasies of Elizabethan survival and to write of the Anglo-Saxon purity of the mountain people, but Lanier Meaders spoke proudly of his Native American ancestry, and the face jug seems to be, like the banjo, an Appalachian trait with an African-American origin. The potters, at least, find the idea reasonable.

Face Jug.
By Lanier Meaders.
1967

Face Jug.
By Lanier Meaders.
1975

Face Jug.
By Lanier Meaders.
Mossy Creek, Georgia.
1991

Now quantities have reversed. Conditioned by ideas from art-appreciation classes so suffused with the idea of the pictorial that the craft of photography has been embraced as an art, and the art of pottery is still called a craft, today's buyers want few churns and many face jugs. Learning the taste of his customers, Lanier Meaders began to fill the kiln with face jugs, and those jugs in time moved steadily from haunting abstraction toward realism and humor. Once rare and known to only a few potters — notably Burlon Craig and the Browns in North Carolina, the Meaders and Hewell families in Georgia — the face jug has become the common product of the Southern potter.

David Meaders says he prefers the pure forms and rippling glazes of the utilitarian ware made by his grandfather Cheever, but what they want now is face jugs. The jugs made by David's father, Reggie, did not follow Lanier's into realism, and David's wife, Anita, has recaptured some of the old strangeness in her jugs, which are, in my opinion, the best of the new lot. Anita is a slim, delicate woman who handles hard work with elegance. Her first need is to create, to make something out of nothing much, shaping wild substances into materializations of the disciplined self. Then, for her, there is the connection to familial lineage, and beyond that to the regional culture of the upland South, her high, hard place. She sells pieces of decor that are culturally resonant, that suggest African-American origins and symbolize the Appalachian segment of the American landscape in their austerity and potential for utility. Anita's deracinated customer buys craft, history, and connection to the land.

Lanier Meaders died in 1998, but the family tradition, which Cheever and Lanier nurtured through a shaky passage, is robust once more. Lanier's old jugs fetch thousands of dollars at shows of antiques, and the working potters have found a reliable new market. The Meaders family's pot, like the Native American pot, has become a high-class souvenir, tending through decoration to art, tending through reference to cultural symbol. Set in its own place, the work's values deepen.

Wanda Aragon is a master of the ceramic tradition of Acoma, a village more than a thousand years old, built atop a mesa in the dry wideness of New Mexico. To locate the values that elevate things into art, we are inclined to focus on objects, contemplating products. Wanda concentrates on process, finding the qualities that define art first in technology. Her art accepts and perfects the gifts of her land. Clay is mined out with a prayer. Rock hard, it is ground down on a stone and dampened with water, which is as rare and precious in New Mexico as it is abundant and terrible in Bangladesh. Wanda's sister, Lilly Salvador, whose work has been purchased by museums of fine art in Boston and Cincinnati, says that when they make their pottery, their minds are filled with prayers for dampness. Cusped and whirling clouds flow and break over curved surfaces. Slanted lines are driving rain. Spots are snow. "All our designs, "says Wanda Aragon, "are a prayer for rain."

Driving their cattle in the mountains, Wanda and her husband, Marvis, stay on the lookout for rocks that might be powdered into paint to decorate their pottery. They search, too, for shards, for bits of ancient pottery that are ground to dust and mixed in the clay for temper. That dust becomes the blood of the clay body — the pot will contain the pots of the ancestors, whose pots contained the pots of their ancestors. Old blood revives with dampness, and a squeeze of pliable clay becomes the seed of a fresh form. The new pot is shaped in the bottom of a broken old bowl, borrowing its shape, and then, damp and vulnerable, it is lifted out tenderly and allowed to stand on its own. The base is ready to receive the coils through which it will grow, widening and rising into a new being. Slipped, then painted with earthy color in fine and dense designs, the new pot is clothed and prepared for the trial by fire.

Not long ago, the potters at Acoma would not call a pot traditional unless it had been fired outdoors, exposed to risk beneath the sky. But so much work goes into creation, into raising and scraping and decorating the fine walls, and so much at home

Marvis and Wanda Aragon. Acoma. 1987

Lilly Salvador. Acoma, New Mexico. 1988

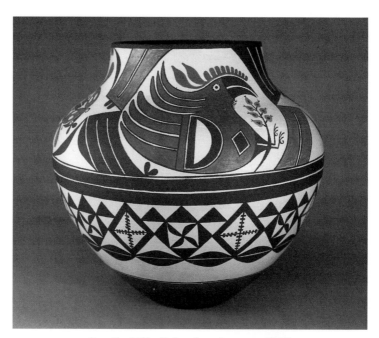

Jar. By Lilly Salvador. Acoma. 1997

Jar. By Wanda Aragon. Acoma. 1987

depends on sale, that electric kilns have slowly come into acceptance. But there is no compromise in materials. Traditional pottery is made of the earth and shaped by hand. Things molded
out of purchased clay and painted with synthetic colors are called
ceramics. At Acoma, the difference between the two — between
"traditional" pottery and "ceramics" — is the difference between
art and other things.

Wanda Aragon's splendid water jar rises out of her arid place.
Local and adamantly natural substances are processed in the old
way, the laborious way, into signs of the conscientious self.
Wanda's pot contains her skill and will and taste. Next, it contains the teaching of her mother, the great master Frances Torivio,
who turned ninety-three when I was writing this chapter in April
of 1998.

As in Georgia, the pottery of the American Indian communities of New Mexico and Arizona can be read as emblematic of a
broad region, but its strength depends on talented individuals
working in family lineages. The most famous potter at Acoma
was Lucy Lewis, who developed new ideas for decoration
through study of old potsherds. She died in 1992, but the daughters she taught, Emma Lewis Mitchell and Dolores Lewis Garcia,
continue her fine line, and her burly son, Drew, is one of the men
who have recently turned successfully to pottery. In the period
between 1930 and 1960, when the idea of the modern was still
fresh with promise and the world was distracted by war, the traditional arts hit their low point in history. At Acoma, in those
days, when the ceramic tradition could have descended through
shortcuts into cheap souvenirs for tourists, Lucy Lewis was one
of those who held to the old, high standards. Frances Torivio
was another. Frances taught her daughters, Ruth, Lilly, and
Wanda. Then Lilly and Wanda taught their daughters. With
Wanda's encouragement, her husband, Marvis, took up the art,
and he told me that, while pottery is now a women's craft, in his
grandfather's days, before men were forced to accept paid employment away from home, they made ceremonial vessels in the

kiva. Now Wanda's daughter-in-law, Delores J. Aragon, has emerged as a leader in the new generation of potters.

Wanda Aragon follows her mother as an artist and a teacher. While responding to her mother's models, and repeating the geometric designs that belong to her family, Wanda also reaches farther back, self-consciously effecting revival through the study of Acoma's old works that have been preserved in museum collections. Searching through storerooms and leafing through books, Wanda has decided that the finest works of her tradition were made in the 1880s. Their bold geometry suits her personal style. The fit of their ornament to their three-dimensional forms would excite any designer. And Wanda has brought their spirit to new life in wonders of technical mastery.

Her works in clay write Wanda Aragon's signature on the world. They entail her environment, remember her teacher, and revive her tradition at the greatest moment it knew before the present. Outstripping the past in precision of execution, Wanda's creations display the sure touch of her hand and her great gift as a designer. An artist, she enters the market with confidence, and in the hectic commercial scene, she is triumphant, victorious because she has won a plenitude of awards in competitions, because she earns enough money to be able to do her art, and because her success has not required her to abandon her standards, the contract to excellence she has made between herself and her tradition.

At the Native American arts fairs where Wanda Aragon sells her work, the exhibitors array their creations on tables before them, and answer the same questions again with unbelievable grace and patience. Trying to gauge the worth of the things they lift for inspection, Anglo buyers ask how long they took to make and what they mean. The answers emphasize the tedious labor involved and the historical and sacred significance of the objects, investing commodities with cultural meanings and smoothing the transaction that brings the artists money, and, as Wanda stresses, that might bring them new friends. At the same time, she tells me, the artists enjoy visiting with each other, trading goods and ideas. The market is a locus for friendship and information, as well as commerce.

At such a fair, Wanda's mother, Frances Torivio, learned a new form from another Native American potter who told her the tourists loved them, and she became the first at Acoma to model the storyteller. The form had its origin at Cochiti pueblo. Though the Cochiti tradition, like that of Acoma, has always been dominated by useful vessels, a figurative strain was added in the late nineteenth century. Potters at Cochiti made caricatures of outsiders and images of mothers singing to children. When Helen Cordero of Cochiti found her talent in midlife, she turned from pottery to shaping figures of clay. One of the first times she exhibited her work, Alexander Girard, a designer and manic collector of folk art, bought everything she had made and commissioned a larger singing mother with a greater number of children. Helen Cordero thought of her grandfather, a famed storyteller and anthropological informant, and she shaped a statue of him telling a tale to his five grandchildren. Since she was one of those children, it was a contextual self portrait, and since her grandfather was one who talked to outsiders, telling them about his culture, her sculpture fit the dynamic of cultural exchange that accompanies the commercial exchange in the market. Her figure was the first storyteller.

That was 1964. Since that time, more than three hundred potters in thirteen pueblos have made storytellers. It has become, Alexander Girard told me, "a regular storyteller industry." Helen Cordero died in 1994, but her storyteller has risen into a regional symbol. Visitors to the Southwest purchase Indians made by Indians out of the earth.

When Frances Torivio became the first at Acoma to make a storyteller, she was attracted by more than commercial potential. The idea suited her expressive style and her wonderful sense of humor, and her little storytellers are distinct in the crowd. Ethel Shields, a potter at Acoma, has pursued the possibilities of the comic by creating storytellers of beasts and tourists. The grinning bear who sits in for the grandfather comments ironically on the tourist's perception of the Indian as somehow natural and wild. The tourist modeled in clay, a camera slung around his neck, bounces stereotypes back. Buying souvenirs, visitors take home images of themselves. During exchange, misunderstanding is wittily acknowledged and graciously submerged in good humor. Ethel Shields finds her work fun.

In a different mood, Frances Torivio's daughters, Wanda Aragon and Lilly Salvador, shape their storytellers with painstaking attention to craft, Wanda's embodying her desire for clean design, Lilly's revealing her interest in narrative detail. To every show, Lilly brings a pretty storyteller, and positioning it among her creations, she asks it to assist her in the difficult business of selling. It is with them as it is with the Bengali sculptors who make toys between commissions for *murtis*. The money Wanda and Lilly gain through the sale of little statues enables them to keep to their main work, praying for rain while shaping clay into water jars that are dressed with geometric designs to present their tradition in its best modern moment.

The fine pottery of Acoma describes relations among habitat, heritage, and the talented self, and it tells of our times. The pots of Acoma, like those of northern Georgia, exhibit at once accommodation and resistance. Accommodating themselves to the desires of their patrons, the potters of Acoma make images, statuettes of adults telling tales to children that have, like the face jugs of Georgia, antecedents in history, but which, like the face jugs, have become common in response to the market's demands for figurative art.

At the same time, like traditional artists throughout the world, they have stepped out of the rush for modernity and returned reverently to ideas from the past. Acting in a spirit of revitalization, they resist the technological progress that divides people from the earth and separates the mind from the hands, reducing art to design. In a time dominated by industrial production, potters at Acoma and in Georgia have determined to hold to elder

Lilly Salvador. Indian Market. Indianapolis, Indiana. 1996

Storytellers. By Frances Torivio. Acoma. 1988

techniques, digging their own clay and forming it in their own hands, while their nimble minds direct the process of creation. This mix of accommodation and resistance establishes a frame of adaptive revival within which forms and techniques hold steady but functions shift.

Once, the pot of Acoma, like that of Bangladesh, was for carrying water. It is still used in ceremonial circumstances, during worship, but no one today would carry the workaday water in a jar worth a thousand dollars in a gallery in Santa Fe. The use now is ornamental for both the potter and her patron, but the functional shift is the graceful consequence of the manifold reality of art. When it was made to use, the water jar of Acoma was also, like the *kalshi* of Bengal, decorative in form, proportion, and detail, so its relocation in a decorative setting requires no radical alteration of technique or form, though it inspires greater precision in ornamentation. Enhancing and refining ornament, artists challenge themselves and invest their works with a quality that excites the eye and attracts the attention of buyers who understand the art incompletely. In the new age, the potters of Acoma and Georgia do not surrender their tradition. They drive it toward new perfection.

Turkey

If the functional shift from utilitarian to ornamental seems modern, or even, perhaps, postmodern, come to a place where pottery has been decorative for half a millennium. Fine ceramics have been made continuously since the late fifteenth century in Kütahya, a lovely city in the mountains of western Turkey.

When I arrived in Kütahya in 1985, the masters told me there were twenty-three ateliers in the city. In 1997, I was told that no one knew the number, maybe it was two hundred. A year later the estimate had risen by fifty. Most of the shops are tiny operations: a man or woman working alone beneath a bulb in the kitchen, decorating plates purchased from a large atelier, and then signing them with the name of a firm that might last for only a few months. But the masters tell me that thirty of the workshops are solid and the market for their ware is strong. Turks have money and love to shop, tourists are coming in steadily increasing numbers, and the potters have participated in Turkey's rapid rise to prosperity. A third of the city's population is involved in the production and sale of ware that is painted underglaze on a composite white body.

The chief products are two. They make tiles to revet the walls of the concrete mosques being built throughout the nation as signs of faith and local pride. They make plates, domestic in scale and form, that are hung on the wall to do in the home what tiles do in the mosque, bringing brightness through their materials and meaning through their decoration.

Tile or plate, flower vase or water jar, the ware is called *çini*. The word is cognate with "china." It designates a ceramic type, like "stoneware" or "porcelain." The ware was developed in response to the stunning wonder of Chinese porcelain. But *çini* is compositionally unlike porcelain. It can be fired at a lower temperature so that the rich color can be applied under the glaze, rather than enameled over the glaze in the East Asian manner, which requires sequential firings, risking loss in the kiln.

The word *çini* also names the firms that produce the ware. Süsler Çini, an atelier of the middle size, was founded in 1950 by Ali Özker. (I like these dates and names, for they remind us that traditional pottery is not the spawn of superorganic forces, but the creation of real individuals at work in time.) When I showed up in Kütahya, İhsan Erdeyer, the master at Süsler, welcomed me into understanding of his craft. In a city that its workers call the city of jealousy as well as the city of *çini*, where some of the masters protect generally known facts as though they were deep secrets, İhsan is famed for his generosity. I watched the work while İhsan explained how six natural materials — kaolin, sand, chalk for whiteness, quartz for brightness, and two clays for plasticity — were mixed, milled, dampened, and strained through silk to make the refined white substance (they call it mud) that was thrown on the wheel for hollow ware, jiggered on the wheel for plates, and patted into molds for tiles.

Süsler Çini was a rambling half-timbered building enclosing a courtyard. In the dusty dark, İhsan Erdeyer managed a team of workers who jumped at his every quiet word. İhsan directed the shaping of forms, then he recentered them on the wheel and shaved them to clarity before slipping them with a whiter, brighter coating of clay. Fired, then painted in two stages by young women and men, the ware was glazed by the master in a fritted lead solution, and then fired again.

At the old Süsler, the master stacked the ware into delicate, perilous columns within a domed and cylindrical kiln, sunken in the floor. Then one of İhsan's workers went down and shoved dry pine into the firing chamber, while the heat rose slowly and held steady at a point above eight hundred and sixty and below nine hundred degrees centigrade. They judged the fire solely by eye, peeping through glassed spy holes, maintaining the heat at the perfect pitch for ten or twelve hours, and then letting the kiln cool slowly. If the heat is too low, the glaze will not convert, the ware will not shine. If the heat get too high, the colors run, smudging the design. If the kiln cools too quickly, the glaze will crackle and craze. In some traditions — the Raku of Japan providing a fine instance — the masters invite accidental effects in firing, but not in Kütahya. The wish is for total control over natural forces — earth and air, water and fire — a control that is materialized in a pure white body and sharply defined forms, spread with a sheet of transparent glaze.

The aesthetic has not changed, but the work has gotten easier. In an effort to banish smoke from the sky, the municipal government has decreed electric kilns to be obligatory in new workshops. The temperature in the electric kiln is easier to regulate, and the hard labor of stoking the kiln has ended. Some old masters decry a decline in quality; they miss a depth in brilliance that came from wood-firing, but they have to be pleased by a

İhsan Erdeyer.
Süsler Çini. Kütahya, Turkey. 1987

Mustafa Oruç. Nakış Çini. Kütahya. 1994

decrease in the number of pieces lost in each kiln. When Süsler Çini was torn down in 1991, making way for a high-rise apartment building, İhsan Erdeyer moved his operation into his old home, rebuilding it into a workshop, where two electric kilns stand on the ground floor, and the decorators work upstairs. The shop's effort coalesces in pieces of *çini* that appear to the eye like gemstones set on snow beneath a clean mountain stream.

Overseeing his squad, the master works to assure the material richness upon which the beauty of *çini* is based. Should you ask whether the ware is art or not, the potters in Kütahya, like those in Acoma, would exemplify the rule that quality must be distinguished within kind. They would tell you that some is art, some is not. Most *çini* is only "factory work," the city's stock in trade, the basis of its economy, but some is "special work," unquestionably art — the Turkish word is *sanat*.

Art in Kütahya depends upon a small number of great masters who both design and paint the ware, and who are obliged to teach as well as create. The greatest was Ahmet Şahin, the twentieth century's grand master of Islamic ceramics.

Ahmet Şahin became a hero to his city in 1927, when he was only twenty. At the beginning of the twentieth century, half of Kütahya's workers were Armenians. They left to repair the tiles on the Dome of the Rock, never to return, and today their descendants make a variety of Kütahya *çini* in Jerusalem. During the Turkish War of Independence, in the violent aftermath of the First World War, Mehmet Emin, the city's leading master, was killed. The Armenians were gone, the old master was dead, and in the early days of the Turkish Republic, Kütahya's tradition seemed at an end. Then Ahmet Şahin formed a partnership with Hakkı Çinicioğlu, Mehmet Emin's son, and they made a few gigantic, intricately painted vases that inspired the city and brought the workers back to work. Since that time, while quality has waxed and waned, the *çini* industry has provided steady employment to Kütahya's people. In 1927, there were two young men in the trade.

Now it supplies the income for something like forty-five thousand people.

The partners parted. Hakkı Çinicioğlu established a firm to produce the city's normal ware. Ahmet Şahin, they say today, was *tek adam* — the one man in the past who was dedicated to quality. He became Kütahya's great designer, drawing patterns on paper that were pricked into stencils in the workshops to pounce designs onto the slipped, biscuit surface for painting. Drawn in black, filled with color, Ahmet Şahin's designs were transferred to seventy percent of Kütahya's tiles and plates, and his taste diffused through commerce to become general in Turkey. He designed for the ateliers, and he painted his own designs with manly firmness to challenge the city as a whole, to keep the standards high.

His art, Ahmet Şahin told me, is the greatest of all. The painter buys paint and brushes, paints his picture, and he is done. Easy. But Ahmet Şahin ground his own paint. He made his own brushes out of the bone from a goose's wing and the hair from a donkey's mane. He painted his picture, and then submitted it to the judgment of the flame. Standing back while God decided, Ahmet Şahin waited anxiously for the kiln to be opened. He was downcast by every failure and exhilarated by every blessed success. *Çini*, he said, is a rose picked from the fire.

Ahmet Şahin wanted no other work, and when he was working, he said, he never knew fatigue or melancholy. At eighty-four, he still sat by the window of his home on the hillside, painting beautifully, and he told me to tell them to put a brush, some paint, and a few raw pieces in his coffin, so he could keep working on his journey to the other land. When I came in 1993, he wrapped me in a hug and emitted an old man's wail. He eyesight was gone. He could not work. The Ahmet Şahin who was his nation's greatest master had vanished. I was able to arrange a belated award for him from the Turkish government, but the days that remained were filled only with waiting.

Ahmet Şahin. Kütahya. 1991

He told me he was satisfied, for he had left his art in good hands. When Ahmet Şahin died at the end of 1996, a new generation had risen around him. His grandson Ahmet Hürriyet Şahin and Ahmet's wife, Nurten, had learned the art from Zafer, Ahmet Şahin's son.

At first, Ahmet and Nurten worked in their apartment. Then in 1989, a businessman set them up as the managers of a new atelier, Işıl Çini, where they used Ahmet Şahin's old designs and led a team of young workers in the production of factory ware of the highest quality. Soon their partner in business double-crossed them, leaving them with a huge debt that they worked off slowly. Nurten would get her son off to school, and then, smoking too much, she would lose herself in delicious creative concentration. Next to her husband and son, she said, she loved her work the most. After the publication of my book on Turkish art with Nurten's portrait on the cover, a big businessman in Istanbul, fantasizing a global market for çini, opened a massive modern workshop in Kütahya, Doğuş Çini, in 1996. Ahmet was named master of the works. Nurten was charged to teach her style to a studio full of young women and men. The businessman could only think of their creations as commodities, as so many potatoes or radios to sell. He pressed them to expand production and slight the art, but there is no room in Nurten for compromise on standards. When profits rose too slowly, he abruptly dissolved their partnership in the summer of 1998. Betrayed again by their capitalist, Ahmet and Nurten returned to their apartment with debts to pay and plates to paint. Despite it all, in times of hope and heartbreak, Nurten Şahin has kept her head, and her work has steadily improved, coming closer and closer to that sweet spot in design where complexity and clarity meet.

In the study of a traditional art like pottery, it is no fitful struggle to bring both women and men into the story, and it has gotten easier, for a softening of gendered distinctions is one aspect of contemporary art. Men are now potters at Acoma. Women have long worked as decorators in Kütahya, but now they are gaining names. Nurten Şahin is first. It is hard, she says, to be an artist in the modern world, impossible to be a female artist, but she is one of three who lead the city's art today, who brought satisfaction to Ahmet Şahin at the end of his life. The others are İbrahim Erdeyer and Mehmet Gürsoy.

When I met İbrahim and Mehmet in 1985, they were painting plates in the Süsler Çini outlet on Kütahya's main street. Since then, both of them have gone from success to success, artistically and financially. In 1997, we zipped around Kütahya in İbrahim's new van and Mehmet's white Mercedes.

İbrahim Erdeyer was raised in the potteries. He mixed the mud in boyhood and fired the kiln as a teenager, learning the whole trade from his father, İhsan, the master of Süsler Çini. Understanding his desire and recognizing his skills, İhsan freed İbrahim to paint and put him in charge of commerce. A man of great charm, in whom, Nurten Şahin says, there is no badness at all, İbrahim surrenders his summers to the hard job of selling, traveling the road and expanding the business. In the quiet of winter, when the soft snow falls, he wields the brush with consummate artistry.

In 1987, Mehmet Gürsoy formed a new partnership called İznik Çini. His intention was to recreate the excellence of the *çini* of the sixteenth century that is named today for the town of İznik, though it was made in its own day in both İznik and Kütahya. Partnerships are volatile, fragile things in Kütahya. His four original partners and many of his students have left him, carrying the İznik Çini aesthetic into other shops, and Mehmet is the master of an atelier where he teaches bright young women, three of whom, he says, have passed him as painters of *çini*. Mehmet is a great teacher.

Mehmet Gürsoy endured criticism for naming his shop after another city, and for focusing so tightly on the works of the masters he calls his teachers: the dead potters of the sixteenth century. But their palette of six colors featuring a luscious red, and their harmonious floral designs, have become his own. Mehmet's

Nurten and Ahmet Hürriyet Şahin. 1994

İbrahim Erdeyer and Mehmet Gürsoy. Kütahya. 1993

goal, he said when he began, was not freedom or novelty, but excellence. Willingly accepting the restraints of tradition in order to learn, Mehmet narrowed his vision to force progress. By 1991, the works in his atelier were approaching the past in material quality, and by trading the loose handling of the old works for modern Kütahya's impeccable precision, Mehmet believed they had surpassed the past in painting. Another five years and the revival was complete. Basing his concept on the masterpieces of the sixteenth century, Mehmet first added flourishes that he called "aesthetic in the last degree," and then he exploded the old patterns across the surface of his plates. His dazzling, energetic works refer to the past but emphatically belong to the present, suiting the opulent decor of the Turkish middle-class home. Meanwhile, İbrahim Erdeyer has continued on his widening course, and Nurten Şahin has turned to the chests filled with Ahmet Şahin's old drawings. She has rededicated herself to the revival of Kütahya's designs of the earlier twentieth century, though she recombines them freely, renders them in the palette of the sixteenth century, and lifts their execution to dizzying new heights of exactitude.

Their styles are distinct. Going through a stack of plates from Kütahya, I do not have to look for signatures. As James Joyce said, the whole work of art is a signature. İbrahim Erdeyer paints in a solid, robust manner, like Ahmet Şahin's. Mehmet Gürsoy's plates dance with dainty detail. Nurten Şahin's works seem supernatural in precision, while remaining clean in overall look. Though he came late to the trade, a fourth artist has joined the others at the pinnacle of modern achievement. Kerim Keçecigil learned in Mehmet Gürsoy's atelier, and while his designs resemble Mehmet's, his fine handling is more like Nurten's. When İbrahim, Mehmet, Nurten, and Kerim bear down in concentration, the result is certainly art.

Turkish artisans describe works of art as devices created in devotion and designed to lead the viewer, step by step, to higher understanding. First, the work pleases the body. Through the aesthetic, it appeals to the eye. Attracted into the work, the eye draws the mind behind it, and the work is revealed to be meaningful. Informed, instructed, the mind knows the world and arouses the soul to its beauty. The soul lifts in bliss and fills with love for God.

God is beautiful, the potters say, and God's beauty collects beauty. The first beauty of the *çini* plate lies in its material excellence — the smooth white body and gleaming clear glaze. These are the gifts of the master of the works, men like İhsan Erdeyer at Süsler Çini. The second beauty is the gift of the painter who draws the outlines in suave sweeps and fills them with deep color.

Painters learn to "read" the design, to unlock its logic, while painting. After a couple of repetitions, the design has been mastered, and the artist is free to forget everything except the point at the end of the brush. Time stops. Creation is all. They call the emotion of that moment *aşk* — devotion, passion, love. Calm and intense in concentration, they give themselves in love to their work, and the work of art is, by definition, the object that contains the love of its creator.

The Western critic seems unable to see the passion in things unless they fuss for attention through innovative abandon and exhibitionistic deviance. But artists in Kütahya feel passion as an inner force that lifts them out of the common place and allows them to drive through meticulous craft toward a transcendent perfection. In Kütahya, the foundation of art is laid in a repetitive, ritualized state of meditative creation that brings natural substances through love into beauty.

The aesthetic quality of Kütahya's ceramics abides in technical mastery, in radiant materials and fastidious painting. Then, pulled through the eye by beauty, the mind is engaged by historical reference. In acts of revitalization, bringing the excellence of thirteenth-century Konya, fifteenth-century Bursa, sixteenth-century Kütahya and İznik, and twentieth-century Kütahya, into fresh being, the potters celebrate the tradition that was given, Mehmet Gürsoy says, as a special gift from God to the Turkish nation. In association with works from the past, modern Kütahya *çini* becomes a symbol for its creators and their patrons of the place they share: this city, this region, this grand country. The masterpieces of the sixteenth century, so dominant in the thinking of the potters, carry them back not only to a time of artistic excellence, but as well to a time of Turkish greatness, when the Ottoman Empire stretched from Morocco to Iran, from the Sudan to the gates of Vienna, and Turkish power was founded upon Islamic precept.

The wish for perfection, displayed in technical mastery, is part of the desire to unify with unity itself, the perfect order of the universe. The quest for perfection leads modern artists into connection with those artists from the past who received God's gift and bequeathed models of excellence to the future. Taking inspiration from old models, the artists make historical references in their own, but their vision lifts beyond history. Old works of art are, like the things of nature, like the cow of the Holy Koran, signs to guide life, and built upon personal passion, retrieving history, the artful ceramics of Kütahya achieve their highest significance in the sacred.

Modern works cluster into three main classes of design. One is calligraphic. Writing God's word in the Arabic script, the artist draws a prayer. The most usual text is the opening formula of the Holy Koran: In the name of God, the Merciful, the Compassionate. It is called the *Besmele*, and tradition says that the one who writes the *Besmele* beautifully will be blessed. The *Besmele* is a prayer for beginnings. It launches action with an appeal to God's mercy. Plates and tiles bearing the *Besmele* are commonly hung above the door to be the last thing seen, the last words spoken before entering the turmoil of the day.

In Ahmet Şahin's youth, Turks used the Arabic script, and he created original calligraphic designs. Today's Turks use the Latin alphabet. The Arabic script, purified in sacred connotation, has become the possession of professional calligraphers in Istanbul. Understanding the complexities of the calligrapher's art, pot-

The *Besmele*. Plate by Nurten Şahin. 1993.
Collection of the Indiana University Art Museum

The *Besmele*. Tiles by Ahmet Şahin. 1990.
Collection of the Museum of International Folk Art

ters in Kütahya restrict their effort to making faithful copies of the works of great masters, both living and dead.

Nurten Şahin gained her first fame, and attracted many imitators, by creating two new designs for calligraphic plates. She took the general idea from Kütahya's recent tradition, refining it graphically while arranging a frame of arabesques around a rendition of the *Besmele* that was given shape by Ahmet Şahin. Her work is a prayer. At once it repeats the word of God and offers an homage to her husband's grandfather, her city's own master.

The second class of design is geometric. Wondrously diverse in detail, but one in structure, geometric designs are radially symmetrical. From a point at the center, the design expands in all directions, enfolding and controlling multiplicity in a single pattern — inscribed in a circle or pulsing toward infinity — that represents abstractly the totalizing, unifying power of the universe. While lecturing on Turkish art, I have found that Westerners generally believe that the Koran prohibits representation. Their own art leads them to feel that it is natural to make pictures of things, of the human form in particular, and only a restrictive ideology could have produced the aniconic qualities of Islamic art. But representation is not prohibited in the Holy Koran, and Islamic art is rich in representation.

They paint pictures of people in Kütahya. For Turks, they paint plates with portraits drawn from photographs. For foreign tourists, obsessed with the pictorial and charmed by the oriental, they fill busy plates with men on horseback, lifted from old miniature paintings. No hard rule prevents them from making pictures of people, but the masters consider them unimportant and consign them to the less talented decorators. Their sale supports the whole atelier, freeing the best artists to concentrate on the most important works. Those works are also representational. Calligraphic plates represent the word of God. Geometric plates represent the encompassing will of God. Theological presuppositions orient artistic actions differently. The Christian God made man in His image and appeared on the earth in human form,

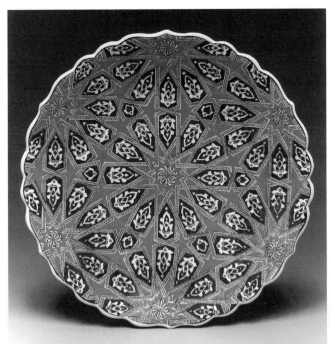

Plate in the design
of the interlocked star.
By İbrahim Erdeyer.
Kütahya, Turkey.
1994

Tile panel. By Ahmet Hürriyet Şahin. 1994

and the Western artistic tradition continues to fixate on the bodily. The God of the Muslim is without form. God's presence is imaged in words, in patterns, in signs.

The flower is a sign. The cycles of seed and blossom, blossom and seed, display, like the geometric design on the plate, the deep order of the universe. The bright flower on the dull landscape, like the star in the night sky, like the word revealed in the Holy Koran, attests to God's presence. It is a sign of the world's inherent beauty, of grace abounding.

Kütahya's third main class of design is floral. Calligraphic and geometric designs owe little to the magnificent *çini* of the sixteenth century. They are based on Kütahya's twentieth-century tradition, though they can also reach deeply into time. Written designs repeat the creations of the great calligraphers of the past, especially the sixteenth-century master Ahmet Karahisari. Geometric designs often overleap the Ottomans to remember the Seljuks of Konya, who shaped the first Turkish state in Anatolia during the thirteenth century. But today's floral designs are founded upon the masterpieces of sixteenth-century *çini*, and they make clear reference to nature.

The flower ornaments nature, as art ornaments the human environment. With amazing frequency, the world's artists match their art to nature's by choosing the beautiful, useless flower when they turn to decoration. Flowers accompany the statues of the deities on the altars of Buddhism, Hinduism, and Catholicism. Where no icon is worshiped, in Muslim, Jewish, and Protestant contexts, flowers still bloom on the face of art. The picture of a flower evinces an affection for nature, and flowers provide a worldly foretoken of the garden of paradise. Those ideas are raised by floral imagery, but the artists of Kütahya deepen meaning in subtle interpretation.

Mehmet Gürsoy tells us first to note that the flower is not realistic. Some are fantastic, dream flowers, but even when they are tulips and roses and carnations, they are solid and supernaturally perfect. The flowers on the plate are not the blossoms

Floral tile.
By Mehmet Gürsoy.
Kütahya. 1993

The works on this
page were given
by the artists to the
collection of the
Indiana University
Art Museum.

Floral plate. By İbrahim Erdeyer. 1994

that wither and die on the hillside. They are not renditions of the transitory surface, shadowed in time, but revelations of eternal essences; they are to flowers as the soul is to the body. Made abstract to be symbolic, the flowers on the plate, Mehmet says, stand for human beings, not for their mortal bodies, but for their immortal souls.

Then note, Mehmet says, that all the flowers, though they are of different varieties, spring from one root. A clump of grass or a dot of red, that root, he says, is a symbol of God's will, like the point at the center of the geometric design. We are not in the realm of mere botany. From one root, different kinds of flowers grow: some are tulips and some are roses, some are large and some are small, some are red and some are blue. And from the will of God, different kinds of people grow: some are women and others men, some are tall and others short, some are black and others white. Only God is one. Nature is diverse and imperfect. People are different at birth, and they are further differentiated by conditions. Some live long lives, other die young, and all are blown by the winds of chance. Mehmet's plate pictures the inner reality of existence. Beautiful forms lift from one root. They rise and sway and break in the wind, but together they shape a balanced composition within a perfect circle.

Balance, Mehmet says, is the key to the aesthetics of design. Accomplished most easily in symmetry, as it is on the geometric plate, balance is more challenging to the artist and livelier to the eye in asymmetrical configurations. On the floral plate, asymmetry signals worldly conditions, the winds that whip the garden, while the prevailing balance reveals the harmony that can be achieved when people live in accord with the deep rule of the universe.

Mehmet Gürsoy's floral plate exposes the inner order of life, the genetic and circumstantial differences among people, and it mounts a rhetoric for peace. Our differences are owed to God's will. Our lives unfold only within the compass of God's design. As different flowers form a balanced pattern, so should we, the people of the earth, cooperate in the creation of a beautiful whole.

Mehmet's plate comes from love, and it asks us to love God by loving the others with whom we live, braving the storms of the moment in the circle of God's eternal love.

For Mehmet Gürsoy, work is devotion, and the work of art is a prayer — just as it is for Haripada Pal. Their religions seem complete in their difference. Islam is rigorously monotheistic and aniconic in its art. Hinduism is polymorphous and iconic in the extreme. Mevlana Celaleddin Rumi, the great mystic of Seljuk Konya and a hero to the potters of Kütahya, teaches in one of his parables that different people — he specifically mentions Hindus, their tradition being so strange to the Muslim — have developed different styles of worship, but God understands the unity of love that lies beyond the difference of communal custom. The Muslim potter of Turkey and the Hindu potter of Bangladesh both materialize their idea of the sacred in shaped and painted clay. The aesthetic is not incidental to their effort. It is essential. Both Muslim and Hindu potters bring the formless into form through beauty, and beauty serves society. The smooth, bright object attracts the eye and draws the soul in love toward God, and the soul commands the body to righteous social conduct.

Through common work, the potter of Kütahya comes into connection at the nexus of value, bringing material, aesthetic, social, and religious forces into union. Work eventuates in rich, shimmering objects and in lives that are happy enough — happy enough because daily labor brings personal integration (when physical, emotional, and intellectual capacities fuse in concentration) and social integration (when the artist works in a team to produce things that others actually want) and spiritual integration (when the creation accomplishes and portrays the self in the cosmos). Work brings the worker pride and power.

At the age of sixteen, Fevziye Yeşildere fills with worth because the works of her hands exhibit her skill, because they connect her to her teacher, Mehmet Gürsoy, and to her place, a city where elegant ceramics have been made for five hundred years. Even if scholars simplify their study and banish Muslim artistry to a dead past by attributing the finest old *çini* to another city — İznik, where the tradition died in the eighteenth century — her city's art, the kind she can make, has attained global recognition as one of the artistic treasures of humankind. Fevziye will not pursue the potter's trade when she marries and moves to Germany, but she will not lose the strength she gained in her apprenticeship. She will become a woman of the modern world, but she will remain free of the debilitating anxieties that bedevil people who have never known creation in their own hands.

That is one purpose of art. It brings confidence to its creators. Those who make things know who they are. They have been tested and found able. Then art exhibits value. The artist's creations work in the world, embodying cultural complexities and shaping relations among people, between people and the environment, between people and the forces that rule creation.

The way that the potter's art contains value — and so communicative potential — came home to me clearly when I took Mehmet Gürsoy and İbrahim Erdeyer to New Mexico, where they attended the opening of an exhibition I arranged of Turkish art and demonstrated their skills at the Museum of International Folk Art. They were shocked at first by the high prices that sentimental people seemed willing to pay for Native American pottery that struck them as mediocre. Then we went to Acoma, to meet Wanda Aragon and Lilly Salvador, and they were thrilled by what they saw and excited to speak, through my translation, with their American colleagues.

The first thing they appreciated in the Acoma pottery was its material quality. The thin and even walls, as delicate as shells, demonstrated control over natural substances and technological procedures. Next they admired the brushwork. Like the Kütahya plate, the Acoma pot displays fine, smooth lines and a dense, unmottled fill of color. Lilly said she liked the bright colors of the Turkish plates, and she would like such a blue for her pottery, but she said she was obliged by religious stricture to use only natural materials. She had to content herself with gray and

Fevziye Yeşildere displaying a plate she painted.
Kütahya, Turkey. 1994

Mehmet Gürsoy, İbrahim Erdeyer, Wanda and Marvis Aragon. 1991

Parrot pot.
By Wanda Aragon.
Acoma, New Mexico.
1998

Çini plate. By Mehmet Gürsoy. Kütahya, Turkey. 1993

shades of buff and brown. Mehmet said he understood, but he was no heretic. He, too, ground minerals down and mixed them with slip for his paint. They agreed on materials, they agreed on fineness of body and brushwork, and they agreed on design.

The Turks took the Acoma designs to be signs of sacred unity. Native Americans, they believed, were true Muslims. They had received the word in the days of the beginning and had held to the right path through time, though they did not know the Holy Koran. Acoma's pottery was not ornamented with trivial images from the transitory surface of things, with depictions of mere bodies. It displayed geometric designs that rotated endlessly to symbolize the unity of universal order, and if the designs reflected the world through imagery, the figures were abstract, not naturalistic, and they were restricted in topic to flowers and birds. The Acoma pot might show a parrot, the bringer of water — a visualization of the potter's prayer for dampness. On the Kütahya plate, a fabulous bird — the flower of the air — often blends into the floral designs, symbolizing the artist who could fly free, disrupting harmony, but who chooses the moral option, melding into the social order and contributing to the world's need for loving and balanced behavior.

Wanda Aragon and Lilly Salvador, Mehmet Gürsoy and İbrahim Erdeyer: all practice the potter's art by selecting the best from the past and holding to old forms and techniques, by adjusting to their times with electric kilns, and by creating the future in traditional designs painted with an exactitude and innovative panache that surpasses their historic models. They come from places far apart and radically different in development. The Americans are women, the Turks are men. Their pottery is different in appearance but alike in its engagement with nature, its commitment to technical mastery, its respect for the past, its geometric and floral designs, its decorative presence, its commercial utility, and its submission to sacred power.

The potter's art brings us, through value, toward human unity as well as cultural difference. I have one more story to tell.

Japan

As Kütahya is to Turkey, Arita is to Japan. It is a city of potters on Kyushu, where a Korean potter named Ri Sampei discovered kaolin early in the seventeenth century, and fine porcelain has been made from that time to this. Arita's porcelain, like Kütahya's *çini*, developed in response to Chinese porcelain but achieved, within half a century, its own distinct character.

Like the Pals of Bangladesh, the potters of Arita make both vessels and statues. That mix seems general in East Asia. Many of Japan's renowned centers for pottery — Bizen, Echizen, Hagi, Kutani, Kyoto, Mino, Seto, Shigaraki — also produce sculpture in clay. At Jingdezhen, China's city of porcelain, potters continue to shape images of the Buddhist deities. Potters at Dehua, China's second city of porcelain, made the creation of lustrous white figures into a specialty in the seventeenth and eighteenth centuries, and porcelain images from Dehua for sale in San Francisco's Chinatown attest to a modern revival of the old quality. Arita's statues, especially of Kannon, the bodhisattva of mercy, recall Dehua's works in their exquisite delicacy, witnessing to a continuity of Chinese influence upon Japanese porcelain.

Arita's main output is tableware: plates and bowls and cups. As in Kütahya it is graded, with a mass of cheap goods at the bottom and a clutch of masterpieces at the top. The finest plate or vase is marked by technical mastery and an attention to historic precedent. Japan is the world's center for ceramic revival. For centuries, Japanese potters, like Chinese potters, have copied and reinterpreted old masterpieces. In 1926, Soetsu Yanagi, Kanjiro Kawai, and Shoji Hamada — the last two of them potters — founded the Mingei movement. Built upon the negative reaction to westernization of the late nineteenth century, inspired by William Morris, and incorporating Buddhist concepts of selfhood, Mingei has pushed creation along certain lines, establishing a cultural climate within which potters in large numbers find worthwhile employment, and the process of revitalization is fostered. Many of those designated as living national treasures in Japan are potters who have experimented in our days to recover the excellence of past practice.

At Arita, some artists reproduce the heavily ornamented ware called Imari that was made in the past at Arita for export to Europe. Some artists work in the soft graphic style of the Chinese literati, and others in the two elegant styles developed in the seventeenth century to suit a Japanese sensibility: the solemn, aristocratic Nabeshima, and the spacious, brilliant Kakiemon.

About 1643, in the twentieth year of his family's work in porcelain, Sakaida Kakiemon used Chinese techniques to naturalize porcelain to Japan in open, asymmetrical designs and a range of bright color, featuring a sweet green and a rich red. A century earlier, potters in Turkey had similarly expanded upon the blue-and-white palette derived from Chinese porcelain, adding new hues, notably the green of grass in springtime and the ripe red of the tomato. And, as Kakiemon would at Arita, the Turkish potters applied their new colors to asymmetrically balanced designs that welcomed nature's beauties: flowers and birds. Late in the nineteenth century, and twice in the twentieth (in Ahmet Şahin's day and again in Mehmet Gürsoy's), the potters of Kütahya returned to the works of the sixteenth century for guidance, struggling to reachieve the white ground, vibrant colors, and transparent glaze of their tradition at its highest point. At the Kakiemon workshop in Arita, in the time of the twelfth and thirteenth masters in the Kakiemon line, a team assembled to rediscover the milk-white ground and gem-like colors of the seventeenth century. In 1953, they succeeded. One in that team was Sadao Tatebayashi, and in subsequent years, as a designer and the leading painter at the Kakiemon kiln, he achieved national recognition as an artist.

In 1978, Sadao Tatebayashi left the Kakiemon workshop and established his own kiln, where his son Hirohisa is the master today. Across from his workshop, in his elegant showroom, Hirohisa has placed a photograph of his father, who died in 1992, and arranged around it an exhibition of his beautiful creations, building a museum to his tradition, much as Lars Andersson has in his pottery at Raus. Like Lars, Hirohisa is dedicated to preserving his teacher's standards, and as Wanda Aragon honors her mother and Haripada Pal honors his grandfather, Hirohisa honors his father in his work. Hirohisa has a box full of his father's designs drawn in pencil on paper, and he uses them, as Nurten Şahin uses Ahmet Şahin's, to create masterpieces that, like those of C. J. Meaders, incarnate his familial heritage, and, like those of the masters of Kütahya, bring the deep history of his city into new vitality.

Hirohisa Tatebayashi told me that there are one hundred and seventy workshops in the Arita area. Twenty percent of them, he says, resemble his in that they use hand techniques of shaping and decorating. None of those shops, he states calmly, make things more beautiful than his.

Hirohisa divides human endeavor into spheres, and envisions human accomplishment to be like a mountain range, rising to peaks of excellence. During our talk, he chose three spheres from life to illustrate his idea. In the realm of education, lazy students, wishing no more than jobs and money, study only at exam time and form a wide base of mediocrity, while a few true intellectuals rise to the heights of wisdom. The poor boy, unable to go to the university, might be doomed to toil in a noodle shop, but still a rare few strive to be the best and ascend to the top of the noodle shop business. Others are potters. Among the potters, most pass their days in dull labor, but a few dedicate themselves to greatness and climb to the summit of their realm of endeavor, becoming equal to the greatest professor or noodle shop man or political leader. Hirohisa's son learned his father's trade, but wishing more money than a potter can earn, he went to college to become prosperous and mediocre, while Hirohisa, by continuing his father's work and connecting through his father to the great Kakiemon tradition, has risen, in his own estimation, to the very apex of ceramic achievement.

Hirohisa Tatebayashi and his daughter Chinatsu.
Arita, Japan. 1994

Porcelain plate from Hirohisa Tatebayashi's kiln.
Arita, Japan. 1994

Hirohisa's concept sorts well with the thinking of Turkish artisans. The Western critic is tempted to give a simple answer to the complex question of what is art and what is not by identifying art with certain media, so that a painting is art, no matter how bad, and a pot is craft, no matter how grand. But the Turkish artisan considers the medium to be no more than a matter of fate. Some are born to be painters, others to be potters, some to be calligraphers, others basketmakers. While the artisans rank calligraphy as the greatest art and basketmaking as the humblest, they argue that what makes art is not the medium — not fate, but will: the dedication of the worker to excellence. Bad calligraphy is not art. Excellent baskets are.

Hirohisa Tatebayashi is willing to place himself among the world's best potters. Others are his equals, but no one is his superior, and yet he will not accept the name of artist. Artists, he says, are arrogant folk who wish it to seem as though they created in splendid isolation, away from the world and its people. Potters might be called artists when they work alone, digging their own clay, throwing and glazing it, but, Hirohisa says, porcelain is an art too complex to indulge individualistic urges or support egotistical claims. It takes ten years to learn the work of the wheel, ten years to learn the work of the kiln, ten years to learn glazing, ten years to learn to draw the design, and ten years to learn to fill it with color. No individual can have mastered the whole trade, so all must work as members of a team under the supervision of a master who understands the whole process.

Hirohisa's excellence lies in management, and he has assembled the best team possible. He has a young man who throws and trims the forms. Then Hirohisa operates the kiln, which was once fed wood but now burns gas. He fires the piece at nine hundred degrees centigrade, matching the peak heat in Kütahya. Then the biscuit ware is painted in blue by a woman who is one of the four decorators in the shop. This is a risk, because the piece receives much effort before it is given its highest firing. It is glazed with a solution of ash, crushed stone, and white glass, and then fired at thirteen hundred degrees. At that high heat, Hirohisa says, the fire gets down into the flesh of the pot. Then over the glaze the decorators add the outline and the infill of color, and the piece returns to the kiln for one or two more firings — it depends on the paint and the weather — at eight hundred degrees.

In the upright romantic critique, division in labor is lamented as a consequence of industrialization, but specialization is normal in any complex technology. Describing the work at Jingdezhen in the early eighteenth century, in the era of handwork when there were three thousand kilns in the city, a French missionary estimated that each piece of porcelain had absorbed the contribution of seventy people. In his astonishing early history of the Staffordshire potteries, published in 1829, Simeon Shaw wrote that specialization had increased with industrialization, when the potteries produced molded statues and sets of china for the English masses, but even in the days before 1760, when the potters wrought by hand in family shops, they divided the work among them by specialty. So it was, and so it is in Kütahya. The plate that İbrahim Erdeyer paints was made of mud mixed by boys in his father's employ, and it was shaped, glazed, and fired by İhsan with the help of a team of young laborers. İbrahim signs his own name discreetly on the front, and he writes the name of his family's firm in large letters on the back. The gleaming porcelain vase by Hirohisa Tatebayashi was thrown by Chitoshi Matsuda, painted by Chizuko Shimimoto to a design by Sadao Tatebayashi, glazed and fired by Hirohisa, and signed with the name of their kiln.

As the manager of a team, the master of a kiln, Hirohisa Tatebayashi stands higher than the artist. And that is how it is in Turkey. The artist, the *sanatkâr*, creates beautifully, but the master, the *usta*, does more. The masters are artists. They create. But they also manage a workshop, and as part of their managerial duties they teach, standing in a parental role to their workers, guiding them to correctness in art and life, and running the business on which their livelihoods depend. One can claim to be an artist, but only society grants the higher title of master. The artist is talented. The master is talented and socially responsible. The wild artist might achieve the highest prestige in individualistic societies. But in the mature society, to be the master of a pottery is a finer thing.

In Japan, the master of a pottery is called *sensei*. The same title is given to teachers in schools. The educational implications of the terms *sensei* and *usta* fit ateliers like Hirohisa Tatebayashi's in Arita or Mehmet Gürsoy's in Kütahya. As Mehmet emerged as an artist in the eighties, he told me his goal was to become the loving master of a workshop. He would teach and his students would become his hands, performing to his will. His goal has been met. When we tape-recorded his life history, İbrahim Erdeyer said he wished to be remembered, not as an artist or businessman, but as a teacher. At Seto in Japan, Hiroshige Kato, the twelfth in the familial line of masters at the Kasen Toen, proudly told me that his vast workshop admitted young people and instructed them, giving them practical experience before they left to follow the chance of their own careers.

Contrasting the pottery of Kütahya with the painting of Europe, Ahmet Şahin said that traditional arts, like his, rarely accomplish shocking novelty, but they rarely fail. Quality is steady, and one reason is the system of the atelier. The atelier is an educational institution, training young workers who leave to seek better jobs, circulating through the community, renewing and unifying the general tradition while preventing stagnation and preserving standards. Split by specialization, housing experts in every phase of a complex technology, the large atelier serves the community's artists who work alone. Early in the eighteenth century, Kenzan Ogata could rely for forms and firing on the masters of Kyoto, and in the middle of the twentieth, Ahmet Şahin was supported by the masters of Kütahya. He took biscuit ware from the workshops, painted the pieces to his own designs, and then returned them for glazing and firing to masters like İhsan Erdeyer at Süsler Çini. It was an honor to serve the artist who served the city through the creation of new and inspirational works.

Success in the cities of Arita and Kütahya depends on the efficient management of the masters. But in even the largest shop, managerial and educational duties are not divorced from creative action. Hirohisa paints and fires. İhsan throws and glazes. As surely as the commander of an army must have known battle and risen through the ranks, as surely as the effective administrator of a university must have taught and conducted serious research, the master of a pottery must have worked in the mud, learning the entire process and coming to know what the workers can do — when they need instruction and when they must be left alone to practice freely. Excellence in creation demands decisions that, grounded in intimate experience, properly mix direction and liberation. It is necessary to manage, natural to teach, but what is central to mastery is creation.

Hagi is a trim, bright city in the far west of Honshu, on the shores of the Sea of Japan, across from Korea. In the city and its environs, two hundred shops produce Hagi *yaki*, the region's distinctive ware. Few of them are large operations, most are small, and the one I will tell you about is Norio Agawa's, on the banks of the Hashimoto River. When I was there once, a man delivering a load of clay said he addressed the manager of every shop as *sensei*, but Norio Agawa is really a *sensei*. No apprentices await his direction. He deserves the title of respect because of his intense creative energy.

Norio Agawa is not exactly alone. His sunny shop bubbles with the chat and cracks with the laughter of many visitors. His sprightly wife, Motoko, finishes some of the pieces and helps in loading the kiln, and he glazes and fires the creations of his brother Hachiro Higaki, who learned from him. But Norio Agawa sets the shop's quick tempo, and he does it all with his own hands, mixing the clay, shaping, glazing, and firing it.

He does the work, and he taught himself. Teaching, he says, is not important. Learning is. When he married, he was adopted into a family that had been making roofing tiles for ten generations. His wife's father gave him his first lessons in the clay, and many others have provided hints along the way. But Norio Agawa is his own teacher. The masters, he says, will not teach the important things. They guard them jealously and transfer them clandestinely within family lines, though even to their own sons they cannot teach the things that matter most, for they have become lost into old habits beyond the reach of the conscious mind. Only simple things can be taught. Complex things must be learned on your own. So, you study the works of the great masters, then experiment to discover how they were made, and, at last, you teach yourself by doing. Talent is necessary, Norio Agawa says, but the key trait is will, the drive to keep at it until failure converts into success. Mastery comes from getting to know the clay in your hands, from making things repetitiously in great numbers.

Differences in organization and education are only the beginning of the differences between a one-man shop like Norio Agawa's in Hagi and an atelier like Hirohisa Tatebayashi's in Arita. When I stayed with him, I brought as a gift a plate painted by Nurten Şahin. Norio Agawa tapped it, commented that it was low-fired, and then said that other than that it was like the ware of Arita. Its artistry lay in its painting. His artistry, he said, lies in the shaping of form, and he divided all of pottery into two kinds. One is like Arita (or the Kütahya of Nurten Şahin), in which pottery provides a bright foundation for a display of decorative virtuosity. It is a painter's art. The other is like Hagi (or the Raus of Lars Andersson), in which decorative qualities are inchoate in the production of form. It is a sculptor's art.

Hagi's tradition began when the lord of the Mori clan brought two Korean potters to the city at the beginning of the seventeenth century. The aristocratic fashion of the tea ceremony was at its peak, and with those potters Hagi became, and remains, a center of production for tea vessels: teabowls and tea canisters, containers for incense, fresh water, and flowers. Hospitality is the prime principle of the tea ceremony, I was told by Kaneko Nobuhiko, a potter in Hagi, but the tea way elaborated in exchanges between the palace and the monastery, and it deepened

Hachiro Higaki. Hagi, Japan. 1998

Norio Agawa. Hagi. 1994

in the context of Zen. Framed by the philosophy of Zen Buddhism, the tea ceremony raises antinomies, not for synthetic resolution in the Western manner, but so that differences might coexist in tension and the complexity of the world might be known. Simple hospitality is governed by an intricately complex etiquette. The setting is deliberately humble and rustic; the actions are mannered, courtly, and elegant. The frothy green tea is bitter; the small round cake is sweet. The company is pleasant and tranquil; the moment is melancholy, suffused with an awareness of time's passing and the transience of things.

Millions in modern Japan practice the cordial discipline of the tea ceremony. Their vessels must not seem luxurious. They should recall the imperfections of nature and the potter's labor, and yet they must fit an exquisitely refined aesthetic. In making tea ware, enacting his city's old tradition, Norio Agawa moves at every step along a path unlike the one that leads to the smooth beauties of Arita. But his course is no less sophisticated. Out of a distinct sensibility, he creates objects that are profoundly informed by the Buddha's understanding of the nature of the world.

At Arita, the struggle is to achieve an unnaturally flawless, luminous white body, in no way reminiscent of the earth. Norio Agawa commences with two kinds of clay, red from an island to the north, yellow from the hills to the south. The yellow can be used alone, but the red must be mixed to take form. The clays might be mixed loosely to produce streaks of natural color, like the marbled ware of England. More often they are blended thoroughly in different proportions. What is most remarkable is that when Norio Agawa blends them, he adds the fine gravel that was removed from the clay during its process of purification. He returns a natural roughness to the body. His works carry the mottled, subtle hues of the earth and the gritty feel of the soil.

Patting the clay into a soft cone, he centers the lump on the wheel and throws off the hump in the Asian manner, like potters in Bangladesh, shaping form after form from the tip of the spinning mass. He cuts the bowl free, carefully preserving the tracks of his fingers that would be fastidiously shaved away at Arita. It is proverbial in Japan to say that, for tea ware, Raku is first and Hagi is second. The Raku teabowl is made in Kyoto without a wheel. It is pinched into shape, then carved. As his teabowl dries, Norio Agawa might add a Raku touch by slicing angular facets in the lower body, diminishing the regularity of the wheel-thrown form. He completes the bowl by chopping in the notched footring that is emblematic of Hagi's ware.

During its first firing at seven hundred degrees centigrade, the bowl might gain smoky burns, and Norio Agawa adds dark passages with splashes of gray slip before glazing. After the second firing at twelve hundred and twenty degrees, the glaze, a mix of feldspar and ash, will sheathe the form with transparent brightness, and it will turn white in streaks to contrast with the buff and gray beneath and with the matte tones of the clay, displayed low on the vessel where it was washed to prevent the glaze from adhering.

Potters in Hagi strive for two special effects. One comes from firing. By controlling the flow of air and preventing the kiln's atmosphere from settling into a state of either reduction or oxidation, they achieve accidental ornamentation: a dappling of yellow spots, nimbed with pink, upon a field of gray — a look that is likened to the pelt of a fawn at the Asahi Pottery in Uji, to fireflies at twilight in Hagi. Hagi's signal effect comes from the "rice straw white." Norio Agawa gets rice straw from neighboring farmers. He burns it, not to ash, but to charcoal, and mixes it with his usual glaze to get a thicker, richer white. Timing is all: the vessel is gripped by the footring, dipped quickly to coat the exterior, popped up at the surface to fill the interior, swished back and forth to thicken the glaze at the rim, and then flipped over suddenly to let thick vanilla drips ooze sumptuously over the light coat beneath, white upon white.

Turned for lifting, the teabowl is savage at the base — rough as though ripped from the earth. It rises from sharp edges toward smoothness on the sides, where the hands nestle into the grooves left by the potter's fingers. The clean rim awaits the lips.

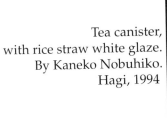

Tea canister,
with rice straw white glaze.
By Kaneko Nobuhiko.
Hagi, 1994

Firefly teabowl.
By Seichi Sakakura.
Hagi, Japan.
1998

Teabowl. By Norio Agawa. Hagi. 1998

With its drips and puddles of satiny white and its rippled, gritty surface, Hagi's ware is a celebration of contrast: it is natural and artificial, controlled and accidental, regular and irregular, rough and smooth, dark and light, shiny and dull, earthy and ethereal. It is like a white cloud descending upon the face of a rocky cliff, or a snowfall on broken ground, or — this is better, given the city's setting by the sea — it is like seafoam adrift on a gravelly beach. Whatever the figure, it needs to fit the Zen tradition, assembling difference and evoking evanescence.

The Hagi style is materialized most dramatically in creations for the tea ceremony. It is subdued, but sustained, in the ware Norio Agawa makes for daily use. A snowy gloss flows down the dimpled, granulated surface of his teapots and cups. His rice bowls come blushing or dove-gray from the kiln.

The potter's performance begins, but does not end the process of creation. Seichi Sakakura, a friend of Norio Agawa's and a maker of tea ware, says that if you place a pot out of touch on a shelf, it weeps, crying to be used. The one who uses it becomes, he says, a new creator as the teabowl continues its existence, transforming through seven stages. With use, the thick white glaze crackles. This is another of Hagi's effects that is at once intentional and accidental, technological and ornamental, for the potter refined the clay so that the emergent web of cracks would suit the vessel, a fine web for small forms, a looser for larger. Then stains grow around the grit. Dark streaks appear. In time, darkening like a storm cloud, the bowl will be broken and repaired with lightning flashes of gold lacquer. Through every phase, in use, the bowl approaches its destiny and increases in value, that value lying in its ability to display the reality of the world: the irreconcilable differences, the inevitable decay.

At Arita, the potter's art yields an object beyond time, made in complete control and mysteriously perfect. At Hagi, the potter's art invites contradiction and accident. In its thrown, burned, and stained fabric, the artifact tells the tales of its mak-

Mustafa Baydemir. Kınık, Bilecik, Turkey. 1985

Teapot. Kınık. 1990

ing and use. It belongs to time. Japanese taste widens to embrace both styles, the one transcendent, the other transient. As they have since the seventeenth century, Japanese potters shape beautiful vessels to radically different aesthetic ends.

Turkish taste displays a comparable breadth. Kütahya's *çini* is like Arita's porcelain in its meticulously painted, gleaming white forms — in its will to control — but the earthenware tradition of Turkey welcomes happy accidents. In the recent past at Çanakkale, jars and bowls were splashed with drips and swirling spatters that recorded the artist's spontaneous gestures, much as canvases by Jackson Pollock do. At Kınık, a village with one hundred and fifty workshops in northwestern Anatolia, the potters dip their jugs and flowerpots in a vat of white slip, and then return them to the wheel. Nudged with a kick, the wheel turns while the slip slides, and the potters drop dots of color or run a spiral of tinted slip into the moving surface. The slip flows, the spiral drifts, distorting to take on the semblance of wavy wood grain, and its descent is hastened by drips tipped from a tin horn. Mustafa Baydemir learned the craft from his father in the 1930s, and he decorated hundreds of pots a day until his death in 1992. No two of them, he said, were the same. Mustafa's art was an art of uncontrol. A participant in the force and counterforce of the universe, he began the process, wedding damp substances in the context of gravity, and then he left completion in the hands of God.

In Hagi, intended accidents are framed by a Buddhist vision of imperfection. At Kınık, intended accidents are framed by the Muslim tenet of submission. Both wares befit the human and belong to the bump and chance of common life. Both are implicitly religious. Through the aesthetic they whisper of the sacred. Then the sacred becomes manifest in representation. In Turkey, the tile or plate of Kütahya is calligraphed with the word of God. In Japan, at Hagi, the potter makes statues.

At the end of the seventeenth century, the great Shinbei Saka pressed Hagi's repertory beyond tea vessels to include sculpture, and before his death in 1968, Geirin Nakano astonished the city with gigantic ceramic images of the Buddhist deities. Many of Shinbei Saka's works remain in museums. Norio Agawa has studied them closely. Once he went to meet Geirin Nakano, but the master would not speak with him, and Norio Agawa has had to figure out sculpture for himself.

The easy way to make a statue, he says, is to take a lump of clay and shape the form by addition and subtraction. The statue of the goddess in Bangladesh is made by packing clay around an armature of wood and straw, then adding clay and carving it away. While the *murti* dries slowly, cracks are filled, and the surface is smoothed with watery layers that prepare it for painting. That technique was used in ancient Japan. It probably came from India through China with Buddhism, and clay statues, technically like those of Bengal and more than a millennium old, remain in the temples of Nara. But those statues were not fired. Even if the flammable core were omitted, such statues would be unsuitable for firing, Norio Agawa said, because differences in the thickness of the walls would lead to cracking in drying and explosions in the kiln.

The solution in Bangladesh is to use molds when images are to be fired. The clay can be pressed into the mold to a steady depth, and the mold will hold the form while it dries. In Hagi, Geirin Nakano used molds for his smaller works, and the master at his kiln today, the marvelously talented Takuo Matsumura, uses his old molds to get new forms that, like the most conscientious masters in Bangladesh, such as Maran Chand Paul in Dhaka, he finishes with painstaking handcraft. But Norio Agawa believes, like Haripada Pal in Dhaka, that molded statues lack life. It takes, he feels, the direct touch, the free-wheeling gesture of the moment, to bless a form with vitality, whether it is a teabowl or the image of a god.

Norio Agawa told me that if you can throw a tea cup on the wheel, you can do anything, and he has developed a way to make statues as though they were pots. His technique is akin to the

Takuo Matsumura. Hagi. 1998

Jurojin,
a god of wisdom.
By Takuo Matsumura.
Hagi, Japan.
1998

Shoki.
By Norio Agawa.
1994

Daruma.
By Norio Agawa.
1998

Hotei. By Norio Agawa. Hagi, Japan. 1994

process used by Native American women, or the Raku potters who raise vessels without wheels. But — and that is, believe me, a big but — instead of circling, pinching, and smoothing clay into symmetrical, spherical forms, he arranges it asymmetrically around the hollow shapes of bodies. It takes deep knowledge of the clay to build forms to the point where the walls want to collapse, to let them dry, just enough, and then to add more, quickly, carefully enclosing the void with a damp, flexible cover that is even in thickness. It takes knowledge, and still more it takes imagination, the mental powers of a great designer, to know how to plan and then fashion a coat of clay around nothing into a vivid representational image. While he works, Norio Agawa takes advantage of his different clays, modeling faces and hands out of the yellow, sweeping robes out of the red, and he ends with a flurry of emphatic, deep incising that charges his expressive figures with his own high-voltage personality. Firing, glazing, and firing them again, just as he would a cup or a bowl, he brings a last layer of life to the statues that stand, glowering and grinning around his workshop.

His images are not intended for temples. Only rarely does Norio Agawa sculpt the icons — the Buddha seated in stillness, Kannon swaying in grace — that are found on public altars. His works fit the decor of the home and garden. They belong to the auspicious, protective order of domestic religion. His repertory is centered among the Seven Gods: Hotei, Benten, and Bishamon, Daikoku and Ebisu, Jurojin and Fukurokuju. Diverse in origin — Buddhist, Hindu, and Taoist — they have been grouped since the fifteenth century and imaged for home consumption in every medium, including ceramics, throughout Japan. These are the deities of good fortune, of longevity and prosperity, who bring music and learning and wealth to balance the sorrow of life. Norio Agawa chooses most often to represent the merry, fat Hotei. A Zen priest in the tenth century, Hotei is a lucky god, always smiling, his bag always full, and he is a bodhisattva, big with compassion for human suffering.

217

Stretching to collect influences, while attending closely to the models left by Hagi's old master Shinbei Saka, Norio Agawa shapes familiar images with wit and warmth. His brother Hachiro Higaki turned to the clay after a career in the merchant marine. He learned Norio's techniques, and he has worked to give some among the Seven Gods a new and peculiarly Japanese cast. When he builds Fukurokuju, a god of longevity, he usually models him to the Chinese figure, but he has also developed a new depiction — no one, Hachiro says, knows what the gods look like — that borrows the brooding mood of Daruma, the monk who brought Zen to China in the sixth century, and who frequently gains monumental presence in Norio's hands.

Norio Agawa constructs images of Japanese heroes and Buddhist deities, but his life's goal is to make the best lion of our days, just as Shinbei Saka made the best lion of his. No extant lion struck him as right, so he embarked on a campaign of research, trading for a molded lion by Geirin Nakano, taking snapshots of old lions, then selecting bits from those he saw and combining them into a lion that is all his own.

The lion is the guardian of the Buddha's way. Lions stand at the entries of temples. For centuries, the citizens of Hagi have bought new lions when they built new houses, placing them in the alcove within, next to the familial altar, where they protect the home from evil and help to keep its occupants on the righteous path of the Buddha. Lions come in pairs. The mouth of the lion to the right is open, the mouth of the one to the left is shut. It is the same with the lions that flank the path to the temple, and with the heroic gods in human form who rage inside the temple's gate, and with the horned demons who glare from the rooftop. The lion of the right opens its mouth to say the sound of the beginning, from which enlightenment flows. The lion of the left closes its mouth to murmur the sound of the end. They speak the sounds of time, separately expressing difference — the female and male, the violent and benign, the start and the finish, existence and extinction — and together they enunciate the syllable of eternity — om —

Fukurokuju. By Hachiro Higaki. Hagi, Japan. 1996

Norio Agawa
at work on a lion.
1998

The lion
in its first phase

Glazed with the rice straw white and fired.
By Norio Agawa. Hagi, Japan. 1998

recalling the place beyond duality, the pure land that abides beyond the world of difference and desire and history.

Norio Agawa works to fulfill his dreams. Pottery is his delight. He makes vessels for the tea ceremony: teabowls, cases for incense, and vases for flowers. He makes cups and bowls for daily use, and he drinks his morning tea from a darkening cup that came from his own hand. He uses the same gritty clay to craft images of the gods and of the lions that guard the Buddhist household.

The circle closes, our tale is told. Like the potter of Bangladesh, Norio Agawa meets the needs of the people with utilitarian ware and sacred statues. The big difference is that he lives in Japan, where tradition is treasured like a dewdrop on a maple leaf in autumn, where the economy, despite talk of crisis, remains miraculous. The effort that brings him personal joy, that eventuates in service to others, also brings him a comfortable living: a big house with a lovely view, two new cars, and an immense, space-age television set.

His seventieth year approaches, but he puts in a long day, every day. Vacations, he says, bring him no pleasure. Work is what he likes, and within work, diversity. He brings a small lion to the end of its first phase, where it must rest and dry, and he shifts quickly to a gigantic lion on a second turntable, sharpening its ferocious snarl and the bristling curls of its mane, until it, too, must wait. He does not stop. His creatures are maturing relentlessly on their own schedules. Holding time's erratic pattern in mind, he switches to another task, pounding, patting, and centering a hillock of pale clay on the wheel and throwing the tall tumblers that were ordered by a customer from the other end of the country, in Tokyo. The board beside him crowds with fresh, pert forms. He looks up at the big clock on the wall and declares it time to quit. The Giants battle the Carp on the box tonight. He will pour himself a tall vodka and milk and relax with baseball. Now it is time to stop. He lifts the board, slides it into the drying rack, centers another lump, and begins again, pulling elegant forms out of the whirling tower of clay.

Work in the Clay

It is good to be a potter. Among the possibilities, architecture is the grandest. It requires the most different skills and provides the most different experiences. In scale and complexity, architecture embodies the richest display of value. But pottery is the most intense of the arts; it brings the most to bear within the smallest compass.

Pottery makes plain the transformation of nature. Clay from the earth blends with water from the sky. The amorphous takes form in the hands. The wet becomes dry in the air. The soft becomes hard and the dull becomes bright in the fire. Cooked, the useless becomes useful.

Pottery displays the values by which human life is shaped. It brings the old and the new, the practical and the aesthetic, the personal and the collective, the social and the economic, the mundane and the spiritual, into presence and connection.

The one who can do all that does enough. The potter has won the right to confidence.

Confidence, stability, quiet pride, easy cheer — these are what I find in the masters of ceramics. They pause to welcome me, then turn back to the work that is their job, their duty, their pleasure. Differences of culture and personality recede into unimportance as potters join in calm intensity, finding what it is to be human through work in the clay. Writing is my craft. It is not more or, I guess, less important than pottery, and practicing it I have been aided by the example of the potters it has been my good fortune to know: Ahmet Şahin, the old master of Kütahya, described by Mehmet Gürsoy as the deeply-rooted tree of which Mehmet and his friends are the branches; Mehmet Gürsoy, who remembers Ahmet Şahin and the masters of sixteenth-century Turkey in creations that situate his personal energy in God's design; İbrahim Erdeyer, Mehmet's friend, who proves that one can be an artist and a thoroughly good human being; Nurten Şahin, who went as a beautiful young woman into the rough

Nurten Şahin.
Kütahya, Turkey.
1993

Haripada Pal.
Dhaka, Bangladesh.
1995

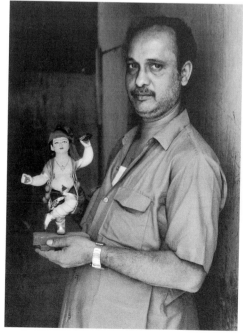

Chester Hewell. Gillsville, Georgia. 1994

Wanda Aragon.
Acoma, New Mexico.
1998

world of men and gained their admiration for her skill; Hirohisa Tatebayashi of Arita, who disdains the name artist because it obscures the collaborative reality of ceramic production; Norio Agawa of Hagi, whose teabowls endure, whose statues of the gods overspill with his own high spirit; Irene Aguilar, Oaxaca, Mexico, whose images of Christ's mother rise serenely out of the tawdry market for souvenirs; Dorothy Auman, Seagrove, North Carolina, practitioner and historian of her tradition, who made the redware plates we use on festive occasions, remembering her; Chester Hewell, Gillsville, Georgia, son and father of potters, who both manages a big factory and turns and burns his region's pots in the old-time way; Mark Hewitt, son of the director at Spode and student of Michael Cardew, now blending the Mingei concept with North Carolina's old tradition into something monumental and fresh, useful, beautiful, and old as hope; Wanda Aragon, Acoma, New Mexico, whose works are the ultimate refinement of her hard environment; Lars Andersson, Raus, Sweden, whose pots beckon the past into burned earth; Haripada Pal, Dhaka, Bangladesh, whose labor is wrapped in philosophical discourse, whose work in the clay is a hymn to God.

I am not a potter. I am a folklorist, a student of ceramics because pottery is a more universal and democratic medium than painting, a better place to begin the search for the world's excellence. I have become an admirer of the maturity of the sincere worker with clay, and I envy the options of the modern potter.

Seizing upon the immanent artfulness of pottery, the potter can withdraw into isolation and ascend along the arc that ends in a transcendence of consciousness. Or, through the earthiness of technique and the compound significance inherent in the committed rearranging of the world, the potter can join the millions remaining on the earth whose daily work brings them, roughly, directly, into awareness of their position in the cosmos.

Västagården. Lima, Dalarna, Sweden. 1989

5

VERNACULAR ARCHITECTURE

BUILDINGS, LIKE POTS and poems, realize culture. Their designers rationalize their actions differently. Some say they design and build as they do because it is the ancient way of their people and place. Others claim that their practice correctly manifests the universally valid laws of science. But all of them create out of the smallness of their own experience.

All architects are born into architectural environments that condition their notions of beauty and bodily comfort and social propriety. Before they have been burdened with knowledge about architecture, their eyes have seen, their fingers have touched, their minds have inquired into the wholeness of their scenes. They have begun collecting scraps of experience without regard to the segregation of facts by logical class. Released from the hug of pleasure and nurture, they have toddled into space, learning to dwell, to feel at home. Those first acts of occupation deposit a core of connection in the memory.

Were it me, were I the one who would come to build, there would be red clay and pale curls of wood. There would be an orchard outside and shotguns in the hallway. Thick white paint on rough pine boards would connote home and call to mind the soft sounds of dogs and old men on the porch, the cool feel of linoleum on the kitchen floor, the smells of bacon frying. A woman's lilt, an endless melody strung of hymns to Jesus, would wander through it, accompanied by the brisk whisks of a broom.

As we grow, memory runs wild, undirected by future projects. Culture accumulates into an inner resource of association and gathers order aesthetically. This feels good, that bad, while experience widens, memories deepen, and culture complicates through learning.

When the builder's attention is narrowed by training, whether in the dusty shop of a master carpenter or the sleek classroom of a university, past experience is not obliterated. It endures in the strange caves of the brain and in the old habits of the muscles as they seek smooth routes through the air. Education adds a layer. In precept and admonition, in pedagogical technique, if not in content, the teacher brings cultural values into the process of transmission. Students obey or rebel. Inwardly, new ideas mix and coexist with old ones, and the mind, fed by the senses, continues to bounce about, unfettered by consistency. Resolution will come in performance, in dedicated, situated instants of concentration, while planning meets accidents and learning continues.

Despite the rigors of training, the architect remains a full person, at once competent and confused. The building shares in its builder's confusions. It seems right, as a result, because it incorporates the experience that the architect shares — not completely, of course, but completely enough — with those who do not build, but who look at buildings and go into them. The building works because it integrates the tight routines of professional practice with the loose expanse of cultural association. The overtly architectural contrivance covertly absorbs the norms of beauty and social exchange and political order with which the architect, as a member of society, has come to feel at ease.

Architecture is like any realization of potential, like any projection of thought. The things of the world — this sentence, that palace — preceded themselves in the mind as plans. Plans blend memories with a reading of the immediate situation. They are realized in things. They can be reversed in analysis. Things become plans, plans disaggregate into sets of decisions, decisions become intentions. All creations bespeak their creators. They stand before us as images of will and wit. In this, architecture is like other things, and there are no differences among kinds of building. All are cultural creations, orderings of experience, like poems and rituals.

Ağzıkarahan, Turkey. 1982

Vale, Guernsey, Channel Islands. 1982

If every building is a cultural fact, the consequence of a collision between intentions and conditions, if differences of culture and circumstance adequately account for differences among buildings, the question is why we persist in calling some of them vernacular. There are answers.

Few kinds of building have been accorded full study. When we isolate from the world a neglected architectural variety and name it vernacular, we have prepared it for analysis. The term marks the transition from the unknown to the known. The study of vernacular architecture is a way that we expand the record, bit by bit. At work, moving toward a complete view of the builder's art, we bring buildings into scrutiny and toward utility in the comprehensive study of humankind.

Buildings are neglected for different reasons. Some are the exotic products of indigenous people in places unknown to us. But others are familiar, maybe too familiar. The architectural historian who lavishes attention yet again on some canonical monument probably lives in a house of a kind that has wholly eluded serious study. Pondering why some buildings get studied and others do not, we are likely to argue that some buildings are important and others are not. Then pondering the emptiness of that answer, we find that important buildings can be interpreted as displays of the values we value — grandeur, perhaps, or originality — while unimportant buildings display values that we have not yet learned to appreciate. Neglect is a sign of ignorance. The term, I repeat, marks the transition from the unknown to the known: we call buildings "vernacular" because they embody values alien to those cherished in the academy. When we called buildings "folk," the implication was that they countered in commonness and tradition the pretense and progress that dominate simple academic schemes. Folk buildings contained a different virtue. The study of vernacular architecture, through its urge toward the comprehensive, accommodates cultural diversity. It welcomes the neglected into study in order to acknowledge the reality of difference and conflict.

Should we wonder why architectural study has aped the study of art in its erection of a canon of important buildings, we will find, on reflection, a host of causes. One of them has to do with the ease of procedure. Selecting a few buildings, a few architects, and then linking them up chronologically, we can borrow the facile techniques of the historian of great men and events. But taking the comprehensive view and recognizing diversity, the study of vernacular architecture drives toward better historical procedures, ones that focus existentially on action and lead to the construction of a multiplex idea of time. We call buildings vernacular to highlight the cultural and contingent nature of all building.

Proposing distinctions and labeling buildings along the way, the study of vernacular architecture is an approach to the whole of the built world. It favors completeness, recognizes diversity, and seeks ways to use buildings as evidence in order to tell better versions of the human story. In the future, it will be obsolete, but now the term "vernacular" is one of the tools we use when we face architectural objects with a wish to crack them open and learn their meanings.

Materialization

Architecture works in space as history works in time. History interrupts time's ceaseless flow, segmenting and reordering it on behalf of the human need for meaning. Architecture intrudes in the limitless expanse of space, dividing it into useful, comprehensible pieces. Converting space into places through disruption, architecture brings meaning to the spatial dimension.

With astronomy as the extreme instance, the architectural impulse begins in exploration and naming. The baby crawls upon a softness that matures in meaning as time passes and names pile up: the softness is a rug, it is a red rug, it is a mediocre late nineteenth-century eagle Kazak. The explorer ventures into unknown territory to parcel and claim it with names that commemorate his heroism. Through time, names accumulate on the land

and combine to recall its history: the sequence of settlement, the conflict between the invader and the native.

The name is a fleeting means for bringing history into space and marking the land as meaningful. Marking becomes firmer with physical alteration, when a trail is blazed through a forest, or one stone is piled on another to set a limit. More stones confirm the limit and rise into walls: the wall the Chinese built that turned the mounted warriors westward toward Europe, the wall the Romans struck across Britain to cede the heathy highlands to the wild men of the north, the walls of forts along the borders, the walls of prisons and gated communities, the walls of the cottage where the bold thresherman, his day's work done, dandles the baby on his knee.

With the act of physical alteration that calls time into space, implying a past and a future, and with the walls that divide space, at once including and excluding, architecture has happened.

Architecture gives physical form to claims and names, to memories and hopes. As a conceptual activity, architecture is a matter of forming ideas into plans, plans into things that other people can see. Architecture shapes relations between people. It is a kind of communication. The mode of its thinking connects architecture to all of culture, but its mode of realization distinguishes it from other varieties of communication. To be architecture, it must be realized in materials.

The decision to create a building is the decision to destroy some part of the material universe. Things are wrecked — trees are toppled, stone is broken, old houses are razed — to make life better. The desire is for improvement. The process of the desire is technological.

Technology is a corollary of human existence. It is the means of our extension into space, as natural to people as swimming is to fish. As life unfolds, every technological act brings changes in two great relations: the one that always connects the human and nonhuman spheres, the other that is built to connect people with one another.

232

Architectural Technology

The relation of the human and nonhuman begins its transformation in the first step of technology, the selection of materials. A distinction between local and imported materials was among the first criteria that writers, in England particularly, used to define vernacular architecture. Vernacular buildings are composed of local materials, they argued. During travel, they enjoyed watching the substrate of the earth rise and form into buildings, crossing the land in bands of sandstone, limestone, and granite, and they deplored the rash of red brick buildings that spread along the railways, oblivious to geological differences. Their taste was built on conventional dichotomies: natural and artificial, native and alien, old and new, local and national, handmade and industrial. The contemporary cynic would find their view easy to deconstruct as elitist and dismiss as sentimental. But they were on to something.

During architectural fieldwork, I have taught myself to concentrate on form, but everywhere I go the people whose houses I study classify buildings by materials, and especially by roofing. I found in Turkey that the local historians separated old houses with flat roofs from new houses with pitched roofs covered by purchased materials. In Bangladesh, village people, thinking less about history than social class, divide buildings by the materials of their walls — stuccoed brick versus puddled mud or bamboo lashed in tension — and by their roofs of thatch or tin. In Africa and Latin America, thatch is comparably yielding to tin, and in the rural United States one age gave way to another when wooden shingles were replaced by shiny sheets of metal.

I learned the lesson of this change first in Ireland. In Ballymenone, a farming community where I drew a plan of every house and classified them into four distinct types, the people classified them into two groups by materials, separating houses that were thatched from those that were roofed with slate or metal.

Joe Murphy, Johnny Drumm, and Tommy Love, masters of thatching, taught me the logic that lay beneath their distinction. Thatch makes good insulation. It is warm in the winter, cool in the summer. Environmentally efficient, thatch is also beautiful. Looking downhill at a house he had recently roofed, Tommy Love said, "When it is new with straw, it shines like gold. The sun glints off it, and it is lovely. It is lovely, right enough."

Efficient and beautiful, thatching is also economical. Its main demand is time, and in Ballymenone they say that the man who made time made plenty. Thatch also requires a knowledge of growing things, the understanding of seeds and soil and weather that farmers develop during time passed in place. The material grows from the ground. It is an endlessly renewable resource, and it is processed and applied by hand, with no need for expensive machinery. Thatching takes knowledge and skill, it is a job for the man called handy, but it is a technology that requires no money.

The problem is that thatch demands regular maintenance and frequent replacement. The metal roof obviates the need for constant intervention; it is effectively permanent. The householder is not obliged to be a craftsman or to be connected — as they were in Ballymenone through trades of aid — with neighbors who are skilled. He manages alone without effort or knowledge or talent or social connection. But metal does not suit the climate. It works little better in cool, humid Ireland than it does in hot, humid Bangladesh, where the tin roof roasts you in summer. And metal is not beautiful. Ellen Cutler said it broke her heart when she used the royalties she received from my first book on Ballymenone to strip the thatch from her home and roof it with metal. Her house, she said, had turned ugly. But she made the change because of "the times that are in it."

Those times, in Ellen Cutler's mind, were characterized by the melting away of intimate social orders in the heat of Ulster's political troubles, and they were marked by shifts in fashion. Mrs.

Tommy Love.
Ballymenone.
1973

Joe Murphy.
Ballymenone.
1983

John Gilleece's house, which he thatches himself.
Ballymenone, Fermanagh, Northern Ireland. 1972

Cutler belonged to a small rural community where it was satisfying to live in the largest, loveliest thatched house. Dick, her son, lived in the same place, but he belonged to a vast rural proletariat. He worked for wages paid by an agricultural entrepreneur. She knew he would never move into a thatched house — so old and cranky, so very Irish — so she ruined its looks, turning it ugly to make it suit him. She was successful. When Mrs. Cutler died in 1981, Dick moved his family up the hill, and, as she had hoped, Cutler blood kept flowing on Cutler land. Her change brought continuity.

The metal roof fits the times. The times demand money. Manufactured in a mill beyond the horizon, moved by rail and road, sheet metal roofing obliges people to collect specimens of their national currency. They are drawn into paying jobs, becoming the little wheels in the big machine that gathers wealth for distant capitalists. Out of the house for most of the day and beat at its end, people have no time to build through cordial conversations the friendships that once brought a thatcher to the house in exchange for agricultural produce.

The connections shaped by thatching — between people and nature, between people and people — were direct and intensely local. The change from thatch to tin signals the surrender of local autonomy. In Ireland, as in Bangladesh, people have chosen to adjust to the times. They have chosen permanence, reliance on distant producers, and participation in the international cash economy.

Not from the perspective of a privileged observer, whether cynical or sentimental, but from the perspective of the people who live the life, we can sum things up. In the shift from local to imported materials, there is a loss in environmental efficiency and a loss in beauty. There is a gain in permanence, which is compensation for a loss of skill and social connection. The loss of the pleasure taken from a job well done, and the burden of the need for cash, must be set against the prestige that is supposed to accrue to the one who purchases expensive objects. Become a consumer, one reorients. Breaking away from the neighbors with their delicate sense of local hierarchy, people come into comparison with others who, they say in Ballymenone, have money like hay. What is lost is security. What is gained is the hope that commodities will somehow balance the account.

The meanings that lie in the selection of materials are social and economic as well as environmental. But the environment sets the stakes. Living wisely in a tight place, people learn the environment. They know how to select from it the right materials for the job. The prime virtue in materials is their ability to alter the climate, shaping a little environment within which architecture can be forgotten and life can go on. It is a matter on which cultures differ, but when people seek separation from nature, which all of them do in bad weather, their actions often glide out of the pragmatic and into the aesthetic.

One of the first to write on Irish vernacular architecture, the Swedish ethnologist Åke Campbell, spoke glowingly of the fit of the thatched Irish house to the green Irish land. The house, he said, belonged like a natural feature, blending in like a rock or a tree. To Campbell, to me, and — this is what actually matters — to the people who labor to make the houses look like they do, Irish houses are things of beauty on the landscape. But the goal of their builders is not to have them melt into nature. In brilliant white, the house cracks out of its setting of green and brown and gray. Ellen Cutler told me how they picked the lumps from the bottom of the limekiln and burst them in boiling water to get the whitest, brightest whitewash. A widow in her seventies, Mrs. Cutler whitewashed the walls regularly to hide the natural tones of the stones and to make her house stand proud in the environment. The weather is wet. The lanes are muddy and rutted. Dampness absorbs light into darkness. In Ballymenone, they

County Galway, Ireland. 1972

County Down, Northern Ireland. 1972

describe the world around them as rough and dull. Smooth and bright, its white walls sparkling, the sun glinting off its roof, the house is a victory over conditions.

It is reasonable for the observer in retreat from the artificiality of industrial environments to see something natural in vernacular architecture. It is equally reasonable for people in daily contention with nature to seek its conquest through processes that smooth the rough and brighten the dull, altering the natural into the artificial. Local materials are their resources, their technologies are powered by their own muscles, but their aim is to create emblems of cultural presence. The bright white house claims the land and names it human.

If vernacular technologies involve local materials and the touch of the hand, their contrast is with industrial systems of production. Vernacular technology depends on direct connections: direct access to materials and direct connections among suppliers, producers, and consumers who simultaneously shape landscapes, social orders, and economic arrangements, while wealth circulates in the vicinity. Industrial production employs imported materials and complex machinery. It depends on expansive political powers that maintain the costly infrastructure of transportation and communication, while supporting through law the right of a small minority to amass great reserves of capital.

The distinction is real and important to preserve, for it helps us assure complexity in historical study. While the globe abounds with instances of the shift to industrial production, technologies based on local skills and materials continue, and they are dominant in many of the world's regions. It is important not to lose the distinction in our thinking. And it is important not to exaggerate its clarity. Vernacular and industrial technologies differ in resources and social organization, but they do not necessarily differ in the attitude toward nature.

Industrial production erases nature. In sheets of metal and slick plastic surfaces, there is no memory of natural origins. People must get up and go outside to remember.

Vacationing folks escape to the woods to forget the city, to relax, to get burned by the sun, bitten by bugs, perhaps to find something like a god in nature. Rolling up logs to build a fancy camp, the city sport leaves them round and brown. They still resemble trees, each distinct in the wall and knobby with knots, and he lets them weather to silver to fit his notion of the natural. A part of nature, his vacation home also alludes to history, to the log cabin that stands firmly in the American consciousness as a mythic sign of the time of the beginning. But the log cabin's builder went into the woods to establish civilization.

The wilderness howled around him, sublime and vast and threatening. He chopped into it bravely, felling trees, hewing their faces flat, lifting them into plumb alignment, and trimming their ends flush at the corner. Chinking the gaps between the logs with shingles or rocks, packed with clay and coated with fine lime plaster, he combined natural substances into smooth, true walls. The trees of the forest were attacked, hacked, split, and made to submit to the plan in his head. They were dropped and raised. They were shifted from the vertical to the horizontal. They were flattened to realize his design in a unified agony of straight lines that sharply marked his disjunction from nature. And then he confirmed his move to artificiality with a consolidating coat of whitewash or a cladding of clapboards. Restorationists tend to strip away these outer layers, leaving the house naked, vulnerable to rot, and creating an image of rusticity to reinforce preconceptions about progress. But the builder intended them from the beginning. Whitewash and clapboarding called up memories of order, of houses in the cities back east, of homes across the water on the tamed landscapes of Ireland and England, and they expressed his hope for improvement. He built to make the world better, to secure a place of control and reason within the mad-

Dovetailed corner-timbering of a log house built on the frontier. Shenandoah County, Virginia. 1969

ness of the wilderness. A man of culture, he built a farmhouse that stood out of the woods in splendid artifice.

Long before the industrial revolution, technologies had elaborated in the West. The towering oak was brought down and dressed into a timber, straight and square. Then the timber was joined into a frame. If wood was to be the cover, trees were sawed and split into slices, regular in size and shape, that were applied in series to make floors and walls and roofs. Or, clay was dug, soured in a pit, and molded into geometric units that were hardened by fire. Then these interchangeable parts were laid by line into walls. Traditional technologies of framing and masonry included a decisive step — the squared timber, the squared brick — in the process by which nature was erased and the human world was created. The timber embedded in the frame or the brick lost in the wall are not reminders of nature but pieces of plans and proofs of human control.

When the materials were still local and the techniques still manual, the straight timber replaced the bent one and the brick replaced the stone. In its products, industrial technology is less a violation of the vernacular than it is an exaggeration of one desire within the Western vernacular: its intention to set the human being in a role of righteous command.

There is a difference, though, between vernacular technology and its exaggeration by industry. When nature loomed tremendous and people fought back with plows and axes, their actions were heroic. When people sit in temperature-controlled offices and decree the continuation of that ancient struggle, their actions seem heartless. But the fact of continuity remains. It is traditional — folk, vernacular, cultural — for Western designers to treat nature as a resource, a convenient means for realizing the plans that are contrived in the freedom of the head. This attitude is exhibited most clearly in the aesthetic of the artificial, the traditional taste for repetitive, identical units (the bricks of the chimney, the windows of the high-rise apartment building) and for smooth, unified surfaces (the adzed timber and planed plank, the tile of the bathroom and the formica of the kitchen).

Aesthetic continuity eases change. The faces of the thatched roof and the metal roof are smooth and bright when new, both slick as a shaved chin. Plywood and sheetrock, asphalt, aluminum, and vinyl have been welcomed to the American country home as perfections of the old wish for artificiality. Clean, repetitive concrete blocks have been gracefully incorporated into rural building practice on both sides of the Atlantic, replacing clean, repetitive bricks and boards. Folded in an Appalachian cove, the manufactured mobile home stands out of the landscape, a compact, sharp unit, in the manner of its handmade predecessor, the log cabin.

But, despite tradition, experience has been disrupted. Nature conquered nonchalantly at a distance is not like nature conquered face on. The hewn timber and the steel beam both display the aesthetic of artificiality, but the tree I topple and hew to smoothness is my victory. I have known the transformation of nature in my own hands. I am powerful. The steel beam mined and milled by another and buried somewhere in the concrete beneath me is so removed from my experience that it seems to hold no message for my mind. But if I stop to think about it, the message is clear. I am powerless, utterly dependent on a system scaled beyond my control or understanding.

In the struggle for freedom, striving to fulfill our humanity through release from delimiting conditions, we have wriggled out of one trap, only to be caught in another. In pushing against the natural environment, fighting for control and nearly winning, we have deployed weapons — increasingly intricate, expensive, and mysterious machines — that have demanded our surrender to the political and economic forces of a cultural environment. We understand the mechanics of our cultural environment no better than our ancestors understood the mechanics of their natural environment. We have entered a new age of magic and fear.

Technology is more than a handy means for materializing designs. Since technology requires disruptive intervention in the universe, it asks for answers to profound questions. One class of question is cosmological. Whether they are articulated in religious or scientific terms, cosmological answers enunciate first principles, locating people in the world and conditioning their right to create through destruction. In one cosmological formulation, people occupy an enchanted realm. The trees and rocks and the very earth are alive with active force. Performing in a world filled with hungry ghosts and wily demons, people combine prayers and charms with skills and procedures into a technology of appeasement. Their products display respect and awe. In another cosmological tradition, the deities have granted command to humankind, or the people have seized it through cunning or courage. Theirs is a technology of mastery. It yields, by increasing division, products that display the clear separation of culture from nature, and that, like as not, contribute to the proliferation of ecological calamities.

Technology demands answers to cosmological questions and to political questions. While they disfigure nature, people configure orders among themselves, organizing a force for work and structuring relations between those who make alterations in the physical environment and those who benefit from them. Doubly cultural, technology unfolds from theories about the human position in the universe and from theories that govern the distribution of power among people.

Social Orders

Technology's political questions do not come into focus in the situation described as ideal by writers on vernacular architecture. In the ideal, design, construction, and use — domains of potential conflict — unify in a single man who gathers materials from his own land to build for himself the building he wants. Such things happen.

In 1938, Richard Hutto built a barn near Oakman, Alabama. He cut the trees on his own farm, dragged them to the site with a mule, and he raised them, alone, into a building. Its form is what scholars call a double-crib barn, and they can trace the plan from Alabama along the mountains to Pennsylvania, and from Pennsylvania to Central Europe. Mr. Hutto took the form from the memories he developed out of life in his locale. He trimmed the trees, cut them to length, and he notched their ends to interlock at the corner in a variety of timbering that the geographer Fred Kniffen named V-notching. Mr. Hutto called it "roof-topping."

Richard Hutto's barn was all his. It had only him to blame, it seems. But, when we talked in 1964, he attributed its failings to the times in which he worked. He told me he was thinking of tearing it down. It did not satisfy him because he had been forced to build it alone. He did not have the help of a black laborer as Pete Everett did when he built a barn, similar in form and construction, near Pine Hill, Mississippi, one year earlier. Mr. Hutto did it alone, but in the better days of the farther past, he said, a team of neighbors would have gathered to help. With more energy available, the timbers would have been hewn, rather than left in the round. Poles, he called them, not logs. The team would have included experts with the proper tools. The ends of the logs would have been trimmed cleanly with a saw, instead of raggedly with a chopping axe.

Many craftsmen have spoken similarly to me. Enacting the vernacular ideal, they think of themselves as enduring amid decline. When I met Stan Lamprey, a basketmaker in Braunton, a village in Devonshire, England, he was working alone like many American craftsmen, cutting the willows, weaving them into tight baskets, and then selling them to women who used them in shopping and gathering eggs. Stan Lamprey kept making baskets because it was his trade, the source of his pleasure and cash, but he remembered better days, when he worked in Braunton's basket factory. Then the boys did the simple tasks of gathering and preparing the materials, the manager of the factory did the noxious job of commerce, and Stan worked in a sociable place, chatting with his mates, and doing the difficult part of the work that brought him his joy.

When the materials were still local, the skills still manual, the norm in architecture, as in pottery, was not for one person to do everything, from the extraction of materials, through their preparation, to their assembly into usable forms. Work was divided by specialization. Different people filled different roles in a single process, as actors do in a drama, and technology entailed social arrangements.

After more than a decade of rambling fieldwork, during which I came to some understanding of the log buildings of the Appalachian domain, I determined to do it right. With a modest grant, I assembled a team of students — all of them, Howard Marshall, Steve Ohrn, and John Vlach, have gone on to success — and I led them in a survey of the old log buildings of Greene County in southwestern Pennsylvania. It was my best experience as an educator. We learned together in the field.

At work in Greene County, we did not, of course, come to conclusions that would support the idea, so fundamental to the capitalistic mythos, that the frontier was a place of equal opportunity. We found brick mansions as old as the log cabins. In the beginning, there were differences of wealth. The log cabin was more a sign of social class than of rugged individualism. Log buildings did not look like they were made by self-reliant souls who went into the woods with an axe, there to succeed or fail by dint of individual intelligence and industry. Highly consistent in form and technology, the buildings implied a prevalence of collective, rather than individual effort. We did not find competitive individualism at the dawn of American time, but neither did we find the perfect unity of a cultural spirit guiding the hands of the dead. What struck us was how many of the eighty-three buildings we studied could be clustered into small groups, each marked by certain conventions of practice, each signed by a particular master at work within a technological tradition.

John James had not yet published his study of Chartres Cathedral, one of the best of all books on material culture. Examining the great building through exacting measurements, James was able to attribute it, not to a single architect, but to a succession of master masons. Their names are lost, but their peculiarities of technical habit abide in the fabric. Similarly, in details that would become invisible once the building was finished, we discovered builders who had knacks and tricks, particular to them alone. They knew special ways to join sills and frame windows. James named his nameless masons for colors. We named the house carpenters of the frontier after the techniques they used to frame the plate at the top of the wall that received the thrust of the rafters.

In silent wood, the buildings remembered the developed skills of architectural specialists, and, as Warren Roberts has demonstrated, they used a big chest of tools to get the job done. The tools were too many for one man to carry into the wilderness on his back. The builders on the frontier had chopping axes to score the logs, broadaxes to hew them, and saws to make clear cuts. They had augers in different sizes for boring, wedges and froes for splitting, and they had a battery of planes to smooth the boards and edge them with decorative moldings.

A fine, trim house, the log cabin displayed professional practice in its finish and in its most difficult joints. But the rest of the building fluttered with the uncertain touch of the amateur. Though plates and doors were framed consistently and accurately, logs were hewn differently, corner-timbering varied, and there were mistakes in the notches cut to receive the joists. The building — whether a house of one room or an enormous, soaring barn — spoke clearly of a collaboration between a master of the trade and a gathering of willing amateurs. The collaboration we puzzle out of common old buildings or rare old contracts is

easy to understand in places where architecture is not yet dominated by industrial capitalism.

When Paddy McBrien wanted a new home, he went to his
neighbor, the mason Tommy Moore, and asked him to build a
house on the track of Eamon Corrigan's. Track is the word they
use in Ballymenone for plan. The shape of the building is like
the track of a cow in the mud that hardens in the sun, leaving an
exact sign of her passing. Paddy did not begin with principles,
but, like most architects, with historical precedents. Tommy, a
professional, the builder of many houses, suggested one change,
an additional door to ease the flow of internal traffic. Paddy accepted Tommy's advice, and made another change. Though it
would cost him more, he did not want his kitchen to rise inside
to the rafters, where soot and cobwebs collect, for that, the old
local norm, would make "a rum looking shop." He wanted a
neat, flat ceiling, easy to clean, above his kitchen.

Mary McBrien, Paddy's wife, also wanted her kitchen clean.
She approved of the ceiling and requested a hallway, a space to
divide the inside from the outside, where muddy wellingtons
could be left. In the community's old houses, the door — "the
hole the mason left" — broke directly into the kitchen, and it was
left open to welcome visitors, winds, chickens, and filth. Mary
McBrien wanted a separation that would, like Paddy's ceiling,
make her kitchen a tidy box. Later, Paddy and Mary would agree
that they had made an error. Mary felt her work in the kitchen
was lonesome when she could no longer glance out the window
and the open front door toward the action along the road. The
hallway proved to be a bad thing when wakes were held in the
kitchen. You had to upend the coffin and walk it along the twisted
route from the kitchen, through the hallway, and out the front
door. The body bumping inside the box was not, Paddy said, a
sound you liked to hear. But when they built, Paddy and Mary
McBrien wanted a modern house, which they designed in their
minds by making alterations to an old house that stood in view,
across the road and uphill from their own.

Paddy chose the site. It was not on a hilltop, where the old houses stood, but near the road, convenient for vehicles. Tommy and Paddy went to the site and stood in the center of the house, the spot where the hearth would be. They imagined walls around them, then staked them out. It was Paddy's job, then, to cut down trees that grew on his land along the river, to get them home, and square them to become the purlins that would carry the roof across the masonry partitions. His grandfather would have gathered stones. His father would have dug clay and shaped bricks. Paddy made a pile of molded concrete blocks, then Tommy Moore came, and with help from hired laborers and from Paddy himself, he laid the block. The team built the walls, leaving gaps where Tommy marked them. He stood away and located the openings by eye. They look symmetrical in placement, but the measurements I took reveal them to be only roughly so. To finish the job, Tommy subcontracted a carpenter to frame the windows and doors, and to make the furniture, the tables and chairs and dresser of the kitchen.

There Paddy sits, resting with a cup of tea after hard work in the fields. A fire of turf burns on the hearth. The Sacred Heart glows by the door. The house above him is solid proof of his ability to accomplish his dreams. Many minds and many hands conspired, but he was part of the process of design and construction, and now he is free to use the building as he wants. He understands the object he lives in completely, and it teaches him convincingly about the extent and limits of his power in the world. There are things he can do, things he cannot do, but from collaborative creation, he understands about both.

During architectural action, abilities are separated and combined in many ways. When the people of Karagömlek, a village in western Turkey, had collected enough cash from the sale of their carpets to build a new mosque, they hired a master. He was not a member of the community. He came, did his job, got his pay, and left. The master planned the building on the ground, orienting it correctly toward Mecca, and he did the woodwork, framing the window, the

The new mosque. Karagömlek. 1986

Mehmet Öztürk at the gate of his new mosque.
Karagömlek, Çanakkale, Turkey. 1994

door, and the roof, and making the stepped *minber* inside where the *hoca* delivers the sermon on Fridays. My friend Mehmet Öztürk and his neighbors took time away from farming; they gathered and raised the masonry walls. The money won from international commerce, from the sale of their beautiful new carpets, was used to tighten the communal bonds of those who work together at the loom and in the fields, who build together, and who worship together in their own bright white mosque.

Prospering, as an energetic merchant can on the pervious, dangerous border between Pakistan and Afghanistan, Attollah decided to make a gift to his community, a village on the outskirts of Peshawar. A new mosque would bring him prestige, while affirming his intention to belong to the community that differences in riches can disturb so easily.

Attollah hired a young master named Fazul. They drew up no plan. A need for plans seems natural to the architectural historian, but we should not be surprised when we find none. Plans drawn on paper are indications of cultural distance. The amount of detail on a plan is an exact measure of the differences that separate those who conjoin in a building project. The more minimal the plan, the more completely the architectural idea abides in the separate minds of the client and the architect. For Attollah and Fazul, a few words were enough. They both knew what mosques looked like. All Fazul needed to know was the size of the budget. Then he staked out the plan. His laborers dug up the soil, shaped it into adobe bricks, and the building went up. Attollah, pleased with the result, proud of his generosity, joins his neighbors for prayer in the cool interior of the new village mosque.

It is like that on the other side of the Indian subcontinent, when the executive committee of a Hindu temple comes to the sculptor Haripada Pal in Dhaka city. There are no plans and few words. They name a deity. They state a sum. The rest is entirely up to Haripada. He prays and crafts the clay image that is installed in the temple. There he and his patrons join with all the members of the Hindu community to receive through prayer the blessings of God. In communal action, personal differences are not suppressed. They are exploited for the common good. The patron's ability to pay connects with the artist's ability to create, and everyone in the community benefits as differences intermesh in a new unity.

In describing buildings as the creations of their occupants, writers on vernacular architecture choose a simple and concrete way to speak of unity. Design, construction, and use come to oneness in a single mind. In one mind, there is room aplenty for conflict, and the possibilities for conflict proliferate when the designer, the builder, and the user are different people. And when they are, social organization is necessary, and social organizations are apt to shape in conformity with the political orders prevalent in society.

Division in labor is normal in complex architectural technologies. Real complications bring differences among the workers and between the producers who can make things and the consumers who cannot make things. But difference coincides easily with unity when designers, builders, and users connect in culture. The idea of cultural unity is the point behind the scholarly creation of the ideal of the builder-occupant. What makes vernacular architecture is not an occupant who builds but a cultural congruity among design, construction, and use.

When different people share in culture, in basic assumptions about what is right and what is wrong, about what a building should be, when they are of like mind about things, their social arrangements can be built on a political order that is simultaneously hierarchical and collaborative. During interaction, people are assigned roles — in one moment obliged to follow, in another obliged to lead. While the walls of his house are rising, Paddy McBrien is one of the crew, a follower. But when the storm clouds gather and the hay lies on the spread, Paddy, renowned as an agricultural expert, steps into the lead. His neighbors submit to his direction and form a single force. In the fields, Paddy's neighbor Peter Flanagan, an impoverished farm laborer, is one of the hands. At night, courtly Peter Flanagan opens his fiddle case and takes command. Successful farmers and professional masons assemble into a respectful audience for his performance. On the basis of neighborly reciprocity and cooperation, they build unity out of difference.

In the beginning, there was difference. Again we can say that the industrial process is a hyperbolic extension of one feature in the old tradition, in this case its rational division of labor for efficiency in production. Again we can say that, despite continuity, there is a disruption in experience. Cultural unity — congruence in design, construction, and use — does not depend on connections made face to face. The objects of material culture are suited to long-range communication. Carried by trade over great stretches of space, now as always, objects can inspire cultural connections between people at a distance. An industrial product, designed by one person and manufactured by many laborers in a big building, can perfectly satisfy the desire of an unknown consumer. It is possible. The designer and consumer might be one in culture. But when hierarchical arrangements expand, unchecked by direct collaborative interaction, then they can harden into a politics of dominance and submission.

Then designers, divorced from consumers, plan houses that they would be unwilling to occupy themselves, and that do not fit the needs of their users. We have the disaster of public housing projects. Then managers, lacking intimate knowledge of the work that must be done, demand the impossible and arrange procedures in strict bureaucratic fashion, leaving little room for the workers to uphold their own standards, or find satisfaction in their daily labor by bringing projects to completion. We have workers who trade their lives for wages, waiting for the unfulfillment of weekends and vacations. Then consumers are reduced to choosing from a set of things, no one of which meets their needs. We have consumers with no option but to purchase commodities that bring them no real joy. As direct social connections disassemble, hierarchical political orders solidify, and malaise shapes into apathy, vague rage, and small fears in search of causes.

With industrial production, a traditional wish for separation from nature, and a traditional pattern of division in work, both extend from order to alienation. In relations between the human and nonhuman spheres, alienation brings bodily comfort. Separated clearly from nature, freed from environmental constraints, cooled when it is hot, heated when it is cold, people feel comfortable. In the relations among people, alienation hastens the pursuit of wealth. Unlimited by obligations owed to other people, no longer locked into a community built on reciprocity and collaboration, people are free to get rich. In the change to alienation, the gain is comfort for many, great wealth for a few.

The loss is more difficult to tally. We have to strain to see the reality of the alternative through curtains of rhetoric, some dropped by the nostalgic, more by the apologists for capitalism.

The old life was simple, we are told. Absurd. Life was anything but simple when people in small groups, interrupted by storms and epidemics and marching armies, managed to raise their own food, make their own clothing, and build their own shelter, while creating their own music, literature, art, science, and philosophy.

It is less fatuous to speak of homegeneity. When I ask people in Turkish villages how they organize work at the loom or in the fields, how they control the flow of water, how they collect to build their own mosques, they answer that they have *birlik,* unity. But their unity is an ideology designed to embrace multiplicity. From living with them, I know they are not homogeneous, if homogeneous means lacking in individuality. Everywhere I go, I find the same range of personality. In the agricultural communities of the mountains of Turkey, the hills of Ireland, or the delta of Bengal, the people are as diverse in psychological makeup, as various in private opinion, as my colleagues in the university. What they have, that my colleagues have in only a diminished version, is a theory of unity. That theory, held in separate minds, draws people into constant engagement.

Engagement — a fit contrast to alienation — puts us on the track. The great poet W. B. Yeats was close when he said that country people, living hard up against life, have their minds ground sharp. Wisdom is too strong a word, but living in connection, engaged on the one hand with nature, engaged on the other with the neighbors, people know what they know. Their knowledge does not bob on the surface. It sinks and melts into the wholeness of their experience. They might be ignorant about distant matters, but they know who they are. Identity is not a hot topic among them.

Finding the rhythm of the universe during common work, they have learned how to make the land yield fuel and food, fibers to spin, and straw to cover the roof. At work with others, they have created their landscape of trim hedges, neat fields, and white houses on the hilltop. They have built the world they inhabit. In action, in engagement, they have learned from the environment about nature, and from the neighbors about human nature. They have learned what is possible and what is not, and they know they are capable. They know how to set priorities and act decisively. I am talking about the people called peasants. They know how, as individuals, they fit in the world. That knowing leads them to wisdom about as often as freedom leads people to great riches in another place. What they do not have is comfort and wealth. What they do have is confidence.

In Ballymenone, they speak of confidence in terms of faith and trust. You know the local environment, and you have faith that God will provide. He does. Hugh Nolan said he remembered no year so bad that the farmers, working diligently, failed to make their crop, the source of their food and cash. In this place, even in the time of the Famine, in the bad old days of greedy landlords, the people endured. They found wild herbs on the mountainside, fish in the river. Faith and trust. You can trust people to act properly when they come through the open door

Paddy McBrien's house. Ballymenone. 1972

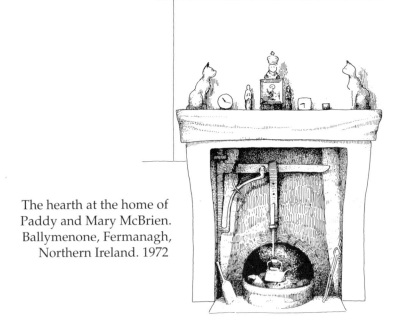

The hearth at the home of
Paddy and Mary McBrien.
Ballymenone, Fermanagh,
Northern Ireland. 1972

of your home. You can trust them to help in times of need. With you, they hold to a neighborly ethic, realized in little acts of reciprocity and cooperation, and founded upon our Lord's commandment to love your neighbor as yourself. In fact, they do not even like one another as particular individuals in particular moments. Differences of personality beget a plenitude of insults, fistfights, and lawsuits. Love is a sacred ideology, the foundation of the social system of trust. In bad times, when troubles strike, the neighbors assemble, someone takes the lead, and the crop is saved, the burned house is rebuilt, the lonely old man is fed.

Paddy McBrien sits in his house. He is a man of power. He knows exactly how his house was planned and built. It protects him adequately from the weather and provides a warm stage for social play. The neighbors round about know exactly who Paddy is. If he falls, they will lift him.

Secure in faith and trust, engaged with the environment, engaged with the neighbors, restricted in freedom, people are confident. They are not very comfortable, they are not rich at all. But they are not bent by the breeze of every fashion, disoriented by every change, frightened by every little noise. They are not lost in quiet desperation with only commodities to use in the struggle to construct a self.

Composition

We began with walls. It would have been as logical to start at the hearth. But I thought of the endless expanse of space, divided it with walls, and then wrote about what it takes to build them, how natural resources are processed and labor is organized. Had I begun at the hearth, where natural resources are transformed by fire into food, I would have made a beginning at the sociable center of life. Then imagining walls around us, just as Paddy McBrien and Tommy Moore did when they stood in the grass and planned Paddy's house, I would have concentrated, not on the walls themselves, on the materials of their building, but on the way they create divisions. Having two sides, walls work to include and exclude. Simultaneously, they make interiors and exteriors.

Architecture divides space for differential experience. It provides an exterior to see and an interior to use. One problem the designer must solve is how to make the exterior and the interior fit together in a composition.

Though they mix in many buildings, there are two distinct approaches to composing a relation between the interior and the exterior. In one, a geometric figure provides a base for a unified envelope. Internal subdivisions, the conventions of use within, do not register on the exterior. The tipi of the Great Plains and the yurt of Central Asia are circular on plan, one shaped as a cone, the other as a hemisphere. Their geometric exteriors cover, rather than expose, the actions patterned internally around a central fire. In another approach to design, the exterior is the consequence of the life inside.

Standing in the gap between the medieval and the modern, the Wealden house of southern England displays its internal arrangements to a viewer from afar. Where there is a second story, it jetties forward, making its presence known. Windows, different in size and glazing, separate the rooms where people sit from the storerooms where agricultural wealth is kept. From the relation between the offset entry and the lofty hall in the middle, visitors are able to predict accurately the route they will travel from the wet, windy world to the warm place of rest and social exchange. The Wealden house stood as a proud monument to prosperity, and yet it remained generously accessible. It fit its transitional moment in history by belonging at once to the family and the community.

Looking ahead in time from the Wealden house, we will watch the jetties retract into smooth walls. The windows will settle on a single size and space themselves evenly. The door will shift to dead center. The new English house will become a geometric

Wealden house of the fifteenth century.
Weald and Downland Museum. Singleton, Sussex. 1979

Early modern house.
Cressing, Essex, England. 1973

St. Andrew's.
Nether Wallop,
Hampshire,
England.
1972

Illtyd and Rhidian.
Llanrhidian,
Glamorgan,
Wales. 1972

Rood screen. Holy Trinity.
Long Sutton, Somerset, England. 1978

unit that hides its internal operations. Pride will continue, but acts of entry will be interrupted. Visitors will no longer know where they will go or what they will find, once the door is opened and they are ushered along a passage through partitions.

Looking backward, we can see that the Wealden house was designed on the model of the parish church. Stepping down from the tower on the west, to the commodious nave, to the lower chancel on the east, the parish church assembled forms around uses. Its internal volumes expanded to shape its external appearance. The walls enclosed liturgical action. A door on the side, offset toward the rear of the nave and announced by a porch, tells you that you will enter, turn, and then proceed toward the rood screen that divides the nave from the sacred place of the priest. In like manner, you enter the Wealden house, turn, then walk toward the warm place of the master, the priest of the hearth. Behind him, a wall separates the hall where you are welcome from the private apartments reserved for the family. The Wealden house borrows authority from the church. Like the church, it builds form out of use, inviting people in, channeling their motion, then blocking them with a wall that breaks the interior into accessible and inaccessible domains.

Where space breaks internally, the community comes to oneness. In their church, the people assemble before the rood screen, taking communion, drinking the wine that is the blood, eating the wafer that is the flesh, creating among themselves the mystic body of the church. In the house, at exactly the same point in the plan, people sit together, drinking and eating, forming friendships and ratifying the sacred order of their community.

We call buildings like the Wealden house vernacular to give them distance, to prevent ourselves from casually using our own cultural assumptions during interpretations of buildings created by other people. In the study of vernacular architecture, one assumption we must dispense with is the familiar dichotomy of the public and private. Modern law makes clear distinctions between the public and the private, between kinds of real estate that individuals can and cannot alienate by sale, between places of access and places of trespass. People in rural communities construct a realm of rights between the public and the private. They shape a middle zone on the landscape where members of the community have rights of way and permission to exploit collective resources, picking windfalls in the forest, grazing herds on the commons. An understanding of architecture requires, at least, a recognition of the central realm of communal space, lying between private space and public. The nave of the parish church and the hall of the Wealden house were not precisely public or private. They were communal. Open to the community, they were not like the highway that was open to everyone, nor were they like the chancel of the church or the bedroom of the house that were open to only a select few.

The scene can be imagined: men and women, different in station, coming and going, mingling freely in the big smoky hall. In the grand old ballads, the hall was a place for feasts and murders. But exactly how the Wealden house was used is a matter, at last, of conjecture. There is no need to guess about the houses of Ballymenone.

Ballymenone's most common house is not common in Ireland. It is historically akin to the Wealden house, the result of English settlement after the failure of the rebellion of Ulster's chiefs at the end of the sixteenth century. The Wealden house and the old house of Ballymenone are similar in form. Both are centered by an open space rising to the rafters. A hall in England, it is called a kitchen in Ireland. Ballymenone's kitchen is flanked by rooms, a parlor on one side, a bedroom and a pantry on the other. These rooms are private spaces, closed during the day, and entered only by invitation. But the offset front door is open to everyone who walks across the fields. It is bad manners to knock, worse manners to stop guests at the door. They enter, walk across the kitchen floor, and sit down by the fire, receiving hot tea and joining conversations that were going before they came, that will continue after they have gone. The space flowing from the hearth

Peter Flanagan's house.
Ballymenone, County Fermanagh, Northern Ireland. 1973

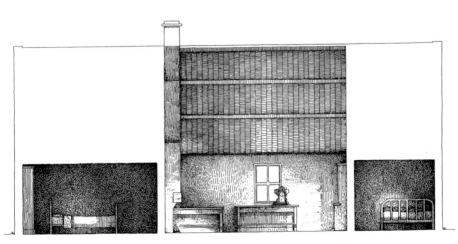

Longitudinal section of Peter Flanagan's house.

and through the front door, running from fire to fire on the hill-sides, expanding through the fields and down to the bog where people have the right to cut turf for fuel and raise vegetables — all that space is not private. People cross it and use it within customary limitations. It is not private, nor is it public. Public space is restricted to the narrow tracks of the roads that cut through the countryside, carrying people who do not know the local etiquette and who, therefore, cannot enter communal space properly.

Communal space opens between the public and the private. As in the cognate houses of Ballymenone, as in the church of the parish, space in the Wealden house probably did not divide into public and private at the front door. The house, instead, divided the communal from the private at the wall beyond the high hall.

Not until houses became geometric units did private space and domestic space become coterminous. Even then the discrimination is not fine enough. The partitioned interior of the geometric unit contained working spaces to the rear that were entered casually, convivial spaces to the front that were entered formally, and procreational spaces that visitors entered at the risk of their lives. Access was different to the kitchen, the parlor, and the bedroom. Unifying those spaces with the name private thwarts rather than advances architectural analysis. In the house of my boyhood and in the house where I live today, the neighbors come through the back door and into the kitchen without knocking. People I do not know come to the front door and wait. If they get in, they go where I take them, probably to the kitchen. The bedrooms are for the family. The exception is my daughter's room, which, being her house, often fills with her friends, who burn incense and listen to old-time rock and roll. This is to speak only of the house. Around it run outer rings, porches and yards, that segment space still more. The simple duality of private and public suffices for lawyers, but it is not complex enough or subtle enough to organize architectural study. The public and the private lie at the opposite ends of a wide spectrum of distinct spatial experiences.

Displaying its interior upon its exterior, the old Wealden house extended a communal welcome, and then divided space internally. It was like the parish church, and it differed from later houses in the way that the parish church, a building for the community, differed in its day from the great cathedral. A truly public building, the cathedral presented an imposing, geometrically composed facade. Like the human face, the facade was bilaterally symmetrical. The unity of two parts was also tripartite: like the triumphal arches of Rome, a tall door was flanked by lower doors, all offering points of beginning for motion toward the triumph over death represented by the cross.

In England's domestic architecture, the aim of composition shifted. The old house had no facade. Its exterior was the consequence of its interior. Its interior was the result of patterns of use. Patterns of use brought communal and familial orders into interaction. The new house was simpler. It had a facade. A regular arrangement of regular openings, the facade obstructed entry, obliterating communal space in a wall that divided public space from an assembly of domestic places. To the public, the new house offered, like the cathedral, a mask of grandeur, figured in bilateral symmetry.

England's change in domestic architecture, accomplished between the sixteenth and eighteenth centuries, was a shift from organic design, in which the exterior is the skin of the inside, to geometric design, in which the outside masks the interior behind a facade. The facade, a smooth surface punctured by repetitive openings, displays the aesthetic of artificiality. Like an industrial product, it hides rather than exposing the processes that lie behind it. But the geometric facade came long before industrialization, just as geometrically contrived building materials did. These smooth, repetitive things — the symmetrical facade, the squared timber and the squared brick — manifest the desire for order that drove the development of industrial procedures.

Walls separate insides from outsides. Buildings link insides with outsides. One linkage is created through the massing of

Ellen Cutler. Ballymenone. 1976

volumes, perhaps organically, perhaps geometrically, and often in a combination of these approaches to composition. Another connection is made through ornament.

Architectural Decoration

Ornament creates an exciting tension within architectural experience when the inside and outside are treated differently. Ellen Cutler whitewashes the exterior of her house in Ballymenone. The whitewash confirms the unity of the building and separates it cleanly from its natural surround of muddy lanes and grassy fields. On its exterior, her house is solid and singular, artful in its massing and its unrelieved whiteness. Step over the threshold. The brightness of the whitewash continues in the buffed and polished surfaces of the things she calls ornaments: the brass candlesticks and enameled dogs on the mantel, the pictures and plates on the walls. But similarities are swept away by differences. The hard, plain unity of the exterior yields to the softness of textiles, to a busy, glittery dance of little things, to a rainbow of color and a happy cacophony of pattern.

The walls of her kitchen darken from smoke nearly as often as the walls outside darken in the wet weather. Nearly as often as she whitewashes the exterior, she papers the kitchen, covering its walls with running, repetitive patterns of medallions. Mud tracked in by the damned old men, when they come from the fields for their tea, causes her to scrub the floor every day. So it will shine, she covers the floor with a smooth sheet of linoleum that brings another pattern to her kitchen. And more patterns come on the strips of cloth that cover the tables, curtain the openings, and run along the shelves of the mantel and dresser.

Mrs. Cutler painted the fireplace green with big red dots, like the berries on the holly at Christmas. On the dresser, built into the wall across from the hearth, she arranges plates so they will sparkle or glimmer or glow with the mood of the fire. She calls the dresser's plates "delph." Her plates were manufactured in

Ellen Cutler's dresser.
Ballymenone.
1977

Ellen Cutler's house.
Ballymenone, Fermanagh, Northern Ireland. 1972

England and Ireland, but her name recalls the city in Holland where beautiful blue-and-white plates were made in the seventeenth and eighteenth centuries, and then exported to England and England's colonies to be put on domestic display. Ellen Cutler defines delph as "not for using." The plates for the day's meals are hidden out of sight. The ones displayed on the dresser are washed often and lovingly. It makes her, she says, "happy as money" to wash them, bathing them like babies in a basin, and setting them up in neat gleaming rows on the shelves of her dresser.

Each of the plates on the dresser was a gift from a neighbor, a friend, a member of her family. Like friendships, plates last forever with care and break in one careless moment. Plates make apt gifts, and assembled on her dresser, her plates are her friends. Her social network could be accurately reconstructed from a list of the people who gave her the plates that she loves enough to display on the dresser and wash once a week.

Smoke from the hearth swiftly films the plates with dullness. Always gleaming and clean, the delph of her dresser is the art exhibit of a "house-proud" woman. Luminosity is the primary intent of her aesthetic, and her plates shine in bright counterpoint to the necessary mess of a workaday farmhouse. The plates reflect light through her kitchen, and they add to its lively mix of color and pattern. White and green and cobalt blue, the plates carry transfer-printed pictures. Like the plates displayed on the walls of a Turkish home, the plates on Ellen Cutler's dresser were inspired by Chinese porcelain. Things to see, not things to use in eating, they carry, like Turkish plates, pictures of things not eaten. They do not show wheat and sheep, but flowers and birds, the lovely ornaments of nature that Mrs. Cutler calls God's messengers.

The difference between the outside and inside is as sharp in the home of İsmail and Narin Yıldız in the magnificent village of Gökyurt in central Anatolia. The exterior is a massive expanse of stone, pierced by small windows. A large door swings to admit you to the runway through the middle of the house, a frank place for agricultural work. At Mrs. Cutler's, the cattle live in a byre built onto the end of the house. Here the cattle live on the floor below. On this, the top level of the Yıldız home, useful pots and baskets are lined into neat rows, and small doors open through the thick walls. You step out of your shoes, over the threshold, and into the interior. The floor spreads with soft, piled carpets, rich in color and pattern. Cloth in bright floral patterns covers the soft cushions on the floor and on the inbuilt seats along the walls. A shelf carries tinned copper bowls and enameled plates around the room near the ceiling. Like the delph on Ellen Cutler's dresser, the silvery vessels, a row of little moons, receive and transmit the light from the fire dancing on the hearth.

In Mrs. Cutler's lovely whitewashed and thatched house, one framed picture on the wall shows a lovely whitewashed and thatched house. Stretched in another frame, a piece of cloth is embroidered "Lead Me and Guide Me." In the Yıldız home, the framed pictures bear glittery calligraphed inscriptions of Koranic texts. The only book in Mrs. Cutler's kitchen, her Bible, rests on the windowsill. The only book in the Yıldız home, the Holy Koran, hangs in an embroidered bag on a wall by the fireplace. In both houses, pots full of flowers stand in the light in the windows, welcoming natural beauty to the interior.

What is true of these two houses, one in Ireland, one in Turkey, is true generally of farmhouses in Ireland and Turkey, and what is true at the western limits of Europe and Asia is true, too, of many places in North America, both rural and urban. In northern New England and the Maritime Provinces, on the farms of the Southern Mountains and the ranches of the West, among Hispanic and Native American people in the Southwest, the French in Louisiana and Quebec, African Americans in the South, and Irish Americans in the big cities of the Northeast, the house is often austere without and ornamented within, at once hard and soft, plain and fancy, restrained and expressive.

The Yıldız house.
Gökyurt.
1987

Gökyurt. Konya, Turkey. 1987

The house presents a hard, clean, undecorated exterior to see and a cozy, ornamented interior to use. In its elevation, the house unfolds from a logic of engineering and makes an appeal to the intellect. As a device for communication, the exterior unites the viewer and the occupant in rationality. Internally, the house comforts the body and delights the senses. It provides soft seats and a titillating array of textures, patterns, and colors. The weary bones find rest, the eye finds excitement. As a device for communication, unfolding from the householder's interests and taste, the interior stimulates engagement. Mrs. Cutler and Mrs. Yıldız make tea at the hearth. The tea does what the room does. It restores and pleases the guest. Ellen Cutler and Narin Yıldız serve the tea, and then sit with their guests in talk. The talk does what the tea does. It makes friendships possible.

During the study of traditions in which men are the builders of walls, students are often frustrated in the search for the contribution made to architecture by the half of society who are women. In discovering a few women who design and build — like the earnest woman William Morris put to work as a stone mason in his utopian novel *News from Nowhere* — scholars are distracted from the solution to their problem. The problem is an inadequate definition of architecture. If buildings are distinct among the things of material culture precisely because they have both interiors and exteriors, and if buildings are the creations of their creators, then the search for women in architecture should not baffle us.

Divisions in labor are apt to clarify in line with other divisions made in society. Architectural practice is split by gender as well as by class and age and political power. There are traditions in which women do the building. Women dominated architecture in central North America before the European conquest. Africa offers numerous instances of women who build and of women and men who build together. But in many places, men build the house and women build the home within it.

The problem, as I said, lies in the definition. The prevalence of men in the record indicates that architecture has been reduced to a matter of building the walls and arranging the look of the elevation. The exterior is crucial to the serious work of sheltering people from the climate and proposing an image of civil order. The interior is crucial to the serious work of raising families and building communities through intimate exchange. The lack of interest in interiors is part of an art-historical orientation to architecture as a sort of sculpture that can be adequately represented by slides of elevations projected in dark classrooms. Teaching becomes easy and contributes to a gross simplification of the architectural reality. The house is reduced to a shelter and a sign of status and public order that can be accommodated easily by histories that serve economic and political interests. If the intimate ordering of common life mattered in history as much as it does in reality, then the interior would matter, families would matter, communities would matter, and women would be in the story. Architecture would be defined correctly, and buildings would assume the powerful role they deserve in history.

One real problem cannot be avoided. Houses are enclosures for domestic environments. When men build the walls and women arrange the space within, what men create is likely to outlast what women create. The textiles spread on the floor and the crockery arrayed on the dresser are easily swept away by time. When Dick Cutler moved his family into Ellen Cutler's house after her death, her dresser of delph displayed to him, as it had to her, communal connections and an old-fashioned taste. The difference was that he hated what she loved. He took an axe, smashed the china to bits, and threw it out in the street. James Deetz has discovered the residue of such violence in archaeological sites in North America and South Africa. But potsherds cannot be reassembled into an understanding as rich as the one Mrs. Cutler gave me when we sat at her hearth and chatted. The walls of her house survive. But her interior has been replaced by another. It is gone.

After the people are gone, and the old house stands empty, stripped of its possessions, it offers better information about its male creators than it does about its female creators. Maybe the name of a woman as well as a man can be teased out of the documents, but her contribution is more transient than his. The solution is to switch from archaeology to ethnography, leaving the empty Wealden house and entering the house of Ballymenone, stepping through the doorway, turning past the dresser of delph, and coming to the glowing hearth where women and men collaborate in hospitality.

Ethnographic study builds in our understanding a sturdy alternative to familiar experience. It ought to enhance our capacity for historical guesswork. Surely, it will lead us to a more comprehensive definition of architecture. That definition will, at the least, alert us to what we cannot know when all we have to study is an empty house in ruins.

We are luckier in the study of old buildings when the ornamental urge of the interior fuses permanently in architectural fabric and spills through the openings to appear on the exterior. Ornament can turn the building inside-out by making the facade into an exhibition of painting and sculpture, as it does in the houses of Nubia and the temples of South India. Much more frequently, external ornament is restrained by the Ruskinian ideal. It reinforces the massing, and provides a foretaste of the delights inside, by clustering at the entry, running around the windows, and marking the edges of the form, its conjunctions of different planes.

When the building's exterior exhibits two aesthetics, one of massing and one of ornament, it speaks at once of two needs. Those needs cut different tracks through time, doubling the building's utility as historical evidence. In its basic massing of tower, nave, and chancel, the English parish church remained stable for centuries. At the same time, the shapes of doors and windows, and the types of ornament that ran along the eaves, climbed the tower, and filled the interior, changed frequently and quickly in harmony with international ecclesiastical fashion.

The form of the parish church remained stable because it was designed to meet the needs of people at worship, and those needs did not change. The congregation needed to connect to God and to one another. The form of the church was right for the work. Details did change because people wanted the church of their parish to symbolize their collective success. They banked extra wealth into a communal building that marked their progress. The church changed to fulfill their need for pride. In meeting two needs at once — building and symbolizing community — their church simultaneously displayed patterns of continuity and patterns of change.

Complexity in Architectural Time

Temporal mixing characterizes the buildings called vernacular. The English parish church, a world wonder of architectural creativity, carries the vernacular idea deeply into time. If vernacular buildings tick with many clocks, changing different components at different rates to display continuity and change at once, then they contrast with buildings that belong perfectly to one moment in time. Nonvernacular buildings are wholly original, new in every detail. Here we have come prematurely to an important conclusion. No building is entirely new. If it were, it would be utterly incomprehensible. Rejecting every old convention, lacking windows and doors, serving no function of shelter or social division, the thing might be sculpture, but it would not be a building. No matter how grandiose or revolutionary the creation, there must be some tradition, some presence of the common and continuous — of the qualities called folk — or people would not be able to understand it or use it. In their mixing of the old and the new, all buildings are vernacular, the products of real people in real situations. But within practice, attitudes differ.

In the nineteenth century, American designers created houses that were intended to be different from the common run — dif-

ferent and better. The designers offered their plans through publications to people who wanted houses that would signal their
estate and separate them from their neighbors. The house was
new, but look at its plan, and you will find that the designer did
exactly what Paddy and Mary McBrien did when they wanted a
new house. He took an old house and remodeled it, adding or
subtracting doors and partitions.

It will come as a surprise to you, but there are still historians
who think society is layered like a cake, with a few leaders at the
top and many followers below. They make the job of history easy
by treating the written record as the wellspring of ideas that
trickle down to the masses. But, with regard to architectural form
and order, the nineteenth-century publication was not a source
for novelty so much as it was a mechanism for recycling. It was
a new cog in the ongoing apparatus of vernacular design. The
new plan in the new book would not have seemed wholly alien
to the builder and his client because it was adapted out of the
cultural experience they shared with the designer. The plan they
found in print, then, was easy to modify, normally by simplify-
ing it in the direction of houses they already knew — houses like
those from which the designer lifted his inspiration. Repeatedly,
nineteenth-century books offered tricky versions of eighteenth-
century plans. The builder's source might be the book, but the
book's source was the builder's old tradition.

In most localities in the United States, we find a few nineteenth-century houses built right out of the book by insecure rich
people who chose to align themselves with unknown others. In
the same places, we find many nineteenth-century houses that
combined new ideas out of books with old ideas from the vicinity. At once fashionable and familiar, those houses conspicuously
mixed change with continuity.

The Yankee builder was not daunted by the arrival of a novel
form in the earlier nineteenth century. The new Greek Revival
house was a little temple with a portico; it positioned a gabled

Greek Revival house.
Sullivan County,
New York.
1968

Greek Revival house:
the single-wing form.
Otsego County,
New York.
1965

Late, western version of the single-wing house.
Madison, Wisconsin. 1992

Northern Greek Revival: side-hall, temple-form house with wings.
Otsego County, New York. 1968

Southern Greek Revival: I-house with a portico.
Sevier County, Tennessee. 1975

block symmetrically between flanking wings. The Yankee builder had two basic arrangements at hand. One of them went back to the seventeenth century in New England, then on to the sixteenth century in southeastern England. It raised a chimney between a hall and a parlor, and placed a kitchen centrally within a run of rooms across the rear. The other, belonging to the eighteenth century, provided a corridor for circulation among the rooms, and set the kitchen in a back wing. The Yankee builder used both of these ideas to make something like a Greek Revival house. In the gabled block, he set the hall and parlor in a line, often running a corridor along the side. Then dispensing with one of the flanking wings as frivolous, he moved the kitchen into the other, increased its size, and gave it a door to the front, so that old friends could come on in. The ornamental door in the main gabled block was for formal entry, and the farther the house moved west, the more likely the builder was to skip it altogether. The Yankee builder's house looked enough like the new house, and it acted enough like the old houses.

The Southern builder did it more easily. He took an eighteenth-century house with rooms on either side of a hallway, then added a gabled portico, a false front of fashion, behind which the house remained unchanged in form and use. Southern builders, like Northern builders, were knotted into the national network of communication that brought them new ideas through publications. But they reacted differently. The difference in the Northern and Southern response reveals a difference in culture that was hardening toward war in the period of the Greek Revival, the 1830s and 1840s. The Southern builder held the national fashion on the porch, like an unwelcome guest. The Northern builder invited it in, reshaping his whole house to suit the times, while preserving the intimate arrangement of space that the people of his place knew how to use.

Nineteenth-century builders merged the old and the new in their houses. The plans in the books that inspired them did quite the same thing. They blended the old and the new. A purer novelty lay in the book's ornamental details. Disconnected from direct use, ancillary to the building's internal functioning, decorative details were easy to change. Symbolizing pride in the nineteenth-century house, as in the medieval church, they accomplished their social work by newness. Still, the designer tended to place the ornaments on the houses in his book in accord with traditional practice. They gathered at the openings and ran along the edges of the form, just as in the Middle Ages. The builder borrowed easily from the book, taking new details and popping them into the old spots. It was enough for his house to seem Italianate — up to date in the decades after the Civil War — if he tucked a row of brackets under the eaves and rounded the tops of the windows. A lower pitch to the roof would cap it off correctly. The house was fashionable, new in its detail, but its form was most likely an Italianate revision of the Greek Revival modification of the Georgian house of the eighteenth century.

Since decorative details alone could signify fashion, and since they fit into the composition at conventional points, around openings and along edges, it was not hard for builders to create houses that were fashionable and familiar at once. Old forms were gussied up with flashy ornaments. The nineteenth-century builder's creations tell, then, a simple story, comparable to that of the parish church. It is a story of social continuity and stylish change. The plan held steady while ornaments came and went, and the building displays a hierarchy of value that usefully challenges the simple, progressive narrative of the historian. The building says clearly that social interaction matters more than shifts in fashion, that local orders matter more than national orders. It says that what continues matters more than what changes. A history that tells only a tale of change misses the most important part of history. Its story is trivial.

The hierarchy of value in the English parish church, where the continuity of sacred action was more important than the changes that signaled worldly pride, sets a clear pattern. The pattern, though simple and schematic, captures the reality in America well enough for many regions. But it misses the excitement in the North.

The book was part of the system of vernacular design, and the book was part of the system of industrial capitalism. The plan in the book made architecture into a commodity. Some people simply bought what they were sold, building as they were told. Others bought selectively, choosing bits to arrange into proof of their awareness of fashion. And many played with their new commodities, ordering and reordering them willfully to suit themselves. The Northern landscape is peppered with extravagant confections, but the clearest sign of the new spirit — of the builders' victory over their cultural conditions — lies in the blatant mixing of decorative styles.

The builders' innovative creations are ignored by critics who should be thrilled by their creativity, but who continue to fixate on the rare big house built lazily out of the book, proving that it is not creativity but class prejudice that focuses their study. The builders' creations madden the modern observer charged with the task of classifying buildings by style. Those dead people are supposed to move obediently from Greek to Gothic to Italianate, then on to Queen Anne. What they did, instead, was to bundle influences into a single decorative style for which the best name is the nonspecialist's label of Victorian. They took doorways from the Greek Revival, jigsawed trim and pointy gables from the Gothic, brackets from the Italianate, and combined them into a new vocabulary of ornament that they applied in the traditional manner to buildings that broke all the rules, departed from the national sequence, and stood as meaningful symbols of pride in their localities.

Especially after the Civil War in the Deep South and in the westering reach of the North, the builders did not comply. They engaged in exhilarated play with commodities. In their willingness to pick and choose and make ungainly combinations, they

Gothic gable and Greek Revival doorway.
Wintersport, Maine. 1978

displayed a spirit we claim for ourselves, thinking of it as so peculiar to these late days that we call it postmodern. In fact, that spirit has been with us since the parish churches of the Middle Ages that are marvelous precisely because of their impurity, their energetic accumulations and assemblies. The difference is that the builder in medieval England or Victorian America played with commodities on the surface of a deep and abiding order. Postmodern play takes place in the air above nothing.

Compositional Levels

Now the walls belong to a composition. Acts of composition bring interiors and exteriors together, massing and ornamenting buildings into units that contain diversity. Then composition expands, and meanings complicate, as buildings are set in relation, one to the other in space. While building walls, people perform on a complex field of influence, balancing the natural and the cultural. By weighing the influences of the natural environment against social and economic influences, we will have a way to begin a consideration of the expansive orders of composition.

It is hot on the vast, flat delta of Bengal, so hot that the climate must figure powerfully in architectural planning. At home in the village, cooking takes place outdoors in fair weather. The heat of the fire disperses, and the woman at work gains a touch of relief from the winds that find their way from the river. It is tropically hot, and it is wet. Rain is an insufficient name for the downpours of summer. In the rainy season, the fire for cooking is moved beneath a roof that is pitched steeply to shed the water. The roof is held aloft by impaled posts. Between the posts, bamboo screens make frail walls. Coolness comes in, the heat of the fire escapes.

A source of heat as well as sustenance, the kitchen stands away from the other buildings that comprise the home. Normally the family is a joint one, made up of brothers, their wives and children, and the old father and mother, should they linger in

Kazipara.
Rupshi, Rupganj,
Bangladesh.
1995

Gillande.
Manikganj. 1987

Norpara. Shimulia, Bangladesh. 1996

life. The members of the joint family pool their resources of labor and capital for the common good. The wife of one of the brothers is detailed for kitchen duty, freeing the others for agricultural work.

Each nuclear unit has its own separate building. Like the kitchen, it is entered directly; opening the door brings fresh air to the people inside. Unlike the kitchen, it is often partitioned. It is a private place for sleeping and the keeping of goods. Visiting, like cooking, takes place outside, in the shade beneath the trees. In wet weather, people shift for talk to the verandas that cross the fronts of the buildings.

Every village exhibits a mix of architectural technologies. The walls might be raised of layers of clay or blocks of clay that make a cave of coolness inside. They might be built of impaled posts and bamboo screens that admit stirrings of air. Clay walls melt and bamboo walls break away in the floods that lift slowly over the flat terrain. Walls go, the place remains, and people rebuild on the old site, not every year, if it is the will of God, but once or twice in a lifetime. Fragile constructions employing local materials seem adaptive in the environment, but the people want freedom from conditions. Sturdy brick walls are what they would have if they could afford them, and gathering a little money, they work for permanence. They replace wooden posts with squared concrete beams, sunken in the soil to carry the light walls that are framed on the ground and then raised. Increasingly, the walls and roof are covered with the sheets of corrugated iron that people call tin.

But local materials — clay and wood and thatch — are still the norm. One neighbor builds thick clay walls, another lives behind flimsy screens of twill-woven bamboo. The simultaneity of different techniques shows that no one of them is truly suitable; the climate is extreme.

The unity of planning shows that this is the best that can be done. Whether the family is rich or poor, whether the buildings are large or small, built of bamboo and thatch or concrete and iron, they stand independently. There is a kitchen, there are bedrooms for every couple, and each one is a building with its own walls. The house — the *bari* — is a cluster of houses, open to the sky. Each building is raised above the flood on its own earthen plinth. All are protected from the sun by the trees that grow around them. Every building stands alone to receive every blessing of breeze.

The village home of Bangladesh meets the family's needs for connection and separation, while modifying as well as it can the natural conditions of heat and damp.

For contrast, come to Dalarna in central Sweden, where it is cold and the snow drifts in heaps. The fire for cooking is tucked in a corner. An open hearth in the past, a stove today, it sends heat toward the table where people sit to eat in the opposite corner. Cozy, curtained beds run in a snug row along the back wall, warmed by the fire. Step out of the room, and you are not outside as you would be in Bangladesh. You stand in a chilly lobby. Closing the door behind you, before opening the door to the exterior, you prevent cold air from getting into the house.

The old Swedish house is a unit, compressed around sources of heat. The walls are built of logs, trimmed to ride tightly one upon the other. There are no chinks for winds to sneak through as there are in the log houses of the United States. The walls are solid wood, a fine insulation, and they are thick and airtight. The mass of the building is unified by paint, and it is centered by a narrow, gabled porch. Though Dalarna is famed in the annals of folk art for the vivid decoration of the interior, the porch carries the only decorative detail applied to the exterior. The porch calls attention to the door and provides protection from the weather while the door is opened. Inside in the lobby, there is a choice of three doors: the door on one side leading to a parlor, the door in the middle leading to a bedroom, the door on the other side leading to the room for daily life, where food is cooked and consumed, where people gather for talk by day and sleep at

Tibble.
Leksand. 1991

Tibble.
Leksand, Dalarna,
Sweden. 1989

Fräsgården. Leksboda, Dalarna, Sweden. 1989

night. All of these rooms have fireplaces that together build heat in the middle of the house.

Within its straight, heavy timber walls, the house of Dalarna gathers the kitchen together with different places for sleeping and with formal and informal locations for socializing. Under one roof, it assembles activities that are scattered in the village home of Bangladesh. In both places, the houses exhibit the knowledge that people develop during lives of environmental engagement. Adjusting intelligently to different conditions, the farming people of Bangladesh and central Sweden create houses that exemplify distinctly different formal arrangements — one of dispersal, the other of compression.

Things tend to fly apart or collapse. During composition, the designer must reconcile the contrary pulls of centrifugal and centripetal forces, accommodating both at once in plans that are liable to move in one direction or the other: toward dispersal or toward compression. At the domestic level, where cooking and eating, sleeping and entertaining combine, the designers of Bengal choose dispersal, while the designers of Dalarna choose compression. Environmental understanding is crucial to their decisions. Let us shift now to the next level of complexity in composition, where domestic work connects with work of other kinds.

In Bangladesh, the buildings that are the bedrooms and kitchen of the family stand among others. There are agricultural buildings, sheds to store produce and shelter cattle, and when the village has a craft specialty, there is a workshop for weavers or potters, carpenters or smiths. Screens and verandas make connections, and the buildings shape into a neat square around an open courtyard, with the houses for sleeping in a line along the rear. The shop to the front provides one entry. An offbeat opening at a corner provides another route to the courtyard where work goes on, where food is cooked and pots are made.

Returning to Dalarna, we expect compression and get a little, for the agricultural buildings often run together, but the situation is more similar than different. The house makes one side of a square, the back side as in Bangladesh, and, as in Bangladesh, all doors open into the courtyard. Entry is made through a barn in front or through a gateway on the side.

At this more expansive level of design, planners in Bengal and Dalarna perform similarly. They build the house as part of a larger compositional unit that forms a square around a courtyard. It is not that they have forgotten about the climate. That would be impossible. But arranging buildings primarily for efficiency in work, and not separating domestic work from agricultural and industrial work, they create a courtyard that facilitates circulation among all the buildings. In doing so, they choose a plan that is tight enough for the Swedish farmer, who must work through the cold and snow, and loose enough for the Bengali farmer, who must work through the heat and rain. Their plan, by establishing order through the geometric figure of the square, asserts an ascendancy of the rational over the natural. And their plan, at once open and closed, locates a midpoint between the extremes of compression and dispersal.

The world of architecture contains examples aplenty of more compressed designs. On the pastoral highlands of the British Isles, notably in Devon and Wales, the separate steading was centered by a longhouse. Retreating from the wide, wild world around it, the longhouse was an agricultural fortress, housing the stock at one end and the people at the other, beneath a single roof. Writers from the seventeenth century allow us to picture the Irish house of those days. It was a thatched longhouse, framed of crucks, with walls of mud or wattle and daub. The interior was one space, narrow, lengthy, and unpartitioned, with a fire in the middle, a place at one end for the people, at the other end for the cows. In Ballymenone, the little piece of Ireland I know, the old house, like Mrs. Cutler's, set the dwelling, the stable for the horses, and the byre for the cows, in one long range. But there was no internal communication from one part to the other. Solid

In this longhouse, an instance of compressed design, the people live to the left, the cattle to the right of the chimney, under one roof. Dartmoor, Devonshire, England. 1972

Dispersal begins when the house separates from the working buildings. St. Hilary, Glamorgan, Wales. 1972

walls separated the house from the agricultural buildings attached to its ends. Modernizing farmers have torn the agricultural buildings down and rebuilt them. They preserve the old axial arrangement but increase the separation between the domestic and the agricultural by opening space between the buildings. The change in time, in Ireland as well as in Scotland, England, and Wales, leads away from compression and toward dispersal. The climate did not change.

For an example of a truly dispersed plan, the farm of the southern Midwest in the United States will do. Fences separate and enclose the farm as a whole. From the main road, a long lane leads to the buildings. A fence follows the lane and divides the farmstead into two separate spheres. One is centered upon the house, the other on the barn. The framed house is painted glossy white and ornamented modestly on the porch. Internally it offers a parlor to the front, a kitchen on the rear. Behind the house, small buildings stand in attendance upon the kitchen. The plain framed barn is weathered to gray or painted red, and around it cluster small agricultural buildings, a crib for corn, houses for poultry and hogs.

Formally in the longhouse, experientially in the open squares of Bangladesh and Sweden, domestic work mingles with agricultural work. On the Midwestern farm, kinds of work separate clearly in space and gather gendered associations. With a fence between the house and barn, the Midwestern farm displays a pattern that was developed in the countryside of Britain and North America, and then perfected during industrialization.

On the farm, domestic space, associated with a clean and comfortable life, becomes the woman's realm. The man leaves the house to the woman and goes to another place to do the work that is really work, the work that brings cash. The hunt for money brings him into the tanglement of capitalism. In Bengal, it is dramatically different. The plan unites the kitchen, the bedrooms, the shed for the cow, and the workshop. Within the open space these buildings define, one woman cooks dinner, the others join the men, fanning rice and making pots.

In planning, as in technology, the rural tradition of the West was exaggerated during industrialization. Clarifying the separation implicit in the farmstead by locating the place for work far from the place for living, industrialization bequeathed to us the stereotyped roles against which we fight with so little success.

If we shift up another level in design, from the familial to the communal, we will find the designers in Bengal and Dalarna again performing similarly. The square farmsteads pack tightly into a village, where buildings jumbled in numbers give the place a dense urban feel. Nearly continuous walls run along the lanes. Behind them, courtyards open for work, and then the lanes run out of the village, leading to a spacious countryside. There are no buildings. The fields spread wide. The family's land is parceled and scattered through the open fields. Divided but unfenced, the fields offer no hindrance to cooperation. Bits of tillage owned by neighbors interlock into a green mosaic of communal unity.

The communities of Bengal and Dalarna are both examples of the agricultural openfield village. It is the structural opposite of the dispersed landscapes of Ireland or the American Midwest. The openfield village consolidates housing and scatters the family's holdings. On the dispersed landscape, the houses are scattered and the family's holdings are consolidated in the fields that surround the dwelling.

Beyond the buildings of the village, beyond the open fields that fan around it, lie other places where members of the community exploit their customary rights. Bengalis use the river and its banks for bathing, beaching boats, and processing clay to make pottery. Swedish farmers cut timber on certain hillsides, and they have places in the high pastures where cattle are driven in the summer. Then the village builds connections beyond its communal space. Roads join the village to a market town, and more

Tibble. Leksand, Dalarna, Sweden. 1992

Kagajipara. Dhamrai, Bangladesh. 1995

roads join the town to the big city. Produce leaves along that route. Cash and goods and the world's new ideas return along it. The city needs the village — the source of its food — more than the village needs the city, but they interconnect in trade. They always have. The idea of isolation is an explanatory convenience in bad history. It dismisses village tradition as the product of ignorance, rather than recognizing it to be the product of choice, which it is.

Central to choice is the building not yet mentioned. Swedish villages connect into parishes. In the old days by communal boat, and now by private automobile, the people of different villages assemble in the parish church to hear the word of the Lord. In Bangladesh, villages are more likely to have their own mosques, but similarities continue. The villages on the delta of Bengal are separate entities, each built on a single foundation, a platform of clay raised by hand above the flood, each sheltered by a single roof, shaped by the trees that stand and branch to weave a canopy overhead. Then the villages straggle together on their mounds, as Swedish villages do along the main roads, and while many villages have mosques, other villages have no religious building, and the people of different villages assemble for worship in public mosques or Hindu temples.

Church, mosque, or temple, it is the largest, finest building of the community, constructed of materials more permanent than those of the houses, and decorated with donations made by members of the congregation. In this most firm and beautiful of environments, the word spoken is love. The sense of unity that people achieve in worship filters through all of life, giving them strength and restraint — the faith and trust of engaged existence. The sacred ideology of union, learned in the church or mosque or temple, becomes real in the cooperative arrangements that make village life possible, when people who do not necessarily like each other pray together on holy days, work together in the wide fields, and sit together at night, enduring again the dull company of those they choose to love.

Forms and Causes

Now, understanding something about building in Bangladesh and central Sweden, areas that are strikingly different in climate and prosperity, yet comparable in architecture, we can turn to causation. Founded upon faith, conjoining the familial with the communal, an idea of social order seems to be the prime condition of design when architects in Bengal or Dalarna plan relations among buildings. The environment sets an outer ring of constraint. Its conditions are brought into consideration whenever they do not contradict the more fundamental concerns that are sacred, social, and economic. There is logic in that formulation, but it is not so easy as that.

The most successful historical movement of our time, in my estimation, has been dedicated to the study of the landscape of the British Isles. By treating the land itself as the primary text and reading it closely during painstaking fieldwork, by building a geographical base for understanding and then bringing the more fragmentary and less democratic written record to bear during the construction of explanations, scholars have shaped a sweeping new view of history that attends to both continuity and change, while focusing on general cultural processes and not on the doings of a few errant princes. In England, W.G. Hoskins gave eloquent, public voice to the movement. In Ireland, the great spokesman was E. Estyn Evans.

One conclusion, reached early in the study of the English landscape, divided the whole into two zones. There was a highland pastoral zone of thin soil and steep slopes, where people lived in longhouses on separate farms, tending the cattle that grazed around them. There was a lowland agricultural zone of heavy, arable soil, where families drew together in tight villages and went out to work cooperatively in the open fields. The distinction is too neat, and generations of scholars have qualified it extensively in new research. But a great pattern remains. From

England, the island at one end of the Eurasian landmass, to Japan, the island at the other, when the soil is fit to the plow, people tend to settle in openfield villages.

Bengal and Dalarna are radically different in climate, but they share other environmental conditions. Both belong to the lowland zone. Both have good soil and open land. It rolls in Sweden, it is relentlessly flat in Bengal, but it is naturally disposed to agriculture. Processes differ in the dry cultivation of wheat and the wet cultivation of rice, but in the days before machinery — our days in Bangladesh — agricultural technology required energy to be built through human cooperation. And the need for cooperation led to compact settlement. And villages borrowed an economically useful ideology of oneness from religious scripture. But, of course, that is too simple. Were it an adequate explanation, the scholar's trim old division of the land into highland and lowland zones would not have gotten so muddled by later research.

If people responded, naturally or mechanically, to steep slopes and thin soil by settling on separate farms, then mountainous Anatolia would be, like the moorland of Devon, a place of longhouses deposited on independent steadings. The environment does not determine. It establishes one of the conditions of choice, and the Turks chose the communal way, settling the mountains in villages. The minaret points out of the mass of houses on the crest of a rocky ridge, or the houses run in terraced rows along the slope, facing downhill into the warmth. The fields spread into a green patchwork below. The gray mountain rises above, where sheep and goats pick among the rocks. The view is still more dramatic in northern Pakistan. There the valleys are sectioned into fields, and the mosque and the houses of the village perch on the steep sides of towering, snowy peaks. Although Ireland is a hilly display of separate farms, the pattern of rundale led in the rocky west to a clustering of houses and a division of fields comparable to Turkey's.

Paşaköy. Çanakkale, Turkey. 1990

Damlacık. Adıyaman, Turkey. 1989

In human affairs, it could always be different. People choose. Though their economy was pastoral, their land was steep and stony, the Turks chose the openfield village. They built villages, too, on the flat, fat lowlands, uniting their landscape into an objective demonstration of their option for community. That it was a choice, and not some force in the environment, is proved by places along the Black Sea where Turkish farmers live in dispersed settlements.

Turks choose to build villages in unsuitable places. Bengalis and Swedes choose to build villages on land right for agriculture. The land did not invent the plan. People brought the plan with them when they came, and they made it work in the places they settled.

If people always built compactly on land suitable for agriculture, then the United States would be largely a place of openfield villages. But in the mountains and on the plains, the United States is Turkey's opposite. It is unified by dispersed settlement. As in Turkey, there are exceptions that test the rule, reveal it to be imperfect, and prove that the landscape is shaped by willful action.

The American pattern of dispersal is interrupted by images of compression, compression so extreme that buildings come together, connect, and pile upon one another in the Native American villages of the Southwest. At Acoma, at Taos, at Cochiti and Santa Clara, the church stands aside when men and women carrying rattles and wisps of evergreen come out of the kiva to dance in lines, separating and converging, transcribing the lineaments of a monumental sacred architecture in the dust and air. Their Hispanic neighbors built openfield villages on the European model. The Catholic church stands in the plaza, an open square enclosed by the houses that string along its sides. The fields, divided by allotment, run beyond into an open expanse.

The most spectacular exception to the American rule — oppositional by intention — is the Mormon village. Fine small farmhouses, Midwestern in form, stand on a foursquare grid like that of a Midwestern town, but the farmer's holdings are cast through

Pueblo. Taos, New Mexico. 1987

Plaza. San José, New Mexico. 1990

Mormon village. Paris, Idaho. 1990

Separate farm. King William County, Virginia. 1978

the fields that spread beyond the village. The vast, mountainous backdrop does little to disturb the comparison. Viewed across the fields, the village of Utah or southern Idaho, with its tall temple and low gathering of houses, offers an image out of old England. In medieval England and nineteenth-century Utah, villages were asserted into space by people who made clear-headed decisions. They chose to build as they did in order to exploit the environment efficiently through agriculture, and in order to shape a social order that brought the familial and the communal together on the base of the sacred.

By genetic dispensation, people are beings of memory, imagination, and will. They choose, and they live only in the world where every choice is made on a field of cause and consequence too large and complex to control or know completely. The result of choice is history.

History

In Virginia and in Massachusetts, the first English settlement was a village. Providing protection and a familiar experience, the village brought unity to the disparate populations gathered at Jamestown and Plymouth. At the time of settlement, early in the seventeenth century, the England they left was in the midst of the most revolutionary change since the Neolithic. Openfield villages a thousand years old still stood on the lowlands, but the process of enclosure, powered by money and law, was reordering the landscape.

The open fields were surveyed, divided, consolidated, and fenced — enclosed — and separate farms were created on the arable lowlands. Village people resisted, leveling new walls, uprooting new hedges, and formulating loose customs into firm traditions designed to counter the expansion of law. Their heroic actions — like those of the Luddites in early industrial times who burned the mills to the ground — attracted the attention and won the sympathy of intellectuals, and the study of custom and tradition, of folklore, was born in England. The power of the village people was great enough to slow things down, to force compromises, and to preserve some openfield villages from destruction. But theirs was the weaker power in the conflict. Their choices were canceled by choices made by people who had more money and better weaponry. The big pattern in time was clear.

On the landscape, the openfield village was replaced by the separate farm. The change from the village to the farm was a change in social order from the communal to the familial. In the village, the dwelling was part of a larger architectural composition that embedded the family securely in the community. On the landscape of separate farms, the dwelling stands alone, and people might or might not work to construct a larger community. The new pattern isolates the family.

The change from the village to the farm was a change from sacred to secular orders. The church standing at the center of the village was the source of the precepts that people used in constructing a customary order for life. On the landscape of separate farms, no church stands in view. People live apart, and local customs come into conflict and compromise with the civil codes devised by the state to increase its dominion. The new pattern replaces collaborative experience with secular doctrine, uniting isolated families by law and political order.

The change from the village to the farm was a change in the economy from collective to individual enterprise. In the village, maintenance was the goal, cooperation was the means, and cooperation required restraint and engendered trust. On the landscape of separate farms, the family works for itself, and its own energies and resources apparently set the only limits for its economic success. In the new pattern, the isolated family operates within a legal framework, and the goal is profit.

My summary is painfully schematic. Its purpose is not to erect categories, classifying the village as sacred, the farm as secular. The purpose is to reveal shifts in emphasis, tendencies in time that give us some purchase on the slow, tremendous change during which one architectural form was replaced by another. Since architecture is not a system unto itself, the architectural change provides the clearest evidence of a cultural change that happened at different times in different places. That cultural change led from a communal order that mixed social and economic goals on a sacred base to an order in which profit took precedence, and the family was isolated as a unit of enterprise within a massive system based on the laws of the state and the needs of the capitalist.

That change is not inevitable. If it were, no villages would remain, and yet villages still dominate the agricultural landscape of Eurasia. In England, though, the openfield village is nearly gone. W. G. Hoskins estimated that half of England's arable land had been enclosed by 1700. When a single landlord owned the earth of the village, he let the farmers complete the harvest, then sent them packing in the winter's cold, demolishing their houses and collecting their strips of tillage into immense hedged pastures where sheep could graze, growing wool for sale. In villages where ownership was divided among many freeholders, they gathered, consolidated their fields, fenced them, and eventually built separate farmsteads. The process that private owners began was completed by the government in the eighteenth and nineteenth centuries. The four and a half million acres that had been open fields in 1700 were reduced to a few hundred when Hoskins wrote in 1955. He mentioned four villages that had survived somehow, and I followed his book to one of them, Braunton in Devon, where I lived for a few months in 1978.

The spire of Saint Brannock's ancient church lifts a golden cock over the tight rows of houses. At the corners, farmhouses stake out the neat plan of the town that was built by Anglo-Saxon pioneers next to the mission church founded by Saint Brannock. He sailed a stone across from Wales to bring the Good News to the heathens of Devon. At first he built on Chapel Hill, high above the valley cut by the River Caen. Every night his work was undone. Then God told him to build below, where he would find a sow with her farrow. At that fertile site, he built his church, and harnessing a team of wild deer to the task, Saint Brannock was the first to plow the rich alluvial soil. The church Saint Brannock built in the sixth century was rebuilt in the thirteenth. The open fields laid out in the eighth century, though diminished in scope and the number of holdings, remain to be seen. Braunton's Great Field is striped with long, curving strips, attached in random alternation to households in the village. Its sections are marked by bondstones, and its strips are separated only by narrow balks of grass called landsherds.

Braunton's view of history is put on display in an annual pageant. It takes place in the nave of the church, and it begins with the arrival of Saint Brannock, played by the priest, Father Budge. Then comes a long series of splendidly dressed kings and queens, who stand aside and do nothing, while the people of the village, played by the people of the village, do all the action and have all the fun. Their play, like their church building, exhibits the mutability of fashion and temporal power, and the stability of common life.

The farmers of Braunton know their place is unusual, but their question is not how their big prosperous village survived. It is why other people changed from the village to the agricultural units they call "ring-fence farms."

Ernie Hartnoll, whose family has worked Town Farm since the days of the Domesday survey, answered his own question when he told me that openfield villages, like his Braunton, are "bad for farming, but good for farmers." He meant that it is hard to manage an efficient operation when the farmer, moving on his tractor from one of his fields to another, gets stuck in traffic, but the village is good for human beings. Children can walk to school and play with their mates in the fresh air. Women are not shut up in a farmhouse, far from their neighbors; they visit casually, do their shopping on foot, and run the businesses of the village. At night, men and women walk to their local, greet the landlord, and lift a few pints with their friends.

304

Saint Brannock's.
Braunton.
1978

Landsherd separating holdings on Pitlands field.
The Great Field. Braunton, Devon, England. 1978

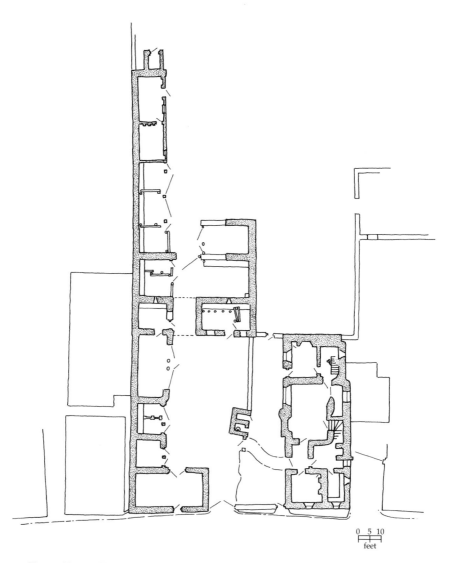

0 5 10
feet

Town Farm. Braunton.
Ernie Hartnoll's Town Farm exemplifies the village pattern that England
shares with Sweden and Bangladesh. The farmstead (above) collects the
main buildings around a courtyard, the house to the right, the barn, shop,
and stable to the left. The shippen for cows closes the courtyard, then
sheds for pigs on the right, carts, root crops, and chickens on the left, run
toward the orchard in the rear. It is located on North Street in the town.
The fields (see the map on the facing page) are scattered south and east.

Braunton. Devonshire, England.
The railroad and the new highway that cut along the River Caen have
been omitted to reveal the old plan. A dotted line shows the extent of
the village in 1978. St. Brannock's Church is marked by a cross. Buildings
strung along the old streets are hatched. Town Farm is black. Town
Farm's dispersed holdings are stippled, arable in the Great Field to the
southwest, pastures on Braunton Down to the east.

Bad economically, an impediment to enterprise, the village is good socially. It yielded to arrangements that were the reverse when profit took command.

England's change has not happened, and will not happen, everywhere. But the pattern in time is by no means restricted to England. In southern Sweden, the village was replaced by the farm, exactly as in England. What makes Dalarna in central Sweden so distinct, so special in the Swedish view of nationhood, is that the farmers of Dalarna fought the agents of change, and openfield villages, like those in the very different environments of Turkey and Bangladesh, remain common.

The American Landscape

The purpose of this excursion has been to understand the choice that made the American landscape. Living in villages in Jamestown and Plymouth, English people understood village life, and they knew of an alternative: enclosure. In both places, they abandoned the village for separate farms. They did not risk their lives on a black ocean to repeat the old but to create the new. They came to get rich. Religious rhetoric and the resistance of the native people could retard but not stop the spread of enclosure.

Jamestown and Plymouth might have been twin points of origin for a landscape unified by enclosure. Instead, history led to regional difference. In New England, the Puritans fought dispersal and isolation, returning by choice to the openfield village. They located a meetinghouse at the center of town and scattered tillage in strips through the open fields, rededicating themselves to the way of the Lord. New England developed in tension between the opposed energies of compression and dispersal. Villages predominated in some areas, notably the lowlands of the Connecticut Valley. In other places, high, rough, and marginal, the farmhouses stood alone. The scene in the South was simpler. Houses, churches, and even courthouses stood apart. Old Virginia was the first impeccably capitalistic landscape.

Pennsylvania, last to be settled and culturally most diverse, presents a swelling, green landscape of separate farms. In Pennsylvania, a synthesis of German, English, and Irish practice was established on independent family farms, and that pattern — call it American — was perfected in the Valley of Virginia and then extended through the Midwest. As time passed and people pressed westward, regional differences diminished. In the wake of genocide, the land of the interior was surveyed, gridded, and enclosed. States have cities, counties have towns, the countryside spreads with separate family farms.

Then as the skies widened and dried, the farms expanded in size. The ranch of the West was like the plantation of the South, a commercial operation in the open air, an immense factory without walls. The owner hires a boss, the boss directs the hands, and they produce a commodity — cattle, protein on hoof, rather than the tobacco or cotton or sugar of the plantation, or the clocks and locks and firearms of the compact, mechanized factories of old New England. The widening dispersal was not ordered by a sacred, communal vision, but by civil law and a network of trade.

A white wooden steeple points above a gathering of white wooden farmhouses: the village was reality in New England, and it lingers dimly in the historical imagination, tempering free enterprise slightly with vague talk about community values, and occasionally inspiring evanescent experiments in communal living. The Mormons revived the idea of the village in the West. A few urban neighborhoods have the old village feel. But the big pattern was clear from the beginning, and it endures in subdivisions, called estates or ranches or parks, where houses stand in isolation, each on its own grassy plot.

The American landscape says that people chose to exchange the confidence of communal life for the excitement of the pursuit for wealth. In daily experience, it might have been only a gentle, nearly imperceptible shift in common conduct as people worked and lived in contentment among their neighbors. In history, it was a great watershed.

The people had chosen. At the communal level of design, they shifted from compressed to dispersed arrangements. When we move down a level, we will find the same culture at work, trading compressed plans, in which many functions combine, for dispersed plans in which functions separate by logical category. Before the philosophers, the rural builders were aggressive rationalists.

Advancing the cause of enclosure on lowland terrain, American farmers chose change. When people came from the uplands of Europe, looking for land they knew how to use, and then settled the American uplands with separate farms, their actions can be taken as continuous. But change was trapped in continuity. Keeping to tradition, they should have built longhouses in the mountainy wilderness as people did in the pioneering phase of British settlement. Instead, they planned their farms into division, setting the house here, the barn there, and surrounding each of them with ancillary outbuildings.

At the communal level, they chose dispersal over compression, isolating the family. Similarly favoring dispersal in planning the farm, they divided the family unit into its domestic and working halves. In the United States, highland and lowland zones are alike in their separate farms, and they are alike in farms that separate the house from the barn.

Tax records from the end of the eighteenth century provide two instances of buildings in Pennsylvania that housed the people and their cattle under one roof. Two out of many thousands: a dramatic change had been completed in two generations. In the areas of Central Europe from which the Pennsylvania Germans came, buildings analogous to the longhouses of Britain, buildings that were dwellings and barns at once, were the norm. Although German immigrants constructed a few unified buildings in eighteenth-century Pennsylvania, as they would in nineteenth-century Wisconsin and Missouri, they developed for themselves a distinct version of the general American practice. They continued to build the house and barn in a line, but rather

Cumberland County, Pennsylvania. 1971

Frederick County, Maryland. 1972

than attaching them, they separated them, like the modernizing farmers of Ballymenone. From southeastern Pennsylvania, through central Maryland, and into the Valley of Virginia, the house and barn align along a slope, facing downhill toward the sun. The farther west and south they went, the more likely the house was to be English in origin, but the big beautiful barn was Germanic, and the two of them stood together, separated by fences and open space. Their alignment recalls the unified buildings of Europe. Their separation makes them fit America, where the domestic separated from the agricultural, making way for industrialization.

There must be exceptions, and Thomas Hubka has documented one of them handsomely. In northern New England, during the nineteenth century, farmers moved their houses and barns into connection in a hopeless effort to restore order during defeat. Prosperity had gone west to flat farmland where the big machines could roll, where agriculture and industrial capitalism could come into productive collusion.

The wish for separation, displayed on the landscape of separate farms and on farms that separate the house from the barn, will continue to drive planning when we shift down a level, to the domestic.

An Entry to History

I discovered history in houses. In 1966, I selected a small area in the middle of Virginia for study. A wide, loose survey convinced me that the area would make a good sample of the large architectural region of the Chesapeake Bay. Acting happily within the frame for research crafted by my mentor Fred Kniffen, I intended to depict the geographical personality of the region through its buildings. I made a quick record of every house and drew careful measured plans of many. Old houses dutifully exhibited a distinct regional character, but the more I analyzed them, the more I felt that the big story was historical change. My training in social science, in days dominated by synchronic systematizing, did little to prepare me for the job at hand.

Houses spoke of history. The old house had a square hall with a narrower parlor built on its end. The front door gave access immediately to the interior, and it was set a touch off center to expose the internal workings to view. With one step, the visitor enters the hall, then turns toward the fire where the work of cooking and entertainment takes place.

The new house was a type that Fred Kniffen named the I-house, achieving immortality by contributing a word to the common language. Two stories high, but only one room deep, the I-house is tall and slender in profile, like the letter. The I-house presents a wide bilaterally symmetrical facade that hides the interior. One side looks like the other, and it is hard to say where you will go once you get in. Upon entering, you do not stand in a room where people sit. You are in an unheated, unlit corridor — a hallway, a way to the hall — out of which you must be led to the sociable place.

Choosing to build a new house instead of an old one is a progressive step, a stretch perhaps for status. But anything can be made to signify status. The tiny teahouse that was designed to evoke poverty and the hermit's hut were buildings of high status in aristocratic Japan. Analysis should not be displaced by quick ascriptions of status. What we need to know, through formal analysis, is what changes during change. The shift from the hall-and-parlor house to the I-house was a compositional move in massing from the organic to the geometric. The change in massing disrupts entry, separating insiders from outsiders. Separation was accomplished internally by the hallway and externally by the facade. The hall-and-parlor house offers a gently asymmetrical array of openings that reveal the interior. The front of the I-house covers the interior with a geometric image of order.

I found old houses smaller than the hall-and-parlor house, some with only one room. Small houses are less likely to survive than large ones, so we can imagine many more in the past, but enough remained to exemplify their forms. I found houses larger than the I-house, some with the heavy double-pile depth of the Georgian ideal, rather than the slim plan of the I-house that balanced one room on each side of the hallway. The house of one room and the Georgian mansion stood at the opposite ends of a scale of size, which probably approximated a scale of wealth, but these antiquarian details do nothing to alter the pattern of change that led from open to closed plans, and from asymmetrical to symmetrical facades.

Features once restricted to the rare mansions of the gentry began to become general in domestic design during the 1760s, a time of intensifying tension. Determining that the architectural change in the Chesapeake region took place on the eve of the American Revolution, I interpreted the shift from one house to the other as material evidence of the change in social arrangements that brought the war that built the nation. Houses told of a retreat from the community of immediate experience, where people might be radicals, loyalists, or unconcerned, where differences were stiffening along lines of class and race and persuasion — it was a time of hot revival and cool deism, of conflict between the old Church and the New Light.

If order is lacking in the world, if the people mingling in space cannot be trusted to carry order within themselves, if their conduct is threatening or impolite, then order must be built into buildings that block and direct them. The I-house stopped people and channeled them with its hallway. Then compensating for experiential disorder with conceptual order, it projected an abstract and rational message on its facade. At once tripartite and bilaterally symmetrical, divisible by both odd and even numbers, the front of the I-house puts on public display a unified image that firmly contains division. The facade was designed on principles that traditionally — on the cathedral, in the carving and painting of furniture, in the structure of the folktale and ballad, in the ranking of society — signal the presence of control in communication.

Change in Virginia.
Above: Open and asymmetrical; left, partitioned house of one bay; right, hall-and-parlor house. Below: Closed and symmetrical; left, I-house; right, Georgian house. This is an early example; the conventional Georgian house has back rooms equal in size to the front rooms and a hallway consistent in width. The I-house most often has a facade with three openings per floor, like the hall-and-parlor house, though it was also built with five openings in the Georgian manner. Characteristically, the hall-and-parlor house has one story, though it was also built in two-story versions. The I-house and Georgian house are characteristically two stories high, though, especially south of Virginia, one-story houses have plans like I-houses and Georgian houses.

Hall-and-parlor house. Madison County, Virginia. 1977

I-house. Surry County, Virginia. 1975

The architectural change fit the times. Trading the immediate community for an abstract vision out of which a new union could be built, the I-house in Virginia was one symptom of the change in the hearts and minds of men that made the Revolution. The old house belonged to the little community of engagement, of constant and direct exchange. The new house belonged to an overarching concept of manifest and self-evident reason — to a political nation as yet unborn. The farmers acted. The politicians got the message and followed along, completing the process later in a tripartite, symmetrically composed constitution.

My idea, however uncongenial to conventional presumptions about leaders and followers in history, gained support through architectural comparison. When I was trying to make sense of the data in Virginia, I had not yet been to England, and new to history, I still thought of temporal developments in national terms. The most obvious and provocatively supportive comparison did not cross my mind. In southern England, there was a pronounced shift from organic to geometric massing before the English Revolution. My thinking at the time turned to places in America I did know. Building houses that were internally closed by a hallway and masked externally by a symmetrical facade, people in Virginia came into alignment with people in New England.

Old England differs regionally in its traditional housing. As is the case in Ireland, houses with chimneys in the middle dominate toward the east, houses with chimneys on the gable ends dominate in the west. The patterning, through, is not sharp in England. English immigrants to America would have known of both ways to build, and there was much architectural diversity during the first phase of settlement. But slowly American regions consolidated and peeled apart.

In New England and Virginia, the common plan united a hall with a parlor. But the chimney was set in the middle in New England, between the hall and parlor, and chimneys flanked the ends of the house in Virginia, one for the hall, one for the parlor.

Both regions exhibit continuity. People from the east of England came to New England, people from the west of England came to Virginia, and they settled into their new places with familiar dwellings. It takes great exertion to preserve continuity despite differences of space and time, but the volition of the early builders becomes easier to appreciate when we note that their choices were environmentally correct. They knew different kinds of houses, and they eventually selected the right one for the weather. In cold New England, the central chimney radiates heat throughout the house. In hot Virginia, chimneys set at the ends of the house leave its center open to the circulation of air through opposed doors and windows.

If environmental adaptation during continuity told the whole story, then the architects of New England would have built the kind of house that was most common in southeastern England. It would have worked in the climate, for its chimney was located between the hall and the parlor. Then, on the usual house of southeastern England, a third room opened off the hall, standing in service to the hearth during the preparation of food. Service, hall, parlor: these three spaces were arranged in a neat line in the narrow houses of England. But architects in New England did not build houses like that. Instead, they chose a rare form from southeastern England and brought it to dominance in New England. Their house, the saltbox house, seems quaint today, but in the early seventeenth century, it was the newest of all English houses, streamlined and ultramodern.

In the saltbox house, the service wing was moved from the end to the rear and covered by the long descent of the roof that gives the house its profile and name. The first effect of this change is a separation between insiders and outsiders. With the service wing out of sight on the rear, the facade can be composed in perfect tripartite, bilateral symmetry. It baffles entry. Open the door, and you are baffled again. You are not in a room. You are in a vestibule, like the lobby of the Swedish house that keeps chilly

The typical house of southeastern England. Robertsbridge, East Sussex. 1982

Saltbox house. Southminster, Essex, England. 1973

Saltbox. Southampton, Long Island. 1970

winds out, and you are in a social lock, like the hallway of later Virginia, that keeps unwelcome visitors out.

The second effect of the saltbox plan is a separation made among the people who live inside. Attached to the rear of the house, the service wing gains access to the central chimney. It becomes a full working kitchen. Formerly the hall mixed cooking and entertainment. The lofty hall of the Wealden house, like the kitchen of the houses in Ballymenone, was at once the kitchen and the living room. The new arrangement relieves the hall of work, leaving it cleaner, and it purifies the kitchen into a place for domestic labor. If the family has servants, then differences between the householders and the servants clarify in architectural fabric. If the family has no servants, then someone from the family must be designated a servant, removed from the social arena of the hall, and exiled to a smoky back place. Class and gender distinctions merge and harden.

When the functions that were compressed in the hall are dispersed through the house, a particular point has been reached in history. Division will elaborate in the future when a dining room is added, but the arrival of a second kitchen, a place for cooking meals that is distinct from the place for entertainment, allows us to date with precision the moment when the gender roles of modern times came into being. Together with the separation of the barn from the house, the advent of the second kitchen tells us that the roles, which some consider natural and eternal, were constructed in our culture not so long ago.

Selected out of the English repertory for use in seventeenth-century New England, the saltbox house was a thoroughly modern creation. It presented a symmetrical facade, a closed interior, and a second kitchen.

When a new form arrived in the eighteenth century, New England builders doubled their options. Called Georgian, for it became common in the long period when men named George sat on England's throne, the new form was an English version of

The Georgian house of New England. Sag Harbor, Long Island. 1970

The New England compromise: saltbox interior in a Georgian box, with Greek Revival trim. Portsmouth, New Hampshire. 1976

a Dutch version of an Italian version of an original from the eastern Mediterranean. The Georgian form offered a symmetrical facade and a central hallway. It was familiar enough to gain easy acceptance, yet new enough to serve as a symbol of fashion and progress. From the environmental standpoint, it was foolish to trade the central chimney, a source of heat, for a central hallway designed to move the air in hot climates. But the Georgian form worked socially like the saltbox house, separating insiders from outsiders and putting the kitchen to the rear. And like the saltbox house in its day, the Georgian house was all the rage. So some people built Georgian houses. For them, clearly, fashion and social order mattered more than the climate. But more people compromised cleverly, stuffing their old interior into a new box, symmetrical from the side as well as the front, and betrayed as old-fashioned, and environmentally sane, by the big chimney that poked above the roof in the middle.

In the Georgian period, the new houses of New England and Virginia were closed internally by a lobby or a hallway, and they were masked by a symmetrical facade. Continuities with past practice left the regions distinct. The chimneys of the I-house, like those of the hall-and-parlor house, were built externally on the ends in the western English manner. In New England, the chimney rose through the middle of the house, as it did in eastern England, or a fashionable hallway bisected the house, and when it did, the chimneys were not usually set on the ends, as they were in Virginia. They conserved heat by standing internally between the front and rear rooms. But the differences were slight, the similarities great.

Once the houses of the North and South had gained symmetrical facades, they were subjected to a process of compositional segmentation that brought New England and Virginia together with Pennsylvania. The plan was fractured along its internal partitions to create houses that were conceptually parts of houses. By eliminating the rooms to one side of the central chimney or the central hallway, designers created a narrow house,

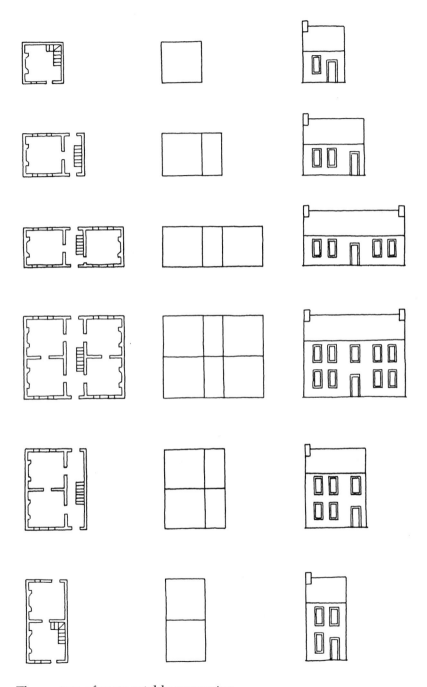

The system of segmentable symmetry.
Houses combine plans from the left column with facades from the right.

Two-thirds of the New England central-chimney house. East Hampton, Long Island. 1970

Two-thirds of an I-house. Winchester, Virginia. 1975

One-third of an I-house. Crisfield, Maryland. 1969

two-thirds of the whole, that suited cramped city lots. They did not stop there. The old urban house of England arranged the hall and parlor in single file, one behind the other. Designers rationalized that old house into one-third of the Georgian form, producing the terraced houses that typify English cities on both sides of the Atlantic; Philadelphia's streets are lined with them. The process by which houses were designed for city living unified urban and rural America within a single system of architectural options.

The fractional house solved the problem of tight urban space. It also solved the problem of limited resources in the countryside, providing less prosperous people with a way to participate in the big architectural change. In Virginia, even the smallest dwellings — the cabins built by slaves on the plantations and the cabins built out of logs by farmers on the slopes of the Blue Ridge — were brought into alignment. Of one room and one story, they were redesigned to be one-twelfth of the Georgian mansion. Architecture told you exactly where you stood in the unified order. With one square room, one chimney, one window, and one door, you were at the bottom. And architecture trained your aspirations. Your small house was not a miniaturized version of a large one, doomed for all time to smallness, as houses often were in England. It was a full-scale fragment of a big house. In time, it would expand with a shed on the rear, perhaps another room on the end. People of modest means built houses in the countryside that were one-third or two-thirds of the whole, and sometimes their heirs got lucky and added to the house, completing the scheme. The prevailing symmetry of the system marked asymmetry as incomplete, and it pushed action toward the achievement of logical unity.

The segmentable, symmetrical box, developed first in New England, came to unify the landscape of the eastern seaboard. I have found this distinctively American pattern to be common in only one other place. On the island of Guernsey, houses also changed from open to closed plans, and from asymmetrical to symmetrical facades. The symmetrical house of Guernsey — an I-house exactly — was also segmented, not only in the usual way, by having one story instead of two, but in the American way too: the house might be a full one, with a room on either side of a central hallway, or it might be two-thirds of the whole, with a hallway to the side that provides a roundabout entry to the room next to it.

Guernsey supports the thrust of my argument. Like America, Guernsey is divided from England by water, and like America, it is culturally heterogeneous. The segmentable, symmetrical house overarched tense differences between English and French people on Guernsey, as it overarched differences between English and German people where they met in Pennsylvania, and as it overarched differences of wealth and persuasion in New England and Virginia. Replacing experiential confusion with abstract reason, a single architectural system brought houses into unity. It ranked them within a single order. It contained and directed progressive motion.

Closed, symmetrical, segmentable houses unified the American land, but regional differences were not at an end. Pennsylvania had its German sections, with houses that refused to fit neatly into the Georgian order. The North was a place of big houses, the South of big spaces. The landscape of Virginia had become modern, wholly enclosed, when designers in New England were still planning medieval villages. The architects of New England had settled on a fully modern dwelling, the saltbox house, when Southerners were still building houses that admitted visitors directly in the medieval way. A piece of the explanation is that Northern houses, set close together, used partitions to do what Southern houses, set far apart, used spatial expanse to do — to divide people from one another. In housing, though, New England got there first. But Virginians and Pennsylvanians were catching up, and the regions came into alignment, just when alignment was necessary, on the eve of the American Revolution.

Through architectural comparison, Virginia has become part of a massive, transatlantic region, unified by historical action. By breaking the village into separate farms, by breaking the longhouse into a house and a barn, by breaking the house out of contact with a facade and hallway, and then fragmenting its interior by function, people had broken up their little world, and they were ready to break up the big one. First they killed the king in England. Then they rebelled in America.

Comparison in Ireland

Thinking like that about the architectural change in Virginia, I proposed to test the idea with something like science. I knew from the superb writings of E. Estyn Evans that Ireland divided into two great architectural regions. The houses of the east, where the English settled, had central chimneys and linear plans like those of southeastern England. The houses of the Celtic west had chimneys on the ends, and they were socially open and pierced asymmetrically like the hall-and-parlor houses of Virginia. I knew, as well, that the Georgian form was introduced to Ireland in the eighteenth century, just as it was in Virginia. My idea was this: though it was present on the landscape, the Georgian form would not become adopted into common building practice until the people were ready, until they were ready to trade the little community they knew for an abstract concept that would bring them into national alliance with people they did not know. That, I surmised, would happen a decade or so before the successful revolution of 1916.

My hypothesis was this: along the border in western Ireland, houses would change from open to closed and from asymmetrical to symmetrical at the beginning of the twentieth century. The cause would be a hardening of political commitment that turned the neighbors away from each other, built factions, broke the community, and shaped new domestic arrangements in advance of the shaping of a national political order. Since writers at the time did not describe the newer houses, I could learn whether I was right only by going to Ireland.

In 1972, I settled in Ballymenone in southwestern Ulster, where my research would go on for a decade. The forms I found were not the forms I predicted. The old house was socially open and asymmetrical, right enough, but it was unlike the western Irish house of the books, and I took it for English in origin. As for the new house: I was expecting a country Georgian form that resembled the I-house. There are I-houses in eastern Ireland, but the new house in Ballymenone did not strike a hallway through the center. The hallway ran transversely, like the hallways in the houses of the Scottish Highlands. It looked different but worked comparably. Like the lobby of New England or the hallway of Virginia, it disrupted entry by setting an intermediate space between the world outside and the kitchen inside. And when the hallway came, the facade took on a tripartite, bilaterally symmetrical configuration. And soon after, the house sprouted a second kitchen on the rear.

In functional terms, the change in Ireland was precisely like the change in Virginia, and it happened exactly when I thought it would. The big difference was that I could know much more about the Irish change. I did not have to construct motives out of analysis. I could talk to people. They taught me generously, and my thinking was much improved.

Dating stumped me in Virginia. I dated undated buildings on analogy with dated ones in the wider region. In Ireland, people could tell me when houses were built. The first house of the new kind was built in 1900, and it was built by a Protestant policeman in a largely Catholic neighborhood — exactly the kind of person who would wish to withdraw behind a symmetrical facade. The last house of the old kind was built in 1958. The change took a long time in Ireland, and I see now that it took longer in Virginia than I had guessed.

Without intimate knowledge of community doings in eighteenth-century Virginia, I had to make a stretch to connect a lo-

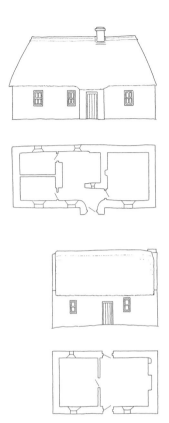

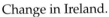

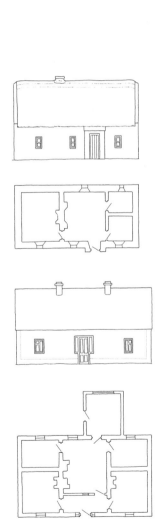

Change in Ireland.
Left: The common traditional Irish houses; above, the eastern type; below, the western type. Both of those types appear, though rarely, in Ballymenone. Right: The common houses of Ballymenone; above, the old type, open and asymmetrical; below, the new type, closed and symmetrical with a second kitchen on the rear.

Ballymenone's old house (see also p. 263).
Bellanaleck, Fermanagh, Northern Ireland. 1972

Ballymenone's new house (see also p. 256).
Springfield, Fermanagh, Northern Ireland. 1972

cal change with the big changes recorded by historians. In Ballymenone, people could tell me about the small events that transferred big historical patterns into community life. When the first house of the new kind was built in Ballymenone, the large argument was about the relationship of Mother England to her colony, just as it was in Virginia when the I-house was invented out of the Georgian pattern. The little event that brought the big argument into Ballymenone was Billy Price attacking the band.

Here is the story as Hugh Nolan and Michael Boyle told it to me. A wealthy Protestant land owner suddenly decided not to rent two fields to the Catholic priest as he had in the past. Catholic farmers gathered and marched to a Protestant pub, beating drums and playing flutes, mounting a musical boycott. On their way home, they passed a field where a Protestant farmer, one Billy Price, was at work with a graip, turning sods. He was so enraged that he took up the weapon and attacked the band. Billy Price got a drubbing, and the boys of the band threw rocks through his windows, wrecking his house. That was the environment in which a Protestant policeman decided to build a new kind of dwelling.

Differences between radicals and loyalists, between Protestants and Catholics sharpened, and the revolution in the future did not resolve the issue in Ulster, as your newspaper will tell you. Increasingly both Catholics and Protestants chose to build houses on the new model. It was that kind of house that Tommy Moore built for Paddy McBrien in 1944. New starts were not common, but remodeling was, and most people — not all, but most — chose to add an enclosed porch, built of concrete blocks, to the front of the house that did outside what the hallway did inside.

The new house separates people from their neighbors — and it offers a truce. Standing alone, the house presents on its front a sign of rational order that transcends communal differences. The porch outside or the hallway inside becomes a transitional place where people, perhaps opposed in political orientation, can negotiate their differences politely.

In Ballymenone, I understood the architectural change much better. The old house welcomes everyone, and some people, especially those living far from the public routes through the community, continued to live in houses of the old kind in my days. The door was open. People walked in. The host trusted them to behave properly. They sat down and took tea. The new house acknowledges disorder. Standing near the public routes, the house makes it difficult to get inside. But once the guests have found their way to the hearth, they sit, drink tea, and the chat circles in the same old way. The new house enables continuity. But its people say that things have changed, and changed for the worse. They miss the easy exchanges of the past, but they live in this world, not that one, and the new house helps them manage.

Intimate information permitted me to refine my ideas of cause and effect in Ballymenone. The cause is immediate social disorder. The result is an object that compensates for disorder with devices that increase privacy and offer public symbols of conceptual order. The object marks the historical instant of a shift in cultural priorities. It dates the arrival of modernity.

When the enclosed landscape carries an open house, as it did in western Ireland and early Virginia, or when the compact village incorporates a closed house, as in Dalarna or early New England, the message is mixed. But when the fields are enclosed and the house is closed, the modern world has been created. Community is not dead, but it has lost dominance, and families live within political and economic systems that are too complex and expansive to understand or command. Social order dissolves, and the individual takes control, responsibly building a house that asserts an honorable point of rationality in a context of chaos.

Since the architectural change was so recent in Ballymenone, I was able to see clearly how the change in housing was one in a chain of changes. In Virginia, I could only drop general patterns into the void that opened before the time of the hall-and-parlor house. I could see the great change of enclosure, and I could see the pattern of environmental adaptation within continuity as people came and built houses in Virginia that were formally like those in England.

But in Ballymenone I learned that the change from open to closed houses followed hard upon another change. During that earlier change, houses of the old type were rebuilt in permanent materials. Wonderful new archaeological research in Virginia reveals that, in the time before the period of the buildings I examined, houses had been constructed of posts stuck in the soil, as they still are in Bangladesh. Then they were framed upon masonry foundations, rebuilt in more permanent materials. In Ireland, the modest old house was built with mud walls, or it was framed of jointed crucks impaled in the earth. As in Virginia, the old technology continued to be used in outbuildings, but the houses in Ballymenone became solid and permanent. Whitewash covered walls of stone or brick, and once houses were permanent, the local designers turned slowly then to symmetrical fronts and fragmented interiors.

It was not at first a double change. Impermanent and permanent materials were both local, taken from the land and processed by hand. But the wish for permanence established a precondition for the acceptance of imported, expensive, industrial materials.

The conditions of the shift from impermanent to permanent materials are patently clear in Ireland. The change happened in the era of the Land League's victory, during the last quarter of the nineteenth century. A massive meeting of the Land League took place right in Ballymenone. The Chief, the great Parnell himself, stood on the hill behind the thatched home of Hugh Patrick Owens and addressed a vast crowd of local farmers. Then, Hugh Patrick told me, they marched and fought and won for themselves the right to own the land they worked. Owning the land, he said, secure in their tenure, the people then built houses permanently upon it. The despicable landlord no longer owned the house. The people who lived in the house owned it outright, and it was worth their effort to rebuild the walls in firm materials and to make the interior more comfortable.

Now think of farmers in Virginia. They have come to a wild new place. It is not theirs, nor a landlord's, but nature's. They build expediently and work the land. At last, gaining wealth enough from agricultural labor, feeling secure in their tenure, they rebuild the old house, making it solid and fine. Then as differences in wealth mingle with differences in political and religious orientation, and community life becomes untenable, they rebuild again.

The sequence of change — from impermanent to permanent, from open to closed — locates the houses of Ireland and Virginia in the big pattern with which Eric Mercer frames his excellent book on the vernacular houses of England. In the beginning, the house was impermanent. At the end, it is permanent. In the middle of that pattern lies the transitional moment that W. G. Hoskins called the Great Rebuilding. In England, at different times, in different places, the walls of the houses were rebuilt in permanent materials and their interiors were fragmented by partitions. An early product of that change was the saltbox house, developed out of the Wealden house late in the sixteenth century in southern England. Later products include the I-house of eighteenth-century Virginia and the new house of twentieth-century Ballymenone.

The United States in the Nineteenth Century

Returning to the American story, we can envision a moment of unity, the most coherent instant in American history, when after the Revolution segmentable houses with symmetrical facades and closed interiors could be found from one end of the new nation to the other. That is as modern as things ever got.

In his excellent introduction to American architecture, Dell Upton comments correctly that the nineteenth century has been studied less well than the centuries that precede and follow it.

334

Nineteenth-century house
in the Georgian form.
Veazie, Maine. 1978

Nineteenth-century house
in the Georgian form,
Gothic and Italianate trim.
Oley, Pennsylvania. 1979

Nineteenth-century I-house with a Gothic gable.
Albemarle County, Virginia. 1966

One reason is that scholars seem to believe that the directions apparent in the eighteenth century continue through the nineteenth. Another is that, with the nineteenth century, there is a sudden flood of paper with words printed on it, and historians can relax at home, reading written texts that are easy to understand instead of the architectural texts that give them fits. But there is absolutely no alternative to fieldwork, to direct and patient study of real buildings in great numbers. The written texts of the nineteenth century are pertinent, but, alas, the story conveniently constructed out of them violently misrepresents the reality.

In a simplified telling, the eighteenth century was a time of convergence. The nineteenth century was a time of divergence, of the simultaneity of many big patterns at once.

One pattern was continuity. Up in the high blue mountains of the South, people continued to build open houses through the nineteenth century. Their small farms connected along the ridges and creeks into loose communities like Ireland's. Set apart, their wooden houses, built on old Irish or English plans, welcomed neighbors directly to the hearth. They stood in knowing contrast to the I-houses on the big farms in the valleys, separating the mountaineers who fought for union from the tuckahoes of the lowlands who fought for slavery's cause.

Down in eastern Virginia, builders seem to have achieved what they wanted in the I-house. It must have suited their sense of propriety, and they continued to build it in the new century. The Civil War came, devastated the land, and ended. In the new era after the war, Virginians built I-houses. There is nothing magical about turns of the century: I-houses were built into the 1930s. Northern New England also displays continuity. Houses with eighteenth-century plans were built before the Civil War and after the Civil War. In many rural places, 1880 would make a better end to the eighteenth century than 1800.

A second pattern was an extension of the eighteenth-century process into new territory. In some of the areas where houses remained open and asymmetrical, they were brought into the new order during the nineteenth century. In the hilly Piedmont of Virginia and North Carolina, people replaced medieval houses with eighteenth-century houses about 1850. Chris Wilson has documented the same change as taking place in the urban housing of Hispanic New Mexico between 1870 and 1910.

A third pattern involved the dismantling of the eighteenth-century accomplishment. In the Southern Appalachian region, throughout the southern Midwest, and in the West, notably in Mormon Utah, people built houses of the I-house kind, but they diminished the bulk. The house stood less than a full two stories high. Its symmetrical facade promised a central hallway, but, by eliminating one of the side walls of the hallway, the builders opened the interior to old hall-and-parlor patterns of use. From the Tennessee Valley westward and southward, architects brought about a similar change in a different way. They built geometrically massed houses with central corridors, but they omitted the front and rear walls of the hallway to create the dog-trot house. Good in hot weather, the dogtrot house sucks the exterior into the interior. The wide open hallway — people who live in such houses call it a hall, not a dogtrot — makes a fine place for cool sitting and casual visiting.

When the eighteenth-century plan was dismantled, the result blended the old and the new. A similar compromise characterizes a fourth pattern — one of fresh design. Presented at the end of the eighteenth century with the Georgian concept, architects redesigned medieval houses so that they had apparently symmetrical facades, but rather than centering a door between windows, they brought two doors to the front so that the house could be entered directly in the old way. That is the pattern of the saddlebag house of the Southern Appalachian domain, of the Deep South, and the southern Midwest. And it is the pattern of houses built by German people in Pennsylvania and French people in Louisiana.

German house.
York County,
Pennsylvania.
1967

Saddlebag house.
Stokes County,
North Carolina.
1965

Shotgun houses. Louisville, Kentucky. 1994

The people who designed the fresh compromises in the nineteenth century are customarily neglected in simple national narratives. Southern Mountaineers, Pennsylvania Dutch, Cajuns in Louisiana — these are the people the old folklorists approached in their search for ancient songs and stories. Their houses provide tangible, measureable, objective evidence of the presence among them of something that brings them together and separates them from the historian's mainstream.

The people who are obviously missing from the list in the last paragraph created a fifth pattern, one of a continuity unconnected to developments in Virginia and Massachusetts. Native American people continued to build houses through the nineteenth century that were designed entirely on indigenous principles. Today in New Mexico and Arizona, many American Indian people live in houses that have nothing to do with their setting in the political entity of the United States. Throughout the nineteenth century, Hispanic architects in the rural Southwest built adobe homes of rooms strung in strings, bent around corners, and arranged along the sides of open courtyards. Their houses owed nothing to commotions in the world of the Anglos.

Another dramatic example is the shotgun house that John Vlach has studied so well. Developed in Haiti out of African and native forms, then brought to New Orleans, the shotgun house is an African-American contribution to the landscape. From Louisiana, the shotgun house diffused east and west, and it was carried against the grain of history, up the Mississippi and along the Ohio River, where it was adopted in the cities by new immigrants from Europe. A narrow run of rooms with a door in the gable end, the shotgun house breaks the American pattern in size and orientation. It is formally distinct, unrelated to the houses brought west from the Atlantic, but like the houses created in compromise, its entry is direct. Nothing architectural blocks your way in.

Native American and Hispanic people in the Southwest; African Americans in the Mississippi Valley; farming people in the

Southern Mountains, the southern Midwest, and the Deep South; Germans in Pennsylvania, Cajuns in Louisiana, Mormons in Utah — all connect in their reluctance to build baffles into their houses that would divide them from their neighbors. Join these objectively more sociable folks together, and they make a large minority of people who did not comply with the great change of the eighteenth century. If we bring the patterns together, all five of them, we will have gathered a clear majority of the houses of the nineteenth century, but I have not yet mentioned the pattern that dominates architectural histories of the period. Something is seriously wrong with research as it is conventionally practiced.

The sixth is the pattern of the books. In line with a developmental succession that began with the fashionable saltbox house, then proceeded to replace it with the Georgian house, designers in the nineteenth century looked around them, imagined improvements, and published books full of earnest advice. Some people followed their directions. They built the houses that historians use to divide the past into a neat series of periods, each one replacing the last on the track that leads to the present.

More of America's nineteenth-century designers created a seventh pattern. They selected ideas out of books, then they mixed them up and created a practice of accommodation and excitement. Their range of action was wide. At one extreme, prevalent from Pennsylvania and Virginia through the uplands of the South and West, the builders plucked a few ornamental details from the book and located them conventionally on the houses of continuity and compromise. At the other extreme, builders drew ideas from publications, blended them surprisingly, and invented synthetic new forms, especially in the era of the Greek Revival in upstate New York and the era of the Italianate in the Midwest and Deep South.

If we combine the pretentious, timid practice of the sixth pattern with the brave, innovative practice of the seventh pattern, we will not overbalance the view of the nineteenth century as a

Synthesis: Greek, Gothic, and Italianate. Bucksport, Maine. 1978

Accumulation: Greek with Italianate and Gothic additions.
Otsego County, New York. 1968

time dominated by different varieties of fluid, traditional practice that were aided rather than destroyed by new technologies. But the builders of the sixth and seventh patterns, though a minority, pointed the way to the future in the nineteenth century, just as the builders of the saltbox house, though a tiny minority in North America, did in their day. Early in the seventeenth century, architects in New England lit upon a modern form — symmetrical, closed, fragmented — that would not become general for nearly two centuries. During the nineteenth century, while others continued in the modern vein, or turned backward through the revival of open plans to premodern times, some architects established a postmodern practice. They accumulated commodities and arranged them to suit themselves.

Other options have not closed, but the twentieth century (a period that begins about 1920) is characterized by people who consume houses, reshape them through remodeling, and make them habitable through the organization of goods into domestic environments. People buy houses with an eye to their sale, and the home is less the house than it is a collection of portable furnishings that can be arranged familiarly in rented apartments, or in restored old houses, or in plastic-clad Queen Anne Revival-French Provincial mansions in the suburbs.

Pattern in Time

My argument is done. Architecture provides a prime resource to the one who would write a better history. I will contrive a conclusion with a summary. Our history breaks into three great periods. Its dynamic depends upon impurity.

First is the period of the village, a time of compressed housing and dispersed fields. The great creation of the period was the largest, most permanent, most lavishly adorned building of the community. Collective resources were banked and the collective will was materialized in a sacred edifice that was built to last, when houses were not. It should humble us some that the

Urnes stave church. Sogn, Norway. 1995

San José. Trampas, New Mexico. 1987

religious buildings of this period are the world's greatest architectural creations: the parish churches of England, the stave churches of Norway, the earthen mosques of West Africa, the towering temples of India — Chartres Cathedral, the Selimiye at Edirne, the Todaiji at Nara.

In the beginning, there was the village, a neolithic invention, and in the beginning, there was enclosure. Valiant people carved farms out of the waste and built longhouses to shelter themselves and their stock against wolves and cattle raids. Enclosure expanded steadily, chewing away the wilderness on the margins, but it was blocked on the fat lowlands where enterprise was entangled in intricate webs of rights and obligations. Village people wanted to prosper, but no more than they wanted to live in confidence among their neighbors. Their cooperative arrangements worked economically, and their religion gave them a vision of unity. They wanted to prosper, but they understood that an appetite for worldly goods than ran beyond necessity was avarice — a sin as deadly as gluttony or fornication. The aim of life was sufficiently clarified by Christ's message that it is easier for a camel to go through the eye of a needle than it is for a rich man to enter the kingdom of God.

Still, as new routes to profit opened through international commerce, enclosure came down to the lowlands. Where men once plowed, sheep came to graze, growing English wool for the merchants of Northern Europe. Then pious reformers did to Christianity what the enclosers were doing to the landscape. They improved it through division, breaking it into pieces. With the religious disunion of the Reformation, greed was released, enclosure increased, and the saltbox house was invented.

The second period is the period of the house. The big buildings of the period were not religious but political. They were government cathedrals where secular power made its public display. They were factories where laws were manufactured to fill the void left by religion. In the United States, a dome was lifted from the religious tradition and set as a crown upon a bilaterally symmetrical, tripartite mass in Washington city. Smaller domes on state capitols, and still smaller domes on county courthouses, spread a network of civil command over the nation. The political buildings were big, but the great creation of the period was the family home.

In their asymmetry and openness, the first houses were fit to communal experience. They belonged to the period of the village. With enclosure, the house was broken out of the collective composition of the village. It came to stand apart — apart from other houses, and apart from the church. The church was disestablished on the enclosed landscape long before it was disestablished by law. As ownership of the land solidified, so did the house. It was rebuilt in permanent materials. Then, as though at last awakening to its aloneness, the house drew a cloak of symmetry over itself and, in hiding, commenced to subdivide its interior, transferring the class structures of the larger society into the little community of the family.

The new house centered the world. It stood away from the church and away from the barn in the midst of fields enclosed by fences. The capitol building of a miniature state, built upon the ruins of community, the house beamed a message of control and order over a shattered landscape. What builders created in houses, politicians then tried to create in society. But what builders created in houses was realized less effectively in politics than it was in technology. People expressed their desire for control and order through technical procedures, just as they did in the massing and ornamentation of geometric houses. At first with manual methods, and then with big machines, artisans made things in increasingly exact repetitious units and with increasingly smooth artificial surfaces.

When a closed house stood on an enclosed landscape, the modern age began. Local powers went down to defeat, while a new power expanded. Dedicated to material gain, protected by new laws and advanced by new machines, this new power signaled its victory in buildings composed of imported, industrial materials.

At the extreme limit of enclosure, the gargantuan pile of the country house stood on its estate, among gardens and parks, surrounded by high stone walls with spiky iron gates; down a lane ran rows of cottages where servants and agricultural laborers tried to live. Into the same position in the structure, next came the plantation with its big house and squalid quarters where human beings were held in captivity. Then it was the industrialist's mansion and a row of identical little dwellings for the mill hands. Putting the capital won from enclosure to work, the princes of industry built factories that served them as vast pastures and cotton fields had served others. They adopted and perfected the rational division of labor that was traditional to complex technologies. They appropriated the abundance of cheap labor that had been generated by the destruction of the villages. They exploited the disruption in family unity that was marked by the separation of the kitchen from the hall and the barn from the house.

No longer able to find good work in the countryside, laborers in need of cash left home. Daughters left the kitchen, fathers left the barn. They assembled in big buildings, filling slots in rigid, hierarchical schemes, and the factory produced great wealth for a few, and for the millions it made industrial commodities.

Third is the period of the commodity. The period's big building does not belong to religion or politics, but to business. At first, in a time of transition, it was the horizontal block of the factory, with its smooth brick walls, its endless rows of identical windows, its racket and smoke. Then it was a vertical marvel of engineering, a ludicrously phallic skyscraper where nothing was made.

As industrial capitalism expanded, some people continued to live in the period of the house. Others turned back toward the period of the village with new open homes. But slowly people came into conformity. They worked for wages, went shopping, and filled their houses with stuff. In this there was nothing new.

Industrial landscape. West Aliquippa, Pennsylvania. 1970

Archaeology teaches that people have always consumed commodities. Across the landscape of prehistoric Europe run the trade routes of the commerce in amber. A bibelot from India was found in the wreckage of Pompeii. Shards of pottery from England, Holland, and China are sifted out of the soil at American colonial sites. The difference is this: at one time, commodities made ornaments of peripheral importance in houses that people built to their own specifications with the help of their handy neighbors. But as industrialization continued, houses themselves became commodities, and people were assigned the difficult task of shaping their personalities out of things made by other people.

How people have handled their assignment is a topic of high importance. Happiness in this age depends in part on consumers finding ways to explore creativity and achieve humanity that are as fulfilling as the common work of the potter or farmer. Cooking might be one, gardening and decorating the home might be others. But there have been few studies of how individuals in the United States, at the end of the twentieth century, compose commodities into expressions of their identities. There is not much evidence, so I speak as a cultural informant, and not as a student of culture, when I opine that the patterns of the twentieth century, hidden behind the walls of the house, are even more various and divergent than those of the nineteenth century. I end this little history with a call for research: during the next century, the study of vernacular architecture should include patient ethnographic investigation of how commodities are assembled into domestic environments.

Three neat periods: if such a scheme is convincing at all, it is probably because it is, like the facade of the I-house, tripartite and bilaterally symmetrical. The front of the house has three parts, a middle one with a door, flanked by two with windows. My historical sketch also has three parts (village, house, commodity), just as ostensibly comprehensive accounts of society have three classes (upper, middle, lower). At the same time — the simultaneity of odd and even numbers being the key to its

pretense to unity — the facade of the house is bilaterally symmetrical. A vertical line at the center will divide it into equal
halves, and my triple pattern also divides into halves at industrialization in the middle of the middle period. I can speak at
once of three periods and of preindustrial and industrial eras,
just as we can divide the triple order of society into the halves of
a professional class and a working class. Schemes that are simultaneously triple and double seem complete.

Insisting that the three periods are no more than a construction of convenience, I know that all histories are such constructions, and I believe my sketch could be elaborated into a history
of the United States better than the one my daughter is taught in
high school. But that is not my goal. Histories confined by national boundaries are, at best, transitional and fractional, pieces
of the picture we need. What interests me is how architecture
can help us puzzle the big picture together.

The three periods could aid in planning a program of research.
With so many things available for study, it is wise to focus on the
ones that are richest in significance. In medieval Europe, the object is the large and beautiful church. In America, between 1650
and 1920, the object is the house. In these late days, buildings are
consumed by many but designed by few. Professional architects
and professional planners have conspired with capitalists to steal
from people their right to architectural design. Since people can
be understood only from their own creations, from what they
say and make, and not from what others say about them or make
for them, our attention will concentrate on things smaller than
churches or houses — pots perhaps — and our work will be to
learn how they are made and marketed, what they mean, and
how they are arranged into satisfying new assemblies. Norio
Agawa makes ceramics. Ellen Cutler receives ceramic pieces and
builds them into a display on the dresser in her kitchen. Both of
them express themselves in art. Both make texts for us to study.

Selecting significant forms is part of the job. Work has begun,
and now the goal is to develop a method of comparison, free

from mere chronology, that will help us understand general principles of historical action through the study of material culture. I have used architecture to illustrate how material culture can be read. Differences between local and imported materials, interiors and exteriors, massing and ornament, compression and dispersal at different levels of design — such distinctions prepare us for formal analysis, cultural interpretation, and historical comparison.

Historical comparison: when I came to the mountains of western Turkey in 1985, I found the people in the villages reorganizing their houses. During subsequent visits over a decade, I watched the process that people could tell me about in Ireland, that I had to dope out of analysis in Virginia.

When they were nomads, moving up to the high pastures in the summer and down to sheltered glens in the winter, the people built domed homes of felt stretched over staked frames. Settling permanently on the site of their winter encampment, they built houses of the same kind, with impaled frames and coats of felt. Once they were secure in their possession of the land, they rebuilt their houses in permanent materials. As in prehistoric England and modern West Africa, round forms were squared off. The walls were built of heavy logs, notched at the corners, or more often of stone. The roofs were flat. They required constant maintenance, as thatching does in Ireland. After every rain, men went up to pack the earthen roofs with stone rollers. When it rained, the roof leaked, so the people borrowed ideas from the houses they saw in the towns where they sold their produce, their wheat and beans and carpets. A few houses with flat roofs remain, but now most houses have hipped roofs covered with purchased tiles.

With its walls of stone and its roof of tile, the house was permanent and snug. The exterior of the house was the outside of the inside. Doors gave direct access to the interior, where carpets covered the earthen floors, cushions were lined along the walls, and a fire flickered on the hearth.

New house. Çınarpınar, Çanakkale, Turkey. 1990

Village mosque. Çınarpınar, Çanakkale, Turkey. 1990

Then, beginning in the 1960s, village people started to build houses with central hallways and bilaterally symmetrical facades, astonishingly like the I-houses of eighteenth-century Virginia. I asked why they were making the change. They said they wanted their houses to be cleaner. People in Ballymenone told me the same thing. But the answer only rearranges the question. In fact, their old houses were impeccably clean. Why did they suddenly think the house should be cleaner? They said that the new houses came with depopulation. People left for the cities, seeking jobs in factories. Those who stayed in the Turkish village were like those who survived the Famine in Ireland. A bad event had good results. The farmers who remained had more land. Expanding their agricultural holdings, they produced a surplus and accumulated wealth. Wealth brought goods — tractors, televisions, refrigerators — and differences of wealth disturbed communal unity. The wealthier people built bigger houses that symbolized their economic success, protected their belongings, and gave them, they said, more privacy.

Farmers in the mountains of western Turkey are in the middle of a change that Irish farmers remember. The old people in Ballymenone are balanced in their evaluation. The change, they say, was good for the family, but bad for the community. The young people in Ballymenone, knowing the old system only in its days of decline, think the change was nothing but good. Turkish farmers say that the community is less cohesive than it was, but life was too hard in the past. A little loss of social coherence is a small price to pay for the gain in comfort, and anyway, they say, the change has brought no serious rupture to the community. The person highest in status is not the one with the biggest house and the most goods. It is the woman who is the best weaver and who teaches generously, it is the man who understands farming and leads the work in the fields, and above all, it is the person who is known to be a true Muslim.

Their houses are changing, but they live in a compact village. The houses stand close together. The fields are not enclosed; they expand into an unfenced patchwork of brilliant green. At harvest, teams of neighbors gather and reap the golden grain. Their cooperative economic arrangements are firm, and their faith is strong. Some of their new wealth goes into improving their homes, but even more conspicuously it is invested in the village mosque. Old mosques are being refurbished. Bright white new mosques are being built. And life is good, all praise to God.

Turkish farmers live simultaneously in the period of the village and the period of the house. Not really. They live in exactly the same time that you and I do, with as much right, and more capacity, to create the future. Predictions are only projections out of the few fragments of the present and past that chance to stick in the mind. No one knows whether their way or our way will prevail, but my prediction is that both will endure.

Out of my fieldwork, facts from Turkey come into association with facts from Ireland and America. Despite chronology, we see the similarities and the differences in historical action. Understanding expands. Facts combine to build the principles by which facts are interpreted. Facts do not dissipate into anecdotery. They become meaningful. As understanding increases, patterns at once clarify and complicate beyond all control. Any hope for evolutionary law — for a history of the world based on the history of the United States or England or France — dissolves in the empirical welter. History's big picture is a patterned picture of diversity.

Examined closely, analyzed formally on the ground of compassion, then manipulated into comparative arrangements, material culture breaks open to reveal the complexity of time, its simultaneous urges to progress, revitalization, and stability. Material culture gives us hope. Many routes lie open to the future.

Bakhti Nasar at work.
Khwazakhela, Swat, Pakistan. 1997

ACKNOWLEDGMENTS

My grandfather was a carpenter. In his shop, my interest in material culture was born, and I dedicated my first book to him. Fred Kniffen took me in and shaped my career, teaching me how to convert enthusiasms into a profession. I dedicated my second book to Mr. Kniffen. Two books I dedicated to my father who delighted in buying and selling antiques, who nurtured my early concerns with art and history. This book I dedicate to my mates in the trade, old comrades in the study of material culture, Jim Deetz and Warren Roberts. Before he faced the knife in the last of a long series of operations, I told Warren that this book was for him and Jim. We lost Warren to death on the first day of February in 1999.

Through Jim and Warren, I give this book to all my colleagues in the movement for the study of material culture. First among them I must name again Fred Kniffen, and then E. Estyn Evans, James Marston Fitch, and Robert Plant Armstrong, and then these friends with whom I have worked, along with Jim Deetz and Warren Roberts, to bring meaning to the artifactual record: Jennifer Attebery, James Ayres, Alison Bell, Charles Bergengren, Hande Birkalan, Jean-Paul Bourdier, Charles Briggs, Simon Bronner, John Burrison, John Carswell, Tom Carter, Catherine Cresswell, Marsh Davis, Walter Denny, Shannon Docherty, Karen Duffy, Alan Gailey, Ritchie Garrison, Reha Günay, Bernie Herman, Mark Hewitt, Tom Hubka, Marjorie Hunt, Susan Isaacs, Jason Jackson, Mike Jones, Sung-Kyun Kim, John Kirk, Peirce Lewis, Jiang Lu, Firoz Mahmud, Seth Mallios, Howard Marshall, Patrick McNaughton, Don McTernan, John Moe, Baqi'e Badawi Muhammad, Peter Nabokov, Paul Oliver, Marion Nelson, Jerry Pocius, Jules Prown, Irwin Richman, Ralph Rinzler, Bob St. George, Tom Schlereth, Muhittin Serin, Roy Sieber, Chris Sturbaum, Nancy Sweezy, Takashi Takahara, George Thompson, Bob Thompson, Dell Upton, Serena Van Buskirk, John Vlach, Mats Widbom, Chris Wilson, Wilbur Zelinsky, and Terry Zug.

I have learned from all of them, as I have from my colleagues in folklore. In addition to the folklorists among those listed in the paragraph above, I wish to record my gratitude to these friends: Mustafa Zaman Abbasi, Roger Abrahams, Ali Ashour Al-Jafar, Bente Alver, Ron Baker, İlhan Başgöz, Dick Bauman, Dan Ben-Amos, Mary Ellen Brown, Bruce Buckley, Shafiqur Rahman Chowdhury, Bob Cochran, Tris Coffin, Cece Conway, Özkul Çobanoğlu, Linda Dégh, Sandy Dolby, Dick Dorson, Alan Dundes, Hasan El-Shamy, Burt Feintuch, Bill Ferris, Kenny Goldstein, Bill Hansen, Lee Haring, Lauri Honko, Dell Hymes, Sandy Ives, Bill Ivey, Alan Jabbour, Roger Janelli, Kersti Jobs-Byörklöf, John Johnson, Suzi Jones, Shamsuzzaman Khan, Barbro Klein, Billy Lightfoot, Orvar Löfgren, John McDowell, Felix Oinas, Elliott Oring, Arzu Öztürkmen, Barry Lee Pearson, Phil Peek, Shipra Sarkar, Greg Schrempp, Amy Shuman, Beverly Stoeltje, Ruth Stone, John Szwed, Barre Toelken, Sue Tuohy, Bill Wiggins, Bert Wilson, and Don Yoder.

Folklorists are lucky that their circles of learning widen through fieldwork beyond the academy. I have learned the most from the teachers I found in the midst of ethnography: Norio Agawa, Siraj Ahmad, Sebire Aktaş, Showkat Ali, Marvis and Wanda Aragon, Ahmet Balcı, Otis Banks, Hagop Barın, Hank Barnes, Mustafa Baydemir, Sait and Lütfü Bayhan, Bilal Hossain Bikrampuri, Ömer Bilge, John B. Brendel, Ellen Cutler, İbrahim Erdeyer, İhsan Erdeyer, T. E. Everett, Peter Flanagan, Mehmet Gürsoy, Ernie and Vinnie Hartnoll, Chester Hewell, Hachiro Higaki, William Houck, Sirajul Islam, Osman Kaya, Mustafa Kesici, Muzaffer Kılıç, Stanley Lamprey, John O. Livingston, Bimal Chandra Mandal, Joseph Murphy, Hugh Nolan, Sıtkı Olçar, Nezihe Özkan, Mehmet Öztürk, Amulya Chandra Pal, Haripada Pal, Maran Chand Paul, Ola Belle Reed, Lilly Salvador, Mustafa Sargın, Ahmet Sefa, Lou Sesher, Yusuf Sezer, Ahmet Şahin, Ahmet Hürriyet and Nurten Şahin, Zafer Şahin, Hirohisa Tatebayashi, and N. T. Ward.

The idea for this book arose in a conversation with my friend John Gallman, director of the Indiana University Press. John and his fine staff proved helpful from the beginning to the end; John, Jane Lyle, Susan Barnett, Sharon Sklar, and Zig Zeigler made suggestions that I incorporated into the writing and design. I work within a capable team. Karen Duffy and Kathy Foster read the text, nudging me toward clarity. Kathy Sitarski and John McGuigan got the back matter onto disks. Michael Cavanagh and Kevin Montague printed my photographs, and the pictures of Turkish plates and tiles in chapter four are theirs. Finally, using the drawings I made of every page, Bruce Carpenter got it all into the computer.

Happy in my work, busy at my craft, always excited by teaching, I am refreshed by my students and warmed by friends around me: Bruce and Inta Carpenter, Karen Duffy, Tom and Ellen Ehrlich, İbrahim and Ayşe Erdeyer, Marshall Fishwick, Allen and Polly Grimshaw, Mehmet and Tülay Gürsoy, Bill Hansen and Mary Beth Hannah-Hansen, Charles Lave and Bethany Mendenhall, Firoz and Daisy Mahmud, John McDowell and Pat Glushko, John McGuigan, John and Mona Pearson, Shaheen and Salma Rahman, Barbara Roberts, Mohammad Ayub and Fouzia Salahuddin, Greg Schrempp, Ahmet Hürriyet and Nurten Şahin, and Takashi Takahara. In a sentence of their own, I thank David Logan, my friend of four decades, the one I can count on to share my outrage at the outrageous, and George Jevremović, companion in travel and brother to the end.

I miss old teachers and friends: Fred Kniffen, Estyn Evans, Erving Goffman, Kenny Goldstein, Hugh Nolan, Ralph Rinzler, Ahmet Şahin, and now Warren Roberts. I miss my father and mother, but I have a family in Judy and Bill, in Wally and Isabella, and I have the joy of my children, Polly, Harry, Lydia, and Ellen Adair. I am glad that Harry brought Lori into our lives, and the two of them have given us the sunshine of Katie Rose and Carly.

At last, I am most thankful for Kathleen, my love. I am proud of her, grateful to her, and I dedicated my biggest book to her. Our marriage is as near to perfection as human things get. An old wooden house on the west side of town, filled with books and pots and carpets, is my home, my place in the world, because Kathy and Ellen Adair live there.

NOTES

Onward

Pp. 1–3. Though the results are always humbling, my usual models for writing are set by my favorite books, Melville's *Moby-Dick* and Joyce's *Ulysses*. In writing this one, I was inspired by Faulkner's *Go Down, Moses*, which can be taken as a collection of short stories, but is read better as a novel built by theme rather than plot. Here the main themes are history and art. On history my best writings are *Folk Housing in Middle Virginia: A Structural Analysis of Historic Artifacts* (Knoxville: University of Tennessee Press, 1976) and *Passing the Time in Ballymenone: Culture and History of an Ulster Community* (Philadelphia: University of Pennsylvania Press, 1982; Bloomington: Indiana University Press, 1995). Two papers prepared me for this book's address to history: "Folklore and History," *Minnesota History* 50:5 (1987): 188–92; and "The Practice and Purpose of History," *Journal of American History* 81:3 (1994): 961–68. On art my best writings are *Turkish Traditional Art Today* (Bloomington: Indiana University Press, 1993) and *Art and Life in Bangladesh* (Bloomington: Indiana University Press, 1997). The progress of my thought on folk art is marked in these publications: *Pattern in the Material Folk Culture of the Eastern United States* (Philadelphia: University of Pennsylvania Press, 1969), pp. 28–33; "Folk Art," in Richard M. Dorson, ed., *Folklore and Folklife: An Introduction* (Chicago: University of Chicago Press, 1972), pp. 253–80, reprinted in T. J. Schlereth, ed., *Material Culture Studies in America* (Nashville: AASLH, 1982), pp. 124–40; "Folk Art," *Encyclopedia Americana* (New

York: Americana Corporation, 1976), XI, pp. 486–92; "The Idea of Folk Art," in John Michael Vlach and Simon J. Bronner, eds., *Folk Art and Art Worlds* (Ann Arbor: UMI Research Press, 1986), pp. 269–74, reprinted and translated into Swedish in Beate Sydhoff, ed., *Folkkonsten: All Tradition Är Förändring* (Stockholm: Kulturhuset, 1992), pp. 13–16, 189–92; "The Spirit of Swedish Folk Art," in Barbro Klein and Mats Widbom, eds., *Swedish Folk Art: All Tradition Is Change* (New York: Abrams, 1994), pp. 247–55; and the book *The Spirit of Folk Art* (New York: Abrams and Museum of International Folk Art, 1989), which seems to have put the definitional question to rest with the idea that "fine art" is our folk art and "folk art" is the fine art of other people.

History

P. 5. This chapter blends and extends the notes for two talks, the first given at the Institute for Advanced Study at Indiana University in 1996, the other delivered as the keynote address of the Missouri Conference on History in 1997. Written to be this book's opening chapter, the paper was published as *History's Dark Places*, Distinguished Lecturer Series 8 (Bloomington: Indiana University Institute for Advanced Study, 1998).

P. 5. All scholars should read Jean-Paul Sartre's "A Plea for Intellectuals," a lecture of 1965, published in *Between Existentialism and Marxism* (New York: William Morrow, 1976). With James Agee, I believe that passion should lift us out of professionalism and into seriousness; see

Let Us Now Praise Famous Men (Boston: Houghton Mifflin, 1960, pub. 1941), p. xv.

P. 6. Claude Lévi-Strauss demonstrates his concept of myth in his great series on mythology. He is his own best guide to that massive work: Claude Lévi-Strauss, *Myth and Meaning* (New York: Schocken, 1978); Claude Lévi-Strauss, *Anthropology and Myth: Lectures 1951–1982* (Oxford: Basil Blackwell, 1987), parts 2 and 3; Claude Lévi-Strauss and Didier Eribon, *Conversations with Claude Lévi-Strauss* (Chicago: University of Chicago Press, 1991), part 2. I believe he illustrates his method best in two shorter books: Claude Lévi-Strauss, *The Way of the Masks* (Seattle: University of Washington Press, 1982) and *The Story of Lynx* (Chicago: University of Chicago Press, 1995). The best introduction to the man is his marvelous *Tristes Tropiques* (New York: Atheneum, 1975, pub. 1955). The best introduction to Bronislaw Malinowski is his book—like *Tristes Tropiques,* a great influence on my own effort—*Argonauts of the Western Pacific* (London: George Routledge, 1922). It contains excellent mythic analysis. Malinowski's classic statement on myth as the charter of society comes in his essay "Myth in Primitive Psychology," in Malinowski, *Magic, Science and Religion and Other Essays* (Prospect Heights: Waveland Press, 1992, pub. 1948), pp. 100–101.

P. 6. Robert Penn Warren, *The Legacy of the Civil War: Meditations on the Centennial* (New York: Random House, 1961), pp. 107–9. I find my first experiences with history captured in the opening pages of Robert Penn Warren's *Jefferson Davis Gets His Citizenship Back* (Lexington: University Press of Kentucky, 1980).

P. 7. V. S. Naipaul, *Finding the Center: Two Narratives* (New York: Alfred A. Knopf, 1984), pp. 45–46. Darkness connects in Naipaul with the idea of a missing history. His account of his first trip to India was titled *An Area of Darkness* (London: Penguin, 1968), and note the comments in his story of his trip through the southern United States, *A Turn in the South* (New York: Vintage International, 1990), pp. 9–11, 36, 198. His superb book on the writer's problem also contains good thoughts on history: *The Enigma of Arrival* (New York: Vintage, 1988), pp. 143–47, 353. In his novel of Hindu life in Trinidad, *A House for Mr Biswas* (New York: Alfred A. Knopf, 1991, pub. 1961), p. 45, Naipaul calls the school's history "unreal." The real history lies in darkness. Then in *A Way in the World* (New York: Alfred A. Knopf, 1994), continuing the chronological line of *A House for Mr Biswas* and the mood of *The Enigma of Arrival,* he probes the darkness, discovering in memory, landscape, and documents paths into unknown history; see pp. 10–11, 43, 56–66 (Naipaul's *Tristes Tropiques),* 72–76, 105, 213–14, 326.

P. 8. In opposition, I pair Claude Lévi-Strauss, *The Savage Mind* (Chicago: University of Chicago Press, 1966) and Jean-Paul Sartre, *Search for a Method* (New York: Alfred A. Knopf, 1963).

Pp. 9–12. For Ahmet Balcı, see my book *Turkish Traditional Art Today,* chapter 19.

P. 12. Fernand Braudel, *On History* (Chicago: University of Chicago Press, 1980). See too his monumental study *The Mediterranean and the Mediterranean World in the Age of Philip II* (New York: Harper and Row, 1972), especially pp. 186–87, 460, 734, 798–800, 1073, 1242–45.

Pp. 12–21. Hugh Nolan is one of the stars of my book *Passing the Time in Ballymenone.* He is featured as well in my books *All Silver and No Brass: An Irish Christmas Mumming* (Bloomington: Indiana University Press, 1976; Philadelphia: University of Pennsylvania Press, 1983) and *Irish Folktales* (New York: Pantheon, 1985). Mr. Nolan's stories and the argument I sketch here are given in full in *Passing the Time in Ballymenone.*

Pp. 16–17. During his fine treatment of storytelling, N. Scott Momaday, poet and novelist, describes the spatial organization of Native American history in *The Man Made of Words: Essays, Stories, Passages* (New York: St. Martin's Press, 1997), pp. 36, 74–76, 207. At the end of their outstanding historical study, *Like People You See in a Dream: First Contact in Six Papuan Societies* (Stanford: Stanford University Press, 1991), p. 303, Edward L. Schieffelin and Robert Crittenden comment on the spatial organization of historical knowledge in New Guinea. Evliya Çelebi's *Seyahatname,* one of the best of all history books, has been rendered in modern Turkish: Tevfik Temelkuran, Necati Aktaş, and Mümin Çevik, eds., *Evliya Çelebi: Seyahatnamesi,* 10 vols (Istanbul: Ücdal Neşriyat, 1978–1984). It would be a grand thing if the entire work could be translated into English and edited with the care that Robert Dankoff gave to one of its sections in *Evliya Çelebi in Bitlis: The Relevant Section of the Seyahatname* (Leiden: E. J. Brill, 1990). Fernand Braudel's sketch of the global whole comes in *A History of Civilizations* (London: Penguin, 1993).

P. 21. Historians on religion: Marc Bloch, *Feudal Society* (Chicago: University of Chicago Press, 1961), I, pp. 81–87; Douglas Southall Freeman, *Lee's Lieutenants: A Study in Command* (New York: Charles Scribner's Sons, 1943), I, p. xxviii.

Pp. 21–24. Haripada Pal tells his story in my book *Art and Life in Bangladesh,* chapter 6.

P. 27. I handled tradition as a way of creating the future out of the past in "Tradition," *Journal of American Folklore* 108:430 (1995): 395–412.

Pp. 29–30. Milton murmurs: Christopher Hill, *Milton and the English Revolution* (New York: Viking Press, 1977), p. 99.

P. 30. One of the very best books on American history is Laurel Thatcher Ulrich's *A Midwife's Tale: The Life of Martha Ballard, Based on Her Diary, 1785–1812* (New York: Vintage Books, 1990).

P. 39. The pinched critic might fault Geoffrey Keating for his inclusion of the mythic and legendary in history, but in defending the cultural importance of the factually questionable, Keating (who lived from about 1570 to 1650) was ahead of his times and ours. See the comments in Dermod O'Connor's influential translation, *Keating's General History of Ireland* (Dublin: James Duffy, 1861), pp. 61, 63, 183, 190–92, 280–81, 342, 362, 364. This century's text is David Comyn and Patrick S. Dinneen, eds., *The History of Ireland by Geoffrey Keating, D.D.,* 4 vols. (London: Irish Texts Society, 1902–1914). Two thousand years before Keating, Herodotus adopted a comparable attitude. The open and inclusive, circumspect and skeptical style of Herodotus is stressed by Carolyn Dewald in her excellent introduction to Robin Waterfield's new translation of *The Histories* (Oxford: Oxford University Press, 1998), and for rich instances, see Herodotus' own words on pp. 34, 80, 94, 102, 117–18, 139, 219, 300, 320, 414, 451, 509, 513, 546. Herodotus tells a historian's tale, beginning with the theft of women and ending with the failure of the invasion of Xerxes, and (as he says, pp. 244–45) he seeks digressions, exploring the interests of the geographer, the anthropologist, and the folklorist. From my book's standpoint, what is remarkable is not only how interested Herodotus is in material culture, but how often he uses material culture to link parts of his tale and to pivot between his narrative and his geographical and cultural digressions; see pp. 44, 60, 75, 86, 94, 130–32, 152, 168, 171, 194–95, 211, 256, 263, 325, 427, 484, 574. Herodotus describes material culture less as his narrative takes over, but it remains for him symbolic of culture and useful in his compositional task.

Material Culture

P. 41. This chapter began as a talk that ended an excellent conference on material culture, held in St. John's, Newfoundland, in 1986. Little of that talk survived in the written version: "Studying Material Culture Today," in Gerald L. Pocius, ed., *Living in a Material World: Canadian and American Approaches to Material Culture* (St. John's: Institute of Social and Economic Research, 1991), pp. 253–66. Not much of that version survives in this one. Before writing this chapter, I had published several statements on material culture, its importance and method, especially in the books *Pattern in the Material Folk Culture of the Eastern United States, Folk Housing in Middle Virginia, Passing the Time in Ballymenone, The Spirit of Folk Art, Turkish Traditional*

Art Today, and *Art and Life in Bangladesh,* and in these papers: "Structure and Function, Folklore and the Artifact," *Semiotica* 7:4 (1973): 313–51; "Archaeology and Folklore: Common Anxieties, Common Hopes," in Leland Ferguson, ed., *Historical Archaeology and the Importance of Material Things* (Columbia: Society for Historical Archaeology, 1977), pp. 23–35; "Meaningful Things and Appropriate Myths: The Artifact's Place in American Studies," *Prospects* 3 (1977): 1–49, reprinted in Robert Blair St. George, *Material Life in America, 1600–1860* (Boston: Northeastern University Press, 1988), pp. 63–92; and "Folkloristic Study of the American Artifact: Objects and Objectives," in Richard M. Dorson, ed., *Handbook of American Folklore* (Bloomington: Indiana University Press, 1983), pp. 376–83.

P. 41. Ralph Waldo Emerson, *Nature* (East Aurora: Roycrofters, 1905, pub. 1836), pp. 9, 32.

Pp. 41–42. I link Robert Plant Armstrong and Michael Baxandall, for I believe them to be the best writers on art of our times. See Armstrong's trilogy: *The Affecting Presence: An Essay in Humanistic Anthropology* (Urbana: University of Illinois Press, 1971); *Wellspring: On the Myth and Source of Culture* (Berkeley: University of California Press, 1975); *The Powers of Presence: Consciousness, Myth, and Affecting Presence* (Philadelphia: University of Pennsylvania Press, 1981). Baxandall outlines his method in *Patterns of Intention: On the Historical Explanation of Pictures* (New Haven: Yale University Press, 1981), and he exemplifies it elegantly in *Painting and Experience in Fifteenth-Century Italy: A Primer in the Social History of Pictorial Style* (New York: Oxford University Press, 1974) and *The*

Limewood Sculptors of Renaissance Germany (New Haven: Yale University Press, 1985).

Pp. 48–58. Aysel Öztürk and her tradition are introduced in my book *Turkish Traditional Art Today,* chapters 18, 20–21.

P. 61. On sets: Noam Chomsky, *Syntactic Structures* (The Hague: Mouton, 1957); Vladimir Propp, *Morphology of the Folktale* (Austin: University of Texas Press for the American Folklore Society, 1968); the works by Robert Plant Armstrong cited for pp. 41–42 above; my paper "The Variation of Concepts Within Tradition: Barn Building in Otsego County, New York," in H. J. Walker and W. G. Haag, eds., *Man and Cultural Heritage: Papers in Honor of Fred B. Kniffen* (Baton Rouge: Louisiana State University School of Geoscience, 1974), pp. 177–235, and the books *Folk Housing in Middle Virginia, Passing the Time in Ballymenone,* and *Turkish Traditional Art Today,* part 4. Another good example is Bill Holm's *Northwest Coast Indian Art: An Analysis of Form* (Seattle: University of Washington Press, 1965).

P. 63. See Noam Chomsky, *Language and Problems of Knowledge: The Managua Lectures* (Cambridge: The MIT Press, 1994), pp. 5–11, 158–62.

P. 66. In a series of papers in the 1960s, Dell Hymes developed the theory of performance that brings such order as there is to contemporary folkloristic study. His basic book on the topic is *Foundations in Sociolinguistics: An Ethnographic Approach* (Philadelphia: University of Pennsylvania Press, 1974). Richard Bauman applies the idea productively to narrative in *Story, Performance, and Event* (Cambridge: Cambridge University Press, 1986).

P. 66. Jean-Paul Sartre, *Nausea* (New York: New Directions, n.d., pub. 1938), pp. 168–69.

P. 66. Robert K. Merton, *On Theoretical Sociology: Five Essays, Old and New* (New York: The Free Press, 1967), chapter 3.

Pp. 68–71. John Ruskin's essay "The Nature of Gothic" was published in the second volume of *The Stones of Venice* (London: Smith, Elder, 1853). William Morris published it as a separate book (Hammersmith: Kelmscott Press, 1892), and I quote from the first page of the preface that Morris wrote for the Kelmscott edition. Among the many biographical writings on Morris, I recommend these especially: J. W. Mackail, *The Life of William Morris,* 2 vols. (London: Longmans, Green, 1899); E. P. Thompson, *William Morris: Romantic to Revolutionary* (New York: Pantheon, 1977); Jack Lindsay, *William Morris: His Life and Work* (New York: Taplinger, 1979); Fiona MacCarthy, *William Morris: A Life for Our Time* (New York: Alfred A. Knopf, 1995). Among the many books on aspects of his achievement, these are among the ones that are germane to material culture and biographically valuable: Gerald H. Crow, *William Morris: Designer* (London: The Studio: 1934); Paul Thompson, *The Work of William Morris* (New York: Viking Press, 1967); Ray Watkinson, *William Morris as Designer* (New York: Reinhold, 1967); A. Charles Sewter, *The Stained Glass of William Morris and His Circle,* 2 vols. (New Haven: Yale University Press for the Mellon Center, 1974–1975); Oliver Fairclough and Emmeline Leary, *Textiles by William Morris and Morris & Co., 1861–1940* (London: Thames and Hudson, 1981); Linda Parry, *William Morris Textiles* (New York: Crescent Books, 1994); Duncan Robinson, *William*

Morris, Edward Burne-Jones and the Kelm-scott Chaucer (London: Gordon Fraser, 1982); William S. Peterson, *The Kelm-scott Press: A History of William Morris's Typographical Adventure* (Berkeley: University of California Press, 1991); and Charles Harvey and Jon Press, *William Morris: Design and Enterprise in Victorian Britain* (Manchester: Manchester University Press, 1991). Many books trace his influence; for examples: Nikolaus Pevsner, *Pioneers of the Modern Movement: From William Morris to Walter Gropius* (London: Faber and Faber, 1936); Susan Otis Thompson, *American Book Design and William Morris* (New York: R. R. Bowker, 1977); and *William Morris Today* (London: Institute of Contemporary Arts, 1984). The key collections of his essays on material culture are: William Morris, *Hopes and Fears for Art* (London: Ellis and White, 1882); *Signs of Change* (London: Reeves and Turner, 1888); and *Architecture, Industry, and Wealth: Collected Papers* (London: Longmans, Green, 1902). I quote from the last volume (p. 59) on the utility to designers of the principles in the western Turkish carpet. The portrait of Morris on p. 69 was taken from the frontispiece of Aymer Vallance's *William Morris: His Art, His Writings, and His Public Life* (London: George Bell, 1898).

P. 71. I cite one major book for each of these great masters of material culture: Ananda K. Coomaraswamy, *Christian and Oriental Philosophy of Art* (New York: Dover, 1956, pub. 1943); Soetsu Yanagi, *The Unknown Craftsman: A Japanese Insight into Beauty* (Tokyo: Kodansha, 1978); Sigurd Erixon, *Svensk Byggnadskultur* (Stockholm: Aktiebolaget Bokverk, 1947); Richard Weiss, *Häuser und Landschaften der Schweiz* (Erlenbach-

Zurich: Eugen Rentsch, 1959); Ruth L. Bunzel, *The Pueblo Potter: A Study of Creative Imagination in Primitive Art* (New York: Dover, 1972, pub. 1929); Gladys A. Reichard, *Navajo Shepherd and Weaver* (Glorietta: Rio Grande Press, 1971, pub. 1936); E. Estyn Evans, *Irish Folk Ways* (New York: Devin-Adair, 1957); H. Jesse Walker and Randall A. Detro, eds., *Cultural Diffusion and Landscapes: Selections by Fred B. Kniffen* (Baton Rouge: Geoscience Publications, 1990).

P. 71. Exemplary works in the interdisciplinary study of material culture are these papers by Jules David Prown: "Style as Evidence," *Winterthur Portfolio* 15:3 (1980): 197–210; and "Mind in Matter: An Introduction to Material Culture Theory and Method," *Winterthur Portfolio* 17:1 (1982): 1–19.

P. 72. Writers on the left: Agee, *Let Us Now Praise Famous Men;* Oscar Lewis, *Five Families: Mexican Case Studies in the Culture of Poverty* (New York: Basic Books, 1959); and these books by the great E. P. Thompson: *The Making of the English Working Class* (New York: Vintage Books, 1963); *Whigs and Hunters: The Origin of the Black Act* (New York: Pantheon, 1975); *Customs in Common* (New York: The New Press, 1991); *Making History: Writings on History and Culture* (New York: The New Press, 1994).

P. 73. Early folkloristic fieldwork with craftsmen in America: Ralph Rinzler and Robert Sayers, *The Meaders Family: North Georgia Potters* (Washington: Smithsonian Institution Press, 1980); Michael Owen Jones, *The Hand Made Object and Its Maker* (Berkeley: University of California Press, 1975), revised as *Craftsman of the Cumberlands: Tradition and Creativity* (Lexington: University Press of Ken-

NOTES TO PAGES 74–108

tucky, 1989); Henry Glassie, "William Houck: Maker of Pounded Ash Adirondack Pack-Baskets," *Keystone Folklore Quarterly* 12:1 (1967): 23–54, reprinted as a separate monograph, the third in the series Studies in American Crafts (Oneida: Madison County Historical Society, 1980).

P. 74. Dell Hymes, ed., *Reinventing Anthropology* (New York: Pantheon, 1972); Dell Hymes, *"In Vain I Tried to Tell You"*: *Essays in Native American Ethnopoetics* (Philadelphia: University of Pennsylvania Press, 1981).

P. 81. Michael Owen Jones wrote a prospectus on remodeling as a focus for material culture study in "L.A. Add-ons and Re-dos: Renovation in Folk Art and Architectural Design," in Ian M. B. Quimby and Scott T. Swank, eds., *Perspectives on American Folk Art* (New York: W.W. Norton for Winterthur, 1980), pp. 325–63.

One Life

P. 87. Rewritten but not changed basically, this chapter was first published as "A Master of the Art of Carpet Repair: The Life of Hagop Barın," *Oriental Rug Review* 9:6 (1989): 32–38; 10:1 (1989): 16–22; 10:2 (1990): 38–43.

Pp. 90–91. I sample the enormous bibliography on Turkish rugs in *Turkish Traditional Art Today,* pp. 899–906. A lovely selection of tapestry-woven kilims can be found in Yanni Petsopoulos and Belkıs Balpınar, *Kilims: Masterpieces from Turkey* (New York: Rizzoli, 1991). Belkıs Balpınar Acar introduces the variety of Turkish flat-weaving techniques in *Kilim, Cicim, Zili, Sumak: Türk Düz Dokuma Yaygıları* (Istanbul: Eren, 1982), though

she does not include the warp-faced *cecim* techniques that are common in eastern Turkey; see my *Turkish Traditional Art Today,* pp. 201–19, 386–90, 900–901. The best collection of Turkish piled carpets is W. Brüggemann and H. Böhmer, *Rugs of the Peasants and Nomads of Anatolia* (Munich: Kunst und Antiquitäten, 1983).

Pp. 92–93. While stressing fine, urban examples of traditional housing in Kayseri, Vacit İmamoğlu describes houses related to the one Hagop Barın remembers in *Geleneksel Kayseri Evleri* (Ankara: Türkiye Halk Bankası, 1992).

Pp. 93–94. Brian Morehouse presents a comprehensive Turkish collection in *Yastiks: Cushion Covers and Storage Bags of Anatolia* (Philadelphia: ICOC, 1996).

P. 106. Gladys A. Reichard describes Navajo teaching by demonstration in *Spider Woman: A Story of Navajo Weavers and Chanters* (New York: Macmillan, 1934), pp. 21, 36–37.

P. 108. There is a solid bibliography on New Mexican carved wooden *santos:* José E. Espinosa, *Saints in the Valleys: Christian Sacred Images in the History, Life and Folk Art of Spanish New Mexico* (Albuquerque: University of New Mexico Press, 1967); William Wroth, *Christian Images in Hispanic New Mexico: The Taylor Museum Collection of Santos* (Colorado Springs: Taylor Museum, 1982); William Wroth, *Images of Penance, Images of Mercy: Southwestern Santos in the Late Nineteenth Century* (Norman: University of Oklahoma Press for the Taylor Museum, 1991); Charles L. Briggs, *The Wood Carvers of Córdova, New Mexico: Social Dimensions of an Artistic "Revival"* (Knoxville: University of Tennessee Press, 1980); and

Laurie Beth Kalb, *Crafting Devotions: Tradition in Contemporary New Mexico Santos* (Albuquerque: University of New Mexico Press, 1994). My reference is to the artists who learned through repair described in Mari Lyn Salvador, *Contemporary Santero Traditions from Northern New Mexico* (Albuquerque: Maxwell Museum of Anthropology, 1995), pp. 11, 73, 77.

P. 111. I wish to call attention to the similarity of the views of Hagop Barın and Norio Agawa (pp. 205–6). We tend to make simple distinctions in education, contrasting those who are self-taught with those who were formally trained in the university, the atelier, or at the hearth (subdividing formal instruction into academic and nonacademic varieties without acknowledging that a single system, that of the atelier, has produced the greatest masters of both "folk art" and "fine art"). But Hagop Barın and Norio Agawa both describe a mixed experience. For both men there was a prime teacher—a tailor for one, a tilemaker for the other—and both say they taught themselves through practice. Peter Flanagan, the great musician of Ballymenone, told me the same thing. His father, Phil, was a great musician, an inspiration, but Peter taught himself by playing. The middle way these men describe seems close to the norm for the artist's learning, and it helps to account for the blend of stability and innovation that characterizes all art.

Pp. 125–26. I describe and picture Abdülkadir Uçaroğlu's plate in *Turkish Traditional Art Today*, pp. 556–57.

P. 128. The information on Turks in Germany comes from İlhan Başgöz and Norman Furniss, eds., *Turkish Workers in Europe: An Interdisciplinary Study* (Bloomington: Indiana University Turkish Studies, 1985), especially pp. 3, 26, 40, 42, 67.

The Potter's Art

P. 143. This chapter combines, updates, and extends two talks presented to the National Council on Education for the Ceramic Arts. The first, given in 1993, was published as "Values in Clay," *The Studio Potter* 22:2 (1994): 2–7. The second, given as the keynote address of the annual conference in 1998, will be published in the *NCECA Journal*. Like the others in this book, this essay is based on my own fieldwork, but that is not necessarily lonely work, and on many of the adventures that brought me information I was accompanied by dear friends. Shafiqur Rahman Chowdhury, Firoz Mahmud, and Shamsuzzaman Khan were often with me in Bangladesh. Orvar Löfgren went with me to Raus in Sweden. John Burrison and I traveled together in Georgia. Karen Duffy has been with me during many visits with Wanda Aragon and Lilly Salvador. Takashi Takahara was with me during my second visit to Hagi. Here I thank them all for their help and friendship.

P. 145. The information on Bangladesh briefly recapitulates the findings from my book *Art and Life in Bangladesh*. Statistics come from Mohammad Shah Jalal, *Traditional Pottery in Bangladesh* (Dhaka: International Voluntary Services, 1987), pp. 15–16, and the tables following p. 55.

P. 148. The aesthetic of the modern *murti* is continuous with that of the sculpture of Gupta, Pala, and Sena times as described by Stella Kramrisch in Barbara Stoler Miller, ed., *Exploring India's Sacred Art: Selected Writings of Stella Kramrisch* (Philadelphia: University of Pennsylvania Press, 1983), pp. 217–22; Joanna Gottfried Williams, *The Art of Gupta India: Empire and Province* (Princeton: Princeton University Press, 1982), pp. 61, 69–70; S. K. Saraswati, *A Survey of Indian Sculpture* (Calcutta: K. L. Mukhopadhyay, 1957), pp. 124–26; and A. K. M. Shamsul Alam, *Sculptural Art of Bangladesh: Pre-Muslim Period* (Dhaka: Department of Archaeology and Museums, 1985), pp. 66–67.

P. 148. The quality of ripe, fecund youthfulness found in Hindu art is found as well in the Yoruba art of West Africa; see: Armstrong, *Wellspring*, pp. 33–35; and Robert Farris Thompson, *Black Gods and Kings: Yoruba Art at UCLA* (Bloomington: Indiana University Press, 1978), chapter 8.

P. 150. Pratapaditya Pal, *Hindu Religion and Iconology: According to the Tantrasāra* (Los Angeles: Vichitra Press, 1981), pp. 58–67, suggests the variety of images of Kali. For Kali: David Kinsley, *Hindu Goddesses: Visions of the Divine Feminine in the Hindu Religious Tradition* (Berkeley: University of California Press, 1988), chapter 8; Ajit Mookerjee, *Kali: The Feminine Force* (Rochester: Destiny Books, 1988).

P. 157. Louise Allison Cort noted the similarity of the vessel and the image in India in "The Role of the Potter in South Asia," in Michael W. Meister, ed., *Making Things in South Asia: The Role of the Artist and Craftsman* (Philadelphia: University of Pennsylvania Department of

South Asia Regional Studies, 1988), p. 167.

P. 158. Raus in the days before Lars Andersson is described by Otto von Friesen in *Krukan från Raus* (Stockholm: Nordiska Museet, 1976).

P. 160. The Meaders family has been excellently documented: Allen H. Eaton, *Handicrafts of the Southern Highlands* (New York: Russell Sage Foundation, 1937), pp. 212–14; Rinzler and Sayers, *Meaders Family*; Nancy Sweezy, *Raised in Clay: The Southern Pottery Tradition* (Washington: Smithsonian Institution Press, 1984), pp. 98–111; John A. Burrison, *The Meaders Family of Mossy Creek: Eighty Years of North Georgia Folk Pottery* (Atlanta: Georgia State University Art Gallery, 1976); and John A. Burrison, *Brothers in Clay: The Story of Georgia Folk Pottery* (Athens: University of Georgia Press, 1983), chapters 6 and 16.

P. 163. The face jug: John Michael Vlach, *The Afro-American Tradition in Decorative Arts* (Cleveland: Cleveland Museum of Art, 1978), pp. 81–94; John Michael Vlach, "International Encounters at the Crossroads of Clay: European, Asian and African Influences on Edgefield Pottery," in Catherine Wilson Horne, ed., *Crossroads of Clay: The Southern Alkaline-Glazed Stoneware Tradition* (Columbia: McKissick Museum, 1990), pp. 27–36; Cinda K. Baldwin, *Great and Noble Jar: Traditional Stoneware of South Carolina* (Athens: University of Georgia Press, 1995), pp. 79–90; Burrison, *Brothers in Clay*, pp. 76, 229, 235, 269; Charles G. Zug, III, *Turners and Burners: Folk Potters of North Carolina* (Chapel Hill: University of North Carolina Press, 1986), pp. 384–86; Charles G. Zug, III, *Burlon Craig: An Open Window into the Past* (Raleigh: North

Carolina State University Foundations Gallery, 1994), pp. 6–21; and Steve Siporin, *American Folk Masters: The National Heritage Fellows* (New York: Abrams and Museum of International Folk Art, 1992), pp. 98–103. Today's explosion in the production of face jugs is documented in Robert C. Lock, *The Traditional Potters of Seagrove, North Carolina* (Greensboro: Antiques and Collectibles Press, 1994), pp. 184–90; and William W. Ivey, *North Carolina and Southern Folk Pottery: A Pictorial Survey* (Seagrove: Museum of North Carolina Pottery, 1992).

P. 163. See Cecelia Conway, *African Banjo Echoes in Appalachia: A Study of Folk Traditions* (Knoxville: University of Tennessee Press, 1995).

P. 166. Acoma's tradition: Jonathan Batkin, *Pottery of the Pueblos of New Mexico: 1700–1940* (Colorado Springs: Taylor Museum, 1987), pp. 136–47, 154–56; Francis H. Harlow, *Two Hundred Years of Historic Pueblo Pottery: The Gallegos Collection* (Santa Fe: Morning Star Gallery, 1990), plates 15–30; Larry Frank and Francis H. Harlow, *Historic Pottery of the Pueblo Indians: 1600–1880* (West Chester: Schiffer, 1990), pp. 121–35; Alfred E. Dittert, Jr. and Fred Plog, *Generations in Clay: Pueblo Pottery of the American Southwest* (Flagstaff: Northland Press, 1980), pp. 43–44, 77, 119; Stephen Trimble, *Talking with the Clay: The Art of Pueblo Pottery* (Santa Fe: School of American Research Press, 1987), pp. 73–80; and Rick Dillingham, *Fourteen Families in Pueblo Pottery* (Albuquerque: University of New Mexico Press, 1994), pp. 82–103. The great book remains Bunzel's *Pueblo Potter,* and the most complete book on Acoma is Rick Dillingham, with Me-

linda Elliott, *Acoma and Laguna Pottery* (Santa Fe: School of American Research Press, 1992). In *Acoma and Laguna,* Dillingham brings the story to the present, mentioning Wanda Aragon's interest in revival: pp. 185, 194, 200–201. On p. 182, he shows a jar by her mother, Frances Torivio, and on p. 84, he shows a jar by Wanda. Works by Lilly Salvador can be found in Jonathan L. Fairbanks, *Collecting American Decorative Arts and Sculpture: 1971–1991* (Boston: Museum of Fine Arts, 1991), pp. 27, 89; and Bill Mercer, *Singing the Clay: Pueblo Pottery of the Southwest, Yesterday and Today* (Cincinnati: Cincinnati Art Museum, 1995), p. 9. Lillian Peaster includes Frances Torivio, Lilly Salvador, and Wanda Aragon in *Pueblo Pottery Families* (Atglen: Schiffer, 1997), pp. 11–15. Robert Nichols has written a brief introduction to Wanda Aragon and her family in "Keeping Tradition Alive," *Focus/Santa Fe* (Oct.–Dec. 1995): 14–15.

P. 169. Lucy Lewis and her family: Susan Peterson, *Lucy M. Lewis: American Indian Potter* (Tokyo: Kodansha, 1984); Susan Peterson, *Pottery by American Indian Women: The Legacy of Generations* (New York: Abbeville Press, 1998), pp. 74–83, 132–41; Dillingham, *Fourteen Families in Pueblo Pottery,* pp. 92–103; Frederick J. Dockstader, *A Tribute to Lucy M. Lewis: Acoma Potter* (Fullerton: Museum of North Orange County, 1975).

P. 171. The storyteller: Barbara A. Babcock and Guy and Doris Monthan, *The Pueblo Storyteller: Development of a Figurative Ceramic Tradition* (Tucson: University of Arizona Press, 1986); Mark Bahti, *Pueblo Stories and Storytellers* (Tucson: Treasure Chest Publications, 1988); Glassie, *Spirit of Folk Art,* pp. 44–49.

P. 174. The early work at Kütahya is described by Oktay Aslanapa in *Osmanlılar Devrinde Kütahya Çinileri* (Istanbul: Sanat Tarihi Enstitüsü, 1949). John Carswell describes the middle period in *Kütahya Tiles and Pottery from the Armenian Cathedral of St. James, Jerusalem*, 2 vols. (Oxford: Oxford University Press, 1972). Şebnem Akalın and Hülya Yılmaz Bilgi present a fine collection, ranging from the eighteenth century to the early twentieth, in *Delights of Kütahya: Kütahya Tiles and Pottery in the Suna and İnan Kıraç Collection* (Istanbul: Suna and İnan Kıraç Research Institute, 1997). Another collection, largely from the same period, is presented by John Carswell in "Kütahya Tiles and Ceramics," in Sevgi Gönül, ed., *Turkish Tiles and Ceramics* (Istanbul: Sadberk Hanım Museum, 1991), pp. 49–102. For the twentieth century: Faruk Şahin, "Kütahya Seramik Teknolojisi ve Çini Fırınları Hakkında Görüşler," *Sanat Tarihi Yıllığı* 9 (1982): 133–64; Rıfat Çini, *Kütahya in Turkish Tile Making* (Istanbul: Uycan Yayınları, 1991); Yılmaz Uyar, ed., *Sıtkı Olçar: From Ceramic to Tile: A Master the Kiln Soul* (Istanbul: Promat A. Ş., 1995); and Glassie, *Turkish Traditional Art Today*, pp. 425–562, 856–72.

P. 178. See Yael Olenik, *The Armenian Pottery of Jerusalem* (Tel Aviv: Haaretz Museum, 1986).

P. 182. Today the great *çini* of the sixteenth century is generally attributed to İznik. In its own day, it was made in both İznik and Kütahya, and when we are faced with a particular piece, it is, with rare exceptions, impossible to know whether it was made in İznik or Kütahya. Long ago, in his *Victoria and Albert Museum Guide to the Collection of Tiles* (London: Board of Education, 1939), p. 19, Arthur Lane commented that Kütahya ware could not be distinguished from that of İznik until the eighteenth century. In the third chapter of his *Later Islamic Pottery: Persia, Syria, Egypt, Turkey* (London: Faber and Faber, 1957), Arthur Lane established the developmental scheme that still provides the basis for thinking about sixteenth-century *çini*. That great ware has received excellent descriptive study; see: Tahsin Öz, *Turkish Ceramics* (Ankara: Turkish Press, Broadcasting and Tourist Department, 1957); Gönül Öney, *Türk Çini Sanatı* (Istanbul: Yapı ve Kredi Bankası, 1976); Walter B. Denny, *The Ceramics of the Mosque of Rüstem Pasha and the Environment of Change* (New York: Garland, 1977); Nurhan Atasoy and Julian Raby, *Iznik: The Pottery of Ottoman Turkey* (London: Thames and Hudson, Alexandria Press, 1989); and John Carswell, *Iznik Pottery* (London: British Museum Press, 1998).

P. 184. James Joyce, *Finnegans Wake* (New York: Viking, 1939), p. 115.

P. 185. I take my stand with the artisans of Turkey. There are thinkers in consumer societies who wish to steal art from its creators, reducing the aesthetic to a matter of the beholder's taste, and defining art in terms of their own reactions, but I believe that art is defined by the gift made to materials by the creator in the instant of concentration, and that the observer's responsibility is not to react positively or negatively in line with a supposedly refined sensibility, but to work, learning to appreciate the artist's gift, however strange it might at first appear. Turks call that gift, that presence in things which defines them as art, *aşk*: passion, devotion, love. It is what Wassily Kandinsky called soul and inner necessity: *Concern-*

ing the Spiritual in Art (New York: George Wittenborn, 1955, pub. 1912), pp. 52, 70; and Wassily Kandinsky and Franz Marc, eds., *The Blaue Reiter Almanac* (New York: Viking Press, 1974, pub. 1912), p. 153. It is what Bernard Leach called sincerity: *A Potter's Book* (Levittown: Transatlantic Arts, 1973), pp. 17–18. It is what Daisetz T. Suzuki called sincerity and devotion: *Zen and Japanese Culture* (Princeton: Princeton University Press, 1970), p. 226. It is what Ananda Coomaraswamy called care and honesty: *The Transformation of Nature in Art* (Cambridge: Harvard University Press, 1935), p. 90.

P. 188. On the issue of representation in Islamic art: Titus Burckhardt, *Art of Islam: Language and Meaning* (Westerham: World of Islam Festival, 1976), chapter 3; Oleg Grabar, *The Formation of Islamic Art* (New Haven: Yale University Press, 1977), pp. 75–103; Thomas W. Arnold, *Painting in Islam: A Study of the Place of the Pictorial in Muslim Culture* (New York: Dover, 1965, pub. 1938), pp. 4–7; Glassie, *Turkish Traditional Art Today*, chapters 5, 23; Yusuf Al-Qaradawi, *The Lawful and the Prohibited in Islam* (Indianapolis: American Trust Publications, 1960) pp. 100–120.

P. 193. Mevlana Celaleddin Rumi's story begins in the second book at verse 1720 of the *Mesnevi*. A full translation of that vast work was prepared by Reynold A. Nicholson, *The Mathnawi of Jalalu'ddin Rumi*, 8 vols. (London: Luzac, 1925–1940). Nicholson included an abbreviated version of the story in *Tales of Mystic Meaning* (Oxford: Oneworld, 1995), pp. 95–97. I took it from Mevlana's *Mesnevi*, translated and edited by Veled İzbudak and Abdülbaki Gölpınarlı (Istanbul: Milli Eğitim Bakınlığı Yayınlarlı, 1990), II, pp. 132–39.

P. 198. Examples of figurative ceramics from Japan: Richard S. Cleveland, *200 Years of Japanese Porcelain* (St. Louis: City Art Museum, 1970), pp. 55, 96–97; Hugo Munsterberg, *The Ceramic Art of Japan* (Rutland: Charles E. Tuttle, 1964), pp. 44, 96, 122, 155, 177, 221; Donald A. Wood, Teruhisa Tanaka, and Frank Chance, *Echizen: Eight Hundred Years of Japanese Stoneware* (Birmingham: Birmingham Museum of Art, 1994), pp. 70–71; Janet Barriskill, *Visiting the Mino Kilns, With a Translation of Arakawa Toyozo's "The Traditions and Techniques of Mino Pottery"* (Broadway: Wild Peony, 1995), pp. 28, 37, 121; Louise Allison Cort, *Seto and Mino Ceramics: Japanese Collections in the Freer Gallery of Art* (Washington: Smithsonian Institution, 1992), pp. 163–64; Louise Allison Cort, *Shigaraki, Potters' Valley* (Tokyo: Kodansha, 1979), pp. 266–67; and Tsugio Mikami, *The Art of Japanese Ceramics* (New York: Weatherhill, 1972), pp. 71, 124, 145, 174. In Mikami's book, the photograph on p. 124 shows a medieval stoneware lion from Seto in the seated form that continues to characterize work at Seto, in contrast to the pouncing form that has been characteristic of Hagi since the seventeenth century (see pp. 218–21).

P. 198. Figurative ceramics from China: He Li, *Chinese Ceramics: A New Comprehensive Survey from the Asian Art Museum of San Francisco* (New York: Rizzoli, 1996), pp. 9–10, 139, 272, 311, 331–32; Wanda Garnsey and Rewi Alley, *China: Ancient Kilns and Modern Ceramics, A Guide to the Potteries* (Canberra: Australian National University Press, 1983), pp. 106–32; Robert Tichane, *Ching-Te-Chen: Views of a Porcelain City* (Painted Post: New York State Institute for Glaze Research, 1983), pp. 35, 37, 74, 99; Hincheung Lovell, ed., *Jingdezhen Wares: The Yuan Evolution* (Hong Kong: Oriental Ceramic Society, 1984), pp. 26–27, 54–57, 90–93; P. J. Donnelly, *Blanc De Chine: The Porcelain of Téhua in Fukien* (London: Faber and Faber, 1969), pp. 8–41; and Fredrikke S. Scollard and Terese Tse Bartholomew, *Shiwan Ceramics: Beauty, Color, and Passion* (San Francisco: Chinese Culture Foundation, 1994). The white figures of Dehua were imitated in Korea as well as Japan; see W. B. Honey *Corean Pottery* (New York: D. Van Nostrand, 1948), p. 16.

P. 198. For Mingei, see the introductory essays by Pearce and the Yanagis to Sori Yanagi, ed., *Mingei: Masterpieces of Japanese Folkcraft* (Tokyo: Kodansha, 1991); these good essays by Robert Moes: *Mingei: Japanese Folk Art from the Brooklyn Museum Collection* (New York: Universe, 1985), pp. 11–20, and *Mingei: Japanese Folk Art from the Montgomery Collection* (Alexandria: Art Services International, 1995), pp. 19–42, and "Edward Morse, Yanagi Soetsu and the Japanese Folk Art Movement," in Erica Hamilton Weeder, ed., *Japanese Folk Art: A Triumph of Simplicity* (New York: Japan Society, 1992), pp. 20–27; Yuko Kikuchi, "Hamada and the *Mingei* Movement," in Timothy Wilcox, ed., *Shoji Hamada: Master Potter* (London: Lund Humphries, 1998), pp. 22–25; Brian Moeran, *Lost Innocence: Folk Craft Potters of Onta, Japan* (Berkeley: University of California Press, 1984), pp. 12–27; and Richard L. Wilson, *Inside Japanese Ceramics: A Primer of Materials, Techniques, and Traditions* (New York: Weatherhill, 1995), pp. 32–34.

P. 199. Potters among the living national treasures: Masataka Ogawa and Tsune Sugimura, *The Enduring Crafts of Japan:*

33 Living National Treasures (New York: Walker/Weatherhill, 1968), pp. 5–42; Jan Fontein, ed., *Living National Treasures of Japan* (Boston: Museum of Fine Arts, 1983), pp. 16–18, 264–66.

P. 199. Kakiemon: Takeshi Nagatake, *Kakiemon* (Tokyo: Kodansha, 1981), pp. 6–12, 38–39; Kenji Adachi and Mitsuhiko Hasebe, *Japanese Painted Porcelain: Modern Masterpieces in Overglaze Enamel* (New York: Weatherhill, 1980), pp. 16–17, 233–34, plates 38–44, 84–85, 91, 162–64; Mikami, *Art of Japanese Ceramics*, pp. 164–65; Munsterberg, *Ceramic Art of Japan*, p. 141; Fontein, *Living National Treasures*, pp. 265–66.

P. 203. The missionary's report from Jingdezhen: Tichane, *Ching-Te-Chen*, pp. 57, 70, 73.

P. 203. Simeon Shaw comments on early divisions in labor in *History of the Staffordshire Potteries* (New York: Praeger, 1970, pub. 1829), pp. 104, 166.

P. 204. Richard L. Wilson, *The Art of Ogata Kenzan: Persona and Production in Japanese Ceramics* (New York: Weatherhill, 1991), pp. 115–16.

Pp. 206–207. A. L. Sadler wrote a full study of the tea ceremony in *Cha-no-yu: The Japanese Tea Ceremony* (Rutland: Charles E. Tuttle, 1963, pub. 1933). I think the best brief introduction is Soshitsu Sen XV, *Tea Life, Tea Mind* (New York: Weatherhill for the Urasenke Foundation, 1979). The relation of the tea ceremony to Zen is described by Suzuki, *Zen and Japanese Culture*, chapters 8–10; and by Hugo Munsterberg, *Zen and Oriental Art* (Rutland: Charles E. Tuttle, 1993), chapter 5. On the teabowl, tea utensils, and their aesthetics: Tadanari Mitsuoka, *Ceramic Art of Japan* (Tokyo:

Japan Travel Bureau, 1949), pp. 170–72; Rand Castile, *The Way of Tea* (New York: Weatherhill, 1971), part 3; Ryoichi Fujioka, *Shino and Oribe Ceramics* (Tokyo: Kodansha, 1977), pp. 35–36, 157–61; Munsterberg, *Ceramic Art of Japan*, chapter 6. Seiroku Noma has written a magnificent general survey of Japanese art; the tea ceremony and its arts are treated in the fifth chapter of the second volume: *The Arts of Japan* (Tokyo: Kodansha, 1978). In his truly excellent introduction to Japanese pottery, Richard Wilson describes aesthetics effectively, treats the centers where tea ware is made, including Hagi, and illustrates the making of a Raku teabowl: *Inside Japanese Ceramics*, pp. 25–31, 41–45, 55–58, 164–76. A wonderful collection of Raku teabowls is assembled in the catalog *Chojiro: 400 Years Memorial Exhibition of Raku* (Kyoto: Raku Museum, 1988).

P. 209. Fawn-spot ware at Asahi: Mitoko Matsubayashi, *The Asahi Pottery in Uji* (Uji: Asahi Pottery, 1991), pp. 50, 56–61.

P. 213. Çanakkale pottery: Gönül Öney, *Türk Devri Çanakkale Seramikleri* (Ankara: Çanakkale Seramik Fabrikaları, 1971); Gönül Öney, "Çanakkale Ceramics," in Gönül, ed., *Turkish Tiles and Ceramics*, pp. 103–43; Ara Altun, *Çanakkale Ceramics: Suna and İnan Kıraç Collection* (Istanbul: Vehbi Koç Vakfı, 1996). Kınık pottery: Güngör Güner, *Anadolu'da Yaşamakta Olan İlkel Çömlekçilik* (Istanbul: Ak Yayınları, 1988), pp. 74–77; Glassie, *Turkish Traditional Art Today*, chapter 13.

P. 217. Reiko Chiba introduces the Seven Gods briefly in *The Seven Lucky Gods of Japan* (Rutland: Charles E. Tuttle, 1966). They are described as ceramic images in

Hazel H. Gorham, *Japanese and Oriental Ceramics* (Rutland: Charles E. Tuttle, 1990), pp. 218–19.

P. 225. My friend Mark Hewitt points one clear route to the future. For his work see: Charles G. Zug, III, *Mark Hewitt: Stuck in the Mud* (Cullowhee: Western Carolina University Beck Gallery, 1992); Charles Millard, *Mark Hewitt: Potter* (Raleigh: North Carolina State University Visual Arts Center, 1997). Every morning I take my coffee from the breakfast table to my desk in a mug made by Mark.

Vernacular Architecture

P. 227. Toward the beginning of this essay, a few fragments survive from a talk I gave at a conference on vernacular architecture at the Middle East Technical University in Ankara, Turkey, in 1982. That talk was printed as "Vernacular Architecture and Society," *Material Culture* 16:1 (1984): 4–24, and it has been reprinted in: Simon J. Bronner, ed., *American Material Culture and Folklife: A Prologue and Dialogue* (Ann Arbor: UMI Research Press, 1985), pp. 47–62; Daniel W. Ingersoll, Jr. and Gordon Bronitsky, eds. *Mirror and Metaphor: Material and Social Constructions of Reality* (Lanham: University Press of America, 1987), pp. 229–45; Mete Turan, ed., *Vernacular Architecture: Paradigms of Environmental Response* (Aldershot: Avebury, 1990), pp. 271–84; and *Traditional Dwellings and Settlements Review* 1:2 (1990): 9–21. This essay starts where the old one did, then it goes in directions that would have been impossible for me in 1982, when my fieldwork had been limited to the eastern United States, Britain, and Ireland.

P. 231. Another reason for architectural history following art history is provided by Dell Upton in *Architecture in the United States* (Oxford: Oxford University Press, 1998), pp. 262–72, when he describes architects, insecure in their identity and wishing to separate themselves from builders, adopting the pose of the artist. One consequence of their pose is a restriction in the use of the professional title. Whether or not they were trained professionally, painters are painters, poets are poets, but some writers call designers of buildings architects only if they were educated and licensed in a particular way. The greatest poets—Homer, Shakespeare—were not trained in the university, and there is no good reason why designers of cathedrals or chicken coops, though not trained in the university, should not be called architects.

Pp. 233–37. I tell about the change in roofing in *Passing the Time in Ballymenone*, pp. 414–22; *Turkish Traditional Art Today*, pp. 261, 635; and *Art and Life in Bangladesh*, pp. 254–55. The pattern I found in Turkey is also found in the Southwest: Nancy Hunter Warren, *Villages of Hispanic New Mexico* (Santa Fe: School of American Research Press, 1987), chapter 4; Charles L. Briggs, *Competence in Performance: The Creativity of Tradition in Mexicano Verbal Art* (Philadelphia: University of Pennsylvania Press, 1988), p. 77.

P. 237. Åke Campbell's attractive evaluation has often been repeated, for example in the excellent *Atlas of the Irish Rural Landscape* (Cork: Cork University Press, 1997), p. 147, edited by F. H. A. Aalen, Kevin Whelan, and Matthew Stout. In his first report of the five weeks he spent in fieldwork in 1934, "Irish Fields and Houses: A Study of Rural Culture,"

Béaloideas 5:1 (1935): 57–74, Campbell described a farm in Kerry and offered a series of highly important observations, connecting Ireland to the highland pastoral tradition, and noting two basic house types, one with the chimney on the gable, the other with the chimney set centrally, and he generalized (p. 58): "The humanizing of the landscape has developed until the natural landscape is now almost wholly defaced."

Pp. 240–42. The log cabin is so important to American views of the self that scholars have lost their cool in arguments over its origins. The main old texts are: Henry C. Mercer, *The Origin of Log Houses in the United States* (Doylestown: Bucks County Historical Society, 1976, pub. 1924) and Harold R. Shurtleff, *The Log Cabin Myth* (Gloucester: Peter Smith, 1967, pub. 1939). Fred Kniffen allowed me to co-author with him the paper that summed things up in the sixties: "Building in Wood in the Eastern United States: A Time-Place Perspective," *The Geographical Review* 56:1 (1966): 40–66, reprinted in Dell Upton and John Michael Vlach, eds., *Common Places: Readings in American Vernacular Architecture* (Athens: University of Georgia Press, 1986), pp. 159–81. I still believe that I got the story about right in my first paper, published when I was still an undergraduate: "The Appalachian Log Cabin," *Mountain Life and Work* 39:4 (1963): 5–14, reprinted in: W. K. McNeil, ed., *Appalachian Images in Folk and Popular Culture* (Ann Arbor: UMI Research Press, 1989), pp. 307–14; and George O. Carney, ed., *Baseball, Barns, and Bluegrass: A Geography of American Folklife* (Lanham: Rowman and Littlefield, 1998), pp. 19–28. That old paper was much refined as "The Types of the Southern Mountain Cabin," in Jan H. Brunvand, *The Study of American Folklore* (New York: W.W. Norton, 1968), pp. 338–70. Horizontal log construction was brought by many different groups to North America, but the variety that became dominant on the eastern frontier was that of the Pennsylvania Germans, though modified through synthesis with techniques from English framing. Since there is no necessary connection in origin between technology and form, the most usual form of the log cabin was not German, but English or Irish. Among the many good regional studies of American log buildings are these: Terry G. Jordan, *Texas Log Buildings: A Folk Architecture* (Austin: University of Texas Press, 1978); Warren E. Roberts, *Log Buildings in Southern Indiana* (Bloomington: Trickster Press, 1996, pub. 1984); Donald A. Hutslar, *Log Construction in the Ohio Country, 1750–1850* (Athens: Ohio University Press, 1992); John Morgan, *The Log House in East Tennessee* (Knoxville: University of Tennessee Press, 1990); Charles E. Martin, *Hollybush: Folk Building and Social Change in an Appalachian Community* (Knoxville: University of Tennessee Press, 1984), chapters 2–3; and Jennifer Eastman Attebery, *Building with Logs: Western Log Construction in Context* (Moscow: University of Idaho Press, 1998).

P. 245. The double-crib barn is type B in Charles H. Dornbusch and John K. Heyl, *Pennsylvania German Barns* (Allentown: Schlechter's, 1958). I described the southern extension of the form in "The Pennsylvania Barn in the South: Part I," *Pennsylvania Folklife* 15:2 (1965/66): 8–19; and I did a better job with it in "The Double-Crib Barn in South-Central Pennsylvania," *Pioneer America* 1:1 (1969): 9–16; 1:2

(1969): 40–45; 2:1 (1970): 47–52; 2:2 (1970): 23–34. In his good book *The Pennsylvania Barn: Its Origin, Evolution, and Distribution in North America* (Baltimore: Johns Hopkins University Press, 1992), Robert F. Ensminger does not treat the double-crib barn, which is unfortunate because it holds the key to much of the formal development of the large banked barns of Pennsylvania. An elaboration of the double-crib form is documented by Marian Moffett and Lawrence Wodehouse in *East Tennessee Cantilever Barns* (Knoxville: University of Tennessee Press, 1993). The common transverse-crib barn was a transformation of the double-crib: Glassie, *Pattern in the Material Folk Culture of the Eastern United States*, pp. 88–99; Terry G. Jordan-Bychkov, "Transverse-Crib Barns, The Upland South, and Pennsylvania Extended," *Material Culture* 30:2 (1998): 5–31.

Pp. 245–46. In his excellent book on traditional pottery in Georgia, *Brothers in Clay*, p. 9, John Burrison comments that the one-man shop was not the norm in the past; it is a twentieth-century expedient. Norio Agawa's operation, described at the end of the fourth chapter of this book, depends on one man, but he does not do everything himself. His clay is mined and refined by others, then delivered to him ready for use.

Pp. 246–47. I have never published the results of our work in Greene County, but a full report, "Architecture in Log in Southwestern Pennsylvania," was submitted to the Information Office of Northern Ireland in 1973, and it became the basis for architectural replication at the Ulster-American Folk Park, Camphill, Omagh, County Tyrone, Northern Ireland.

NOTES TO PAGES 247-73

P. 247. John James, *Chartres: The Masons Who Built a Legend* (London: Routledge and Kegan Paul, 1982).

P. 247. Warren Roberts, "The Tools Used in Building Log Houses in Indiana," in Upton and Vlach, *Common Places*, pp. 182–203.

Pp. 248–49. I illustrate Paddy McBrien's house in *Passing the Time in Ballymenone*, pp. 387, 412–13.

Pp. 249–51. Karagömlek's new mosques: Glassie, *Turkish Traditional Art Today*, pp. 742–46.

P. 251. A builder in Ethiopia said that architectural plans are only for people who don't know what they are doing: Naigzy Gebremedhin, "Some Traditional Types of Housing in Ethiopia," in Paul Oliver, ed., *Shelter in Africa* (New York: Praeger, 1971), p. 120.

Pp. 258–61. The Wealden house: M. W. Barley, *The English Farmhouse and Cottage* (London: Routledge and Kegan Paul, 1961), pp.26–30; Eric Mercer, *English Vernacular Houses* (London: Royal Commission on Historical Monuments, 1975), pp. 11–14; Richard Harris, *Discovering Timber-Framed Buildings* (Aylesbury: Shire, 1978), pp. 65–67; R. W. Brunskill, *Houses* (London: Collins, 1982), pp. 58–61; R. T. Mason, *Framed Buildings of the Weald* (Horsham: Coach, 1969), chapters 2–3; and Anthony Quiney, *Kent Houses* (Woodbridge: Antique Collectors' Club, 1993), pp. 137–56.

Pp. 267–69. Mrs. Cutler's kitchen is the prime text of chapter 13 in my *Passing the Time in Ballymenone*, and I feature Gökyurt in the chapter on vernacular architecture in *Turkish Traditional Art To-*day, pp. 264–71. For more on the Irish dresser, see Claudia Kinmonth, *Irish Country Furniture: 1700–1959* (New Haven: Yale University Press, 1993), chapter 3.

P. 272. Dell Upton describes the search for women in architecture in *Architecture in the United States*, pp. 272–79. William Morris, *News from Nowhere; or, an Epoch of Rest, Being Some Chapters from a Utopian Romance* (Hammersmith: Kelmscott Press, 1892), chapter 26. In chapter 15, on work, art, and the kind of commercial colonialism that is called globalization today, William Morris makes a concise presentation of the essentials of his thinking.

P. 272. My generalization on North America comes straight from this excellent book: Peter Nabokov and Robert Easton, *Native American Architecture* (New York: Oxford University Press, 1989), p. 30. For women as builders in Africa: Susan Denyer, *African Traditional Architecture* (New York: Africana, 1978), p. 92; Labelle Prussin, *Architecture in Northern Ghana* (Berkeley: University of California Press, 1969), pp. 57–58, 97; Jean-Paul Bourdier and Trinh T. Minh-ha, *African Spaces: Designs for Living in Upper Volta* (New York: Africana, 1985), pp. 45, 47, 105–6, 162–63; T. C. Anyamba and A. A. Adebaye, *Traditional Architecture: Settlement, Evolution and Built Form* (Nairobi: Jomo Kenyatta Foundation, 1993), p. 20; and Franco Frescura, *Rural Shelter in Southern Africa* (Johannesburg: Ravan Press, 1981), p. 14.

P. 273. See James Deetz, *Flowerdew Hundred: The Archaeology of a Virginia Plantation, 1619–1864* (Charlottesville: University Press of Virginia, 1993), pp. 124–32.

P. 274. See: Marian Wenzel, *House Decoration in Nubia* (London: Duckworth, 1972); Stella Kramrisch, *The Hindu Temple*, 2 vols. (Delhi: Motilal Banarsidass, 1996, pub. 1946).

Pp. 276–79. Talbot Hamlin's *Greek Revival Architecture: Being an Account of Important Trends in American Architecture and American Life Prior to the War Between the States* (New York: Dover, 1964, pub. 1944) introduces the style without attending to formal transformations, leaving a wonderful topic for one who would settle into the analysis of the houses of the period in New York, Ohio, and Michigan. Examples can be found in Richard N. Campen, *Architecture of the Western Reserve, 1800–1900* (Cleveland: Press of Case Western Reserve University, 1971). Fred W. Peterson analyzes the western single-wing variety of the Greek Revival form in his good book *Homes in the Heartland: Balloon Frame Farmhouses of the Upper Midwest, 1850–1900* (Lawrence: University of Kansas Press, 1992), chapter 5.

P. 281. In *American Architecture Since 1780: A Guide to the Styles* (Cambridge: The MIT Press, 1969), Marcus Whiffen presents the sequence of styles clearly. The problem is that very few houses fit the sequence neatly.

Pp. 283–86. I describe the architecture of Bangladesh in the first chapter *of Art and Life in Bangladesh.* See also: A. K. M. Islam, *A Bangladesh Village: Political Conflict and Cohesion* (Prospect Heights: Waveland Press, 1987, pub. 1974), pp. 44–48, 55–58, 61, 67–68; Khondkar Iftekhar Ahmed, *Up to the Waist in Mud: Earth-Based Architecture in Rural Bangladesh* (Dhaka: University Press, 1994), pp. 6–15, 25–31, 43–44, 47–48, 94–95, 105, 107, 112, 115, 118; Syed Mahmudul Hasan, "Folk Architecture of Bangladesh," in Shamsuzzaman Khan, ed., *Folklore of Bangladesh* (Dhaka: Bangla Academy, 1987), pp. 424–45; and Saif-ul-Haq, "Architecture within the Folk Tradition: A Representation from Bangladesh," *Traditional Dwellings and Settlements Review* 5:2 (1994): 61–72.

Pp. 286–88. As is the case throughout this book, the information from Sweden is based on my own fieldwork, but I know Sweden less well than I do Bangladesh (or Ireland or Turkey) and I wish to acknowledge the help of good friends: Kersti Jobs-Björklöf, Mats Widbom, and Christer Ekelund. Two excellent publications deal with the villages I visited: Roland Andersson, *Byar och Färbodar i Leksands Kommun: Kulturhistorisk Miljönalys* (Leksand: Dalarna Museum, 1983) and Lillie Hågglund, *Bilder Från Ullvi by* (Leksand: Leksands Kommun, 1983). And I was aided by the excellent report, "The Dwelling as a Cultural Phenomenon," submitted by Christer Ekelund and Mats Widbom to the Swedish Council for Building Research in December 1988.

Pp. 289–91. For the longhouse, see Mercer, *English Vernacular Houses*, chapter 3. W. G. Hoskins describes the longhouses of Devon in the first chapter of *Old Devon* (London: Pan Books, 1966). The architecture of Wales has been studied magnificently. For the Welsh longhouse, see these important works: Iorwerth C. Peate, *The Welsh House: A Study in Folk Culture* (London: The Honourable Society of Cymmrodorion, 1940), chapter 4; Sir Cyril Fox and Lord Raglan, *Monmouthshire House* (Cardiff: National Museum of Wales, 1951–1954), I, pp. 88–90; II, pp. 104–8; III, pp. 82–85; S. R. Jones and J. T. Smith, "The Houses of Breconshire," *Brycheinog* 9 (1963): 5–34; 11 (1965): 50–89; 12 (1966/67): 23–53; and Peter Smith, *Houses of the Welsh Countryside: A Study in Historical Geography* (London: Royal Commission on Ancient and Historical Monuments in Wales, 1988), chapters 4, 9, 10. I report the seventeenth-century sources for Ireland in *Passing the Time in Ballymenone*, pp. 376–79, and describe the linear farm plan on pp. 343–51.

P. 295. D. W. Meinig closes the important book he edited on *The Interpretation of Ordinary Landscapes* (New York: Oxford University Press, 1979) with an essay on the contributions of W. G. Hoskins and J. B. Jackson, two of the most influential of the scholars of the landscape. Jackson is of great importance in the United States; see his *Discovering the Vernacular Landscape* (New Haven: Yale University Press, 1984). Because, as Meinig points out (pp. 203, 229), Hoskins believed above all in the facts, while Jackson proceeds by argument, offering little by way of documentation or demonstration, I would have paired Hoskins with Fred Kniffen if I needed an American master, and I believe the best pairing would be W. G. Hoskins and E. Estyn Evans. Both authored a grand statement: Hoskins, *The Making of the English Landscape* (London: Hodder and Stoughton, 1955); Evans, *The Personality of Ireland: Habitat, Heritage and History* (Cambridge: University Press, 1973). Both wrote a superb local study: Hoskins, *The Midland Peasant: The Economic and Social History of a Leicestershire Village* (London: Macmillan, 1965); Evans, *Mourne Country: Landscape and Life in South Down* (Dundalk: Dundalgan Press, 1967). Both wrote popular accounts of regions:

Hoskins, *Midland England: A Survey of the Country between the Chilterns and the Trent* (London: B. T. Batsford, 1949) and *Devon* (London: Collins, 1954); Evans, *Northern Ireland* (London: Collins, 1951). Both concentrated on the rural, for most of the landscape is rural, but both wrote on cities: Hoskins, *Two Thousand Years in Exeter* (Exeter: James Townsend, 1960); Evans, ed., *Belfast in Its Regional Setting: A Scientific Survey* (Belfast: British Association for the Advancement of Science, 1952). For both there are major collections of essays: Hoskins, *Provincial England: Essays in Social and Economic History* (London: Macmillan, 1965); Evans, *Ireland and the Atlantic Heritage: Selected Writings* (Dublin: Lilliput Press, 1996). Both of these men wrote elegantly and passionately; both were impatient with the impatience of the twentieth century, and while Meinig is right to fault Hoskins for his lack of interest in modern phenomena (pp. 206–9), the intensity of his belief not only led Hoskins to write clearly, it led him to use modern technology to reach a wider audience. The books Hoskins wrote to accompany his television work are exemplary popular presentations of important ideas: *English Landscapes* (London: British Broadcasting Corporation, 1973) and *One Man's England* (London: British Broadcasting Corporation, 1978). Evans used lectures, the radio, and the museum to get his ideas to the public; he was instrumental in founding the Ulster Folk and Transport Museum, one of the very best outdoor museums in the world. Hoskins is, at last, a historian, and he prepared two important guides for local historical research: *Local History in England* (London: Longmans, Green, 1959) and *Fieldwork in Local History* (London: Faber and Faber, 1969). Evans is, at last, a social scientist, a geographer, archaeologist, and ethnologist. He wrote a major statement on Irish archaeology in *Prehistoric and Early Christian Ireland: A Guide* (London: B. T. Batsford, 1966). He wrote two important books on Irish folk culture: *Irish Heritage: The Landscape, The People and Their Work* (Dundalk: W. Tempest, 1963, pub. 1942) and *Irish Folk Ways.* And Evans did not limit himself to Ireland; he wrote *France: A Geographical Introduction* (London: Christophers, 1951, pub. 1937). W. G. Hoskins and E. Estyn Evans both inspired a host of followers who work productively along the trails they blazed. Together they show how exacting study in the field and clear, passionate exposition can bring humanistic and social scientific concerns and methods into unity. Their works best exemplify the hope for historical study in material culture.

Pp. 295–96. The idea of two zones is too simple: Hoskins, *Making of the English Landscape,* p. 38. The village landscape of Japan is described well by Tsuneo Sato, "Tokugawa Villages and Agriculture," in Chie Nakane, Shinzaburo Oishi, and Conrad Totman, eds., *Tokugawa Japan: The Social and Economic Antecedents of Modern Japan* (Tokyo: University of Tokyo Press, 1991), pp. 37–80.

P. 296. I describe the Turkish village in *Turkish Traditional Art Today,* chapter 9. The architecture and dispersed settlement of the eastern Black Sea region are presented by Orhan Özgüner in *Köyde Mimari: Doğu Karadeniz* (Ankara: Orta Doğu Teknik Üniversitesi Mimarlık Fakültesi, 1970). The Irish system of rundale is described by E. Estyn Evans in *Irish Folk Ways,* pp. 20–26, 32–34, and in his introduction to the facsimile re-

print of the fifth edition (1889) of Lord George Hill's *Facts from Gweedore* (Belfast: Institute of Irish Studies, 1971). Rundale—the Irish openfield system— is also described by F. H. A. Aalen in his excellent book *Man and the Landscape in Ireland* (London: Academic Press, 1978), pp. 181–87, 220–25.

Pp. 298–301. Lowry Nelson provides a fine account in *The Mormon Village: A Pattern and Technique of Land Settlement* (Salt Lake City: University of Utah Press, 1952). Thomas Carter describes Mormon houses excellently in his paper "Folk Design in Utah Architecture, 1849–1890," in the book he edited, *Images of an American Land: Vernacular Architecture in the Western United States* (Albuquerque: University of New Mexico Press, 1997), pp. 41–60.

Pp. 301–2. The story of the English village and its enclosure is told by W. G. Hoskins in *Making of the English Landscape,* chapters 2–6. The topic has a vast, complicated, and contentious bibliography, but one clear history is W. E. Tate's *The Enclosure Movement* (New York: Walker and Company, 1967). The movement divides into three great phases: thirteenth to fifteenth centuries, sixteenth and seventeenth, eighteenth and nineteenth. The last, the period of parliamentary enclosure, was marked by a diminishing of argument (Tate, p. 86) but the middle period, most important for America, inspired outrage among intellectuals, like Sir Thomas More, and it drove the peasants to rebellious action; it was the time of the Levellers and the Diggers. Through its long history, the argument for enclosure was that it promoted agricultural improvement and increased profits. The argument against enclosure was that it led to depopulation of the land and to misery for the poor. But the poor were called lazy, their communal culture stood in the way of progress, and enclosure triumphed despite the opposition of Christian moralists. The issues and results are about the same in the United States when poor people are removed from their neighborhoods in the cities by urban renewal or driven from their family farms when their land is taken and made into parks for the pleasure of the prosperous. The spirit of enclosure—progressive, profiteering, and disdainful of poor people and local cultures—continues. Tate ends his calm, balanced history by seeing the enclosure movement as an economic success and a social disaster (p. 175).

Pp. 303–8. W. G. Hoskins, *Making of the English Landscape,* pp. 138–39. For a little on Braunton: Roy Millward and Adrian Robinson, *North Devon and North Cornwall* (London: Macmillan Education, 1971), pp. 73–79; A. H. Slee, *Victorian Days in a Devon Village* (Braunton: S. J. H. Slee, 1978), chapters 1–2.

P. 308. For the New England landscape, see these general statements: John R. Stilgoe, *Common Landscape of America, 1580 to 1845* (New Haven: Yale University Press, 1982), pp. 17–18, 43–58; D. W. Meinig, *The Shaping of America: A Geographical Perspective on 500 Years of History* (New Haven: Yale University Press, 1986), I, pp. 91–109, 243–44, 413–14; and David Hackett Fischer, *Albion's Seed: Four British Folkways in America* (New York: Oxford University Press, 1989), pp. 181–205. And these excellent studies: Sumner Chilton Powell, *Puritan Village: The Formation of a New England Town* (Middletown Wesleyan University Press, 1970, pub. 1963); and J. Ritchie Garrison, *Land-*

scape and Material Life in Franklin County, Massachusetts, 1770–1860 (Knoxville: University of Tennessee Press, 1991), chapter 2.

Pp. 310–12. Tax records: A. L. Shoemaker, ed., *The Pennsylvania Barn* (Kutstown: Pennsylvania Folklife Society, 1959), p. 9. I describe the Pennsylvania farm plan in "Eighteenth-Century Cultural Process in Delaware Valley Folk Building," *Winterthur Portfolio* 7 (1972): 29–57, reprinted in Upton and Vlach, *Common Places,* pp. 394–425. Unified German buildings in the United States: Richard W. E. Perrin, *Historic Wisconsin Buildings: A Survey of Pioneer Architecture, 1835–1870* (Milwaukee: Milwaukee Public Museum, 1962), pp. 14–25; Charles van Ravenswaay, *The Arts and Architecture of German Settlements in Missouri* (Columbia: University of Missouri Press, 1977), pp. 266–67, 279–84.

P. 312. Thomas C. Hubka, *Big House, Little House, Back House, Barn: The Connected Farm Buildings of New England* (Hanover: University Press of New England, 1984). The pattern that Hubka discovered—of farm buildings becoming more unified in the nineteenth century—I had noted in the study of one farm in upstate New York and reported in a paper which, though early and rough, I thought would become a model for fieldwork in its consideration of the whole farm as a unit (as opposed to the focus on building types), and in its blending of oral history, architectural history, and agricultural history; see "The Wedderspoon Farm," *New York Folklore Quarterly* 22:3 (1966): 165–87. But that did not become the norm for research, and it was Tom Hubka who brought the idea to fruition in his excellent book. Now it should be the model for the future.

P. 312–17. I reported my work in *Folk Housing in Middle Virginia*. Generally criticisms of that book have struck me as irrelevant, but in *Housing Culture: Traditional Architecture in an English Landscape* (London: UCL Press, 1993), p. 36, Matthew Johnson is quite right when he says the grammar of building is "unnecessarily cumbersome," and, in retrospect, I had come to his conclusion that constructing two models of competence would have been rhetorically preferable; at the same time, I could not have comprehended the nature of the duality until I had schematized the unity, and the complex conceptualization helped me understand change: in the transitional moment, the builder's competence, simultaneously incorporating two processes of design, was a bit cumbersome. Dell Upton illustrates how a better historian would have handled comparable data in "Vernacular Domestic Architecture in Eighteenth-Century Virginia," in Upton and Vlach, *Common Places*, pp. 315–35. In *The Transformation of Virginia: 1740–1790* (New York: W. W. Norton, 1988, pub. 1982), Rhys Isaac marvelously enriched our understanding of the period of architectural change. Using written sources and making them yield hints about life beyond the world of rich white men, Isaac reveals the political, religious, and especially the religious-political tensions of the period, confirming and deepening the notion of images of order that compensate for disorder on a dispersed landscape; see pp. 30–38, 51–59, 70–81, 116–20, 131–35, 147–77, 183, 197–98, 276, 292–95, 302–6, 310–12, 320–22, 327, 354–55. But nothing basic has been unsettled by later research, and the wonder to me is how close I came, with little time and no money, when I was twenty-five. For more on the architecture of the region: Marcus Whiffen, *The Eighteenth-Century Houses of Williamsburg* (Williamsburg: Colonial Williamsburg Foundation, 1985, pub. 1960); and Henry Chandlee Forman, *The Architecture of the Old South: The Medieval Style, 1585–1850* (Cambridge: Harvard University Press, 1948).

P. 313. The classic statement on the I-house is Fred Kniffen's article "Folk Housing: Key to Diffusion," appropriately taken from *Annals of the Association of American Geographers* 55:4 (1965): 459–77, and reprinted as the first paper in Upton and Vlach, *Common Places*, pp. 3–26. Mr. Kniffen had been using the term for a long time when he wrote that paper; it appears in the article with which, for me, the modern study of American vernacular architecture begins: "Louisiana House Types," *Annals of the Association of American Geographers* 26 (1936): 179–93, reprinted in Philip L. Wagner and Marvin W. Mikesell, eds., *Readings in Cultural Geography* (Chicago: University of Chicago Press, 1962), pp. 157–69.

P. 313. James Deetz argues effectively and correctly against the simplistic notion of "power relations" that replaces analysis in many writings about architecture; see *Flowerdew Hundred,* p. 65.

P. 317. For the change in English houses that took place between 1570 and 1640, before the English Revolution, see the notes to p. 334 below.

P. 318. To say that the climate conditioned the choice of dwelling in New England and Virginia is to state the obvious. James Marston Fitch has written a great book on the environmental influences upon design in *American Building 2: The Environmental Forces That Shape It* (Boston: Houghton Mifflin, 1972). In his earlier book *American Building: The Forces That Shape It* (Boston: Houghton Mifflin, 1948), pp. 10–14, Fitch began by noting the need in New England for heat and in the South for ventilation. Houses were not invented to fulfill those needs, but the houses that were selected from the large English repertory did provide heat in the North and ventilation in the South. Yet, to his excellent study of Virginia's houses in the period of diversity that precedes the period of conformity in every American region, Fraser D. Neiman appends a footnote, declaring consideration of climatic conditions, during explanation of architectural differences between New England and Virginia, to be "environmental determinism at its worst." It is not environmental determinism to consider the climate as an influence on design. Neiman argues further that the environmental rationale for the positioning of chimneys in the South makes no sense because people had separate kitchens. Many houses did not have separate kitchens. Even if they did, there is no basis for assuming that small meals were not prepared in the main house. In my time in Virginia, I never heard anyone use the word "hall" for the room that scholars call a hall. I did, however, hear it called "the fireplace room," and I was told that a fire was kept going in it in all weathers (exactly as in Ireland and in other parts of the South) so visitors could be entertained immediately. But even if the chimney were cold, its position centrally behind a central door would block the flow of air; the location of chimneys in the South seems to have less to do with the creation of heat than with the creation of passages for wind. If we were allowed only one explanation for architectural design, I would

prefer a social explanation to an environmental one. The shift from one monofunctional argument to another is progress: we move from the climate to tradition to social status, and things seem to be going forward. But real advancement would be marked by a shift from single causes to multiple causes, and it is necessary to consider the environment among them. I go on like this because Neiman's paper, "Domestic Architecture at the Clifts Plantation: The Social Context of Early Virginia Building," was reprinted (pp. 292–314) in the most important book on American vernacular architecture, *Common Places* by Upton and Vlach, and because his opinion was repeated by James Deetz in his book, the best of books on American material culture, *In Small Things Forgotten: An Archaeology of Early American Life* (New York: Anchor Books, 1996, pub. 1977), p. 153.

Pp. 318–22. The houses of southeastern England are described in P. Eden, "Smaller Post-medieval Houses in Eastern England," in Lionel Munby, ed., *East Anglian Studies* (Cambridge: W. Heffer, 1968), pp. 71–93. Eden's class J is the usual southeastern type; his class L moves the service to the rear, enabling a symmetrical facade, but it is far less common in England than it is in New England. It is not hard for the American in search of antecedents to find saltbox houses in England, but they are not easily found in the literature, since English authors are correctly concerned with the statistically dominant forms. Harry Forrester does show both the common asymmetrical form and the rarer saltbox form in *The Timber-Framed Houses of Essex: A Short Review of Their Types and Details, 14th to 18th Centuries* (Chelmsford: Tindal Press, 1959), pp. 14–20. There is an excellent bibliography on early New England houses: J. Frederick Kelly, *The Early Domestic Architecture of Connecticut* (New Haven: Yale University Press, 1924); Anthony N. B. Garvan, *Architecture and Town Planning in Colonial Connecticut* (New Haven: Yale University Press, 1951); Clay Lancaster, *The Architecture of Historic Nantucket* (New York: McGraw-Hill, 1972); Abbott Lowell Cummings, *The Framed Houses of Massachusetts Bay, 1625–1725* (Cambridge: Harvard University Press, 1979). The best introduction, I believe, to early New England architecture is Robert Blair St. George, "'Set Thine House in Order': The Domestication of the Yeomanry in Seventeenth-Century New England," in Jonathan L. Fairbanks and Robert F. Trent, eds., *New England Begins: The Seventeenth Century* (Boston: Museum of Fine Arts, 1982), II, pp. 159–351, revised in Upton and Vlach, *Common Places*, pp. 336–64.

P. 322. See Dana Arnold, ed., *The Georgian Villa* (Phoenix Mill: Alan Sutton, 1996).

P. 325. The central hallway and symmetrical facade clearly indicate the presence of the Georgian idea in the largest houses. Its presence in the smallest houses is much subtler. The early form of the small house is like the cabin I illustrated on pp. 84–85 of *Folk Housing in Middle Virginia*: the door is set near the center of the front; the plan, while squarish, might be rectangular, and the house might be partitioned internally into a large room and a small one, like a tiny hall-and-parlor house. The later cabin, about the same in size, has the door set far to one end of the front, away from the chimney; the plan is square and gen-

erally unpartitioned. It is conceptually a piece of a large house. I illustrate an example in "Types of the Southern Mountain Cabin," in Brunvand, *Study of American Folklore*, p. 382(7A). Both are English forms from Virginia—the early one pre-Georgian, the later one Georgianized—and both are distinct from the more oblong Irish cabin, for which see my little paper "Irish," in Dell Upton, ed., *America's Architectural Roots: Ethnic Groups That Built America* (Washington: National Trust for Historic Preservation, 1986), pp. 74–79. An example of two-thirds of an I-house that was filled in to complete the form can be found in *Folk Housing in Middle Virginia*, p. 92. The segmentable central-chimney house of the North can be seen in Ernest Allen Connolly's "The Cape Cod House: An Introduction," *Journal of the Society of Architectural Historians* 19:2 (1960): 47–56.

Pp. 325–26. *The Guernsey Farmhouse: A Survey by Members of the Guernsey Society* (St. Peter Port: Toucan Press, 1978) shows clearly the older (hall-and-parlor) and the newer (I-house) forms, but unfortunately it does not picture the fractional forms. Since scholarly values differ, since what is too new to be interesting to historians in one place might be crucial to historians in another, there is no substitute for fieldwork in comparative study.

P. 326. The German house of Pennsylvania typically has a central chimney and a three-room plan that is not amenable to segmentation in the manner of American Georgian houses. Instead, it was built in large and small versions of the whole form. See: Robert C. Bucher, "The Continental Log House," *Pennsylvania Folklife* 12:4 (1962): 14–19; Henry Glassie, "A Central Chimney Continental Log

House," *Pennsylvania Folklife* 18:2 (1968–1969): 32–39; Scott T. Swank, *Arts of the Pennsylvania Germans* (New York: W.W. Norton for Winterthur, 1983), pp. 26–34; and Philip E. Pendleton, *Oley Valley Heritage: The Colonial Years, 1700–1775* (Birdsboro: Pennsylvania German Society, 1994), pp. 57–58, 70–73. Edward C. Chappell excellently documented houses that expressed the German form and houses that synthesized German and British ideas in the Valley of Virginia in "Acculturation in the Shenandoah Valley: Rhenish Houses of the Massanutten Settlement," *Transactions of the American Philosophical Society* 124:1 (1980): 55–89, reprinted in Upton and Vlach, *Common Places,* pp. 27–57. The usual Pennsylvania-German compromise was a house with the old plan and a regularized facade with two front doors; see my paper in *Common Places,* pp. 406–8. Though it looked symmetrical, the facade was usually only approximately so, and the plan was not symmetrical, so even when Georgianized, the German house did not fit into the symmetrical, segmentable system.

Pp. 327–28. Irish farmhouses: Evans, *Irish Heritage,* chapters 7–8; Evans, *Irish Folk Ways,* chapters 4–5; Kevin Danaher, *The Pleasant Land of Ireland* (Cork: Mercier Press, 1970), chapter 2; Kevin Danaher, *Ireland's Vernacular Architecture* (Cork: Mercier Press for The Cultural Relations Committee of Ireland, 1975); and Timothy P. O'Neill, *Life and Tradition in Rural Ireland* (London: J. M. Dent, 1977), chapter 1. Now the best book is Alan Gailey, *Rural Houses of the North of Ireland* (Edinburgh: John Donald, 1984); see especially chapter 8. I tell the story of change in *Passing the Time in Ballymenone,* pp. 376–424. For Georgian

houses in Ireland: Hugh Dixon, *An Introduction to Ulster Architecture* (Belfast: Ulster Architectural Heritage Society, 1975), pp. 37, 39–42, 47, 50; and Maurice Craig, *Classic Irish Houses of the Middle Size* (New York: Architectural Book Publishing Company, 1977).

P. 328. Neither archaeological nor documentary research has solved the problem of dating in Middle Virginia. The best technique remains the quickest one: comparisons made on the basis of material evidence in the buildings—something I would do much better today than I did in 1966. Lacking dates for specific houses, I derived dates for architectural types from houses in the wider region. Then assigning dates to particular houses from an abstract typology, I dated many of those in my small area of study too early, but still got the regional sequence about right, so that, for example, Rhys Isaac in his fine *Transformation of Virginia* can comment in three separate footnotes (pp. 365, 370, 406) that people have told him that my dates are too early, which many are, and yet in his text he can adopt my argument without modification (pp. 72–74, 302–6, 310–12, 327, 334). I suppose that the pattern in the area I studied is much like the one Bernard L. Herman found in another area at the Chesapeake edge; see his *Architecture and Rural Life in Central Delaware, 1700–1900* (Knoxville: University of Tennessee Press, 1987). First comes the shift to more permanent materials, and the landscape is dominated by hall-and-parlor houses. The change to the I-house begins about 1750. So far, the patterns are comparable, but I clamped the period of transition between 1760 and 1810, when, as in Delaware, the hall-and-parlor house continued to be built well into the nineteenth century. The pattern is looser, the change took longer than I thought, but there were hall-and-parlor houses in the beginning (of the record as it exists in buildings), and there were I-houses at the end, and the change from one to the other started before the Revolution.

P. 331. Billy Price and the band: Glassie, *Passing the Time in Ballymenone*, pp. 272–79, 400.

P. 332. As Raymond Williams argues in *The Country and the City* (Oxford: Oxford University Press, 1973), especially chapter 10, people always look backward to a time when community was stronger. Nostalgia seems a permanent state of affairs. But E. P. Thompson, *Making History*, pp. 245–47, counters that something really did change with enclosure, and Thompson supports his case by documenting resistance in *Customs in Common*, chapters 3–4. Thompson, I believe, is right. People seem always to lament the decline in community as part of an argument for preserving community in the future. Since they do, their words do not help us see the big change when it happens. We become trapped in an oscillation between progressive and reactionary rhetorics, and we try to make sense of them, not by studying communities at first hand, but by extrapolating from our little circles of friendship to concoct a dream of a compact, harmonious social entity in the past. Then always finding conflict in the record, we always think community is on the wane. Signs of conflict caused Michael Wood to date the decline of the village to the fourteenth century in *Domesday: A Search for the Roots of England* (New York: Facts on File, 1986), pp. 197–98. But it is not the absence of conflict that signals the presence of community. Conflict is the negative side of the engagement that keeps community alive. All communities are about to break apart. They are held together by volitional conduct, by the constant engagement that results, not from mere friendship, but from a concept of interlinked destiny. Documents, as E. P. Thompson argues in *Customs in Common*, chapter 2, tell us only the views of a privileged few who might be progressive, reactionary, or both. Conflict and longing for the past are part of the continuity of human life. But that does not mean that community is a dream and change a delusion. Material culture tells us exactly when, in the course of time through a particular landscape, engagement, and therefore community, ceases to be a high priority. It is when land and dwelling both become private: when a closed house stands on an enclosed landscape. New England had closed houses in the seventeenth century when Virginia had an enclosed landscape. Then both developed the full modern combination between, say, 1750 and 1840, as Ballymenone did in the twentieth century. The full change happened as early as the sixteenth century in southern England. In much of the world, it has not yet happened and may never happen.

P. 333. See Cary Carson, Norman F. Barka, William M. Kelso, Gary Wheeler Stone, and Dell Upton, "Impermanent Architecture in the Southern Colonies," *Winterthur Portfolio* 16:2/3 (1981): 135–96. James Deetz interprets these important findings in *Flowerdew Hundred*, pp. 53–54, 73–76; and *In Small Things Forgotten*, p. 33.

P. 334. See: Eric Mercer, *English Vernacular Houses*, pp. 1–9, 28–37, 59–62, 74–75; W. G. Hoskins, *Making of the English*

Landscape, pp. 119–24; and Hoskins, *Provincial England,* chapter 7; and see these excellent books by M. W. Barley: *The English Farmhouse and Cottage,* pp. 45–47, 123–25; and *The House and Home* (Greenwich: New York Graphic Society, 1963), pp. 18–26, 40–42.

Pp. 334–36. Upton, *Architecture in the United States,* p. 12. The best treatment we have of the architecture of a single state is Catherine Bishir's *North Carolina Architecture* (Chapel Hill: University of North Carolina Press for The Historic Preservation Foundation of North Carolina, 1990). In it, she surprisingly, accurately, and laudably ends her consideration of the nineteenth century by describing the plain and traditional buildings that are so often neglected in progressive narratives (pp. 287–309).

P. 337. Chris Wilson, "When a Room Is the Hall: The Houses of West Las Vegas, New Mexico," in Carter, *Images of an American Land,* pp. 121–23.

P. 337. The best description of a single house ever written is James Agee's account of the dogtrot house in *Let Us Now Praise Famous Men,* pp. 134–89. Examples of dogtrot houses: Eugene M. Wilson, *Alabama Folk Houses* (Montgomery: Alabama Historical Commission, 1975), pp. 30, 32–39; Howard Wight Marshall, *Folk Architecture in Little Dixie* (Columbia: University of Missouri Press, 1981), pp. 52–57; and Jean Sizemore, *Ozark Vernacular Houses: A Study of Rural Homeplaces in the Arkansas Ozarks, 1830–1930* (Fayetteville: University of Arkansas Press, 1994), pp. 63–73.

Pp. 337–38. Examples of these houses with two front doors: Glassie, *Pattern in the Material Folk Culture of the Eastern United States,* pp. 57–59, 82–83, 103–6,

140–41. The houses of Louisiana are ably presented by Jay D. Edwards in *Louisiana's Remarkable French Vernacular Architecture: 1700–1900* (Baton Rouge: L.S.U. Department of Geography and Anthropology, 1988). For Pennsylvania, see the note to p. 326 above.

P. 339. Native American examples: Peter Nabokov, *Architecture of Acoma Pueblo: The 1934 Historic American Buildings Survey Project* (Santa Fe: Ancient City Press, 1986); Stephen C. Jett and Virginia E. Spencer, *Navajo Architecture* (Tucson: University of Arizona Press, 1981). Hispanic houses of the Southwest: Bainbridge Bunting, *Early Architecture in New Mexico* (Albuquerque: University of New Mexico Press, 1976), chapter 3; Bainbridge Bunting, *Taos Adobes* (Santa Fe: Museum of New Mexico Press, 1964); and Chris Wilson and David Kammer, *La Tierra Amarilla: Its History, Architecture, and Cultural Landscape* (Santa Fe: Museum of New Mexico Press, 1989), chapter 2. The shotgun house: John Michael Vlach, "The Shotgun House: An African Architectural Legacy," in Upton and Vlach, *Common Places,* pp. 58–78; and Philippe Oszuscik, "African-Americans in the American South," in Allen G. Noble, ed., *To Build in a New Land* (Baltimore: Johns Hopkins University Press, 1992), pp. 157–76.

Pp. 342–44. Examples: Alec Clifton-Taylor, *English Parish Churches as Works of Art* (London: B. T. Batsford, 1974); Roar Hauglid, *Norwegische Stabkirchen* (Oslo: Dreyers Forlag, 1970); Jean-Paul Bourdier and Trinh T. Minh-ha, *Drawn from African Dwellings* (Bloomington: Indiana University Press, 1996), chapter 6; and Henri Stierlin, *Hindu India: From Khajuraho to the Temple City of Madurai* (Cologne: Taschen, 1998).

P. 344. Beware histories that begin at the beginning. Time is segmented, given a narrative order with a beginning and an end, only by a historian with a particular interest to explore and case to make. I exemplify historical research as I think it should be practiced (in the Sartrean manner), when I start in the middle of time, at the architectural change in Virginia, and then move backward and forward at once to develop and refine an explanation. Here, playing with historical convention, I assert a beginning at about the year 1000, after the Anglo-Saxons had made the lowlands of Britain into a place of openfield villages, and before their descendants dismantled their creation through enclosure.

P. 344. The attitudes and practices that power modern capitalism were sins and crimes before the Reformation; see R. H. Tawney, *Religion and the Rise of Capitalism* (London: Penguin, 1990, pub. 1926), pp. 43–67, 145–46, 184–85, 232–51. And see Matthew 19:24.

P. 348. Mihaly Csikszentmihalyi and Eugene Rochberg-Halton have written excellently on how people attach meanings to possessions in *The Meaning of Things: Domestic Symbols and the Self* (Cambridge: Cambridge University Press, 1981). The topic that remains is how people create anew by altering and arranging possessions. In architecture, the topic divides. One part is exterior decoration, and Richard Westmacott has written a fine book on *African-American Gardens and Yards in the Rural South* (Knoxville: University of Tennessee Press, 1992). The other aspect is interior decoration, on which I have directed a few theses, the best being Shannon A. Docherty's "Home Decorating: Contemporary American Folk Art," Ph.D. in

Folklore (Bloomington: Indiana University, May 1994). In it, through patient description of real houses, she isolated some of the important patterns in twentieth-century practice.

Pp. 350–53. I describe the change in western Anatolia in *Turkish Traditional Art Today*, pp. 252–64. Turkey helps to clarify the argument. In Virginia, certain Georgian features—hallways and symmetrical facades—began to be adopted generally soon after they were introduced (even if it took a century to complete the Georgianizing process), so it is not obvious that elements of the new style were adopted, not merely because they were new, but because they were socially useful. (Had sheer newness been the goal, Virginians would have accepted the whole Georgian package. Were fashion a sufficient explanation, they would have continued to adopt new forms through the nineteenth century when they continued to build I-houses.) In Ireland, the Georgian form was also introduced in the eighteenth century, but it was not generally adopted until the twentieth, showing clearly that conditions had to develop to the point where people wanted what the style had to offer. In Turkey, houses with central hallways for circulation are an old part of the tradition, quite general by the eighteenth century, but the village people of the northern Aegean did not begin borrowing the idea until the 1960s. To note a change in fashion makes a beginning, but what we must learn from formal analysis is exactly what changed (realizing that change is always accompanied by continuity), and what we must learn from contextual analysis is why there is, in a particular historical moment, a particular mix of change and continuity.

BIBLIOGRAPHY

This bibliography is not a list of the works cited in the notes. In compiling it, my aim was double. I wished to gather writings of particular importance for the argument of this book and to assemble a collection of general use to students of material culture. I kept the list within bounds by restricting it entirely to books in English. Its first section, Orientations, will be less useful than its second, Material Culture. The first section, at least, makes the point that students of material culture must read more than books about material culture, and I offer it because I would feel dishonest if it were omitted. It contains works that influenced my thought and that bear upon this book's conceptual drift. In the second section, I worked to produce a basic bibliography on material culture. It is a place to start, a set of good texts that individually exemplify modes of study and that together suggest the topical range of the field.

Orientations

Abrahams, Roger D. *A Singer and Her Songs: Almeda Riddle's Book of Ballads.* Baton Rouge: Louisiana State University Press, 1970.

_____ . *Singing the Master: The Emergence of African American Culture in the Plantation South.* New York: Pantheon, 1992.

Agee, James, and Walker Evans. *Let Us Now Praise Famous Men.* Boston: Houghton Mifflin, 1960 [1941].

Ali, Ahmed, trans. *Al-Qur'an.* Princeton: Princeton University Press, 1988.

Alver, Bente Gullveig. *Creating the Source Through Folkloristic Fieldwork.* Helsinki: Suomalainen Tiedeaketemia, 1990.

Barnett, H. G. *Innovation: The Basis of Cultural Change.* New York: McGraw-Hill, 1953.

Bauman, Richard. *Story, Performance, and Event: Contextual Studies of Oral Narrative.* Cambridge: Cambridge University Press, 1986.

Beckett, Samuel. *Waiting for Godot.* New York: Grove Press, 1954.

_____ . *Malone Dies.* New York: Grove Press, 1956.

_____ . *The Lost Ones.* New York: Grove Press, 1972.

_____ . *Mercier and Camier.* New York: Grove Press, 1972.

Ben-Amos, Dan, ed. *Folklore Genres.* Austin: University of Texas Press, 1976.

Bercovitch, Sacvan. *The Puritan Origins of the American Self.* New Haven: Yale University Press, 1975.

Berger, Peter L. *Invitation to Sociology: A Humanistic Perspective.* Garden City: Doubleday, 1963.

Bloch, Marc. *The Historian's Craft.* Trans. Peter Putnam. New York: Vintage Books, 1953.

_____ . *Land and Work in Mediaeval Europe.* Trans. J. E. Anderson. New York: Harper and Row, 1969.

_____ . *Feudal Society.* Trans. L. A. Manyon. 2 vols. Chicago: University of Chicago Press, 1964.

Boas, Franz. *Kwakiutl Ethnography.* Ed. Helen Codere. Chicago: University of Chicago Press, 1966.

Botkin, B. A. *Lay My Burden Down: A Folk History of Slavery*. Chicago: University of Chicago Press, 1945.

Braudel, Fernand. *The Mediterranean and the Mediterranean World in the Age of Philip II*. Trans. Sián Reynolds. 2 vols. New York: Harper and Row, 1972.

———. *On History*. Trans. Sarah Matthews. Chicago: University of Chicago Press, 1980.

———. *A History of Civilizations*. Trans. Richard Mayne. New York: Penguin, 1993.

Buchan, David. *The Ballad and the Folk*. London: Routledge and Kegan Paul, 1972.

Burke, Kenneth. *A Grammar of Motives*. Berkeley: University of California Press, 1969.

———. *The Philosophy of Literary Form*. Berkeley: University of California Press, 1973.

Burke, Peter. *Popular Culture in Early Modern Europe*. Aldershot: Wildwood House, 1988 [1978].

Butterfield, Herbert. *The Whig Interpretation of History*. New York: W.W. Norton, 1965.

Camus, Albert. *The Rebel*. Trans. Anthony Bower. London: Hamish Hamilton, 1953.

Chaudhuri, Nirad C. *Hinduism: A Religion to Live By*. New York: Oxford University Press, 1979.

———. *The Autobiography of an Unknown Indian*. Bombay: Jaico Publishing House, 1994 [1951].

Chomsky, Noam. *Syntactic Structures*. The Hague: Mouton, 1957.

———. *Cartesian Linguistics: A Chapter in the History of Rationalist Thought*. New York: Harper and Row, 1966.

———. *Problems of Knowledge and Freedom: The Russell Lectures*. New York: Vintage Books, 1971.

———. *Language and Problems of Knowledge: The Managua Lectures*. Cambridge: The MIT Press, 1994.

Cochran, Robert. *Vance Randolph: An Ozark Life*. Urbana: University of Illinois Press, 1985.

Comyn, David, and Patrick S. Dinneen, eds. *The History of Ireland by Geoffrey Keating, D.D.* 4 vols. London: Irish Texts Society, 1902–1914.

Davis, Burke. *To Appomattox: Nine April Days, 1865*. New York: Rinehart, 1959.

Davis, Susan G. *Parades and Power: Street Theatre in Nineteenth-Century Philadelphia*. Philadelphia: Temple University Press, 1986.

Dégh, Linda. *Folktales and Society: Story-Telling in a Hungarian Peasant Community*. Trans. Emily M. Schossberger. Bloomington: Indiana University Press, 1969 [1962].

———. *Narratives in Society: A Performer-Centered Study of Narration*. Helsinki: Suomalainen Tiedeakatemia, 1995.

Demos, John. *A Little Commonwealth: Family Life in Plymouth Colony*. New York: Oxford University Press, 1970.

Dorson, Richard M. *Bloodstoppers and Bearwalkers: Folk Traditions of the Upper Peninsula*. Cambridge: Harvard University Press, 1952.

———. *American Folklore and the Historian*. Chicago: University of Chicago Press, 1971.

Dundes, Alan. *Interpreting Folklore*. Bloomington: Indiana University Press, 1980.

———. *Two Tales of Crow and Sparrow: A Freudian Folkloristic Essay on Caste and Untouchability*. Lanham: Rowman and Littlefield, 1997.

Ellmann, Richard. *James Joyce.* New York: Oxford University Press, 1982 [1959].

Faulkner, William. *Go Down, Moses.* New York: Vintage International, 1990 [1942].

Freeman, Douglas Southall. *Lee's Lieutenants: A Study in Command.* 3 vols. New York: Charles Scribner's Sons, 1943–1944.

Fryer, Judith. *Felicitous Space: The Imaginative Structures of Edith Wharton and Willa Cather.* Chapel Hill: University of North Carolina Press, 1986.

Frykman, Jonas, and Orvar Löfgren. *Culture Builders: A Historical Anthropology of Middle-Class Life.* Trans. Alan Crozier. New Brunswick: Rutgers University Press, 1987.

Geertz, Clifford. *Works and Lives: The Anthropologist as Author.* Stanford: Stanford University Press, 1988.

Gibbon, Edward. *The History of the Decline and Fall of the Roman Empire.* 12 vols. London: Cadell and Davies, 1807 [1776–1788].

Gillis, John R. *A World of Their Own Making: Myth, Ritual, and the Quest for Family Values.* New York: Basic Books, 1996.

Goffman, Erving. *Presentation of Self in Everyday Life.* Garden City: Doubleday, 1959.

_____. *Behavior in Public Places: Notes on the Social Organization of Gatherings.* New York: Free Press, 1963.

_____. *Relations in Public: Microstudies of the Public Order.* New York: Basic Books, 1971.

_____. *Forms of Talk.* Philadelphia: University of Pennsylvania Press, 1981.

Goldstein, Kenneth S. *A Guide for Field Workers in Folklore.* Hatboro: Folklore Associates, 1964.

Gould, Stephen Jay. *Time's Arrow, Time's Cycle: Myth and Metaphor in the Discovery of Geological Time.* Cambridge: Harvard University Press, 1987.

Gregory, Lady Augusta. *The Kiltartan History Book.* London: T. Fisher Unwin, 1926.

Griaule, Marcel. *Conversations with Ogotemmêli: An Introduction to Dogon Religious Ideas.* London: Oxford University Press, 1970 [1948].

Grimshaw, Allen D. *Collegial Discourse: Professional Conversation Among Peers.* Norwood: Ablex, 1989.

Hansen, William. *Phlegon of Tralles' Book of Marvels.* Exeter: University of Exeter Press, 1996.

Haring, Lee. *Verbal Arts in Madagascar: Performance in Historical Perspective.* Philadelphia: University of Pennsylvania Press, 1992.

Harris, Marvin. *The Rise of Anthropological Theory: A History of Theories of Culture.* New York: Thomas Y. Crowell, 1968.

Hemingway, Ernest. *Death in the Afternoon.* New York: Halcyon House, 1932.

Herodotus. *The Histories.* Trans. Robin Waterfield. Oxford: Oxford University Press, 1998.

Hill, Christopher. *The World Turned Upside Down: Radical Ideas During the English Revolution.* New York: Viking, 1972.

_____. *Change and Continuity in Seventeenth-Century England.* Cambridge: Harvard University Press, 1975.

Holbek, Bengt. *The Interpretation of Fairy Tales: Danish Folklore in a European Perspective.* Helsinki: Suomalainen Tiedeakatemia, 1987.

Hymes, Dell, ed. *Reinventing Anthropology.* New York: Pantheon, 1972.

_____ . *Foundations in Sociolinguistics: An Ethnographic Approach.* Philadelphia: University of Pennsylvania Press, 1974.

_____ . *"In Vain I Tried to Tell You": Essays in Native American Ethnopoetics.* Philadelphia: University of Pennsylvania Press, 1981.

Illick, Joseph E. *At Liberty: The Story of a Community and a Generation: The Bethlehem, Pennsylvania, High School Class of 1952.* Knoxville: University of Tennessee Press, 1989.

Isaac, Rhys. *The Transformation of Virginia: 1740–1790.* New York: W. W. Norton, 1988 [1982].

Ives, Edward D. *Larry Gorman: The Man Who Made the Songs.* Bloomington: Indiana University Press, 1964.

_____ . *Lawrence Doyle: The Farmer-Poet of Prince Edward Island: A Study in Local Songmaking.* Orono: University of Maine Press, 1971.

_____ . *Joe Scott: The Woodsman-Songmaker.* Urbana: University of Illinois Press, 1978.

Joyce, James. *Ulysses.* Paris: Shakespeare and Company, 1922.

Joyner, Charles. *Down by the Riverside: A South Carolina Slave Community.* Urbana: University of Illinois Press, 1984.

Kalupahana, David J. *Buddhist Philosophy: A Historical Analysis.* Honolulu: University of Hawaii Press, 1976.

Keegan, John. *The Face of Battle: A Study of Agincourt, Waterloo and the Somme.* London: Penguin, 1978.

_____ . *The Mask of Command.* London: Penguin, 1987.

_____ . *A History of Warfare.* New York: Alfred A. Knopf, 1993.

Korson, George. *Minstrels of the Mine Patch: Songs and Stories of the Anthracite Industry.* Philadelphia: University of Pennsylvania Press, 1938.

Larkin, Jack. *The Reshaping of Everyday Life, 1790–1840.* New York: Harper and Row, 1988.

Levi, Carlo. *Christ Stopped at Eboli.* Trans. Frances Fernaye. New York: Farrar, Straus and Giroux, 1989 [1947].

Lévi-Strauss, Claude. *Tristes Tropiques.* Trans. John and Doreen Weightman. New York: Atheneum, 1975 [1955].

_____ . *The Savage Mind.* Chicago: University of Chicago Press, 1966.

_____ . *The Story of Lynx.* Trans. Catherine Tihanyi. Chicago: University of Chicago Press, 1995.

Lewis, Bernard. *The Middle East: A Brief History of the Last 2,000 Years.* New York: Scribner, 1995.

Lewis, Oscar. *Five Families: Mexican Case Studies in the Culture of Poverty.* New York: Basic Books, 1959.

Lord, Albert B. *The Singer of Tales.* New York: Atheneum, 1965.

Lowie, Robert H. *The Crow Indians.* New York: Holt, Rinehart and Winston, 1956 [1935].

Macfarlane, Alan. *Reconstructing Historical Communities.* Cambridge: Cambridge University Press, 1977.

Malinowski, Bronislaw. *Argonauts of the Western Pacific: An Account of Native Enterprise and Adventure in the Archipelagoes of Melanesian New Guinea.* London: George Routledge, 1922.

Martin-Perdue, Nancy J., and Charles L. Perdue, Jr. *Talk About Trouble: A New Deal Portrait of Virginians in the Great Depression.* Chapel Hill: University of North Carolina Press, 1996.

McDowell, John. *Sayings of the Ancestors: The Spiritual Life of the Sibundoy Indians.* Lexington: University Press of Kentucky, 1989.

Melville, Herman. *Moby-Dick; or, The Whale.* Berkeley: University of California Press, 1981 [1851].

Merton, Robert K. *On Theoretical Sociology: Five Essays, Old and New.* New York: Free Press, 1967.

Montell, William Lynwood. *The Saga of Coe Ridge: A Study in Oral History.* Knoxville: University of Tennessee Press, 1970.

Murphy, Michael J. *Tyrone Folk Quest.* Belfast: Blackstaff Press, 1981.

Naipaul, V. S. *An Area of Darkness.* London: Penguin, 1964.

_____. *Among the Believers: An Islamic Journey.* New York: Alfred A. Knopf, 1981.

_____. *Finding the Center: Two Narratives.* New York: Alfred A. Knopf, 1984.

_____. *India: A Million Mutinies Now.* New York: Viking, 1990.

Oring, Elliott. *The Jokes of Sigmund Freud: A Study in Humor and Jewish Identity.* Philadelphia: University of Pennsylvania Press, 1984.

Ortiz, Alfonso. *The Tewa World: Space, Time, Being, and Becoming in a Pueblo Society.* Chicago: University of Chicago Press, 1969.

Paredes, Américo. *"With His Pistol in His Hand": A Border Ballad and Its Hero.* Austin: University of Texas Press, 1958.

Powell, Sumner Chilton. *Puritan Village: The Formation of a New England Town.* Middletown: Wesleyan University Press, 1975 [1963].

Propp, Vladimir. *Morphology of the Folktale.* Trans. Laurence Scott and Louis A. Wagner. Austin: University of Texas Press for the American Folklore Society, 1968.

Radcliffe-Brown, A. R. *The Andaman Islanders.* Glencoe: The Free Press, 1948 [1922].

Radhakrishnan, S., ed. *The Bhagavadgita.* New Delhi: HarperCollins, 1993 [1948].

Redfield, Robert. *The Little Community: Viewpoints for the Study of a Human Whole.* Chicago: University of Chicago Press, 1955.

_____. *Peasant Society and Culture: An Anthropological Approach to Civilization.* Chicago: University of Chicago Press, 1956.

Rosenzweig, Roy, and David Thelen. *The Presence of the Past: Popular Uses of History in American Life.* New York: Columbia University Press, 1998.

Sartre, Jean-Paul. *What Is Literature?* Trans. Bernard Frechtman. New York: Philosophical Library, 1949.

_____. *Search for a Method.* Trans. Hazel E. Barnes. New York: Alfred A. Knopf, 1963.

_____. *Between Existentialism and Marxism.* Trans. John Matthews. New York: William Morrow, 1976.

Schieffelin, Edward L., and Robert Crittenden. *Like People You See in a Dream: First Contact in Six Papuan Societies.* Stanford: Stanford University Press, 1991.

Schimmel, Annemarie. *Mystical Dimensions of Islam.* Chapel Hill: University of North Carolina Press, 1975.

Schrempp, Gregory. *Magical Arrows: The Maori, The Greeks, and The Folklore of the Universe.* Madison: University of

Wisconsin Press, 1992.

Simmons, Leo W., ed. *Sun Chief: The Autobiography of a Hopi Indian*. New Haven: Yale University Press, 1942.

Synge, John Millington. *The Aran Islands*. Boston: John W. Luce, 1911.

Tate, W. E. *The Enclosure Movement*. New York: Walker and Company, 1967.

Thompson, E. P. *The Making of the English Working Class*. New York: Vintage Books, 1963.

_____. *Whigs and Hunters: The Origin of the Black Act*. New York: Pantheon, 1975.

_____. *William Morris: Romantic to Revolutionary*. New York: Pantheon, 1977.

_____. *Customs in Common*. New York: The New Press, 1991.

_____. *Making History: Writings on History and Culture*. New York: The New Press, 1994.

Toelken, Barre. *The Dynamics of Folklore*. Logan: Utah State University Press, 1996 [1979].

Turnbull, Colin M. *The Forest People*. New York: Simon and Schuster, 1961.

Turner, Victor W. *The Ritual Process: Structure and Anti-Structure*. Chicago: Aldine, 1969.

Ulrich, Laurel Thatcher. *A Midwife's Tale: The Life of Martha Ballard, Based on Her Diary, 1785–1812*. New York: Vintage Books, 1991.

Wacker, Peter O. *The Musconetcong Valley of New Jersey: A Historical Geography*. New Brunswick: Rutgers University Press, 1968.

Watson, Burton, trans. *The Lotus Sutra*. New York: Columbia University Press, 1993.

Wiggins, William H., Jr. *O Freedom! Afro-American Emancipation Celebrations*.

Knoxville: University of Tennessee Press, 1990.

Williams, Raymond. *The Country and the City*. New York: Oxford University Press, 1973.

_____. *Keywords: A Vocabulary of Culture and Society*. New York: Oxford University Press, 1976.

_____. *Marxism and Literature*. Oxford: Oxford University Press, 1977.

Wolfe, Tom. *The Electric Kool-Aid Acid Test*. New York: Bantam, 1969.

Wolpert, Stanley. *A New History of India*. New York: Oxford University Press, 1993 [1977].

Yeats, William Butler. *The Celtic Twilight*. Dublin: Maunsel, 1902.

_____. *A Vision*. London: Macmillan, 1937.

Material Culture

Aalen, F. H. A. *Man and the Landscape in Ireland*. London: Academic Press, 1978.

Aalen, F. H. A., Kevin Whelan, and Matthew Stout, eds. *Atlas of the Irish Rural Landscape*. Cork: Cork University Press, 1997.

Addy, Sidney Oldall. *The Evolution of the English House*. London: Swan Sonnenschein, 1898.

Appadurai, Arjun, ed. *The Social Life of Things: Commodities in Cultural Perspective*. Cambridge: Cambridge University Press, 1986.

Armstrong, Robert Plant. *The Affecting Presence: An Essay in Humanistic Anthropology*. Urbana: University of Illinois Press, 1971.

_____. *Wellspring: On the Myth and Source of Culture*. Berkeley: University of California Press, 1975.

_____. *The Powers of Presence: Consciousness, Myth, and Affecting Presence*.

Philadelphia: University of Pennsylvania Press, 1981.

Arnold, Dana, ed. *The Georgian Villa.* Phoenix Mill: Alan Sutton, 1996.

Askari, Nasreen, and Rosemary Crill. *Colours of the Indus: Costume and Textiles of Pakistan.* London: Merrell Holberton and Victoria and Albert Museum, 1997.

A:son-Palmqvist, Lena. *Building Traditions among Swedish Settlers in Rural Minnesota: Material Culture—Reflecting Persistence or Decline of Traditions.* Stockholm: Nordiska Museet, 1983.

Atasoy, Nurhan, and Julian Raby. *Iznik: the Pottery of Ottoman Turkey.* London: Alexandria Press, Thames and Hudson, 1989.

Ayres, James A. *The Shell Book of the Home in Britain: Decoration, Design and Construction of Vernacular Interiors, 1500–1850.* London: Faber and Faber, 1981.

_____ . *Two Hundred Years of English Naive Art: 1700–1900.* Alexandria: Art Services International, 1996.

_____ . *Building the Georgian City.* New Haven: Yale University Press for the Mellon Center, 1998.

Barbeau, Marius. *Totem Poles.* 2 vols. Ottawa: National Museum of Canada, 1950.

Barber, Edwin Atlee. *Tulip Ware of the Pennsylvania-German Potters: An Historical Sketch of the Art of Slip-Decoration in the United States.* Philadelphia: Pennsylvania Museum and School of Industrial Art, 1926 [1903].

Barley, M. W. *The English Farmhouse and Cottage.* London: Routledge and Kegan Paul, 1961.

Bascom, William. *African Art in Cultural Perspective: An Introduction.* New York: W.W. Norton, 1973.

Baxandall, Michael. *Painting and Experience in Fifteenth-Century Italy: A Primer in the Social History of Pictorial Style.* Oxford: Oxford University Press, 1974.

_____ . *The Limewood Sculptors of Renaissance Germany.* New Haven: Yale University Press, 1985 [1980].

_____ . *Patterns of Intention: On the Historical Explanation of Pictures.* New Haven: Yale University Press, 1985.

Becker, Howard S. *Art Worlds.* Berkeley: University of California Press, 1982.

Benes, Peter. *The Masks of Orthodoxy: Folk Gravestone Carving in Plymouth Colony, Massachusetts, 1689–1805.* Amherst: University of Massachusetts Press, 1977.

Berliner, Nancy, and Sarah Handler. *Friends of the House: Furniture from China's Towns and Villages.* Salem: Peabody Essex Museum, 1995.

Biebuyck, Daniel, ed. *Tradition and Creativity in Tribal Art.* Berkeley: University of California Press, 1969.

Bishir, Catherine W. *North Carolina Architecture.* Chapel Hill: University of North Carolina Press for The Historic Preservation Foundation of North Carolina, 1990.

Bizley, Alice C. *The Slate Figures of Cornwall.* Marazion: Worden, 1965.

Bluestone, Daniel. *Constructing Chicago.* New Haven: Yale University Press, 1991.

Blurton, T. Richard. *Hindu Art.* Cambridge: Harvard University Press, 1993.

Boas, Franz. *Primitive Art.* New York: Dover, 1955 [1927].

Bogatyrev, Petr. *The Functions of Folk Costume in Moravian Slovakia.* Trans. Richard G. Crum. The Hague: Mouton, 1971 [1937].

Bourdier, Jean-Paul, and Trinh T. Minh-ha. *African Spaces: Designs for Living in Upper Volta.* New York: Africana, 1985.

_____. *Drawn from African Dwellings.* Bloomington: Indiana University Press, 1996.

Boyle, Elizabeth. *The Irish Flowerers.* Belfast: Ulster Folk Museum and Institute of Irish Studies, 1971.

Branch, Daniel Paulk. *Folk Architecture of the Eastern Mediterranean.* New York: Columbia University Press, 1966.

Brand, Stewart. *How Buildings Learn: What Happens After They're Built.* New York: Penguin, 1994.

Bravmann, René A. *Islam and Tribal Art in West Africa.* Cambridge: Cambridge University Press, 1974.

Brears, Peter C. D. *The English Country Pottery: Its History and Techniques.* Newton Abbot: David and Charles, 1971.

_____. *Traditional Food in Yorkshire.* Edinburgh: John Donald, 1987.

Brend, Barbara. *Islamic Art.* Cambridge: Harvard University Press, 1991.

Brewington, M. V. *Chesapeake Bay Log Canoes and Bugeyes.* Cambridge: Cornell Maritime Press, 1963.

Briggs, Charles L. *The Wood Carvers of Córdova, New Mexico: Social Dimensions of an Artistic "Revival."* Knoxville: University of Tennessee Press, 1980.

Bronner, Simon J. *Chain Carvers: Old Men Crafting Meaning.* Lexington: University Press of Kentucky, 1985.

Brüggemann, W., and H. Böhmer, *Rugs of the Peasants and Nomads of Anatolia.* Munich: Kunst und Antiquitäten, 1983.

Brunskill, R. W. *Illustrated Handbook of Vernacular Architecture.* New York: Universe Books, 1970.

_____. *Vernacular Architecture of the Lake Counties: A Field Handbook.* London:

Faber and Faber, 1974.

_____. *Traditional Farm Buildings of Britain.* London: Victor Gollancz, 1982.

Bunting, Bainbridge. *Taos Adobes: Spanish Colonial and Territorial Architecture in the Taos Valley.* Santa Fe: Museum of New Mexico Press, 1964.

Bunzel, Ruth L. *The Pueblo Potter: A Study of Creative Imagination in Primitive Art.* New York: Dover, 1972 [1929].

Burckhardt, Titus. *Art of Islam: Language and Meaning.* Westerham: World of Islam Festival, 1976.

Burrison, John A. *Brothers in Clay: The Story of Georgia Folk Pottery.* Athens: University of Georgia Press, 1983.

Caffyn, Lucy. *Workers' Housing in West Yorkshire, 1750–1920.* London: Royal Commission on the Historical Monuments of England, 1986.

Cardew, Michael. *Pioneer Pottery.* New York: St. Martin's Press, 1969.

Carswell, John. *Iznik Pottery.* London: British Museum Press, 1998.

Carter, Thomas, ed. *Images of an American Land: Vernacular Architecture in the Western United States.* Albuquerque: University of New Mexico Press, 1997.

Chang, K. C., ed. *Settlement Archaeology.* Palo Alto: National Press Books, 1968.

Chapelle, Howard I. *American Small Sailing Craft: Their Design, Development, and Construction.* New York: W.W. Norton, 1951.

Chinnery, Victor. *Oak Furniture in the British Tradition: A History of Early Furniture in the British Isles and New England.* Woodbridge: Antique Collectors' Club, 1979.

Cipolla, Carlo M. *Clocks and Culture.* New York: Walker and Company, 1967.

Coe, Ralph T. *Lost and Found Traditions: Native American Art, 1965–1985.* New York: American Federation of the Arts, 1986.

Cole, Bruce. *The Renaissance Artist at Work: From Pisano to Titian.* New York: Harper and Row, 1983.

Comeaux, Malcolm. *Atchafalaya Swamp Life: Settlement and Folk Occupations.* Baton Rouge: Geoscience and Man, 1972.

Coomaraswamy, Ananda K. *The Arts and Crafts of India and Ceylon.* New Delhi: Today and Tomorrow's Printers and Publishers, 1984 [1913].

_____ . *The Dance of Śiva: Essays on Indian Art and Culture.* New York: Dover, 1985 [1924].

_____ . *The Transformation of Nature in Art.* Cambridge: Harvard University Press, 1935.

_____ . *Christian and Oriental Philosophy of Art.* New York: Dover, 1956 [1943].

Cooper, Patricia, and Norma Bradley Buferd. *The Quilters: Women and Domestic Art: An Oral History.* Garden City: Anchor Books, 1978.

Cort, Louise Allison. *Shigaraki, Potters' Valley.* Tokyo: Kodansha, 1979.

Cort, Louise Allison, and Nakamura Kenji. *A Basketmaker in Rural Japan.* New York: Weatherhill and Sackler Gallery, 1994.

Csikszentmihalyi, Mihaly, and Eugene Rochberg-Halton. *The Meaning of Things: Domestic Symbols and the Self.* Cambridge: Cambridge University Press, 1985.

Cuisenier, Jean. *French Folk Art.* Tokyo: Kodansha, 1977.

Cummings, Abbott Lowell. *The Framed Houses of Massachusetts Bay, 1625–1725.* Cambridge: Harvard University Press, 1979.

Curtis, James. *Mind's Eye, Mind's Truth: FSA Photography Reconsidered.* Philadelphia: Temple University Press, 1989.

Danto, Arthur C. *The Philosophical Disenfranchisement of Art.* New York: Columbia University Press, 1986.

d'Azevedo, Warren L., ed. *The Traditional Artist in African Society.* Bloomington, Indiana University Press, 1973.

Deetz, James. *Invitation to Archaeology.* Garden City: Natural History Press, 1967.

_____ . *Flowerdew Hundred: The Archaeology of a Virginia Plantation, 1619–1864.* Charlottesville: University Press of Virginia, 1993.

_____ . *In Small Things Forgotten: An Archaeology of Early American Life.* New York: Anchor Books, 1996 [1977].

Dillingham, Rick. *Fourteen Families in Pueblo Pottery.* Albuquerque: University of New Mexico Press, 1994.

Dillingham, Rick, and Melinda Elliott, *Acoma and Laguna Pottery.* Santa Fe: School of American Research Press, 1992.

Donnelly, P. J. *Blanc De Chine: The Porcelain of Téhua in Fukien.* London: Faber and Faber, 1969.

Dutt, Gurusaday. *Folk Arts and Crafts of Bengal: The Collected Papers.* Calcutta: Seagull, 1990.

Eames, Penelope. *Furniture in England, France and the Netherlands from the Twelfth to the Fifteenth Century.* London: Furniture History Society, 1977.

Eck, Diana L. *Darśan: Seeing the Divine Image in India.* Chambersburg: Anima Books, 1985.

Eco, Umberto. *Art and Beauty in the Middle Ages.* Trans. Hugh Bredin. New Haven: Yale University Press, 1986 [1959].

Engel, Heinrich. *The Japanese House: A Tradition for Contemporary Architecture.* Rutland: Charles E. Tuttle, 1988 [1964].

Ensminger, Robert F. *The Pennsylvania Barn: Its Origin, Evolution, and Distribution in North America.* Baltimore: Johns Hopkins University Press, 1992.

Espejel, Carlos. *Mexican Folk Ceramics.* Barcelona: Editorial Blume, 1975.

Espinosa, José E. *Saints in the Valleys: Christian Sacred Images in the History, Life and Folk Art of Spanish New Mexico.* Albuquerque: University of New Mexico Press, 1967.

Evans, E. Estyn. *Irish Folk Ways.* New York: Devin-Adair, 1957.

———. *Mourne Country: Landscape and Life in South Down.* Dundalk: Dundalgan Press, 1967.

———. *The Personality of Ireland: Habitat, Heritage and History.* Cambridge: Cambridge University Press, 1973.

———. *Ireland and the Atlantic Heritage.* Dublin: Lilliput Press, 1996.

Evans, Timothy H. *King of the Western Saddle: The Sheridan Saddle and the Art of Don King.* Jackson: University Press of Mississippi, 1998.

Fabian, Monroe H. *The Pennsylvania-German Decorated Chest.* New York: Universe Books, 1978.

Fairbanks, Jonathan L., and Robert F. Trent, eds. *New England Begins: The Seventeenth Century.* 3 vols. Boston: Museum of Fine Arts, 1982.

Fenton, Alexander. *The Northern Isles: Orkney and Shetland.* Edinburgh: John Donald, 1978.

Fenton, Alexander, and Bruce Walker. *The Rural Architecture of Scotland.* Edinburgh: John Donald, 1981.

Ferguson, Leland, ed. *Historical Archaeology and the Importance of Material Things.* Columbia: Society for Historical Archaeology, 1977.

Ferris, William. *Local Color: A Sense of Place in Folk Art.* New York: McGraw-Hill, 1982.

Finley, Ruth E. *Old Patchwork Quilts and the Women Who Made Them.* Philadelphia: J. B. Lippincott, 1929.

Fischer, Eberhard, and Haku Shah. *Rural Craftsmen and Their Work.* Ahmedabad: National Institute of Design, 1970.

Fischer, Joseph, and Thomas Cooper. *The Folk Art of Bali: The Narrative Tradition.* Kuala Lumpur: Oxford University Press, 1998.

Fitch, James Marston. *American Building 2: The Environmental Forces That Shape It.* Boston: Houghton Mifflin, 1972.

———. *Historic Preservation: Curatorial Management of the Built World.* New York: McGraw-Hill, 1982.

Fitchen, John. *The New World Dutch Barn: A Study of Its Characteristics, Its Structural System, and Its Probable Erection Procedures.* Syracuse: Syracuse University Press, 1968.

Fontana, Bernard L., William J. Robinson, Charles W. Cormack, and Ernest J. Leavitt, Jr. *Papago Indian Pottery.* Seattle: University of Washington Press, 1962.

Foster, Kathleen A. *Thomas Eakins Rediscovered: Charles Bregler's Thomas Eakins Collection at the Pennsylvania Academy of the Fine Arts.* New Haven: Yale University Press, 1997.

Fox, Sir Cyril. *The Personality of Britain: Its Influence on Inhabitant and Invader in Prehistoric and Early Historic Times.* Cardiff: National Museum of Wales, 1952 [1932].

Fox, Sir Cyril, and Lord Raglan. *Monmouthshire Houses: A Study of Building Techniques and Smaller House-Plans in the Fifteenth to Seventeenth Centuries.* 3 vols. Cardiff: National Museum of Wales, 1951–1954.

Frescura. Franco. *Rural Shelter in Southern Africa: A Survey of the Architecture, House Forms and Construction Methods of the Black Rural Peoples of Southern Africa.* Johannesburg: Ravan Press, 1981.

Fry, Gladys-Marie. *Stitched from the Soul: Slave Quilts from the Ante-Bellum South.* New York: Dutton Studio and Museum of American Folk Art, 1990.

Fussell, G. E. *The Farmer's Tools: A.D. 1500–1900: A History of British Farm Tools, Implements and Machinery.* London: Andrew Melrose, 1952.

Gailey, Alan. *Rural Houses of the North of Ireland.* Edinburgh: John Donald, 1984.

Gailey, Alan, and Alexander Fenton, eds. *The Spade in Northern and Atlantic Europe.* Belfast: Ulster Folk Museum and Institute of Irish Studies, 1970.

Garrison, J. Ritchie. *Landscape and Material Life in Franklin County, Massachusetts, 1770–1860.* Knoxville: University of Tennessee Press, 1991.

Garvan, Anthony N. B. *Architecture and Town Planning in Colonial Connecticut.* New Haven: Yale University Press, 1951.

Glassie, Henry. *Pattern in the Material Folk Culture of the Eastern United States.* Philadelphia: University of Pennsylvania Press, 1969.

_____ . *Folk Housing in Middle Virginia: A Structural Analysis of Historic Artifacts.* Knoxville: University of Tennessee Press, 1976.

_____ . *Passing the Time in Ballymenone: Culture and History of an Ulster Community.* Philadelphia: University of Pennsylvania Press, 1982.

_____ . *The Spirit of Folk Art.* New York: Abrams and Museum of International Folk Art, 1989.

_____ . *Turkish Traditional Art Today.* Bloomington: Indiana University Press, 1993.

_____ . *Art and Life in Bangladesh.* Bloomington: Indiana University Press, 1997.

Goodwin, Godfrey. *A History of Ottoman Architecture.* London: Thames and Hudson, 1971.

Gowans, Alan. *Images of American Living: Four Centuries of Architecture and Furniture as Cultural Expression.* Philadelphia: J.B. Lippincott, 1964.

Graburn, Nelson H. H., ed. *Ethnic and Tourist Arts: Cultural Expressions of the Fourth World.* Berkeley: University of California Press, 1979.

Griffith, James S. *Beliefs and Holy Places: A Spiritual Geography of the Pimería Alta.* Tucson: University of Arizona Press, 1992.

Hansen, H. J., ed. *European Folk Art.* New York: McGraw-Hill, 1967.

Harper, Douglas. *Working Knowledge: Skill and Community in a Small Shop.* Chicago: University of Chicago Press, 1987.

Hedgecoe, John, and Salma Samar Damluji. *Zillij: The Art of Moroccan Ceramics.* Reading: Garnet, 1992.

Herman, Bernard L. *Architecture and Rural Life in Central Delaware, 1700–1900.* Knoxville: University of Tennessee Press, 1987.

_____ . *The Stolen House.* Charlottesville: University Press of Virginia, 1992.

Hewett, Cecil Alec. *The Development of*

Carpentry, 1200–1700: An Essex Study. Newton Abbot: David and Charles, 1969.

Hill, Sarah H. *Weaving New Worlds: Southeastern Cherokee Women and Their Basketry.* Chapel Hill: University of North Carolina Press, 1997.

Hindle, Brooke, and Steven Lubar. *Engines of Change: The American Industrial Revolution, 1790–1860.* Washington: Smithsonian Institution Press, 1986.

Hofer, Tamás, and Edit Fél. *Hungarian Folk Art.* Oxford: Oxford University Press, 1979.

Holm, Bill. *Northwest Coast Indian Art: An Analysis of Form.* Seattle: University of Washington Press, 1965.

_____. *Smoky-Top: The Art and Times of Willie Seaweed.* Seattle: University of Washington Press, 1983.

Hoskins, W. G. *The Making of the English Landscape.* London: Hodder and Stoughton, 1955.

_____. *The Midland Peasant: The Economic and Social History of a Leicestershire Village.* London: Macmillan, 1965.

_____. *Provincial England: Essays in Social and Economic History.* London: Macmillan, 1965.

_____. *Fieldwork in Local History.* London: Faber and Faber, 1969.

Hubka, Thomas C. *Big House, Little House, Back House, Barn: The Connected Farm Buildings of New England.* Hanover: University Press of New England, 1984.

Hummel, Charles F. *With Hammer in Hand: The Dominy Craftsmen of East Hampton, New York.* Charlottesville: University Press of Virginia for Winterthur, 1968.

Ingersoll, Daniel W., Jr., and Gordon Bronitsky, eds. *Mirror and Metaphor:* *Material and Social Constructions of Reality.* Lanham: University Press of America, 1987.

Ioannou, Noris. *Ceramics in South Australia, 1836–1986: From Folk to Studio Pottery.* Netley: Wakefield Press, 1986.

_____. *The Barossa Folk: Germanic Furniture and Craft Traditions in Australia.* Roseville East: Craftsman House, 1995.

Itoh, Teiji, *The Gardens of Japan.* Tokyo: Kodansha, 1998 [1984].

James, John. *Chartres: The Masons Who Built a Legend.* London: Routledge and Kegan Paul, 1985.

Jenkins, J. Geraint. *The English Farm Wagon: Origins and Structure.* Lingfield: University of Reading, 1961.

_____. *Traditional Country Craftsmen.* London: Routledge and Kegan Paul, 1965.

_____. *Nets and Coracles.* Newton Abbot: David and Charles, 1974.

Jensen, Doreen, and Polly Sargent. *Robes of Power: Totem Poles on Cloth.* Vancouver: University of British Columbia Press, 1986.

Jenyns, Soame. *Ming Pottery and Porcelain.* London: Faber and Faber, 1988 [1953].

Jett, Stephen C., and Virginia E. Spencer. *Navajo Architecture: Forms, History, Distributions.* Tucson: University of Arizona Press, 1981.

Johnson, Matthew. *Housing Culture: Traditional Architecture in an English Landscape.* London: UCL Press, 1993.

Jonaitis, Aldona. *Art of the Northern Tlingit.* Seattle: University of Washington Press, 1986.

_____. *From the Land of the Totem Poles: The Northwest Coast Indian Art Collection of the American Museum of Natural History.* New York: American

Museum of Natural History, 1988.

Jones, Michael Owen. *Craftsman of the Cumberlands: Tradition and Creativity.* Lexington: University Press of Kentucky, 1989 [1975].

Jordan, Terry G. *Texas Log Buildings: A Folk Architecture.* Austin: University of Texas Press, 1978.

Kalter, Johannes, and Margareta Pavaloi, eds. *Uzbekistan: Heirs to the Silk Road.* London: Thames and Hudson, 1997.

Kandinsky, Wassily. *Concerning the Spiritual in Art.* New York: George Wittenborn, 1964 [1912].

Kandinsky, Wassily, and Franz Marc, eds. *The Blaue Reiter Almanac.* New York: Viking Press, 1974 [1912].

Kapp, Leon and Hiroko, and Yoshindo Yoshihara. *The Craft of the Japanese Sword.* Tokyo: Kodansha, 1987.

Kelly, J. Frederick. *The Early Domestic Architecture of Connecticut.* New Haven: Yale University Press, 1924.

Kent, Kate Peck. *Navajo Weaving: Three Centuries of Change.* Santa Fe: School of American Research Press, 1985.

Kerr, Rose. *Chinese Ceramics: Porcelain of the Qing Dynasty, 1644–1911.* London: Victoria and Albert Museum, 1986.

Kindig, Joe, Jr. *Thoughts on the Kentucky Rifle in Its Golden Age.* New York: Trimmer, 1960.

Kingery, W. David, and Pamela B. Vandiver. *Ceramic Masterpieces: Art, Structure, and Technology.* New York: Free Press, 1986.

Kirk, John T. *American Chairs: Queen Anne and Chippendale.* New York: Alfred A. Knopf, 1972.

_____. *American Furniture and the British Tradition to 1830.* New York: Alfred A. Knopf, 1982.

Klein, Barbro, and Mats Widbom, eds. *Swedish Folk Art: All Tradition Is Change.* New York: Abrams, 1994.

Knapp, Ronald G. *China's Traditional Rural Architecture: A Cultural Geography of the Common House.* Honolulu: University of Hawaii Press, 1986.

Koizumi, Kazuko. *Traditional Japanese Furniture.* Trans. Alfred Birnbaum. Tokyo: Kodansha, 1986.

Kostof, Spiro. *Caves of God: The Monastic Environment of Byzantine Cappadocia.* Cambridge: The MIT Press, 1972.

Koverman, Jill Beute, ed. *I Made This Jar: The Life and Works of the Enslaved African-American Potter Dave.* Columbia: McKissick Museum, 1998.

Kramer, Barbara. *Nampeyo and Her Pottery.* Albuquerque: University of New Mexico Press, 1996.

Kramrisch, Stella. *Unknown India: Ritual Art in Tribe and Village.* Philadelphia: Philadelphia Museum of Art, 1968.

_____. *The Hindu Temple.* 2 vols. Delhi: Motilal Banarsidass, 1996 [1946].

Krishna, Nanditha. *Arts and Crafts of Tamilnadu.* Ahmedabad: Mapin, 1992.

Kuban, Doğan. *The Turkish Hayat House.* Istanbul: Eren, 1995.

Kubler, George. *The Shape of Time: Remarks on the History of Things.* New Haven: Yale University Press, 1962.

_____. *The Religious Architecture of New Mexico in the Colonial Period and Since the American Occupation.* Albuquerque: University of New Mexico Press for the School of American Research, 1972.

Küçükerman, Önder. *Turkish House: In Search of Spatial Identity.* Istanbul: Turkish Touring and Automobile Association, 1985 [1978].

Kumar, Nita. *The Artisans of Banaras: Popular Culture and Identity, 1880–1986*. Princeton: Princeton University Press, 1988.

Kuran, Aptullah. *The Mosque in Early Ottoman Architecture*. Chicago: University of Chicago Press, 1968.

_____. *Sinan: The Grand Old Master of Ottoman Architecture*. Washington: Institute of Turkish Studies, 1987.

Lane, Arthur. *Later Islamic Pottery: Persia, Syria, Egypt, Turkey*. London: Faber and Faber, 1957.

Lanier, Gabrielle M., and Bernard L. Herman. *Everyday Architecture of the Mid-Atlantic: Looking at Buildings and Landscapes*. Baltimore: Johns Hopkins University Press, 1997.

Leach, Bernard. *A Potter's Book*. Levittown: Transatlantic Arts, 1973.

_____. *Hamada: Potter*. Tokyo: Kodansha, 1990 [1975].

Le Corbusier. *Towards a New Architecture*. London: Architectural Press, 1952 [1927].

_____. *When the Cathedrals Were White*. New York: McGraw-Hill, 1964 [1947].

_____. *Journey to the East*. Trans. and ed. Ivan Zaknić. Cambridge: The MIT Press, 1989 [1966].

Leone, Mark P., and Parker B. Potter, Jr. *The Recovery of Meaning: Historical Archaeology in the Eastern United States*. Washington: Smithsonian Institution Press, 1988.

Lévi-Strauss, Claude. *The Way of the Masks*. Trans. Sylvia Modelski. Seattle: University of Washington Press, 1982.

Lewis, J. M. *The Ewenny Potteries*. Cardiff: National Museum of Wales, 1982.

Lipman, Jean, and Alice Winchester. *The Flowering of American Folk Art (1776–1876)*. New York: Viking Press and Whitney Museum of Art, 1974.

Long, Amos, Jr. *The Pennsylvania German Family Farm*. Breinigsville: The Pennsylvania German Society, 1972.

L'Orange, H. P. *Art Forms and Civic Life in the Late Roman Empire*. Princeton: Princeton University Press, 1972.

Ludwig, Allan I. *Graven Images: New England Stonecarving and Its Symbols, 1650–1815*. Middletown: Wesleyan University Press, 1966.

Luther, Clair Franklin. *The Hadley Chest*. Hartford: Case, Lockwood and Brainard, 1935.

MacDonald, George F. *Haida Monumental Art: Villages of the Queen Charlotte Islands*. Seattle: University of Washington Press, 1994 [1983].

Macnair, Peter L., Alan L. Hoover, and Kevin Neary. *The Legacy: Tradition and Innovation in Northwest Coast Indian Art*. Seattle: University of Washington Press, 1984.

Mahmud, Firoz. *Prospects of Material Folk Culture Studies and Folklife Museums in Bangladesh*. Dhaka: Bangla Academy, 1993.

Mango, Cyril. *Byzantine Architecture*. New York: Abrams, 1974.

Marriott, Alice. *Maria: The Potter of San Ildefonso*. Norman: University of Oklahoma Press, 1948.

Marshall, Howard Wight. *Folk Architecture in Little Dixie: A Regional Culture in Missouri*. Columbia: University of Missouri Press, 1981.

Martin, Charles E. *Hollybush: Folk Building and Social Change in an Appalachian Community*. Knoxville: University of Tennessee Press, 1984.

McNaughton, Patrick. *The Mande Blacksmiths: Knowledge, Power, and Art in West Africa*. Bloomington: Indiana University Press, 1988.

Meinig, D. W., ed. *The Interpretation of Ordinary Landscapes*. Oxford: Oxford University Press, 1979.

Meirion-Jones, Gwyn I. *The Vernacular Architecture of Brittany: An Essay in Historical Geography*. Edinburgh: John Donald, 1982.

Mercer, Eric. *Furniture, 700–1700*. New York: Meredith Press, 1969.

_____. *English Vernacular Houses: A Study of Traditional Farmhouses and Cottages*. London: Royal Commission on Historical Monuments, 1975.

Mercer, Henry C. *Ancient Carpenters' Tools*. Doylestown: Bucks County Historical Society, 1960 [1929].

Michell, George. *The Hindu Temple: An Introduction to Its Meaning and Forms*. Chicago: University of Chicago Press, 1988 [1977].

Mikami, Tsugio. *The Art of Japanese Ceramics*. New York: Weatherhill, 1972.

Moes, Robert. *Mingei: Japanese Folk Art from the Montgomery Collection*. Alexandria: Art Services International, 1995.

Montgomery, Charles. *American Furniture: The Federal Period*. New York: Viking Press, 1966.

_____. *A History of American Pewter*. New York: Praeger, 1973.

Mookerjee, Ajit. *Ritual Art of India*. New York: Thames and Hudson, 1985.

Morris, Richard. *Churches in the Landscape*. London: Phoenix, 1997 [1989].

Morris, William. *Hopes and Fears for Art*. London: Ellis and White, 1882.

_____. *Signs of Change*. London: Reeves and Turner, 1888.

_____. *Architecture, Industry and Wealth: Collected Papers*. London: Longmans, Green, 1902.

Moughtin, J. C. *Hausa Architecture*. London: Ethnographica, 1985.

Munsterberg, Hugo. *The Folk Arts of Japan*. Rutland: Charles E. Tuttle, 1958.

_____. *The Ceramic Art of Japan: A Handbook for Collectors*. Rutland: Charles E. Tuttle, 1964.

Muraoka, Kageo, and Kichiemon Okamura. *Folk Arts and Crafts of Japan*. Trans. Daphne D. Stegmaier. New York: Weatherhill, 1973.

Murray-Wooley, Carolyn, and Karl Raitz. *Rock Fences of the Bluegrass*. Lexington: University Press of Kentucky, 1992.

Muthesius, Stefan. *The English Terraced House*. New Haven: Yale University Press, 1982.

Nabokov, Peter, and Robert Easton. *Native American Architecture*. New York: Oxford University Press, 1989.

Nahohai, Milford, and Elisa Phelps. *Dialogues with Zuni Potters*. Zuni: Zuni A:shiwi Publishing Company, 1995.

Naismith, Robert J. *Buildings of the Scottish Countryside*. London: Victor Gollancz, 1989.

Nasr, Seyyed Hossein. *Islamic Art and Spirituality*. Albany: State University of New York Press, 1987.

Nelson, Lowry. *The Mormon Village: A Pattern and Technique of Land Settlement*. Salt Lake City: University of Utah Press, 1952.

Nelson, Marion, ed. *Norwegian Folk Art: The Migration of a Tradition*. New York: Abbeville, 1995.

Noble, Allen G., ed. *To Build in a New Land: Ethnic Landscapes in North America*. Baltimore: Johns Hopkins University Press, 1992.

Noble, Allen G., and Hubert G. H. Wilhelm, eds. *Barns of the Midwest*. Athens: Ohio University Press, 1995.

Noma, Seiroku. *The Arts of Japan*. Trans. John Rosenfeld. 2 vols. Tokyo: Kodansha, 1978.

Norberg-Schulz, Christian. *Intentions in Architecture.* Cambridge: The MIT Press, 1965.

_____. *Existence, Space and Architecture.* New York: Praeger, 1971.

_____. *Genius Loci: Towards a Phenomenology of Architecture.* New York: Rizzoli, 1984.

_____. *Nightlands: Nordic Building.* Cambridge: The MIT Press, 1996.

O'Bannon, George. *The Turkoman Carpet.* London: Duckworth, 1974.

Oettinger, Marion, Jr. *The Folk Art of Latin America: Visiones Del Pueblo.* New York: Dutton Studio and Museum of American Folk Art, 1992.

Oliver, Paul, ed. *Shelter in Africa.* New York: Praeger, 1971.

_____, ed. *Encyclopedia of Vernacular Architecture of the World.* 3 vols. Cambridge: Cambridge University Press, 1997.

Opie, James. *Tribal Rugs: Nomadic and Village Weavings from the Near East and Central Asia.* Portland: Tolstoy Press, 1992.

Paccard, André. *Traditional Islamic Craft in Moroccan Architecture.* 2 vols. Saint-Jorioz: Éditions Atelier 74, 1980.

Panofsky, Erwin. *Gothic Architecture and Scholasticism.* New York: World, 1957.

_____. *The Life and Art of Albrecht Dürer.* Princeton: Princeton University Press, 1971 [1945].

Palmer, Gabrielle G. *Sculpture in the Kingdom of Quito.* Albuquerque: University of New Mexico Press, 1987.

Peate, Iorwerth C. *The Welsh House: A Study in Folk Culture.* London: The Honourable Society of Cymmrodorion, 1940.

Peterson, Fred W. *Homes in the Heartland: Balloon Frame Farmhouses of the Upper Midwest, 1850–1920.* Lawrence: University of Kansas Press, 1992.

_____. *Building the Community, Keeping the Faith: German Catholic Vernacular Architecture in a Rural Minnesota Parish.* St. Paul: Minnesota Historical Society Press, 1998.

Peterson, Susan. *Lucy M. Lewis: American Indian Potter.* Tokyo: Kodansha, 1984.

_____. *Pottery by American Indian Women: The Legacy of Generations.* New York: Abbeville, 1997.

Peterson, William S. *The Kelmscott Press: A History of William Morris's Typographical Adventure.* Berkeley: University of California Press, 1991.

Petsopoulos, Yanni, ed. *Tulips, Arabesques and Turbans: Decorative Art from the Ottoman Empire.* New York: Abbeville Press, 1982.

Pevsner, Nikolaus. *Pioneers of the Modern Movement: From William Morris to Walter Gropius.* London: Faber and Faber, 1936.

Philippides, Dimitri. *Greek Traditional Architecture.* 2 vols. Athens: "Melissa," 1983.

Pocius, Gerald L. *Textile Traditions of Eastern Newfoundland.* Ottawa: National Museum of Canada, 1979.

_____. *A Place to Belong: Community Order and Everyday Space in Calvert, Newfoundland.* Athens: University of Georgia Press, 1991.

_____, ed. *Living in a Material World: Canadian and American Approaches to Material Culture.* St. John's: Institute of Social and Economic Research, 1991.

Price, Sally. *Primitive Art in Civilized Places.* Chicago: University of Chicago Press, 1989.

Prown, Jules David. *John Singleton*

Copley. 2 vols. Cambridge: Harvard University Press for the National Gallery of Art, 1966.

Prussin, Labelle. *Architecture in Northern Ghana: A Study of Forms and Functions.* Berkeley: University of California Press, 1969.

Pylkkänen, Riita. *The Use and Traditions of Mediaeval Rugs and Coverlets in Finland.* Helsinki: Archaeological Society of Finland, 1974.

Quiney, Anthony. *Kent Houses: English Domestic Architecture.* Woodbridge: Antique Collectors' Club, 1993.

Ragette, Friedrich. *Architecture in Lebanon: The Lebanese House During the 18th and 19th Centuries.* Beirut: American University of Beirut, 1974.

Rapoport, Amos. *House Form and Culture.* Englewood Cliffs: Prentice-Hall, 1969.

_____. *The Meaning of the Built Environment: A Nonverbal Communication Approach.* Beverly Hills: Sage, 1982.

Rees, Alwyn D. *Life in a Welsh Countryside.* Cardiff: University of Wales Press, 1971 [1950].

Reichard, Gladys A. *Spider Woman: A Story of Navajo Weavers and Chanters.* New York: Macmillan, 1934.

Reina, Ruben E., and Robert M. Hill, III. *The Traditional Pottery of Guatemala.* Austin: University of Texas Press, 1978.

Reps, John W. *Town Planning in Frontier America.* Princeton: Princeton University Press, 1969.

Rinzler, Ralph, and Robert Sayers. *The Meaders Family: North Georgia Potters.* Washington: Smithsonian Institution Press, 1980.

Roberts, Warren E. *Viewpoints on Folklife: Looking at the Overlooked.* Ann Arbor:

UMI Research Press, 1988.

_____. *Log Buildings of Southern Indiana.* Bloomington: Trickster Press, 1996 [1984].

Rugh, Andrea B. *Reveal and Conceal: Dress in Contemporary Egypt.* Syracuse: Syracuse University Press, 1986.

Russell, Carl P. *Guns on the Early Frontiers.* Berkeley: University of California Press, 1962.

Safadi, Yasin Hamid. *Islamic Calligraphy.* London: Thames and Hudson, 1978.

St. George, Robert Blair, ed. *Material Life in America: 1680–1860.* Boston: Northeastern University Press, 1988.

_____. *Conversing by Signs: Poetics of Implication in Colonial New England Culture.* Chapel Hill: University of North Carolina Press, 1998.

Salvador, Mari Lyn. *Contemporary Santero Traditions from Northern New Mexico.* Albuquerque: Maxwell Museum of Anthropology, 1995.

Saqqaf, Abdulaziz, ed. *The Middle East City: Ancient Traditions Confront a Modern World.* New York: Paragon House, 1987.

Saraswati, S. K. *A Survey of Indian Sculpture.* Calcutta: K. I. Mukhopadhyay, 1957.

Sayers, Robert, and Ralph Rinzler. *The Korean Onggi Potter.* Washington: Smithsonian Institution Press, 1987.

Schauss, Hans-Joachim. *Contemporary Polish Folk Artists.* New York: Hippocrene Books, 1987.

Schimmel, Annemarie. *Calligaphy and Islamic Culture.* New York: New York University Press, 1984.

Schlee, Ernst. *German Folk Art.* Tokyo: Kodansha, 1980.

Schlereth, Thomas J., ed. *Material Culture Studies in America.* Nashville: AASLH, 1982.

Seckel, Dietrich. *The Art of Buddhism.* New York: Crown, 1963.

Shah, Haku. *Votive Terracottas of Gujarat.* New York: Mapin International, 1985.

Shaw, Simeon. *History of the Staffordshire Potteries.* New York: Praeger, 1970 [1829].

Shearer, Allistair. *The Hindu Vision: Forms of the Formless.* London: Thames and Hudson, 1993.

Sieber, Roy. *African Furniture and Household Objects.* Bloomington: Indiana University Press, 1980.

Smith, Cyril Stanley. *A Search for Structure: Selected Essays on Science, Art, and History.* Cambridge: The MIT Press, 1982.

Smith, Peter. *Houses of the Welsh Countryside: A Study in Historical Geography.* London: Royal Commission on Ancient and Historical Monuments in Wales, 1988.

Sowden, Harry. *Australian Woolsheds.* North Melbourne: Cassell Australia, 1972.

Stea, David, and Mete Turan. *Placemaking: Production of Built Environment in Two Cultures.* Aldershot: Avebury, 1993.

Steensberg, Axel, and Grith Lerche. *Danish Peasant Furniture.* 2 vols. Copenhagen: Arnold Busck, 1989.

Stilgoe, John R. *Common Landscape of America, 1580 to 1845.* New Haven: Yale University Press, 1982.

Sturt, George. *The Wheelwright's Shop.* Cambridge: Cambridge University Press, 1965 [1923].

Sutton-Smith, Brian. *Toys as Culture.* New York: Gardner Press, 1986.

Swank, Scott T. *Arts of the Pennsylvania Germans.* New York: W. W. Norton for Winterthur, 1983.

Sweezy, Nancy. *Raised in Clay: The Southern Pottery Tradition.* Washington: Smithsonian Institution Press, 1984.

Tanavoli, Parviz. *Shahsavan: Iranian Rugs and Textiles.* New York: Rizzoli, 1985.

Tanner, Clara Lee. *Apache Indian Baskets.* Tucson: University of Arizona Press, 1982.

Tashjian, Dickran and Ann. *Memorials for Children of Change: The Art of Early New England Stonecarving.* Middletown: Wesleyan University Press, 1974.

Taylor, Christopher. *Dorset.* London: Hodder and Stoughton, 1979.

Taylor, Lonn, and Dessa Bokides. *New Mexican Furniture, 1600–1940: The Origins, Survival, and Revival of Furniture Making in the Hispanic Southwest.* Santa Fe: Museum of New Mexico Press, 1987.

Ther, Ulla. *Floral Messages: From Ottoman Court Embroideries to Anatolian Trousseau Chests.* Bremen: Edition Temmen, 1993.

Tichane, Robert. *Ching-Te-Chen: Views of a Porcelain City.* Painted Post: New York State Institute for Glaze Research, 1983.

Thompson, Jon. *Carpet Magic: The Art of Carpets from the Tents, Cottages, and Workshops of Asia.* Wisbech: Barbican Gallery, 1983.

Thompson, Robert Farris. *African Art in Motion: Icon and Act.* Los Angeles: University of California Press, 1974.

_____ . *Flash of the Spirit: African and Afro-American Art and Philosophy.* New York: Vintage Books, 1984.

_____ . *Face of the Gods: Art and Altars of Africa and the African Americas.* New York: Museum for African Art, 1993.

Trent, Robert F. *Hearts and Crowns: Folk*

Chairs of the Connecticut Coast, 1720–1840. New Haven: New Haven Colony Historical Society, 1977.

Tuan, Yi-fu. *Space and Place: The Perspective of Experience.* Minneapolis: University of Minnesota Press, 1977.

Turan, Mete, ed. *Vernacular Architecture: Paradigms of Environmental Response.* Aldershot: Avebury, 1990.

Ungerleider-Mayerson, Joy. *Jewish Folk Art: From Biblical to Modern Times.* New York: Summit Books, 1986.

Upton, Dell. *Holy Things and Profane: Anglican Parish Churches in Colonial Virginia.* Cambridge: The MIT Press, 1986.

_____, ed. *America's Architectural Roots: Ethnic Groups That Built America.* Washington: National Trust for Historic Preservation, 1986.

_____. *Architecture in the United States.* Oxford: Oxford University Press, 1998.

Upton, Dell, and John Michael Vlach, eds. *Common Places: Readings in American Vernacular Architecture.* Athens: University of Georgia Press, 1986.

Van Ravenswaay, Charles. *The Arts and Architecture of German Settlements in Missouri: A Survey of a Vanishing Culture.* Columbia: University of Missouri Press, 1977.

Venturi, Robert. *Complexity and Contradiction in Architecture.* New York: Museum of Modern Art, 1966.

Vlach, John Michael. *The Afro-American Tradition in Decorative Arts.* Cleveland: Cleveland Museum of Art, 1978.

_____. *Charleston Blacksmith: The Work of Philip Simmons.* Columbia: University of South Carolina Press, 1992 [1981].

_____. *Back of the Big House: The Architecture of Plantation Slavery.* Chapel Hill: University of North Carolina Press, 1993.

Vlach, John Michael, and Simon J. Bronner, eds. *Folk Art and Art Worlds.* Ann Arbor: UMI Research Press, 1986.

Walker, H. Jesse, and Randall A. Detro, eds. *Cultural Diffusion and Landscapes: Selections by Fred B. Kniffen.* Baton Rouge: Geoscience Publications, 1990.

Walton, James. *African Village.* Pretoria: J. L. Van Schaik, 1956.

Warren, John, and Ihsan Fethi. *Traditional Houses in Baghdad.* Horsham: Coach, 1982.

Weiser, Frederick S., and Howell J. Heaney. *The Pennsylvania German Fraktur of The Free Library of Philadelphia.* 2 vols. Breinigsville: Pennsylvania German Society, 1976.

Welsch, Roger. *Sod Walls: The Story of the Nebraska Sod House.* Broken Bow: Purcells, 1968.

Wenzel, Marian. *House Decoration in Nubia.* London: Duckworth, 1972.

Westmacott, Richard. *African-American Gardens and Yards in the Rural South.* Knoxville: University of Tennessee Press, 1992.

Whiffen, Marcus. *The Eighteenth-Century Houses of Williamsburg: A Study of Architecture and Building in the Colonial Capital of Virginia.* Williamsburg: Colonial Williamsburg Foundation, 1985 [1960].

Wilson, Chris. *The Myth of Santa Fe: Creating a Modern Regional Tradition.* Albuquerque: University of New Mexico Press, 1997.

Wilson, Richard L. *The Art of Ogata Kenzan: Persona and Production in*

Japanese Ceramics. New York: Weatherhill, 1991.

_____. *Inside Japanese Ceramics: A Primer of Materials, Techniques, and Traditions.* New York: Weatherhill, 1995.

Wood-Jones, Raymond B. *Traditional Domestic Architecture of the Banbury Region.* Manchester: Manchester University Press, 1963.

Wright, Gwendolyn. *Building the Dream: A Social History of Housing in America.* Cambridge: The MIT Press, 1983.

Wulff, Hans E. *The Traditional Crafts of Persia: Their Development, Technology, and Influence on Eastern and Western Civilizations.* Cambridge: The MIT Press, 1966.

Wyatt, Gary. *Spirit Faces: Contemporary Native American Masks from the Northwest.* San Francisco: Chronicle Books, 1995.

Yanagi, Soetsu. *The Unknown Craftsman: A Japanese Insight into Beauty.* Ed. Bernard Leach. Tokyo: Kodansha, 1989 [1972].

Yanagi, Sori, ed. *Mingei: Masterpieces of Japanese Folkcraft.* Tokyo: Kodansha, 1991.

Yutang, Lin. *The Chinese Theory of Art: Translations from the Masters of Chinese Art.* London: Heinemann, 1967.

Zaman, Niaz. *The Art of Kantha Embroidery.* Dhaka: University Press, 1993 [1981].

Zelinsky, Wilbur. *Exploring the Beloved Country: Geographic Forays into American Society and Culture.* Iowa City: University of Iowa Press, 1994.

Zimmer, Heinrich. *Myths and Symbols in Indian Art and Civilization.* Ed. Joseph Campbell. New York: Pantheon, 1946.

Zug, Charles G., III. *Turners and Burners: The Folk Potters of North Carolina.* Chapel Hill: University of North Carolina Press, 1986.

Index

INDEX

MATERIAL CULTURE
was designed by Henry Glassie,
composed by Bruce Carpenter,
printed & bound by Vail-Ballou Press Inc.,
& published by the Indiana University Press.